PRAISE FOR *GOSPEL SERMONS*

Through decades of rummaging around for old German sermon and theological books, I've come across dozens of copies of Walther's "Gospel Postille" and "Epistle Postille." A "postil" comes from a conflation of two Latin words, "post ille" or "after that." In the service the texts are read and "after that" expounded by the preacher. In the years before I could read any German I'd longingly survey the big folio volumes, so beautifully bound, photo of the rather un-photogenic and unlikely force for American Lutheranism, C. F. W. Walther, reproduced in the front matter, looking as well as or better than he ever looked in real life. Below his lithograph is 1 Peter 2:9 scribbled in his own hand, *"Ihr seid ... das königliche Priestertum,"* "You are ... a royal priesthood," his theme verse.

Now, after a century, Walther is still preaching, or preaching again. I'm convinced that amidst all the causes of the Missouri Synod nearly losing its dogmatic compass in the 1960s and early 70s, very significant was that within a generation and a half, she was cut off from her literary patrimony. The new generations could no longer read German and thus lost access to Luther and Walther and other articulate proponents of the faith. It's fairly amazing that we live in a time when translations of classics continue to be published and so marvelously by Concordia Publishing House, which keeps producing the veritable best of the best old and new. As I survey these sermons in English, I think of Pastor Heck burning the midnight oil, bringing them into English already a half century ago. I think of Dr. Walther and all the deep disappointments and sorrows, but also great joys he experienced in the forty years he led the Missouri Synod. And I thank God for his crystal-clear orthodoxy, his total commitment to Scripture and the Confessions, and his burning passion for the Gospel of free forgiveness in Christ.

—Pastor Matthew C. Harrison
President, The Lutheran Church—Missouri Synod

I strongly recommend this collection of C. F. W. Walther's sermons on the Standard Gospels as a model of God's Word's sound pattern of speaking as well as of eloquence and beauty in delivering God's Word unto conviction of sin, the relief of the penitents' guilt and the guidance of every believer's desire to please our good and gracious God. Having used this excellent translation of Heck in my own study for many years, I also commend Concordia Publishing House for now making it more readily available in such an attractive form. This is a "must resource" for all true Lutheran preachers and those all who love sound biblical preaching.

—Rev. Joel R. Baseley
Pastor, Emmanuel Lutheran Church, Dearborn, MI
Owner of/Publisher at Mark V Publications

Good preaching grows not only out of sharp-eyed exegesis but also out of a synoptic awareness of the connection between the text at hand and the entire body of Christian doctrine. In these sermons, C. F. W. Walther, the Missouri Synod's first leader in dogmatics and practical theology, shows his mastery of both fields. Today's preacher can find much food for thought here. You can trace Walther's connections for your hearers, and his work will stimulate you to trace others too.

—Rev. Ken Schurb
Pastor, Zion Lutheran Church, Moberly, MO
Author of *The Old Testament Collection: Preaching Christ in the Old Testament during the Church Year* (CPH, 2010)

In this must-have collection of Walther sermons, the Missouri Synod's first president offers unique insights on the Gospel lessons of the one-year lectionary. It revisits familiar texts through the refreshing lens of an American Lutheran pastor who did not yet have to yield to the political correctness of our day. Discover a "new" Walther—not only a prolific writer and first-class theologian, but also a powerful orator. Featuring key summary points on each sermon, this volume is also a handy reference for pastors wondering "WWWD" ("What Would Walther Do?") with this particular pericope.

—Rev. Christian C. Tiews
Translator of C. F. W. Walther's *Law & Gospel: How to Read and Apply the Bible* (CPH, 2010)
Associate Pastor, Grace Lutheran Church, Tulsa, OK

Donald Heck has afforded an invaluable service to Christ's Church through the translation of Walther's *Gospel Sermons*. Contained herein is both the timeless and timely application of God's Word for the life of His people by the true pastor-theologian C. F. W. Walther, who preached unhesitatingly to the whole person. He boldly proclaimed the power of the Gospel unto salvation in all of its Christ-centered purity and objective scriptural foundation. What is more, the resultant experiential sanctification of those who belong to Christ is vividly described where one learns how to live in the Gospel through faith in Jesus.

—Rev. Dr. Alfonso O. Espinosa, PhD
Contributor to *C. F. W. Walther: Churchman and Theologian* (CPH, 2011)
Senior Pastor, Saint Paul's Lutheran Church, Irvine, CA
Adjunct Professor of Theology, Concordia University, Irvine

Walther's *Gospel Sermons* is a devotional treasure worthy of a place on your bookshelf. CPH should be commended for bringing out this old German treasure from the early years of American confessional Lutheranism and dusting it off with an easy-to-read format that can be enjoyed by English readers of all kinds. Although Walther's style of sermon writing is quite different from what's typically seen in Lutheran preaching today, the devotional value of these well-translated sermons spanning the historic Church Year is priceless for the modern reader, who will certainly grow in faith and appreciation of the past through this resource.

—Rev. Jeremiah J. Gumm
Pastor, Cross of Christ Ev. Lutheran Church (WELS), Liverpool, NY
Editor of Wisconsin Lutheran Seminary's *The Shepherd's Study*
(http://www.wlsce.net/shepherds-study)—A Continuing Education Blog to
Help Pastors Grow through the Discovery of Literature

During his life, Walther was the Missouri Synod's most sought-after preacher, and in the years after his death, he just kept on preaching, in several published volumes. In the homes of our laity, a book of Walther sermons was near to hand, alongside a Luther Bible, both in German. Today, a hundred years after our church's transition to English began, this publication of *Gospel Sermons* resurrects Pastor Walther for a new age. Walther's sermons brim with ennobling rhetoric, doctrinal clarity, persuasive logic, heartfelt love for his hearers and for his Savior, an urgent summons to repentance, a relentless call to forsake cultural idols, and above all, a compelling confidence that Christ has reconciled us sinners to God and won for us an everlasting kingdom. Do we need such sermons today? Yes we do.

—Rev. Thomas J. Egger
Assistant Professor of Exegetical Theology, Concordia Seminary, St. Louis
Contributor to *C. F. W. Walther: Churchman and Theologian* (CPH, 2011)

As well as being an excellent resource for pastors' study and sermon preparation, I heartily endorse Donald E. Heck's translation of C. F. W. Walther's *Gospel Sermons* for use in one's devotional life. Even if presented in an unfamiliar sermonic style, this postil remains surprisingly contemporary, dealing with hopes and struggles, issues and challenges that still touch those who live a century and a half after Walther first delivered these sermons. These pages are not musty relics of a past age but are God's living word of Law and Gospel delivered in refreshingly direct teaching and wise pastoral counsel.

—Rev. Keith Clow
Pastor, Trinity Lutheran Church, Wellsville, MO

Amerikanisch-Lutherische

Evangelien Postille

Predigten

über die evangelischen Pericopen des Kirchenjahrs

von

Carl Ferd. Wilh. Walther

Pfarrer der ersten deutschen ev. luth. Gemeinde zu St. Louis

Neunte Auflage.

Lutherischer Concordia Verlag,

St. Louis.

You are the chosen race,
the royal priesthood, etc. etc.
1 Pet. 2:9
C. F. W. Walther

GOSPEL SERMONS

VOLUME 1

C. F. W. WALTHER

TRANSLATED BY

DONALD E. HECK

CONCORDIA PUBLISHING HOUSE · SAINT LOUIS

Originally published as *Amerikanisch-Lutherische Evangelien Postille Predigten über die evangelischen Pericopen des Kirchenjahrs* [American Lutheran Gospel Postil: Sermons on the Gospel Pericopes of the Church Year] © copyright 1870 by Lutherischer Concordia Verlag, St. Louis.

Scripture quotations are from the ESV Bible® (The Holy Bible, English Standard Version®), copyright © 2001 by Crossway Bibles, a publishing ministry of Good News Publishers. Used by permissions. All rights reserved.

Quotations from the Lutheran Confessions are from *Concordia: The Lutheran Confessions*, second edition; edited by Paul McCain, et al., copyright © 2006 Concordia Publishing House. All rights reserved.

Quotations with the abbreviation *LSB* are from *Lutheran Service Book*, copyright © 2006 Concordia Publishing House. All rights reserved.

Quotations with the abbreviation *TLH* are from *The Lutheran Hymnal*, copyright © 1941 Concordia Publishing House. All rights reserved.

Manufactured in the United States of America

Library of Congress Cataloging-in-Publication Data

Walther, C. F. W. (Carl Ferdinand Wilhelm), 1811–1887.

[Sermons. English. Selections]

Gospel sermons / C.F.W. Walther ; Translated by Donald E. Heck.

pages cm

Includes index.

ISBN 978-0-7586-3889-2

1. Bible. N.T. Gospels--Sermons. 2. Church year sermons. 3. Lutheran Church--Sermons. 4. Sermons, German--Translations into English. I. Heck, Donald E. II. Title.

BS2555.54.W3513 2013

252'.041--dc23   2012041989

1 2 3 4 5 6 7 8 9 10   22 21 20 19 18 17 16 15 14 13

CONTENTS

FOREWORD

Many a day I remember seeing my father, the Rev. Donald E. Heck, at his desk in our home in Livermore, Iowa, and, later, La Valle, Wisconsin, with his German dictionary and the sermons of C. F. W. Walther or George Stoeckhardt nearby. On numerous occasions, I and my siblings helped him in the basement of our Livermore or La Valle home with the mimeographing, collating, and binding of the sermons, with stacks of paper on makeshift sawhorse tables and while listening to classical music. Sometimes we did some of the work in the parish hall of Immanuel Lutheran Church. The work had undoubtedly commenced during our days in Ireton, Iowa, where my father had been a pastor of a rural church outside of the bustling metropolis of 200, and, later, in Livermore, Iowa. Livermore seemed large by comparison, boasting a population of about 500. The work continued into the La Valle years, by then having branched out into the Lutheran Bulletin Insert Service.

The Old Standard Gospels were published by my father from Walther's *Evangelium Postille* in 1955, and they were published with Walther's own Preface, which Walther had written in St. Louis, Missouri, in December 1870. My father later reissued them in a single volume with some improved translation. The translation of the *Lenten Sermons* of George Stoeckhardt, copyrighted in 1958, was completed on August 3, 1962. Then, a couple of years later, Walther's *Year of Grace* was published, the translation having been completed on November 22, 1964.

While the sermonic style of Walther will seem quite different from the typical sermon of today, the theological content of his sermons will remain relevant, since Scripture always remains relevant. In these sermons one will read the author of *The Proper Distinction between Law and Gospel*, applying those twin doctrines in parish settings intended for the laypeople of his congregation, and this, of course, will be one of the primary benefits for those who read these sermons. God's blessings to you as you read.

My siblings—Barbara Haseley, Doris Sherfy, Christine Dea, and Tom Heck—join me in expressing appreciation to Concordia Publishing House for bringing these translations to publication and, along with this endeavor, for the recognition it brings to our father (and to our mother, Lucille Heck, who was also skilled in transcribing and translating letters in the old German script for Concordia Seminary, not to mention keeping us five children from getting underfoot while Dad was doing his work) for his long hours of translation, revision, and publication.

Rev. Dr. Joel D. Heck
Concordia University Texas
Austin, Texas

PREFACE

Since the undersigned is about to publish the present collection of sermons, being urged to from several quarters, he does so only because it might serve as a public testimony on how God's Word is expounded to the congregation of the Lutheran Church in America and especially in the denomination to which the author belongs. The sermons are therefore printed unchanged as to content and form.[1] They originate from the author's almost 30-year activity as pastor of the first German Ev. Lutheran (Joint) congregation of the Unaltered Augsburg Confession in this country, which for some time past consists of four areas with four churches: Trinity, Immanuel, Zion, and Cross Churches. Because the sermons, as was stated, should serve as a testimony, the references appearing in them to the circumstances of the time in which, and to the condition of the congregation before which, they were preached were intentionally not deleted. Therefore, the purpose of the editor also should not be to choose those sermons which best follow the rules, nor even those which conform best to the text, but those which show most clearly the manner in which the counsel of God for our salvation is proclaimed to our beloved hearers, how Law and Gospel, grace and good works, repentance, faith, and sanctification is preached.

Originally it was the author's plan to make such a selection, that every article of Christian doctrine might be found in this book. To attain this purpose, a supplement on the Gospel and Epistle pericopes and so-called occasional sermons on free texts was to be added. However, since it appeared that the book would be too thick and too expensive, this plan had to be abandoned.

None of the author's sermons that have already appeared in print are included in the present collection, so no buyer of this collection having them in his possession need buy them again.

---

[1] Editor's Note: We have updated the grammar and punctuation of the text to allow for easier reading. When able, we have also updated various quotations, such as Scripture, hymn texts, and quotes from the Lutheran Confessions, to modern translations.

Unfortunately, the postils could not be published in complete form, since the author did not think he dared abandon the principle of using in unchanged form only sermons already preached, but the few sermon manuscripts that were loaned out had not been returned to their owner. These sermons are the Sixth Sunday after Epiphany, the Twenty-sixth and Twenty-seventh Sundays after Trinity, and the Second Day after the great festivals of the Church Year, because no manuscripts of those just named were on hand for printing.

That the author unwillingly let his portrait, made without his knowledge, be added, and, that also the beautiful make-up of the book was not arranged at his wish, both rather done entirely at the request of those who did the printing, scarcely needs mention.

May the Lord, who blessed these testimonies when they were delivered from the pulpit, as many children of God confessed they did, bless also those who read them for the sake of Jesus Christ through the working of His Holy Spirit. Amen.

St. Louis, in the State of Missouri, December, 1870.

C. F. W. Walther

INTRODUCTION

By Christoph Barnbrock

SERMONS AS BESTSELLERS

C. F. W. Walther's collection of sermons on the Gospels was a bestseller for Concordia Publishing House in the 1800s. In the first eleven years, starting with the original publication in 1870/71, it was printed eight times, selling tens of thousands of copies. 22,000 copies were sold in this rather short amount of time. Within seven years of the original publication, the sermons were translated into Norwegian.

This interest in the sermons reflects not only the importance of Walther as leading theologian of The Lutheran Church—Missouri Synod in the first decades of its existence but also his extraordinary gifts as a preacher. Now in English, Walther's sermons will give readers today a peek into the powerful preaching of the first president of the LCMS.

HISTORICAL BACKGROUND

The sermons contained in this collection were preached by Walther from about 1840 to 1870, predominantly in congregations of the St. Louis area. Unfortunately, we do not know the specific dates and locations of most of the sermons, since many of the manuscripts on which Walther affixed information such as this are lost. However, some sermons can be dated thanks to a collection of handwritten Walther sermons transcribed from originals by Otto Hanser (now held at the Concordia Historical Institute in the collection of Walther's Papers, Folder 504). Hanser was a student of Walther's and later a pastor in St. Louis. He faithfully copied dozens of Walther's sermons. The volume at CHI contains many of these copies, handwritten, basically arranged according to the order of the Church Year. When available, the dates of the sermons are listed in this volume.[2]

The language in which Walther preached was, of course, German. In the 1850s, more than a third of all immigrants came from Germany (more than 200,000 alone in 1854). During Walther's time Germans were the largest group in St. Louis, with German even being taught and spoken in the public schools.

Those German immigrants were often surprised about the new world they met in the United States. They had to cope with a different political and social system. They had to deal with a huge variety of unknown religious denominations. Some of their illusionary dreams vanished; the United States was not the land of milk and honey as some had expected, but rather a country in which people were forced to work hard, sometimes under difficult circumstances.

When these immigrants heard the Gospel preached in their native language, they felt at home. They heard the Word of God proclaimed according to the Lutheran Confessions as they had in Germany. Walther himself described it in one of his sermons like that: "The Gospel . . . brings to you the heaven on earth [and] it makes this foreign country for you to a new home country."[3]

When Walther published these sermons in 1870, he could look back on a turbulent but nonetheless blessed life in the ministry of the Lord. In the early 1800s the immigrants from Saxony dealt with various irritations and a severe spiritual and theological crisis when their leading theologian, Rev. Martin Stephan, was deposed and the legitimacy of the immigrant group as church stood in question.

It was C. F. W. Walther who was able to solve the theological challenge in a public debate and helped to overcome the crisis that had also caused him deep afflictions. In 1841 a period of upswing and prosperity began. Walther succeeded his brother as pastor of Trinity Church in St. Louis. In 1847 he was elected as the first president of "The German Evangelical Lutheran Synod of Missouri, Ohio, and other States" (today's LCMS). In 1849 he became a professor at Concordia Seminary in St. Louis.

---

[2] I am indebted to Rev. Thomas J. Egger, Assistant Professor of Exegetical Theology, Concordia Seminary, St. Louis, for this information.

[3] C. F. W. Walther, Kirchweihpredigt [1847], in Walther, *Casual-Predigten und Reden. Aus seinem schriftlichen Nachlaß gesammelt* (St. Louis, 1892, 197–207, 205; translation mine).

Until then he was mainly a parish pastor who preached at least once each Sunday (in the afternoon service he was allowed to read a sermon). As was customary, Walther preached mainly on the traditional Gospel lessons (the order of the Gospel readings originating from the seventh century). Sermons on the Epistle lessons were preached less often; other biblical texts were used mainly for special occasions.

In 1849 he served not only as professor but also as the head pastor of the union of LCMS congregations in St. Louis (*Gesamtgemeinde*). In this function he had to preach at least once a month in his home congregation, and on special occasions as president of the Synod (again from 1864 as successor of Friedrich Wyneken) in other congregations of his church body.

When he finally published the sermons on the Gospel lessons, the LCMS had already grown fast. In 1866, about 200 congregations belonged to it. After some painful frictions in the early years of LCMS, it was the 1860s and 70s which brought some reconciliation with church bodies with which there had been various theological conflicts. After that, he and his church were privileged to walk their way with each other for another nearly 20 years during which Walther served as professor and in doing so as teacher for the next generations of preachers.

HOMILETICAL ASPECTS

Walther worked for days on his sermons—rearranging, reformulating, and memorizing. Taking a closer look at the sermons, you can see how carefully they are designed. Each sermon starts with a general introduction, which leads to the theme, which is then explicated in usually two or three parts.

While Walther himself used to be unsatisfied with his own style, the listeners of his day enjoyed his doctrinal approach and his popular way of preaching. His style reflected his unchangeable point of view. His special charisma and his rhetorical design not only attracted believers but also those who were not regular churchgoers.

But what have been Walther's own criteria for good preaching? In his *Pastoral Theology*[4] he lists the following seven aspects: (1) that God's Word alone is preached clearly; (2) that the Word is applied in the right manner; (3) that everything necessary for salvation is proclaimed (repentance, faith,

---

[4] C. F. W. Walther, *Americanisch-Lutherische Pastoraltheologie.* 5th ed. (St. Louis: Concordia, 1906), § 11, 76–77.

sanctification); (4) that the preacher addresses the hearers in their needs and (5) in their special challenges; (6) that the sermon has a proper order; and (7) that it might be not too long.

If you would have asked Walther what the goals of his sermons were, he probably would have answered: "To preach God's Word as Law and Gospel so that the hearers repent from their sins, believe in Jesus Christ as their Savior, and lead a God-pleasing life." And indeed you find these aspects in all of Walther's sermons. But beyond that, you can also discover further intention in Walther's sermons, that is, what he wanted to accomplish when he was preaching.

One basic intention in Walther's sermons is to describe reality in the light of God's Word and to present and represent aspects of this God-shaped truth. We find an example in the sermon for the Fourth Sunday after Easter, where Walther explains basic thoughts on sin, righteousness and judgment.

A second intention found consistently in Walther's sermons is his goal to lead the listeners to overcome situations of spiritual danger, hardships, and despair. You find sermons with such an emphasis for the Second and Thirds Sundays in Lent in which Walther describes how to battle with God Himself and how to be delivered from the kingdom of the devil.

In some of his sermons, Walther tried to convince his hearers by logical conclusions. In the sermon for the Third Sunday in Advent Walther starts to argue and to convince his hearers that Jesus Christ did signs and miracles and that these are an evidence for the fact that Jesus Christ is the Son of God and the Savior of the world.

Another intention of Walther's preaching is to give his listeners orientation. For example, keep in mind the historical situation while reading his sermon for Pentecost. Walther was not simply talking about the Church because it is an interesting dogmatic issue that fits to Pentecost. More than that, he was providing criteria for his listeners where and how to find the true Church among the huge variety of denominations and sects in the American context, with which the German immigrants were not familiar. Thus he contributed to the reduction of spiritual uncertainty and fear.

In the second volume of Walther's *Gospel Sermons*, you will find more frequently sermons in which Walther is showing, motivating, and leading his listeners to act as a Christian in daily life, for example, in the new political context of the United States (sermon for the Twenty-third Sunday after Trinity) or in the light of rising wealth of those days (sermon for the Ninth Sunday after Trinity).

THE ONGOING HISTORY OF WALTHER'S SERMONS

The volume of the first German edition of Walther's *Gospel Sermons*, which lies in front of me on my desk, is more than 140 years old. Its spine is already falling apart. How many hands may it have passed through until a close friend sent it to me? We may assume that this and other copies were used in worship services when no ordained minister was available, in family devotions, and for the personal study of individual Christians.

The age of these sermons can be discovered at some points. Walther's thoughts were, of course, shaped by his personal experiences and circumstances. But it is astonishing how fresh his thoughts seem today. The issues that Walther and his congregation faced are in many ways the same issues we face today. Reading these sermons, you will often feel as if Walther is addressing you personally.

By Donald Heck translating these sermons and by taking this book into your hands, the history of Walther's sermons goes on. People who read these sermons will experience the explanation of God's Word by C. F. W. Walther, who should be seen as a "Servant of the Word," as August R. Suelflow put it in the title of his biography on Walther.

May this publication lead many people to the insight that they are as Christians "a chosen race, a royal priesthood, a holy nation, a people for His [God's] own possession, that you may proclaim the excellencies of Him who called you out of darkness into His marvelous light" (1 Peter 2:9). This was the bible verse Walther put on one of the first pages of the German edition of his Gospel sermons. This also should be the motto of this volume.

FOR FURTHER REFERENCE

Barnbrock, Christoph. *Die Predigten C. F. W. Walthers im Kontext deutscher Auswanderergemeinden in den USA. Hintergründe—Analysen— Perspektiven* (Hamburg: Verlag Dr. Kovač, 2003).

C. F. W. Walther: Churchman and Theologian (St. Louis: Concordia, 2011).

Suelflow, August R. *Servant of the Word: The Life and Ministry of C. F. W. Walther* (St. Louis: Concordia, 2000).

Walther, C. F. W. *Law & Gospel: How to Read and Apply the Bible*, ed. Charles P. Schaum, trans. Christian C. Tiews (St. Louis: Concordia, 2010).

Walther, C. F. W. *The Church and the Office of the Ministry*, trans. J. T. Mueller, rev. and ed. Matthew C. Harrison (St. Louis: Concordia, 2012).

Walther Sermon Inventory. Exhaustive Listing for the Sermons and Addresses of Dr. C. F. W. Walther. Prepared by Thomas Egger (St. Louis: Concordia Historical Institute, 1998).

THE TIME OF CHRISTMAS

ADVENT SEASON

FIRST SUNDAY IN ADVENT (1857)

MATTHEW 21:1–9

Lord Jesus, whenever we began the new Church Year, we had to come before You in shame, because of the sins committed in the past. Today is no exception. We are again laden with the burden of guilt. Lord, are You not tired of having mercy upon us? No! No! You are not. You are God and not man; You are Jesus, "the same yesterday, and today, and forever." Though *we* may forget You, You will not forget us. Though *we* may forsake You, You will never forsake us. Though *we* may be unfaithful to You, You will remain ever faithful. You cannot deny Yourself. " 'For the mountains may depart and the hills be removed, but My steadfast love shall not depart from you, and My covenant of peace shall not be removed,' says the LORD, who has compassion on you" (Isaiah 54:10). Trusting this word of comfort, we on this first day of the new Church Year approach You and beseech You not to remember our unfaithfulness; come again through Word and Sacrament with new grace, new blessings, new protection for Your whole Church, for our city, our congregation, our homes, and for all of us. Even so, come, Lord Jesus. Amen.

Dear friends in Christ Jesus!

"The steadfast love of the LORD never ceases; His mercies never come to an end; they are new every morning" (Lamentations 3:22–23). Thus Jeremiah comforted the believers of the old covenant as they groaned in captivity, and Jerusalem, city and temple, lay in ruins. The Lord's mercies "are new every morning," cried the prophet. How comforting! Sinners cannot have a greater, richer, more precious comfort. Let us ponder the meaning of these words.

"God's mercies are new *every* morning." They never cease as long as morning follows evening. Although God has for thousands of years shown endless mercy to the whole sinful human race, though He has pursued a certain person with nothing but mercy for many years, and though He has, as it were, overwhelmed him with mercy, it still has not ended or reached its goal.

If we *human beings* ever show mercy at all, it is only in a limited amount. Our mercy toward our fellow sinners soon ends. If we have been merciful to them several times, we finally say only too quickly, "That's enough." Should he to whom we had shown mercy prove unthankful or even use our mercy *against* us, our mercy easily and quickly ceases.

The fountain of divine mercy flows on without interruption; even the basest unthankfulness, even the most wanton abuse cannot choke it up, for He is an eternal unfathomable *sea* of love.

Still more. When it says, "God's mercies are *new* every morning," it not only means that they never cease, but that they also never wane. They are always the same, always as great and ardent as at the beginning. They never age.

Our mercy may even burn brightly for a while. Though it may not be completely extinguished when put to the test, it will readily become weaker, and finally it will flow only drop by drop like a nearly empty jar.

Not so God's mercy. It is, as it says, *new* every morning. Not only on the first day of life does it flow over us in a full stream, but each succeeding evening we must sing, "Praise to the Lord, who will prosper your work and defend you, Surely His goodness and mercy shall daily attend you" (*LSB* 790:4). As the sun rises anew each morning with the same brightness with which it has shone upon the world for thousands of years, so does also God's mercy rise anew every morning upon each person in the same measure as in the past.

However, when it says, "God's mercies are *new* every morning," God does not think of how much or how long He has already shown a person mercy. He does not charge it to His account in order to subtract it from His quota of love. But whenever a new day comes around, God acts as though He had *never* shown him mercy, as if *this were the first day* He let him taste His love, as if today He first began to seek him to show Himself a God who wishes salvation. Whenever a new day dawns, God's mercy again takes a person into its arms, even though he should have a million proofs of God's grace, even though in the past they should all have been in vain, because His mercy is *new* every morning.

If Scripture has any comforting word, such as we need today at the beginning of a new Church Year, if it has any comfort after the undeserved, often vainly bestowed mercy in past years, it certainly is this comforting word. If, according to this word, His mercies are new every *morning*, how much more will they be new every *year*! How sure we can be that they will be new today and throughout the new Church Year! The mercy of God consists chiefly in this, that Jesus in the coming Church Year will again come to us with all His grace, as if He had never come to us before. With God's help, that is what I will try to impress deeply upon your hearts today. To this end may He graciously assist you and me.

The text: *Matthew 21:1–9*

The chief reason why this story was chosen as the text to begin the new Church Year is without doubt this, that at the beginning of the year every Christian may be comforted by the knowledge that Jesus will come again. Let me present to you the comforting truth:

Jesus will come again in also this new Church Year

I direct your attention especially to two points:

1. Who will come, and
2. To whom He will come.

I.

Throughout more than 1,800 years Christ has been coming and has come to each of us. Thousands have noticed His presence. But how few have received Him in the past Church Year! How many have rather turned their backs to Him! Are we therefore certain that in the Church Year now beginning Christ will come again? Couldn't He be tired of coming after having come so often in vain? Isn't it possible that the Church Year just passed was the last in which He wanted to come?

No, that is impossible; He has not tired of coming. Today's text shows us that; Christ's coming into Jerusalem is nothing else than a picture of His continual coming to the New Testament Jerusalem, His Church, as He promised, "If anyone loves Me, he will keep My word, and My Father will love him, and We will come to him, and make our home with him" (John 14:23). And, "behold, I am with you always, to the end of the age" (Matthew 28:20).

But is it really so comforting to know that *Jesus* will come again this new Church Year? Is *He* not the holy Son of God and *we* sinners, who have come short of the glory of God? Is *He* not the eternal Judge of all? Does not *our* conscience accuse us of great guilt, if we but look back into our past, or only into last year? Must we not expect that, when Jesus comes, He will come in wrath to punish us as we deserve?

It certainly might seem that way; but let us take a look at today's Gospel. How does it describe that Jesus who wants to come to us again? We read:

> Now when they drew near to Jerusalem and came to Bethphage, to the Mount of Olives, then Jesus sent two disciples, saying to them, "Go into the village in front of you, and immediately you will find a donkey tied, and a colt with her. Untie them and bring them to me. If anyone says anything to you, you shall say, 'The Lord needs them,' and he will send them at once." This took place to fulfill what was spoken by the prophet, saying, "Say to the daughter of Zion, 'Behold, your king is coming to you, humble, and mounted on a donkey, on a colt, the foal of a beast of burden.' " (Matthew 21:1–5)

Who is this Jesus, who offers to come in the new Church Year? Need we fear such a Jesus? Or haven't we really every reason to await Him with longing and welcome Him with joy? Yes, it is true that our Gospel pictures Jesus as an exalted, noble person. It tells us that He is *omniscient*; He knows the thoughts and words of every inhabitant of Bethphage afar off. It tells us that He is almighty; from afar He made the owner of those two animals do His will. But our Gospel also tells us that He did not come as a holy Judge, armed with the terror of righteous judgment, but as a king, a meek king, a king of grace and mercy.

Can any truth be more comforting than this one on this Sunday of the new Church Year? Study everything carefully. Jesus is omniscient; He knows all the sins that we have ever committed, even those we have already forgotten; He knows all the sins that we will commit in the future; He knows exactly the condition of our heart. He knows it better than we ourselves do; He knows our whole great sinful corruption. Yet He does not want to know this as our Judge, who wants to punish our sins, but as our meek King of grace, who comes to forgive them, blot them out, hurl them into the depths of the sea.

Since He is omniscient, He also knows all the trouble in which we are; all the worries that oppress us; all the unheard sighs that arise within us; all the unseen tears we shed; all the wants of body and soul; all our scheming enemies who seek after our souls. He knows therefore all the dangers, distresses, and afflictions toward which we are going. And though He knows that all our trouble and dangers are caused first by our sins, He does not know all this in order to punish us through them as our enemy, to let us be overwhelmed by them without giving comfort or help. He knows all this as our King of grace; He wants to come in order to fill our temporal and spiritual wants, to hear our prayers and sighs, to dry our tears, to turn aside dangers, to protect us against our enemies, to turn all evil to our good, and finally, to free us from all evil by a blessed death.

Not only does He *know* our trouble and *want* to help us, but He is also *almighty*. He can help us when no one else can; He is able to devise a plan when others give up; everything is in His hands. He can even turn the hearts of men like rivers, and therefore direct everything for our temporal and eternal welfare.

And now what should we do when we today hear the cry "Jesus comes!"? Dare we, looking at Jesus' glory and our sins, filled with fear and worry, let our heads fall? No, no! Who dares be afraid when he hears that his meek king is at the same time great, wise, strong, and mighty? At the call "Jesus comes!" we today must much rather lift up our heads and join in the song of jubilation with which the joyful people greeted the entry of the King of grace, "Hosanna to the Son of David! Blessed is He who comes in the name of the Lord! Hosanna in the highest!"

II.

Yet, of what benefit would it be to know that this wonderful King of grace is coming again in the new Church Year, if He would not come to us? Let us secondly find out *to whom He wants to and promises to come.*

We have no difficulty in finding the correct answer to this question. It has already been given in our Gospel in clear and simple words, "This took place to fulfill what was spoken by the prophet, saying, 'Say to the daughter of Zion, "Behold, your King is coming to you, humble, and mounted on a donkey, on a colt, the foal of a beast of burden" ' " (Matthew 21:4–5). Jesus comes to the daughter of Zion. Zion was the name of a mountain upon whose peak the temple was built, and upon whose sides Jerusalem itself lay. Really, the daughter of Zion means the inhabitants of Jerusalem; figuratively, it means the Church of the Old and New Testaments. Consequently, the Church of believers has the promise that Jesus will come to her at all times, therefore also in the new Church Year beginning today.

But must not many of us fear that Jesus will not come to them? That they do not belong to the daughters of Zion? That they are not yet true members of the Church, true believers?

My dear hearers, I have reason to fear that many a one is not yet a daughter of Zion. Bear in mind, when Christ entered Jerusalem, He of course visited His spiritual believing Zion first of all. Yet at the same time He came to all who had come to Jerusalem, even if they were the most miserable and forlorn sinners. Today Jesus comes first of all to His Church, that is, His true believers. Yet in so doing He comes also to all who have joined the Church, even though they may be the most miserable and wretched sinners. You find Christ's Church wherever His Word is preached and the Sacraments are administered. No daughter of Zion, no Church, no salvation, no bliss can be found where these Means of Grace are not used. Whoever does not use God's Word and Sacraments vainly hopes for Christ's coming. He has no part in Christ nor Christ in him. "Rejoice greatly, O daughter of Zion! Shout aloud, O daughter of Jerusalem! Behold, your King is coming to you . . . humble and mounted on a donkey" (Zechariah 9:9), is the message that should be announced only to the daughter of Zion who has His Word and Sacraments.

Happy are all of you who, not despising God's Word, have come today to hear it and have decided to hear the Word of God diligently in the new Church Year! Even if all of you are not yet citizens of the true spiritual Jerusalem, you are nevertheless like those Israelites who shared in Jesus' entry into Jerusalem. No matter who you are, no matter how hopeless you may think things are, be among those who hear Christ's Word. The joyous message, *Jesus comes in this new Church Year*, applies then also to you.

Despair not, oh sinner, you who in the old Church Year have not quite forgotten, forsaken, or lost your Lord Jesus, but have often been untrue to Him, have not kept many a promise made to Him, have been overcome by many a sin, and in many respects have gone backward instead of ahead. Today begins a new Church Year, in which Jesus your king comes to you again with new grace. Oh, accept Him in new faith and new fervent love. Your aging heart will then be new and young, filled through and through with spiritual spring air. In the new Church Year you will strew before Jesus those palm branches of thanks, which you failed to offer Him in the old.

Despair not, even you who in the old Church Year, perhaps tricked by your flesh, the world, or Satan, have lost your Savior who had lived in your heart. Nor you, who have lived without peace and rest, without light and comfort, without power, and hope, oppressed by the feeling of God's displeasure, despair not! A new year of grace, in which Jesus your king comes to you again with new grace, has come to you today. Oh, fall at His feet; accept Him; gladly will He be yours again. Cast off the garments of your own righteousness; let Christ trample them under foot; ask Him for the true garment of His righteousness; yes, hurry to put it on in faith and you also can again sing hosanna today.

Nor should you despair, you who have never experienced how blessed it is to have Jesus for your King of grace; you who have lived hitherto in carnal security, unconcerned about the salvation of your immortal souls; you who have hitherto striven for wealth, peaceful days, and a comfortable life, and have never earnestly concerned yourself about Jesus, yes, perhaps have been His bitter enemy; you who now see that you can never be saved this way. Though you have wasted past years, God now gives you in the new Church Year new grace. Jesus your king comes to and seeks you again in the new year. Only let Him find you. With a repentant heart grasp the outstretched hand of grace and you will experience that with Him is gracious redemption. And though you be tied with a thousand cords of sin and unbelief, Christ will again say, as He did once, "Untie them and bring them to Me," and you will be free.

Behold, the gates of the new Church Year are open. Jesus our king has in this hour already come to us in His Word. He is here. Rise! Hurry to meet Him! Amen.

SECOND SUNDAY IN ADVENT

LUKE 21:25–36

The grace of our Lord Jesus Christ, the love of God, and the communion of the Holy Spirit be with you all. Amen.

Dear friends in Christ Jesus!

That the world in which we live will not last forever, that some day heaven and earth with all it contains will disappear, is a clear teaching of Holy Scripture. It tells us that this great universe serves only a passing purpose; when it has served its purpose, it will be torn down by the very one who built it. According to the Scriptures, the world is only a tent under which men, who are moving toward eternity, remain just for the night; and when the last person has completed his pilgrimage, it will be pulled down. For us it is not an abiding city, that is, it is not our permanent residence, in which we should remain forever, but only the scaffolding of the eternal dwelling place. As the scaffolding will be removed when the real building is completed, so will also the earthly creation be removed when the heavenly one will be finished. Therefore, according to Holy Writ we must expect a Day of Judgment.

In our day many who wish to be looked on as enlightened deny that there will be such a Judgment Day. Idle enthusiasts have always predicted the day and hour in which that great terrible day would come, and lo! it did not come! All, who have most positively foretold the time when the end of the world would come, have been refuted by time itself. All who believed their prophecy have been mocked by the world. Consequently, the world laughs to think that there still are people who have not been made wise by such experiences and despite them assert that some day, the judgment will come. Though the world may laugh, there can be nothing more foolish than to deny that some day the world's Last Day will most certainly come. Not only does Scripture tell us this but even our reason.

First, it is an incontestable principle, that the whole is the sum of its parts. To use a plain example, if all the individual pieces of a thing are of wood, the whole is made of wood. If all the parts of a thing are perishable, the whole must be perishable.

We see that all the separate elements of the world are subject to change and destruction and are therefore perishable. Fire consumes most of the things that compose the world, rust others, water decomposes still others; others crumble away through atmospheric action, and so on. We see how sometimes this, sometimes that, part of the world is desolated, destroyed, or lost to view by floods, earthquakes, or subterranean craters. Even unbelieving scientists and especially astronomers maintain that comets are destroyed planets. In amazement they have at times even announced that certain stars, observed for thousands of years, have sometimes suddenly, sometimes gradually, disappeared from the heavens. We have shown that certain *parts* of the world have been destroyed, hence it is rank folly to maintain that the whole world never can or will be destroyed.

Bear this also in mind. Our earth especially cannot exist without other heavenly bodies. The sun, moon, and stars give it light, warm it, and make it fruitful. Should the sun withdraw only a little farther from the earth, the world would quickly grow cold and all life would cease. Should the sun, on the other hand, draw only a little closer, the water would soon boil away and everything would be burned. Now if the heavenly bodies upon whose existence the world depends, can be changed, yes, destroyed, the earth can also be changed and destroyed.

Moreover, we must add, the world has changed, and changes daily. It is undeniable that the human race has become weaker from century to century. It is evident that men today do not become as old as previously; man falls prey to an increasing number of various kinds of sicknesses; and as men have overpopulated ever more countries, the earth has become ever more impoverished and the means to support people become fewer and fewer. Every reasonable person must therefore perceive even without God's Word, that the earth and mankind cannot exist forever. The earth must of necessity end. And when the last second of the world will come, it will also be true of this world: So far and no further! In short, there must be a Judgment Day even according to the judgment of sound reason. Even the heathen have written that.

We, however, will follow God's Word. It shows us not only that Judgment Day will certainly come but also that in these times we dare never imagine ourselves safe.

The text: *Luke 21:25–36*

On the basis of today's Gospel let me present to you:

How foolish it is in our day to imagine ourselves
safe from Judgment Day

It is foolish because of

1. The signs that have already occurred;
2. The circumstances in which the word finds itself; and,
3. The suddenness with which judgment shall come.

Lord Jesus, who once came into the world to save sinners, and who will come again to judge the quick and the dead, let us in repentance and faith find Thee in Thy manger and on the cross, so that we may see Thee with joy upon the clouds and on Thy throne. To that end bless also this present meditation on Thy Holy Word, for the sake of Thy merciful incarnation. Amen.

I.

God has earnestly forbidden all inquisitiveness on man's part in wanting to discover the exact time of Judgment Day. Christ not only says in the state of humiliation, "But concerning that day or that hour, no one knows, not

11

even the angels in heaven, nor the Son, but only the Father" (Mark 13:32); He also tells His apostles after His resurrection in glory, "It is not for you to know times or seasons that the Father has fixed by His own authority" (Acts 1:7). As little as God will let men know in advance the Day of Judgment, so little does God want to let men ever feel safe from Judgment Day. Rather, the *false* Christian is presented in God's Word as a person who says in his heart, "My master is delayed" (Matthew 24:48), while the true Christians are described as those who "wait for the revealing of our Lord Jesus Christ" (1 Corinthians 1:7).

Therefore, even the apostles told their hearers that Judgment Day is near, and admonished them to hold themselves in readiness. "Children," writes St. John in his first letter, "it is the last hour" (1 John 2:18). Peter writes, "The end of all things is at hand" (1 Peter 4:7). Paul writes, "They were written down for our instruction, on whom the end of the ages has come" (1 Corinthians 10:11). James writes, "Behold, the Judge is standing at the door" (James 5:9). At the beginning of the only prophetic book of the New Testament, we read, "Blessed is the one who reads aloud the words of this prophecy, and blessed are those who hear, and who keep what is written in it, for the time is near" (Revelation 1:3). And finally in Hebrews we read, "Yet a little while, and the coming one will come and will not delay" (Hebrews 10:37).

The apostles used the nearness of Judgment Day as an important reason for their admonitions. Thus for example in Hebrews, "Not neglecting to meet together, as is the habit of some, but encouraging one another, and all the more as you see the Day drawing near" (10:25). And in Philippians, "Let your reasonableness be known to everyone. The Lord is at hand" (4:5).

If even the Christians of apostolic times should not feel safe from the unexpected appearance of Judgment Day, assuredly we in our time dare much less. Yes, nothing can be more foolish than this, *first of all, because of the signs that have already been fulfilled.*

There are certain signs that should precede Judgment Day and announce its nearness to all people. Christ mentions them in our text,

> And there will be signs in sun and moon and stars, and on the earth distress of nations in perplexity because of the roaring of the sea and the waves, people fainting with fear and with foreboding of what is coming on the world. For the powers of the heavens will be shaken. And then they will see the Son of Man coming in a cloud with power and great glory. (Luke 21:25–27)

Many are of the opinion that they can be very calm in regard to the Last Day, because these signs must precede the last great and terrible day. They suppose that they are still to come. But they err; all those signs have occurred in the course of time and take place now in part before our very eyes.

Have not the sun and moon been darkened often? Have not remarkable phenomena in the stars and especially in distant space been noticed? Have not people become so afraid, that they fainted for fear and for waiting for those that should come and in despair have committed suicide? Have not the sea and the waves roared frightfully and swallowed great multitudes of people? Have not the powers of heaven been often shaken? Have not astronomers reported that stars observed for thousands of years have suddenly disappeared?

And have not also all other signs, which according to God's Word should precede Judgment Day, been fulfilled long ago? Have not the times long since passed when nation first rose against nation and kingdom against kingdom? In which pestilence, famine, and earthquakes came time and time again? In which unrighteousness even among baptized Christians increased and love in many grew old? In which many false prophets have arisen and deceived many? Furthermore, has not the Gospel been preached throughout the whole world, not to convert them, but as Christ says, "As a testimony to all nations" (Matthew 24:14)? Has not the great falling away in Christendom, which according to prophecy precedes the day of the Lord, taken place long ago, when the Roman papacy came to power? Is not the long line of Roman popes who have seated themselves in the temple of Christ, that is, in the Church of Christ, the antichrist? Has the antichrist not been revealed to all who cling to God's Word, which has destroyed him? And finally, have not the scoffers of Peter's prophecy, which should be fulfilled in the last days, actually arisen within the very Church of Christ itself?

There is no doubt: all the signs that should precede the unexpected appearance of the Last Day of the world have been fulfilled long ago. Of course, the unbelieving world pays no attention to all these signs. They consider it childish superstition to regard these appearances in nature, especially those in the sky, as signs of the last times. They think that because similar things have constantly occurred, due in part to easily explained natural causes, since astronomers can forecast most exactly eclipses of the sun and moon, it is foolish to attach any significance to these things. But do not be deceived by such thoughts! Even if many of these harbingers might be explained by natural causes, yes, may even be forecast, they still are and remain indisputable signs of the Last Day. The rainbow is and remains the sign that God will never again send a universal, all-destroying flood, even though scientists understand the natural laws that operate to make the rainbow. God has made the rainbow a sign of this and has given it this meaning.

Similarly, all eclipses of the sun and moon, and all other unusual happenings in the heavens, yes, even the frightful roaring of the seas, are and remain undeniable signs of the Last Day. One may always be able to point to natural causes, but Christ has made them the signs of the Last Day and has given them this meaning. All sicknesses and the infirmity of old age have natural causes. Yet both signs, lasting from the cradle to the grave, show in part the certainty, in part the nearness, of death. To be sure, many of those signs have natural causes; and yet God has appointed them to remind the world of the certainty and nearness of its final dissolution. Each recurring sickness of man calls time and time again, "Set your house in order, for you shall die" (Isaiah 38:1). So also all these signs, which have occurred throughout the centuries, have called to the whole world time and time again: Soon, oh world, also your last hour will strike!

Hence, what can be more foolish than to hear how in the past 1,800 years God has again and again announced the nearness of the end of all things through creatures over us and next to us and under us, as though by a trumpet blast, and still remain calm, secure, and carefree, and say, "My master is delayed!"? May the God of grace guard us from such security! The patience of God, to whom a thousand years is as a day and a day as a thousand years, has already waited with the Day of Judgment for 1,800 years. He has patience with us and is not willing that any should perish but that all should come to repentance. But finally, when that hour strikes, which in His counsel He has decided upon, the Lord will also come and will not delay. "Heaven and earth will pass away, but My words," He says and also the word of His return, "will not pass away" (Matthew 24:35). The Jewish people are still before our eyes as a sign of His promised coming. Christ said, "Truly, I say to you, this generation will not pass away until all these things take place," (Matthew 24:34). As certainly as neither time nor oppression, though ever so severe, dared destroy the Jews, this drop in the sea of nations, so certainly will Jesus let that happen for which, as a sign, He has sustained that nation until this hour.

II.

That it is foolish to imagine oneself safe from Judgment Day we see also from *the condition of the world*. Permit me to speak to you of this.

In what condition the world will be before the Last Day, Christ explains in our Gospel: "But watch yourselves lest your hearts be weighed down with dissipation and drunkenness and cares of this life, and that day come upon you suddenly like a trap" (Luke 21:34). In these words Christ warns Christians not to be drawn into the life of the last world. It consists partly in the secure, carefree, voluptuous life, eating, drinking, and carousing, partly in worry, covetousness, and driving oneself to acquire worldly goods. That this is the correct explanation of this word of Christ we see from other related sayings of Christ and the apostles.

Christ says in Matthew 24:14, "This Gospel of the kingdom will be proclaimed throughout the whole world, . . . and then the end will come." But Christ does not say, that by this universal preaching there shall be a universal conversion; He expressly adds, "As a testimony to all nations."

Christ says in Luke 17,

> Just as it was in the days of Noah, so will it be in the days of the Son of Man. They were eating and drinking and marrying and being given in marriage, until the day when Noah entered the ark, and the flood came and destroyed them all. Likewise, just as it was in the days of Lot—they were eating and drinking, buying and selling, planting and building, but on the day when Lot went out from Sodom, fire and sulfur rained from heaven and destroyed them all— so will it be on the day when the Son of Man is revealed. (vv. 26–30)

Christ adds in Luke 18, "Nevertheless when the Son of Man comes, will He find faith on earth?" (v. 8b).

Paul and Peter also give the same description of the condition of the world shortly before the Last Day. Paul writes to the Thessalonians, "That day will not come, unless the rebellion comes first" (2 Thessalonians 2:3). To Timothy, "Now the Spirit expressly says that in later times some will depart from the faith by devoting themselves to deceitful spirits and teachings of demons" (1 Timothy 4:1); for "Understand this, that in the last days there will come times of difficulty. For people will be lovers of self, lovers of money, proud, arrogant, abusive, disobedient to their parents, ungrateful, unholy, having the appearance of godliness, but denying its power" (2 Timothy 3:1–2, 5). And Peter writes, "Knowing this first of all, that scoffers will come in the last days with scoffing, following their own sinful desires. They will say, 'Where is the promise of His coming? For ever since the fathers fell asleep, all things are continuing as they were from the beginning of creation' " (2 Peter 3:3–4).

If we hold the condition of the world of our days against this picture the Holy Scriptures sketch of the condition of the world shortly before the Last Day, can we doubt for an instant that we live in the last times? There is no doubt; the fig tree has leaves and blossoms; the heat of the Last Day approaches. We cannot deny the facts, whether we examine doctrine or life.

As far as *doctrine* is concerned, the Gospel of the kingdom, just as Christ said, is even now being preached to all nations; the great falling away that was foretold is being revealed in Christendom itself, partly in the papacy, partly in the enthusiastic sects and the confusion in religion in our day. Whole armies of baptized scoffers and slanderers have now arisen; they seek to overthrow all religion under the guise of progress and enlightenment, and condemn all holy mysterious doctrines and institutions of Christ as superstition. They make a game of the Bible, God, Christ, heaven, and hell, and merely laugh at and ridicule a belief in the last day.

On the other hand, as far as *daily life* is concerned, most live by the principle: let us eat, drink, and be merry, for tomorrow we die. All sins are committed so brazenly, as though there were no longer a God whom men should fear, and no judgment before which men must appear and give account. They make no secret of their sins, rather boast of them; they regret that they cannot be more open about them. As at the time of the flood and the destruction of Sodom and Gomorrah, they live and plan amid the greatest feeling of security and unconcern; they seek to gather money, build houses, and enjoy the world. And if here and there witnesses for the truth appear, who announce God's threats, wrath, punishment, judgment, and hell, most (just like the inhabitants of Sodom) consider this something laughable. Societies are being constantly organized which have the purpose of ending all Christian discipline, inciting the children against their elders, the citizens against the government, the hearers against the teacher, the poor against the rich. Yes, nowadays no one is ashamed to slander even the estate of matrimony and declare that adultery, divorce, and all other sins are permissible.

Whoever does not see from all this that we have come to the very dregs of time, must of a truth have drunk from this very intoxicating cup of these last, shameful times and become intoxicated.

Dare we be secure? Of a truth, no! Heaven and earth are everywhere calling to us, as though with the voice of thunder, "The Judge is standing at the door." Satan himself is ringing every bell, calling for the last revolt of mankind against his Maker. Oh, let us therefore not sleep, but let us arm ourselves, so that we may be ready that, when Jesus Christ comes to judge the living and the dead, we may welcome Him with joy.

III.

Our Gospel presents a third reason for not considering ourselves safe. It is *the suddenness with which the last day will come*. Jesus says in our text, "For it will come upon all who dwell on the face of the whole earth" (Luke 21:35).

My friends, if God should announce the Last Day only a day, yes, only an hour ahead of time, many would think that he could risk waiting with his conversion and preparation until the announcement came. He could console himself with the thought that in the short appointed respite he could still turn to God and beg for His grace, because God is a merciful God.

But God has cut off this false comfort. The Last Day will come as unexpectedly and suddenly as death comes to most. No unusual indisposition, no sickness, no weakness of age, in short, nothing will announce that day, except what has announced it long ago. It will come as unannounced as a thief in the night, as suddenly as lightning out of the blue sky, and, as our text says, unexpectedly "suddenly like a trap . . . on all who dwell on the face of the whole earth." Even the pious will have received no sign.

As the hunter secretly sets his snare for the wild animal that he wishes to capture and avoids every noise that would betray his presence; as he, while the animal grazes unconcerned in the meadow, suddenly dashes out of the thicket and throws the snare around its neck and feet; as the trembling animal sees itself suddenly caught and tied so that it cannot stir and carried swiftly away to receive the deaththrust with a sharp gleaming knife, so God is also secretly preparing His Last Day for the secure world; He lets no man, yes, no angel or creature know the second in which He will break in upon the world. This great terrible day already hovers over the world, but no one in heaven and on earth suspects the day of the frightening event.

The fateful day dawns, but the world, sleeping in sin, will live on up to this day as it has always lived. In eating and drinking, in marrying and giving in marriage, in building and planting, in laughing and joking, in mocking and slandering. The world will always say to the believers: be still about that Last Day, about your hell and judgment; all that is a jest, a boogeyman, dreamed up by priests in order to frighten children and women.

But see! While they still mock, while they still eat and drink, commit adultery and play, and, blasphemously laughing and joking, while away the hours, suddenly the heavens open and Jesus Christ, clothed with all the fear of a judge, appears on the clouds of heaven. Thousands upon thousands of angels surround Him with flaming swords, the archangel sounds the trumpet, and, as a thousand storms, thunders its crashing sound throughout the quivering creation. The dead arise; the whole world trembles and quakes; the enemies of Christ feel their waiting damnation in their hearts, and their cries fill heaven and earth; at the sight of their Savior only the host of the pious, full of holy delight, sing rejoicingly in a million-voiced hallelujah.

There will be no time for the unconverted to be converted; with the appearance of the Judge, the period of grace has ended. In a second God's wrath, as though it were a mountain, rests upon the souls of all who did not prepare themselves for this day with true repentance. They shall cry woe and shame upon themselves, curse the day of their birth, wish to escape but cannot, wish to hide but cannot; without bringing any results their cry of woe, "to the mountains and rocks, 'Fall on us and hide us from the face of Him who is seated on the throne, and from the wrath of the Lamb, for the great day of Their wrath has come, and who can stand?' " (Revelation 6:16–17), dies away. With a crash the whole creation that had been kept for judgment will collapse, hell will roar up, open its fiery jaws, and eternally swallow all its children.

Bear this in mind, you sinners: we can still live through this terrible scene today, even during this hour!

Up! Up! Flee quickly in faith to the Zoar of the wounds of Jesus Christ. Remain, ah, remain there, and then "But stay awake at all times, praying that you may have strength to escape all these things that are going to take place, and to stand before the Son of Man" (Luke 21:36).

To the Savior, the comfort and refuge of all sinners, be praise and honor forever and ever. Amen.

THIRD SUNDAY IN ADVENT (1843)

MATTHEW 11:2–10

Grace and peace be multiplied unto you through the knowledge of God, and of Jesus our Lord. Amen.

Dear friends in Christ Jesus!

Not only is the world itself a great and glorious miracle of God, but so many miracles take place every day that they cannot be counted. Who can express the greatness of the miracle that the sun has shone for well nigh unto six thousand years without lessening or changing its power, its brightness, its warmth. What a miracle that day and night, since the creation of the world, the countless stars traverse their orbits around the earth without even once being displaced in the least. Astronomers can with almost unfailing certainty forecast far in advance the moment when the sun or other star will rise over our horizon!

What a miracle that this colossal globe, hanging freely in space, unsupported by pillars, has not long ago fallen into the bottomless abyss of space! What a miracle that the freely moving wind and clouds have not long ago laid everything waste, that despite their apparently irregular interweaving on earth, they sometimes water it, sometimes dry it out, and thus have always kept it fruitful! What a miracle that every year as we entrust our seed to the ground it decays, and we see full heads of grain sprouting. Every tree with its twigs, leaves, blossoms, and fruit growing from one seed, every vine with its sweet grapes growing up luxuriantly out of the dry earth, each blade of grass daily unfolding before our eyes is a miracle, whose secrets we can indeed gaze at with astonishment, but which no wise man can explain.

These are the miracles of nature, which loudly proclaim that the world is not an accidental heaped-up mass of raw material but the living masterpiece of an almighty and all-wise God in whom we live and move and have our being.

And yet, my friends, all the puzzling things that we see daily in nature are only improperly called miracles. Really, a miracle is something that cannot be produced in the course of nature and through the powers lying in creatures, but only through God, the Lord of nature, through His new, creative limitless power. That a seed grows up to be a stalk with a full head of grain and multiplies itself a hundredfold is not a real miracle, because this takes place through the powers that God has already placed in nature. But if by His mere word someone makes a thousand loaves from one loaf of bread, He performs a true miracle, because this is contrary to the laws of nature, and surpasses all powers that are inherent in creatures. That a doctor cures the sick by using drugs is not a miracle; but if someone with a word cures a sickness that no drug can cure, He performs a true miracle, because the simple word is a sign of that which has or should occur. That the sun gradually matures the grapes on the vine is not really a miracle; but He who through His mere word turns water into wine does something for which more power is necessary than is found in the whole creation. This again is properly a miracle. Consequently, if we see a miracle, we see the workings of a power that no creature, not even an angel, has—the workings of the almighty Creator.

Every time God sent messengers into the world who had to proclaim something that no man could know, God also conferred upon these messengers the power to perform miracles. In so doing He provided them with the credentials, that what they said was the divine truth. Therefore, everyone must believe them upon pain of God's displeasure.

Today's Gospel shows us that because of the miracles that Jesus Christ did, He demanded faith in Himself. Let us now consider further how the miracles of Jesus Christ prove beyond question that He is truly He whom He claimed to be, namely, the Son of God and the Savior of the world.

The text: *Matthew 11:2–10*

John the Baptist did not doubt in the least that Jesus was the true Messiah, as many mistakenly maintain. Above all, Christ's last words in our text have the purpose of removing such thoughts from the hearts of the people, as though even John, after he was imprisoned because he confessed Christ, was a "reed shaken by the wind" (Matthew 11:7). Although John continually pointed his disciples to Christ as the Lamb of God who takes away the sin of the world, his disciples took offense at the humble form of Jesus Christ. John, therefore, sent his disciples to Christ with the question, "Are You the one who is to come, or shall we look for another?" (Matthew 11:3). John wanted his disciples to hear the evidence from Christ's own mouth, and thus be brought to faith in Him.

Now what did Christ answer? He said, "Go and tell John what you hear and see: the blind receive their sight and the lame walk, lepers are cleansed and the deaf hear, and the dead are raised up, and the poor have good news preached to them. And blessed is the one who is not offended by Me"

(Matthew 11:4–6). Clearly, the Lord refers the doubting disciples first of all to His miracles. Therefore, let us today meditate on this:

The miracles of Jesus Christ prove that He is God's Son
and the Savior of the world.

Let us

1. Examine the power of this evidence, and
2. Consider that no person will therefore have an excuse if he does not believe on Christ.

Lord God, heavenly Father, You have not only borne witness to Your dear Son through Your servant Moses, "And whoever will not listen to My words that he shall speak in My name, I Myself will require it of him" (Deuteronomy 18:19); You did not only call from heaven to all the world, "This is My beloved Son; listen to Him" (Mark 9:7); but You have also given Your only-begotten Son signs and wonders, by which He proved beyond any doubt that You sent Him. Oh, have mercy on us and grant that we may recognize the glory of the works of Your Son, that all of us will believe on Him and be saved. Hear us for the sake of Your Son, our Savior. Amen.

I.

A miracle, as you have heard, is a work that is produced contrary to the laws of nature. It does not have its power in the laws of nature but infinitely surpasses the restricted power of all created beings. No creature, no man, not even an angel can make something out of nothing or change the nature of a thing—only God can. Therefore we read in Psalm 72:18, "Blessed be the LORD, the God of Israel, who alone does wondrous things."

Without a doubt, if we see a miracle performed, we must believe that the person has received this unusual power from God; what such a person says and confirms with miracles has the divine seal of being the absolute truth; it is just as if God Himself had spoken. No deceit is possible in genuine miracles. The secret seal can be stolen from a king; men can forge his handwriting; they can make false documents and credentials in order to pass themselves off as empowered representatives of the king; but no man can enter the secret chambers of God and steal the seal of divine majesty. God must have voluntarily given it to him who has it.

Therefore, God does not demand that we believe a teaching that no person can know except by God's direct revelation, if it is not confirmed by miracles. Christ clearly says, "If I am not doing the works of My Father, then do not believe Me" (John 10:37). How miserable we would be, if we had to receive men as God's messengers and their words as God's words, if they performed no miracles! How could we protect ourselves against false prophets?

Consequently, whenever prophets were sent by God into the world with a new revelation, they were also accredited by the divine seal, the power to do miracles. What amazing works Moses did before the whole nation of Egypt! Even the Egyptian magicians could no longer imitate them with their delusions. They had to cry out, "This is the finger of God" (Exodus 8:19). Was not Aaron's divine mission confirmed when in one night his dry stick became green, blossomed, and bore almonds? Did not Joshua prove his divine call, when at his word sun and moon stood still? And the prophet Elijah, when at his request fire fell from heaven, and the widow's son at Zarephath was raised from the dead? Elisha, when he made solid iron swim; and Isaiah, when he made the shadow on the sundial go back ten degrees? But who can mention all the miracles of the prophets of the Old Testament?

Hence you see saying that little or nothing depends on the miracles related in the Scriptures, but only the excellence of the doctrines it contains, is a godless trick now used to rob the miracles of their divinely attested authority. The very miracles, which no man can do without God's help, prove to us that we are not deceived when we perceive the excellence of the doctrines of Scripture.

Christ's miracles have also a special meaning. He shows two things about Himself: first, that He is more than a prophet, namely the Son of God; and second, that He is that Messiah, or Savior, of the world who had been promised by the prophets. He says of Himself: "Something greater than Solomon is here" (Matthew 12:42); "I and the Father are one" (John 10:30); "Whoever has seen Me has seen the Father" (14:9); "My Father is working until now, and I am working" (5:17); "For whatever the Father does, that the Son does likewise" (5:19); "For as the Father raises the dead and gives them life, so also the Son gives life to whom He will. The Father judges no one, but has given all judgment to the Son, that all may honor the Son" (5:21–23); "I am the way, and the truth, and the life. No one comes to the Father except through Me" (14:6); "You search the Scriptures because you think that in them you have eternal life; and it is they that bear witness about Me" (5:39). Once the question, "Do you believe in the Son of Man?" was asked of a man born blind but now healed. He replied, "And who is He, sir, that I may believe in Him?" Jesus answered, "You have seen Him, and it is He who is speaking to you" (John 9:35–37). Thus Christ witnessed of Himself.

But would any man dare believe Him if He had not proven it by His works? Never! The Old Testament clearly foretold that the true Christ would confirm His office and person with great miracles. Moses said of Him, "The LORD your God will raise up for you a prophet like me from among you, from your brothers—it is to Him you shall listen" (Deuteronomy 18:15). "*Like me*," says Moses; consequently, the Prophet of prophets would have to do miracles as Moses did. This Prophet excelled all other messengers of God by the very greatness and number of His miracles. Furthermore, Isaiah says that the Child of salvation would live up to the name "Wonderful." Even more clearly, he bears witness in another passage: "Say to those who have an anxious heart, 'Be strong; fear not! Behold, your God will come with vengeance' " (i.e., against the seducer, the devil), " 'with the recompense of God. He will come and save you.' Then the eyes of the blind shall be opened, and the ears of the deaf unstopped; then shall the lame man leap like a deer, and the tongue of the mute sing for joy" (Isaiah 35:4–6).

It is clear from this that Jesus could not have been the Savior promised by the prophets if He had not performed miracles. He did not let His power to perform miracles be seen only now and then, but He infinitely excelled all other messengers of God by His miracles.

He did this, first of all, by their astonishing number. As soon as Christ entered upon His office of teaching, He made entire crowds well. We read that almost every step was accompanied with miracles. And yet those related in the Gospels are only a part of those that Christ did. John expressly says at the end of his Gospel, "Now there are also many other things that Jesus did. Were every one of them to be written, I suppose that the world itself could not contain the books that would be written" (John 21:25). The Jews count 150 miracles in the Old Testament; but Christ performed more miracles than all the prophets put together. The people said at the beginning of His ministry, "When the Christ appears, will He do more signs than this man has done?" (John 7:31).

Christ's miracles excel not only in their great number but also in their special glory. Full of astonishment, one person confessed, "Never since the world began has it been heard that anyone opened the eyes of a man born blind" (John 9:32). It was an even greater miracle that Christ could say, "Destroy this temple, and in three days I will raise it up" (2:19). He meant, of course, the temple of His body. He stated that He would rise by His own power. In another passage He said, "No one takes it from Me, but I lay it down of My own accord. I have authority to lay it down, and I have authority to take it up again" (John 10:18). What divine power and glory streams from these words! No prophet had or ever could speak that way. Christ not only uttered them, but also fulfilled them by making Himself alive again on the third day, as He said He would.

Furthermore, the unusual variety of His miracles also shows the superiority of Christ. He did them to all manner of creatures—to the evil spirits whom He drove out of the possessed; to men in every walk of life. He revealed their most secret thoughts. He healed the sick who lay in a fever, those with dropsy, the paralytic, and those with flowing blood. He made the deaf hear, the dumb speak, the blind see, the lame walk, the leprous clean, yes, the dead alive. And He did this not only in their presence, but often being far away from the sufferer whom He helped without having to speak to or see them.

Christ also proved His power by doing miracles in other creatures. At His command, the fish of the sea were compelled to gather in one place. A fish had to bring Him a piece of money for payment of a tax. Because he blessed them, bread and fish had to multiply a thousandfold. At His word the fig tree that bore no fruit had to wither; the water had to change into wine; the enraged waves had to quiet down at His threat; the disciples at that time had to say, "What sort of man is this, that even winds and sea obey Him?" (Matthew 8:27).

However, that He did His miracles in His own name, hence, in His own power, sets Christ above all the prophets and apostles. He proved thereby that He was the very Son of God. To the prayer of a leper, "Lord, if You will, You can make me clean," Christ simply said, "I will; be clean!" (Matthew 8:2–3), and the miracle took place. To the dead daughter of Jairus He said, "Child, arise" (Luke 8:54). To the son of widow of Nain, who was in his casket, "Young man, I say to you, arise" (Luke 7:14). And to Lazarus who was decaying in the grave, "Lazarus, come out" (John 11:43). And see, death and decay fled before the powerful word of Christ!

Moses could not speak that way; he always said, "Thus says the LORD, . . . 'I will strike the water that is in the Nile' " (Exodus 7:17), and so on. Even the apostles had to speak differently. They received their power to perform miracles from Christ, yes, with the command to do them in Christ's name. Peter, for example, said to the lame man at the temple, "In the name of Jesus Christ of Nazareth, rise up and walk!" (Acts 3:6). And so only of Christ can we say, as we can of God the Father, "For He spoke, and it came to be; He commanded, and it stood firm" (Psalm 33:9).

In one more way Christ shows by His miracles that He is no mere prophet but is come as a Savior. The miracles of Christ were not as those of many other prophets, which destroyed and frightened, but helped and cheered. With a word Christ could indeed have smashed His slandering enemies. He could have allowed the godless cities that rejected Him to be swallowed up. He could have made the seeing blind and the speaking speechless.

But Christ's office was not like Moses', which preached damnation. Christ's office was grace. Where Moses turned water into blood, Christ turned it into wine; where Elisha smote an unfaithful servant with leprosy, Christ cleansed those who were burdened with it. Elijah called fire from heaven to fall on the enemies of God; when the apostles demanded the same from Christ, He said, "You do not know what manner of spirit you are of; for the Son of Man came not to destroy people's lives but to save them" (Luke 9:55). When in the garden of Gethsemane Peter cut off the ear of Malchus, Christ healed it in a second, even though Malchus had come to take Christ captive.

These are the glorious miracles of Christ, by which He proves beyond doubt that we must believe Him when He states that He is the Son of God and the Savior of the world. We do not mention the wonderful miracles, which for Christ's sake occurred at His birth, baptism, crucifixion, death, resurrection, and ascension. Hence, He Himself at all times appealed to His works; He said among other things, "The testimony that I have is greater than that of John. For the works that the Father has given Me to accomplish, the very works that I am doing, bear witness about Me" (John 5:36). "Believe me that I am in the Father and the Father is in Me, or else believe on account of the works themselves" (14:11). Christ wants to say: If nothing can convince you, then My works should.

Christ's miracles did not remain without great fruit. Thousands were brought to faith in the Gospel through them. Finally, the high priests and Pharisees took council, saying one to another, "What are we to do? For this man performs many signs. If we let Him go on like this, everyone will believe in Him" John 11:47–48. And not only were the uneducated convinced by Christ's miracles. Even Nicodemus, a leader of the Pharisees, admitted to Christ, "Rabbi, we know that You are a teacher come from God, for no one can do these signs that You do unless God is with him" (John 3:2).

II.

Hence, because of the great miracles that Christ did, no man will have an excuse if he did not believe in Christ. For when in our text Christ, after the illusion to His works, adds, "*Blessed* is the one who is not offended by Me," (Matthew 11:6), He at the same time is uttering a threat: unhappy, eternally lost, will he be who is offended by Me. Permit me in the second place to add a few words about this.

No one can doubt in the least that Christ actually did the miracles that the evangelists relate. They are the most unbiased witnesses. With the greatest frankness and impartiality they reveal their own faults. Would they have done that, had they not been lovers of the truth? Whom could we believe if we did not want to believe such witnesses? And why should they not have wanted to speak the truth? Were the apostles benefited in any earthly way by preaching the words of Christ? Or did they not because of their preaching have to suffer poverty, shame, persecution, yes, even the most cruel death? Will a person tell a lie in order to involve himself deliberately in misfortune? Nothing is more absurd than to believe something like that.

Christ's miracles did not only take place in secret, in a corner, only before the eyes of His friends, as do the alleged miracles of deceivers. They took place before many thousands of witnesses, often in the very presence of Christ's bitterest enemies. Therefore, when after the resurrection of Christ, the apostles referred to His miracles, no one dared contradict them. If that which the disciples mentioned of Christ had not taken place in the presence of all, would they not have answered them, "You lie!"?

Not even the unbelieving Jews could deny Christ's miracles. They are conceded even in the Talmud. But in order to be able to reject Christ despite them, the rabbis have invented the childish fable that Christ could utter the secret name of Jehovah and thereby received the power to perform miracles.

In the very first century of the Christian era the heathen wrote books against Christianity. We have them today—some in their entirety, others in fragments. But it is noteworthy that none of them try to refute Christianity by denying the truth of these miracles. Rather, they admit that they took place, only that in heathenish blindness they ascribe them to magical powers. How can one deny what a whole nation had seen and witnessed? Even Muhammad acknowledged Christ's miracles in his Koran, so that not even a Muslim denies them.

How, therefore, can a person who has rejected Christ excuse himself? What more could Christ have done in order to prove beyond a doubt that He actually is the Son of God and the Savior of the world? Not only could Christ say, "If I had not done among them the works that no one else did, they would not be guilty of sin, but now they have seen and hated both Me and My Father" (John 15:24); but Christ has also directed affairs in such a way that to this very day we are convinced of the certainty of His miracles by thousands of witnesses.

If Christ had spoken only God's *words* and had not also done God's *works*, one could yet excuse himself. As a person blind by nature in spiritual things, he would not have been in a position to test and examine the excellence of this doctrine. But everyone, even a child, can and must see into the divinity of His *works*. Even the most simple can and must recognize that no man can with one word make one born blind see, in an instant heal a body, yes, awaken the dead. Even the most simple can see that whoever does this must be allied with God. His certified statements must be the truth. The true God Himself gives him the testimony that we can believe in Him, yes, should and must believe in Him at the risk of His eternal displeasure and the loss of eternal life.

Jesus Christ has clearly declared: whoever sees Me, sees the Father; the Father is in Me and I am in the Father; I am the Door; I am the Good Shepherd; I am the Bread of Life; I am the Light of the world; I am the Resurrection and the Life; he that believes in Me, though he were dead, yet shall he live. Now how do those, who have not believed that, expect to be excused on that day? Christ's wonderful miracles will rise against them, accuse and condemn them. They will have nothing—nothing with which to excuse themselves.

And if Christ were only one of the prophets or merely a teacher of the truth, there would still be hope that even those could be saved who had erred in respect to His person and unknowingly rejected Him. Christ, however, is the very Son of God, the Judge of the living and the dead, the only Savior, the only Mediator between God and man. Neither is their salvation in any other; there is no other name given among men whereby they should be saved than by Him alone, Jesus Christ, the blessed Son of God and Son of man! Whoever, therefore, rejects Him, rejects His salvation, His bliss, eternal life, and no creature can rescue such a wretched man.

God already by Moses says of Christ, "I will raise up for them a prophet like you from among their brothers," that is, a prophet who like Moses would bring a new state of the kingdom of God on earth, "and I will put My words in His mouth, and He shall speak to them all that I command Him. And whoever will not listen to My words that He shall speak in My name, I Myself will require it of him" (Deuteronomy 18:18–19). God says there is still help for him who does not keep Moses' word. But for him who does not receive the Word of Christ, the greatest of all prophets, there is no help. Christ Himself therefore, says, "unless you believe that I am He you will die in your sins" (John 8:24).

Oh, the eternally deplorable fate of all unbelievers! Who of us will dare reject the divine seal that Christ has produced, that His word is the truth, and that He is the Son of God and the Savior of the world? Oh, may none, none of us permit ourselves to be drawn into the circle of unbelievers! Otherwise we will some day have regrets, useless and eternal regrets.

No, let us with the open eyes of faith take Christ's great signs and miracles into account and say with Peter, "Lord, to whom shall we go? You have the words of eternal life, and we have believed and [from your works and words] have come to know, that You are the Holy One of God" (John 6:68–69). "Hosanna in the highest." Amen.

FOURTH SUNDAY IN ADVENT

JOHN 1:19–28

Grace be with you, mercy and peace, from God the Father, and from the Lord Jesus Christ, the Son of the Father, in truth and love. Amen.

Dear friends in Christ Jesus!

"I believed, even when I spoke" is the way David speaks in Psalm 116:10. Saying this he declares that since he has faith, he must speak of it. The prophet Jeremiah says something similar. He relates that he had to prophecy misfortune to the apostate nation of Israel; and because he reaped nothing but the most bitter scorn and mockery for prophesying this he had intended to be completely silent. He adds, "there is in my heart as it were a burning fire shut up in my bones, and I am weary with holding it in, and I cannot" (Jeremiah 20:9).

From both of these examples, we see that true faith is a flame kindled in the heart of man by God Himself. Faith like a hemmed in fire bursts into a conflagration; it breaks forth in ardent confession.

History proves that this is actually true. Whenever Christian faith reached greater than average heights, Christians became bold confessors. How zealously the apostles availed themselves of every opportunity to express what lived in their hearts! Though Paul was in chains, we hear him joyfully confessing Christ crucified even before the governors Felix and Festus, before King Agrippa and his queen. We see the apostles Peter and John standing unafraid before the Sanhedrin at Jerusalem saying, "Rulers of the people and elders, let it be known to all of you and to all the people of Israel that by the name of Jesus Christ of Nazareth, whom you crucified, whom God raised from the dead—by Him this man is standing before you well. This Jesus is the stone that was rejected by you, the builders, which has become the cornerstone" (Acts 4:8, 10–11). And when they were threatened never to speak to man of this name again, they answered with joyful shining eyes, "We cannot but speak of what we have seen and heard" (Acts 4:20).

We find such zealous confession among Christians during the first three centuries. In those times, death at the stake, at the blood-stained sword, at the threatening jaws of lions, yes, at even the most horrible pain of torture could not hinder staunch Christians from confessing even before the cruelest ruler: We are Christians! With their confession of faith, even weak women and delicate maidens, yes, children, fearlessly and unshakably resisted all the threats of the mighty.

What happened when three hundred years ago the Gospel again poured the spirit of faith upon thousands and thousands of hearts? Lo, confession soon re-echoed from thousands upon thousands of lips. Though the Roman bishop might angrily excommunicate the Evangelical Christians, though the Kaiser might pronounce the fearful ban of empire, though the confession "I am a Lutheran Christian" might be fraught with danger to life and body, he whose heart was full could not remain silent. "I believed, even when I spoke" was true also in those days.

If we compare our times with those, must we not exclaim "Alas! Where is that wonderful golden age of faithful confessors?" Is not Christ reviled these days rather than confessed by most of the very ones who wish to call themselves Christians? Do not most so-called Christian preachers deny that Christ is true God and the Redeemer?

Of course, a great glorious awakening to faith took place among us Germans a few years ago, but where is the frank confession of the whole truth? Do they not claim that every faith is equally good? Do they not call him a proud, haughty person who wishes to confess, "God has permitted me to find the truth in comparison to which all else is error?"

Yes, they say, you should not deny Christ, but why do you want to reject others who do not believe exactly like you do?

My friends, if they only knew what it means to deny *Christ*, they would not speak like that. Alas, Christ is more often denied than one suspects! Permit me therefore to speak to you today on what it really means to deny Christ.

The text: John 1:19–28

In the Gospel just read we are told how John the Baptist was greatly tempted to deny Christ. But we read, "He confessed, and did *not* deny." This prompts me to speak to you today on

Denying Christ.

I will show you:

1. In which way one can deny Christ, and
2. Why one should allow nothing to move him to deny Christ.

Oh Lord Jesus Christ, who for our sakes made a good confession before Pontius Pilate, forgive us when we, perhaps unknowingly, have denied You, and help us in these last calamitous times to remain in the true faith and a joyful confession of Your pure Gospel until our death. Awaken us also today to such a confession through the preaching of Your Holy Word, for the sake of Your saving name. Amen! Amen!

I.

To know how to *confess* Christ means one must know how one can *deny* Him, for the opposite of confession is denial. It is impossible to go a middle road, to remain absolutely neutral. What Christ says applies here: "Whoever is not with Me is against Me, and whoever does not gather with Me scatters" (Matthew 12:30). Today's text presents John the Baptist as an example of a faithful witness and confessor.

John the Baptist spent his youth in the Judean wilderness. Dressed in a rough garment of camel's hair, he with great self-denial lived simply on nothing but locusts and wild honey. He did so not to earn merit but to attract the attention of the people. And so it happened. Through his unusual appearance, John soon drew the attention of the whole nation. When he finally entered manhood and began to preach repentance, to announce the nearness of the long awaited messianic kingdom, and to baptize those who believed his preaching, almost all people thought that John himself was the promised Messiah; or perhaps he was Elijah, whom they supposed would reappear in the days of the Messiah; or perhaps he was a great prophet, who, according to the popular delusion, should appear with the Messiah.

John's authority with the people grew every day. Even the highest authority felt compelled to respect John. It dispatched a distinguished delegation of priests and levites with the question, "Who are you?" Had John answered "I am the Christ, the promised Messiah," without a doubt the excited people would have enthusiastically sworn allegiance to him as their long awaited deliverer and king. And had John then placed himself at the head of the nation, no government would have been able to stem the tide of revolt. As it seems, the delegation expected no other answer. But what did John say? We read, "He confessed, and did not deny, but confessed, 'I am not the Christ.' " Saying this, John withstood the first temptation to the worst and grossest denial of Christ.

But the delegation asked him more, " 'What then? Are you Elijah?' He said, 'I am not.' " They continued to ask, " 'Are you the Prophet?' And he answered, 'No.' " Many might be surprised that John answered these questions with a No. According to Christ's own words, was not John that Elijah who should precede the Messiah? Didn't Christ call him a prophet, yes, the greatest of all prophets? In a certain sense, yes. And yet he denies both!

We see from John's conduct how careful one must be in confessing one's faith. The Jews supposed that John was really that Elijah who had lived a long time ago. But John was called Elijah only because he came "in the *spirit* and *power*" of Elias. He answered his questioners in the sense in which they asked, not dishonestly misconstruing their questions. The same was true in regard to the question whether he was that prophet. In the sense in which he was asked, John certainly was not that prophet, and so he answered with a decisive No! In his confession he wished to make it impossible for them to draw any false conclusion.

Yet the delegation continues and says, " 'Who are you? We need to give an answer to those who sent us. What do you say about yourself?' He said, 'I am the voice of one crying out in the wilderness, "Make straight the way of the Lord," as the prophet Isaiah said.' " We see from his answer how earnestly John thought so that he answered in such a way that he did not deny in the least even those truths that must be offensive to the delegation. John not only said that he was the herald, the forerunner of the Messiah, but that he was also there to prepare hearts for the Messiah through the preaching of repentance. The priests and Levites might have listened to this in anger. They did not believe that the kingdom of the Messiah was an invisible kingdom into which one could enter only by repentance, much less that *they* needed repentance to receive the Messiah.

The previous friendliness of the delegation, which fancied itself holy, now turned into threatening seriousness. They finally said, "Why are you baptizing, if you are neither the Christ, nor Elijah, nor the Prophet?" Joyfully seizing the opportunity given him, John gave the correct clear testimony that that despised Jesus of Nazareth was the Christ, the Messiah, and that he was one of the subjects of His kingdom. He answered, "I baptize with water, but among you stands one you do not know, even He who comes after me, the strap of whose sandal I am not worthy to untie."

From this wonderful example of a most faithful *confessor* we can learn to know how one can deny Christ. Just think: If John had answered the question "Who are you?" with "I am the very Christ whom the people think I am," he would have grossly and clearly denied Christ.

Today those who declare that Jesus is merely a man, though an outstanding and wise one, are guilty of gross denial. They deny that He is the Savior of all men foretold by the prophets, true God and true man in one person. They deny that He died on the cross to pay the debt of sin. Therefore, they also deny that one is righteous before God and saved by faith in Him. In our day the number of such deniers in churches, in the schools, and even among the people, is legion.

To these gross deniers of Christ belong also those who confess Christ with their mouth, but by a life in open sin show that they want to have nothing to do with Christ. Their confession without faith is no confession, but the clanging of iron and the clinking of a tinkling cymbal.

The example of John shows us still more. When he was asked, "Are you Elijah?" or "the Prophet," John felt obliged to answer with a "No" in order not to be guilty of the error that the Jews associated and expressed with this question. We learn this: Even he denies Christ who denies any truth of the Gospel, though it seems ever so unimportant, and helps to confirm any error, though it seems ever so harmless.

How important this is for our day! Not a few suppose that they are faithful confessors because they have not denied that Christ is the Son of God and the Savior of the world. But from the example of John we see that this is by no means enough for a true confession. One must confess everything that Christ said. For example, whoever wishes to confess that Christ is the Son of God, but either from pride in his reason or fear of the world denies that there is a devil, or that the entire Bible, Old and New Testament, is God's Word, or that a person is reborn through Holy Baptism, or that the body and blood of Christ Jesus are truly present in the Holy Supper, and that all communicants receive it, and the like—I say, whoever denies one of these truths, and though it seems most insignificant, denies Christ Himself and His Word. He makes a liar of Christ.

But more! As we have seen, John was very definite in his confession. Therefore, whoever confesses the truth, but in order to evade the mockery of his foes, confesses, in such a way that he can point out the truth, but that his enemies can also interpret the confession in their favor; whoever does not diligently make his confession so clear that even his foes know exactly what he really believes, in the eyes of God such a confession is nothing else than a clear-cut denial.

Furthermore, we find that John did not suppress that truth which he knew would offend his questioners and arouse their anger. It was the truth that he was come to preach to all: "Make straight the way of the Lord." He was to preach that by nature all are unable to receive the Messiah, he was to hold before all their sins, to show all their unrighteousness, and to call all to repentance.

From this we see that Christ can even be denied by suppressing the truth. Whoever confesses many things, but in order to keep the friendship of the world *suppresses* that truth which he knows the world hates; or whoever suppresses the confession of a truth because he knows that peace and unity with the heterodox will be disturbed, considers the friendship of the world and peace with men more important than Christ and His truth. He also denies his Lord. He belongs to that wretched group of Jewish rulers of whom we read, "Nevertheless, many even of the authorities believed in Him, but for fear of the Pharisees they did not confess it, so that they would not be put out of the synagogue; for they loved the glory that comes from man more than the glory that comes from God" (John 12:42–43).

Finally, we heard that when John was asked for the reason of and authority for his baptism, he used this opportunity to confess his oneness with Christ. We see that all those deny Christ who deny His kingdom on earth, His true Church. How many there are in our day who deny Christ who do not suppose they do! For are they who wish to be known as sincere

Christians honestly concerned not merely in being members of any church but of the true Church of Jesus Christ? Do not many nominal and also true believers join a church in which they clearly recognize that truth and error is tolerated as having equal rights? Are not many true believers ashamed these days to join the little flock of orthodox who have at all times remained with the simple words of Christ and whom Christ calls His true disciples? Alas, in these last times it has come to the point that the church is divided into many factions and even those who earnestly wish to be His own unknowingly deny Him.

II.

Next, let us consider why no one should consciously permit himself to deny his Lord.

If ever there was a situation in which a person had reason to deny his faith, John the Baptist must have been in it. The most distinguished of the country questioned him; had he wanted to deny Christ, he could expect that he would be placed on the Jewish throne. If he, on the other hand, had not wanted to deny Christ, he foresaw nothing but hatred, persecution, prison, and finally a violent death. Yes, since all the Jews had such great confidence in him, he could have thought that if he would at first somewhat conceal the truth, he would be able to save even more souls than if he would bluntly disavow their proposal.

But what did John do? Neither enticements nor threats, neither pleasure nor grief, neither honor nor shame, neither life nor death, neither hope nor fear, neither good nor evil could move him to deny his Lord and Master by double-talk or silence. And why? He clung to God's command to be Christ's herald, the voice in the wilderness, "Make straight the way of the Lord!" Love to his Savior and his poor misguided brethren drove him on. Finally, God's earnest threat discouraged him from subtracting or adding anything to His Word; whoever rejects the Lord's Word would in turn find himself rejected.

There you have the reasons why we should let nothing move us to deny Christ knowingly. If we wish to be Christians, we have the earnest call to be Christ's heralds, to glorify His name in word and deed, yes, with our whole life. The Second Commandment forbids taking Christ's name in vain. That happens every time we deny Him. Whenever we pray the Second Petition, we pray for God's assistance to confess Christ before the world. When we were baptized, we permitted ourselves to be drafted into Christ's army under

His banner in battle for His honor. Whenever we deny Christ, we transgress God's holy command; we jeer at our own Lord's Prayer; we break our baptismal covenant; we forsake the host of believing confessors who stand under Christ's cross. We become faithless deserters to the camp of the enemy, the world, and Satan. Though our reason or heart may recommend the denial of a truth under a good pretext, we must, as dear as God's favor and our salvation is, always consider God's command and our holy oath more important.

Even if we had not promised God and God had not commanded us, the love and thanks we owe Christ should move us not to deny Him under any circumstances or for any consideration. Do we not consider it most shameful when a person is ashamed of his faithful friend and denies him behind his back? How much more shameful must we consider denying our best friend in heaven and on earth—He who loved us from eternity, who for our sakes gave us life, yes, left heaven and His glory, who painfully redeemed us from death and hell through a life full of disgrace, suffering, and finally through shedding His blood? Deny Him who, when our salvation was at stake, "in His testimony before Pontius Pilate made the good confession" (1 Timothy 6:13), though He knew that He would be scourged, mocked, spit upon, crowned with thorns, and finally nailed to the cross? What little thanks for this love is our confession that brings such little disgrace?

And do we not owe it to our fellow redeemed not to deny Christ and His truth? Does not Christ say, "The truth will set you free?" Do we not owe it to our neighbor to confess the complete truth? Does not our heart horribly deceive us when we suppose that we can by denying the truth love our neighbor, since only the truth can truly make him free and save him?

Finally, Christ has not only given the wonderful promise, "So everyone who acknowledges Me before men, I also will acknowledge before My Father who is in heaven," but has also added the frightful threat, "whoever denies Me before men, I also will deny before My Father who is in heaven" (Matthew 10:32–33). "Whoever is ashamed of Me and of My words, of him will the Son of Man be ashamed when He comes in His glory and the glory of the Father and of the holy angels" (Luke 9:26). What good does it do us if we by denying Christ should gain the good will of all men, the wealth of the whole world, yes, of the entire universe? We would in death lose all this and after our death we would learn that we had gambled away our souls and salvation only to be eternally lost. Woe, eternal woe to even a Peter, if with bitter tears of repentance he had not heartily bewailed his denial. Even he would have been eternally lost.

On the other hand, what do we lose if we, like John the Baptist, must shed our blood because we do not want to deny Christ by even one word? Then in place of temporal life we will inherit eternal life, in place of temporal disgrace eternal honor, for temporal pain eternal joy and salvation. Let Jesus above all have our hearts by faith—not only our heart, but also our mouth, yes, everything which we are and have. If already here He is all ours by faith, if we also confess Him in such a faith, we will also receive the end of faith, eternal life. Then Christ will there embrace us and be all ours also to see and enjoy, for the apostle testifies to us through the Holy Spirit, "For with the heart one believes and is justified, and with the mouth one confesses and is saved" (Romans 10:10). May Jesus Christ Himself, the author and finisher of our faith, help us for the sake of making a good confession. Amen! Amen!

CHRISTMAS SEASON

CHRISTMAS DAY

LUKE 2:1–14

Lord Jesus! When long ago today You were born into this world, You came to Your own, and Your own received You not. The world for whose salvation You had come remained silent. No welcome, no words of rejoicing were on its lips. The heavenly hosts had to descend in order that Your blessed birth might be celebrated with holy songs of rejoicing. Yet You did not return to heaven in disgust. You did not come because men wanted You but because You wanted them; You came to seek and to save not the holy but sinners, not the whole but the sick. And the message "For unto you is born this day a Savior" should not resound only then but be continually proclaimed from that time on to all generations until the end of time. And You knew that millions would come in spirit to Your manger to worship You and rejoice greatly over Your birth.

And so it has happened, Lord Jesus: the message "For unto you is born this day a Savior" has finally after 1,800 years penetrated even this distant western land; it has reached also us. Its sweet sound rings today in the ears of us all. If *no one* will shelter You today, *we* will, and we will say with a loud voice from hearts filled with joy: Welcome, welcome, dearest, friendliest, sweetest Savior. The inn that we have for You is admittedly a very poor house; it is our dark, empty heart. And what we can give You is also a very wretched gift; it is nothing else than the great guilt of our sin. But You were born to enter sinful hearts and take away sin. Hence with ardent happy confidence we say to You:

Ah, dearest Jesus, holy Child,
Prepare a bed, soft, undefiled,
A quiet chamber set apart
For You to dwell within my heart. Amen. (LSB 358:13)

Friends, whom God has dearly loved, highly honored, and greatly cheered!

That festival that all Christians regard as the most beautiful, the dearest, and the most precious—the holy joyous Christmas season—has again come. Throughout the whole year this festival throws a ray of perfect joy on the Christians' road. Every time he begins the year he sees at its end the holy Christmas season. There it stands as a brightly lit hall, in which after the labor of a wearisome year God lets him enjoy the foretaste of the eternal festival celebration in heaven.

Consequently, even today in all the countries of the earth millions stream into their houses of God and loudly lift up their voices in all the languages of the world in ardent psalms of praise. Wherever just one church bell hangs, it must today call the host of Christians to this festival celebration. Today with dancing the child hurries from the gifts to church and sings only of the invisible gifts of heaven; on tottering feet yet with a heart rejuvenated with joy the feeble grayhead goes along to the courts of the Lord. Today many thousands of poor forget their poverty and feel themselves rich; today many thousands of rich forget their earthly wealth and cannot hear enough of the heavenly treasures, which God today displays to the whole world and also to them. Longingly the sick person, chained to the sickbed, sees the healthy go to the house of God. He forgets his pains and only a hot tear rolls down his pale cheeks at the thought that this year he cannot be counted among the multitudes who celebrate in church. Yes, even he who is otherwise indifferent is today drawn into this universal Christian joy. Like a mighty stream this joy irresistibly carries them along, drawing songs of praise and joy from even their hearts and mouths.

Oh tell me, what, what is it that today excites the world to rejoice? Do we not today hear Christians break forth into that song of praise, which the angels composed and brought from heaven to earth? Oh why, why is it that today all hills and valleys, in north and south, in east and west, re-echo to that great universal heavenly choir song, "Glory to God in the highest, and on earth peace among those with whom He is pleased"?

The cause of this worldwide rejoicing is, as you know, that today more than 1,800 years ago a Child was born in Judea in the city of Bethlehem, naked just as all newborn children are. People said that His father was a carpenter named Joseph; His mother, a poor maiden named Mary; the house in which He was born was a dark, gloomy stall; the first bed that sheltered the Child was a manger; His layette was a swaddling cloth in which He was wrapped. And as small as Bethlehem was, even here no one asked about the

CHRISTMAS

Child. Only some simple shepherds, told of His birth by an unusual phenomenon, came and congratulated the mother on the birth of this Child. This Child seemed to be the most humble of all who were ever born.

Is it this birth that all Christians are celebrating today? Is it possible? Don't the enemies of Christ have reason to laugh at the folly of Christians, because they exult day and night over such a commonplace event as the birth of a Child, yes, that they exult over the birth of a Child in a dark stall?

To be sure, it seems to the proud world as though we Christians must be ashamed of our joy and blush when they ask us: Why are you happy today? And then we must tell them of the stall and the manger and the swaddling clothes. But poor, blind world! It has eyes to see only worldly, passing, empty, pretended grandeur; it is blind to true, heavenly, eternal, and divine glory. Oh, if it could see this, it would today recognize that that stall at Bethlehem is more glorious than all the palaces of the mighty of this world. They would consider that manger more precious than the whole world with all its gold and silver, yes, they would regard those swaddling clothes as a garment more precious than all the splendor with which heaven and earth is clothed.

All right! Let the world laugh at us. We meanwhile will delve into the secrets of the eternal love of God revealed in Bethlehem today. We will ponder the unspeakable, incomparable importance of the poor humble birth of that Child at Bethlehem. May God Himself give us clear eyes, the eyes of a child, the eyes of faith. Let us ask for this in silent prayer.

The text: Luke 2:1–14

On the basis of this story, permit me to speak in greatest simplicity on

The inexpressible importance of the birth of the Child at Bethlehem.

This importance is evidenced in

1. The singular commotion in heaven and Earth;
2. The wonderful union of God and man; and finally,
3. The great purpose that it had and attained.

I.

My friends, after mature reflection I will not promise to preach to you today but only to speak in childish simplicity. Should I think only a little bit on the importance of the birth of the Child at Bethlehem, I see myself placed before giddy heights and unfathomable depths. I must forthwith confess that

39

the importance of this birth is *inexpressible.* Even the angels and archangels cannot completely express its importance in human language. They must, when they are finished speaking, reach for their harps in order at least to praise the Inexpressible in songs of heavenly *praise.* Hence, what more can we mortals do than stammer and stutter?

The day of the birth of the Child at Bethlehem is the most important day of history. The birth itself is the most important event which ever had or ever will take place. It is the birth of Jesus Christ, the Son of God and the Savior of the world.

If in the first place we knew nothing more of this birth than the great *commotion* that took place and still takes place in heaven and on earth because of it, we would have to conclude that this birth must be of the most incomparable and inexpressible importance.

The birth of Jesus Christ did not take place in the manner of men. It was the result of a special secret decree that was decided upon in eternity in the counsel of the triune God. In Scripture it is called, together with the work that originated it, the eternal *plan* of God, in order, as it were, to represent it as the work of God's eternal deep counsel and will. It is also called a "mystery," which was "hidden for ages in God who created all things" (Ephesians 3:9) and which was "realized in Christ Jesus our Lord" (3:11). In another place we read, "[God] chose us in [*Christ*] before the foundation of the world" (1:4). While as yet there was no time, no world, no created heavens or earth; while as yet no man or angel had been called into existence, even then God had decided upon the birth of the Child in Bethlehem. From eternity the thought of letting this happen filled and moved the heart of God. As eternal as God Himself is, so eternal is also His decree to carry out what long ago today took place in Bethlehem. However, as for the sake of this birth great agitations took place *in eternity* in the heart of *God,* so it also set the whole *world* into commotion in the period of *time* which expired before it happened.

Scarcely had the world been created and man fallen, then God at once revealed the birth of the Child at Bethlehem as a mystery of His eternal will, even though this birth should take place 4,000 years later. He said the woman's Seed would bruise the head of the serpent (cf. Genesis 3:15). All of God's messengers who were sent into the world had the special command to proclaim this birth to the world. All patriarchs and prophets pointed to it as to that upon which the salvation of the world hinged. All special preparations that God made among men had the purpose of directing the attention of all to this birth and preparing them for it. That God instituted a covenant with a special nation, chose it for His own, committed His revelation to it for safekeeping, and led it as a shepherd, all that occurred only to make the necessary preparation for that birth. All the mysterious acts, customs, types, and ceremonies commanded by God in the divine service were simply pictures of Him who was to come into the world in Bethlehem. All the works of divine providence great and small, all the conditions of the governments in victory and defeat, in conquest and subjugation, in imprisonment and dethroning of the great, the rise and fall of world monarchies and republics, all this prepared the world for the birth of the Child at Bethlehem. This was the one bright star of hope toward which God directed languishing mankind. Wherever in the first 4,000 years of the world beat a heart in which light, comfort, peace, and hope lived, all this was created alone by the promise of the birth at Bethlehem. It was the fulfillment of the 4,000 years of the longing and hope of all nations.

As great as was the stir that took place in heaven and on earth even before it happened, just so great a stir did this birth create when it finally took place. Without knowing or wanting it, the mighty Caesar Augustus had to serve at the birth of Jesus Christ. According to prophecy, Christ would be born in Bethlehem of Judea; so through God's direction Caesar had to issue a decree that the entire world should be taxed. Because of this decree Mary, the mother, had to go to Bethlehem, so that at the place designated and at the time foretold by the prophets the birth took place. The whole world everywhere was churned into surging masses and on this day moved from place to place. Without suspecting it, the cause of this sea of nations moving today like waves was the birth of that little Child who had entered this world so quietly and so secretly.

The prophet had foretold, "For thus says the LORD of hosts: Yet once more, in a little while, I will shake the heavens and the earth and the sea and the dry land. And I will shake all nations, so that the treasures of all nations shall come in" (Haggai 2:6–7). Even the heavens should be shaken today. And see! this also came to pass. As soon as the little Child was born, the heavens in the dark of night were suddenly parted, night became day, beams of heavenly light streamed from the opened heaven toward earth; an angel, around whom the glory of the Lord shown, appeared and announced to the shepherds and thus to the whole sleeping world that birth which had taken place. But see! yet more; thereupon a multitude of the heavenly host from the throne of the most high God followed the herald, praised God, congratulated the world, and sang in a million-voiced echo-choir, "Glory to God in the highest, and on earth peace among those with whom He is pleased!"

Even heaven's Christmas song did not once awaken the sleeping world; it slept on, unconcerned about the newborn Child. Yet what has happened in the past 1,800 years? The story of the birth at Bethlehem in deepest humility has gone out into all lands unto the ends of the earth—and this story has transformed the world. Whole nations together with their rulers have thrown themselves down before the manger. From century to century, from nation to nation, millions and ever new millions have with one voice confessed and still confess today: if this Child had not been born, we would be completely lost. All investigators declare the birth of this Child to be the most impenetrable object of all human investigation.

Who, therefore, can finish speaking of the importance of this birth, which caused such a stir in heaven and on earth, in the heart of God, among angels and men, in eternity, and at all times? It must be unique; it must be inexpressibly great.

II.

However, we have as it were, only listened at the door of heaven and have afterwards, as it were, merely walked about in the world, inquiring in every quarter as to the meaning of the birth of the Child at Bethlehem. Come! let us now enter the very hut itself, where the little Child lies, and see in our hands this Child Himself, the light of the world. And what does the eye of faith see there? Who is He, who as a little Child lies in the lap of a poor young maiden? Oh, yes, He has the form of merely a human child. No visible rays of glory play around His friendly face. But what does the angel of the Lord say to the amazed shepherds? The angel said to the world, "[He] is Christ the Lord," Jehovah, the God of all, blessed to all eternity.

Oh wonderful message! God and man are united with this birth. God has become a man; a man has become God!

The eternal united with a mortal. The all-powerful united with powerless dust. Eternal love wedded with that which hates her. The Most Holy united with the sinner. The Creator joined with a creature, with His most needy creature, and becomes like its lowliest creature. The Lord of lords before whom all angels and archangels must bow in worshipful adoration shackles Himself to the servants of sin and Satan. He who carries all in His hands and has sown the myriads of stars as seed on the field of the firmament, becomes weak with the weak, helpless with the helpless, and permits Himself to be lifted and carried by sinful hands.

He whom the heavenly Father in His eternal glory today declared to be the image of His essence and the reflection of His glory, the same with Him in divine majesty, the true Son of the living God, the everlasting Father, becomes the child of a human being, a blood relation, a brother of sinners, a fellow-descendant of the forefather of the children of death, a member of the miserable human race which deprived itself of its nobility and became an abomination before angels and all creatures.

He, the eternal light before whom even the light of heaven is darkness, who lives in a light that none can approach, comes down into our dark world in order to become a member of the same family with those who sit in darkness and in the shadow of death.

He, whom the heaven of heavens cannot contain, for whom the skies merely serve as His throne and the earth as His footstool, descends in order to share their huts of earth and clay with the inhabitants of dust. He, who alone writes in and erases from the Book of Life, today permits His name to be enrolled in the list of men as the least and poorest of them.

Oh, great is the mystery of godliness, "[God] was manifested in the flesh!" What mind, I will not say of man, but of the greatest angel, dares look into the depths of this divine counsel revealed today and see bottom? The holy angels with bowed countenance desire to look into it, but finding no bottom in this abyss of God's heart, can only cry out in adoration, "Glory to God in the highest!"

What are all God's miracles compared with this miracle, "the Word became flesh" (John 1:14)? What is the miracle of creation? What is the wonderful structure of the firmament resting upon invisible pillars? What are its countless stars traveling in eternal order in their orbits? What is the miracle of the preservation of each and every living and moving being? What are all these wonders of the power of the Almighty, all these miracles of the wisdom of the Omniscient, all these miracles of the love of the All-loving, about which the morning stars praised God in eternity and all the sons of God shouted for joy? What are all these compared with *that* miracle, that God divested Himself of His divine glory, descended from His throne that stands *over* all the heavens, took not only the form but also the nature of a creature, a creature that had fallen from Him, becomes a man, a man in the form of a servant, a child, a brother of sinners!?

Tell me, what language has words enough to express the importance of such a birth? When the angels had praised it in an earthly language, they quickly hurried back into heaven in order to begin the song there in the language of heaven, that they might celebrate this deed of God in song before His throne forever and ever. What should, what can *we* do? We can do nothing but throw ourselves into the dust and worship and stammer hallelujahs to Him who to the amazement of all creatures today took in Bethlehem not the nature of a holy angel but, mystery of mysteries, miracles of miracles, the nature of a man!

III.

The wretched birth of the Child at Bethlehem is important also in its ultimate purpose and its most blessed results. It is this which in the third place I offer for your meditation.

When a wise man uses great wealth and brings a sacrifice, he has something great in view. But who is wiser than God? What wealth and sacrifice can be greater than the sending of His only-begotten Son in our flesh?

And, what did God have in view? First of all, His honor in heaven; secondly, the peace of all men on earth and eternal goodwill, that is, the happiness of all men and eternal salvation. This is true because the heavenly host sings over the manger, "Glory to God in the highest, and on earth peace among those with whom He is pleased."

Does not this hymn of the angels contain the truth? Oh, yes, indeed! By letting his only-begotten Son become a man God opened the innermost depths of His divine Father-heart. He revealed that He was a God such as no creature could suspect. He showed that He was love itself, radiating throughout heaven and earth, surrounding, covering, and holding everything in His lap. Oh, yes, at the sight of those divine flashes of love the world's cold hollow heart cries, "God is love!" But it does not know of what it speaks, for it does not believe in that miracle in which alone God has revealed the true greatness of His love. The world does not believe in God's incarnation in which shines not only sparks, or rays, but the whole sun of divine love. Once the heavens looked down with delight on this revelation, all the souls of men looked into it with agitated heart—all angels and archangels, all cherubim and seraphim, and all the heavenly thrones and powers and dominions had to sing the great hymn of praise to the Incarnate

Eternal Love, "Glory to God in the highest!" All believers and saints join in; some day they will continue to sing the song of mercy forever and ever.

Why can and should we also join this singing, we who still have such dim eyes for seeing God's glory in His incarnation? Because this miracle of love concerns us most of all. It means peace on earth and eternal goodwill, that is, happiness and eternal salvation. Behold, the humility and misery with which the Son of God enters our world is nothing else than the guilt and misery of our sins, which He took upon Himself. Now it lies on Him and is taken from us. We should be relieved of it forever. That the Son of God was born in a stall is of such great merit that it earned for us the mansions of His Father's house. His lying in a manger merits eternal rest in the lap of God. His wretched swaddling clothes are the shining garments of divine righteousness. His becoming a child makes us His brothers and children of His heavenly Father, gives men a nobility which even the angels do not have; men are now of royal race. When the Son of God descended from heaven and appeared as a citizen of earth, He made this small dwelling place the center of the universe, God's favorite place upon which He looks with unspeakable love and goodwill; yes, the walls of heaven now surround earth. In brief, because the Son of God stooped to our level we are lifted up from the dust to the throne of God's glory.

This is of interest not only to the one or the other person. Had all men at that time been with the shepherds on the field, the angel would have said to them all, also to us, to you and to me, "Fear not, for behold, I bring you good news of great joy," for he adds, "that will be for all the people" (Luke 2:10). For that very reason Christ could not be born in any one man's home, but in a dark stall, so that no person could say that He was born for him alone. Every person should see that he has the same rights in Him as anyone else.

Had God merely *said* that all men must be saved, many might still think that they have some doubts as to whether they are included. But now that God's Son became a man, every human being must say: "Yes, God's Son is also *my* brother. God has becomes friends with me. God must have stopped being angry with me. He must be gracious even to me. God must have wanted me to believe too. He is my Father; I am His dear child."

Oh most blessed birth! As the sun rises and sets on all men, on the evil as on the good, on the child as on the aged, on the poor as on the rich, on the beggar as on the king, so with this birth at Bethlehem the eternal Sun of happiness, grace, and salvation has risen on all men, but never, never to set. As there is no difference in that they are all sinners and none dare exempt himself from this class, so is there now no difference: they are all redeemed, pardoned, saved, and none dare say he is not. The birth of this child has brought happiness to all the millions upon millions who have lived for the past 6,000 years and will live until the last one is born at the end of time.

Is that not joy? Joy for the poor sinners that we are? Joy upon joy? Bliss upon bliss? Ah, my dear fellow-redeemed brothers and sisters, do not say any more, "How can I come to God?" Behold, God has come to you, and therefore, you are already with Him; only believe it, and you will experience it.

Do not say, "How shall I be freed of my sins?" Behold, they are already taken from you. The Child at Bethlehem has taken them upon Himself and carried them away from the presence of God; believe it and you will experience it.

Do not ask, "How does God feel toward me?" Behold, God has already given you the answer to this question in Bethlehem. There He has proved that He loves you in such a way that the angels shout for joy and hell trembles. There He has given you the very best and dearest He has, His most precious treasure, I will not say of heaven, but of his own heart, His only-begotten dearest Son.

Oh, that all who hitherto have viewed this indifferently or despised it would today believe it! How blessed they would be! For even though thousands, though millions have despised the greatest miracle of eternal love for 6,000 years, this fountain of grace and salvation still flows in the very same mighty stream. God with eyes directed to Bethlehem still calls from heaven, "Let the one who is thirsty come; let the one who desires take the water of life without price" (Revelation 22:17). Oh, come then, all come and say with me:

Let me in my arms receive Thee;
On Thy breast Let me rest,
Savior, ne'er to leave Thee. Amen. (TLH 77:12)

FIRST SUNDAY AFTER CHRISTMAS

LUKE 2:33–40

The grace, friendship, and love of the newborn child, our Lord and Savior Jesus Christ, be with you all and fill you with light, comfort, power, life, and joy both now and forever. Amen.

Dear friends in Christ!

Throughout the past festival all of you were urgently exhorted and invited to rejoice in the birth of your Savior. Was that necessary? Would it not have been more necessary for us dull and sinful men to have been admonished to be holy, to follow Christ in His humility, and especially imitate His holy example? Does not the thoughtless person comfort himself too soon rather than too late? Does he not rely much too easily on the grace of Christ? Was not the repeated invitation to Christmas joy therefore superfluous?

To be sure, many think so. We seek all joys and flee all sadness. Who should not therefore rejoice in the Christ Child, who takes away all causes for sadness and brings us joy for time and eternity? Surely, we want to have God as our friend. Who should not the incarnation of God's Son please? Does not God become our brother in him? Is He not reconciled? Does He not extend the hand of friendship?

Surely, we wish that all would find comfort in the troubles of this world and the hope of eternal life in the hour of death. Who should not the appearance of the Savior of the world delight? With Him the only comfort and hope has arisen for all men.

Finally, without a doubt, we wish that all would be saved and have as easy and enjoyable a way to heaven as possible. Who should not be pleased at the arrival of the Savior? He has made the way to heaven easy and enjoyable; God Himself could find a no more beautiful, gentle way for us poor, sinful, weak men.

Would not a person's offense at the incarnation of God be more amazing than the fact that God became a man? Is it not easier to believe in God's great love to men than to believe that there is a person who despises this love, yes, who scorns it? Might we not suppose that even the eternal woes of hell itself would be turned into cries of joy, if suddenly in the midst of its darkness the message resounded, "Fear not, for behold, I bring you good news of great joy that will be for all the people"? Hear that, all of you! For you spirits of hell there "is born this day a Savior," a Redeemer and Deliverer.

Though it appears to be so unbelievable and puzzling, it still is true; our hearts are by nature so profoundly corrupt and hard that even God's most ardent love does not warm it. God's love radiates in vain through heaven and earth; our heart remains steel and stone. It would not melt if God Himself did not again come to our aid, if God Himself did not take away our natural offense and through His grace work true delight in our hearts.

With God's assistance I will now speak at length on how this takes place.

The text: *Luke 2:33–40*

In the Gospel just read we find the little child Jesus in the temple. Mary went there after the expiration of her six-week period to bring her firstborn to the Lord as the Law directed. When she did that, old Simeon came, took the child up in his arms, and confessed that God had revealed to him that this child would be the Savior of all nations. That is why we read in the beginning of our text, "And His father and His mother marveled at what was said about Him."

However, the most important thing is how the old man predicted that men would receive Christ. He said to Mary, "Behold, this child is appointed for the fall and rising of many in Israel, and for a sign that is opposed (and a sword will pierce through your own soul also), so that thoughts from many hearts may be revealed."

Hence, ponder with me:

Christ, an offense to man.

1. By nature all men take offense at Christ, and
2. By God's grace one can be freed of it.

I.

"Behold, this child is appointed for the fall and rising of many in Israel, and for a sign that is opposed." Old father Simeon predicts that this is how men will receive Christ. He says, "Many in Israel," not to show that only the Israelites will feel that way; he really wants to say, that if this shall be His fate even among His elect people, then how much more elsewhere!

And so it is. Not only did Christ offend most as He lay as a poor naked child in the manger. He is today, after the whole world has seen His glory, still "a sign that is opposed." Many appear to have the noblest attitude as long as Christ is not preached. But as soon as Christ is preached, Simeon's dictum is fulfilled in many: In Christ Himself the "thoughts from many hearts may be revealed." The more the truth about Christ is preached, the more He becomes a stone of stumbling and a rock of offense. To preach Christ and to stir up the world against oneself is one and the same. No sooner does the preaching of Christ spread then opposition arises from all sides: With horror the proud wise human reason hears this preaching. All hearts rise against this unbelievable doctrine. All the wise of the world are united to refute this "foolish" Gospel and suppress it. The kings of the earth take counsel to banish from their states those religions that appear dangerous. Those whom men call the most holy, upright, and pious are the very ones who declare that this teaching about Christ is the most dangerous and pernicious of all which is being preached.

However, we dare not suppose that only gross unbelievers and scoffers oppose Christ. Oh no, let us descend into our own heart. Even we who joyfully heard the message of the newborn Christ Child will hear a voice that constantly and clearly opposes Christ.

Tell me, when you heard that the true God and creator of heaven and earth was a little child in Bethlehem; when you were shown that God's love is so infinite and incomprehensible that even the angels cannot grasp it but become dumb with wonder, tell me, did you not hear the voice saying in your heart: Is this really true? Is it really possible that God would stoop so low as to offer His most precious possession, His only-begotten Son, for despicable sinners? Is He really from eternity so anxious and concerned about the salvation of fallen creatures?

May it not be said of many that when they heard the message of the angel and the song of the heavenly host they often said in themselves, as did Nicodemus, "How can these things be?" Has not the thought arisen in many a heart: Is not this only a dream that comforts us today and compels us to wonder at a God whose love is unending? Is it not really a dream that holds no truth and disappears with our life like a fog?

Who of us has felt absolutely no such tidal waves of doubt during the Christmas season? Certainly only a very few, perhaps hardly a soul. And in how many could not this doubt have subdued the heart so completely that it could not rejoice in the Child of their salvation?

See the practical proof in our own hearts of the truth of Simeon's prediction, "[Christ] is appointed for a sign that is opposed."

Why has God given men such a Savior and prescribed such a way to salvation, which is so offensive to our reason? Why does not God preach a Gospel which every man, especially the worldly wise and prudent, would find agreeable? Why did God let His dear Son of all people come in a form and with a teaching that offends every one? Why has God set Christ as a sign that every man shall speak against?

The reason does not lie, let us say, in a secret counsel of God by which He does not want the salvation of all men, but the damnation of many. God also has not done this to make the return to heaven more difficult or to conceal the mystery of grace especially from the wise and prudent.

This is the reason: this is the only way in which we can be renewed to the image of God and be saved. Had God wanted to give the world the kind of a Savior and Gospel it likes, He would have had to send them an earthly Messiah, just like the one the Jewish nation once expected and still does. God would have had to send the wise a great philosopher, not a poor child in a manger; gold and silver to the greedy; good eating and drinking to the pleasure-loving; honor and glory to the proud. In short, God would have had to reveal to the world the kind of gospel that would have flattered its fleshly senses, pride, and arrogance. Yes, that would be the very savior and gospel which the world would want and which no natural heart would oppose.

But just how would that have helped us sinners? We would have been alienated only the more, fallen only the deeper into sin, and become only the more unfit for eternal, heavenly blessedness.

If we were to be helped at all, God would have to send us a Savior who offends our natural heart, in short, the kind of Savior He is and no other. Bear in mind: our natural pride in reason and virtue, our innate trust in our own imagined wisdom and righteousness, and our earthly, fleshly disposition, that is our fall from God. That is the ruin that shuts us out from God and His blessed Communion as long as we remain in it. The true Savior must therefore be of the kind that, if we accept Him, all our false wisdom, all our false righteousness, all our earthly fleshly disposition must be destroyed.

Do not be surprised, my dear hearers, if even you perceive that your reason, heart, and mind oppose the preaching of the Christmas Gospel. Rather remember that if your corrupt heart liked the Gospel, it could not save you; just that which is bitter for your flesh becomes a healing remedy for your soul. The very opposition of your heart shows that it is not human but divine, that it has not arisen in the heart of a sinner, but in the heart of God. Consequently, this verdict applies also to the *Gospel*, "If you were of the world, the world would love you as its own; but because you are not of the world, but I chose you out of the world, therefore the world hates you" (John 15:19).

II.

But let us proceed and hear secondly how through God's grace one can be freed from his natural offense at Christ.

My friends, if this is to take place, two things especially must be worked in us: first, we must confess our resentment toward Christ; then, be filled with dissatisfaction with ourselves.

Many suppose that they already rejoice in Christ. That is the chief reason why Christ has come in vain for them, even for some Christians. Ah, how many there are who diligently read God's Word, diligently and gladly hear the Gospel preaching, and attentively listen when during the holy Christmas season the joyful story of the birth of Jesus Christ is explained. They praise the preaching of Christ and think that they do not need this exhortation. They think: Who shouldn't rejoice in Christ?

However, in thinking that way, their heart is not like the heart of Simeon or Anna. It still clings to the earth; their greatest concern is the temporal, their greatest joy is only that what they enjoy on earth, and they still have sins that they love and cherish and from which they cannot free themselves. Jesus has not yet become their one and all. His grace is not the treasure that they joyfully carry in their heart. His righteousness is not the one of which they boast and in which they are happy and blessed.

Oh, how you deceive yourselves! Believe this: if Jesus does not live alone in your heart; if He is not the only wealth of your soul; if He is not the only sun which shines upon you; if He is not the only good in which your soul finds its rest and peace; if you would not gladly lose everything so that you could have only Jesus; if He still can not make you happy in misfortune, joyful in tribulation, content in poverty, and willing even to die and leave this world with its goods and joys as soon as possible, you have not yet found your true joy in Christ; He still offends you. And it is your resentment toward Christ that you must above all confess, if true joy in Him should enter into your heart.

Moreover, one must also be filled with dissatisfaction with oneself.

If a person is satisfied with himself, if he does not confess that he is a deeply fallen sinner; if he does not feel the trouble of his soul; if he is not earnestly concerned about his salvation; if he has no gnawing hunger and thirst after grace and a righteousness in which he can stand before God; if he does not wait day and night, as old Anna for the comfort of Israel; if he has no fear of God's judgment; if he still thinks quite a lot of himself; if he thinks that he is pious, that God certainly will accept him, then one vainly utters high praise about Christ's grace and friendliness, vainly pictures God's love even in its boundless greatness, vainly urges the mercy of his Savior. On such a heart the sweet Gospel is only wasted; they find no true joy in Christ.

Christ gives joy to those who have not yet perceived the misery of their souls without Him as little as a well-spread table delights the sated, the most wonderful painting the blind, and the most beautiful harmonies the deaf. But if he is grieved over his sinfulness, the Gospel is the dew of heaven which falls upon a parched, withering land, the pardon for one groaning in prison, a rescue ship for him who hangs on a cliff in the middle of the sea, the opening of the doors of heaven to him who struggles with death.

You who do not find such dissatisfaction with yourself, do not be amazed if the past holiday passed over your heads without a trace. Your heart was locked; Christ could not enter in. Tell me, do you want to lock yourselves out completely? Do you want to end this year without Jesus? Oh, take my advice; only God can unlock your heart through His Word. Hence, look first of all in the mirror of the divine Law—ponder its demands and threats, and compare your heart and life with it. At the same time turn to God with heartfelt sighs—beg Him to open the deep spiritual intent of the Law. Picture most vividly the misery of your souls to yourselves, and thus awaken in yourself true hunger and thirst after grace. Oh, how gladly God will hear you! Soon your heart will be so full of grief that you will reproach and condemn yourself for having gone on so long without really and truly knowing Jesus.

But do not remain only with the Law; this is the letter that killeth. If you are to rejoice in Christ, you must, after you have looked into the Law, see God's wrath, become frightened, quickly take the Gospel mirror into your hand, look into that, and there in faith see the comforting picture of the Savior of all sinners, and therefore also your Savior. You will have a far different attitude toward Him; true joy in Him will enter your hearts. As Simeon took the Savior in his arms, so you will take Him up in the arms of faith. If at first the Savior was a stone of stumbling, who caused your fall, and a sign, whom you in the depths of your hearts opposed despite the confession of your mouth, He will, on the other hand, become a rock in whom you will rise from your fall. As the old prophetess Anna, it will be also your desire to serve Christ night and day. And you will find in your Savior a rest, a peace, a joy, which the whole world with its treasures could never have given you. And finally, when your death comes you will fall asleep in sweet peace and will awaken happy and blessed in God's bosom. God, through Jesus Christ, help us all reach this goal. Amen.

NEW YEAR'S DAY

[CIRCUMCISION AND NAME OF JESUS]

LUKE 2:21

Eternal, living, unchangeable God! You are the same, and Your years have no end. We, however, are born and die, come and go, and wander from one year to the next.

We come to You, the eternal and unchangeable, in this morning of a changing year to offer You, the ruler of our life, thanksgiving and praise and glory and adoration for all the good things which You have sent us. Your goodness has preserved us in the old year, Your love providing all necessities, Your faithfulness shielding us from all danger, Your help delivering us in all need, anxiety, and trouble, and Your patience carrying us despite our countless sins. Great things, yes, great things You have done to us whereof we are glad. Oh Lord, do not disdain the wretched praise of our sinful hearts and lips. Receive in Christ the thanks we bring.

Behold, O heavenly Father, today we again come into Your holy presence with prayer and supplications. Do not remember—this we pray above all—do not remember our guilt of the old year in the new which we are entering; blot them out like a cloud, and let them vanish like a fog, that they will never, never be remembered. Do not change Your Fatherly heart toward us; give us again in the new year new grace, and rule us with new forbearance.

The only reason You have permitted us to see this new year is that we might glorify You and seek eternal life. Oh, permit us all to reach this blessed goal.

We especially pray, O God, bless this congregation planted here by Your mercy; bless it in temporal and eternal things. Let each one be honorably successful in his earthly affairs this year. Lay on no one a greater burden than he is able to bear and serves for the salvation of his soul. Give all married people love and faithfulness for a blessed, peaceful marriage. Grant all parents wisdom and zeal to give their children a God-pleasing education. Bestow on all children, young men and women a God-fearing, heavenly-minded, chaste, and obedient heart. Comfort all widows and orphans. Have mercy on all sick, miserable, and tempted. And if according to Your will any of us must die, do not seize him violently in his sins, but graciously prepare him for death, and finally permit him to fall asleep confessing Your name.

Protect our schools and teachers as the apple of Your eye; make them nurseries of Your heavenly kingdom. Be graciously present in our voters meetings and the meetings of our elders. Give them good counsel to carry out Your will. O Lord, help us, O Lord, prosper us, and we will also in that world, where no changes of the year take place, sing a new song with new tongues forever and ever. Amen.

Dear friends in Christ Jesus!

Most people who are not out-and-out godless believe that one cannot begin a new year better than by making good resolutions. Yet if one but considers on New Year's Day how often he had sinned in the past year, the many thousands of benefits God permitted him to enjoy anyhow, how with each new day God's goodness rose over him, how God's Father-hands guided him despite his unfaithfulness, and gave him a new year again, who will not resolve the following: "I will today begin a new life. The sins into which I had so often fallen will not rule me again. The old slowness will not again steal over me. I will zealously serve the Lord and ardently love my brother."

It is only natural that everyone who does not have a completely hardened heart begins the new year with similar resolutions, yet we dare not suppose that this is the proper way to begin a new year. Our good resolutions cannot make good the sins with which we have insulted God in the past, even though we actually carry out every resolution. If the sins of the old year are still charged against us, what good will it do to try to begin the new with a clean slate? If the sins of the old year will continue to accuse us before God, what good will it do to live in the new such a holy and pure life that this new year will not condemn us?

And we must also bear this in mind: Who actually has carried out all his good resolutions? Were not our hearts as full of the same good resolutions last year as today? But have we kept our oaths? Have we done what we promised God a year ago? Have not most of them been left undone? Have not many on the very next day of the year fallen into the old rut and stayed there? Do we serve God if we again appear with good resolutions, lay them as our new year's gift at His feet, and then begin again the old year's way? Luther speaks the truth when he says, "The road to hell is paved with good intentions," that is, the lost have always made good resolutions but never carried them out. Though people are unashamed of the sins in which they live and die, few of them have not at some time or another promised God, even with tears, to live a new life!

In Matthew 21[:28–31] Christ tells the following parable to the Pharisees: " 'A man had two sons. And he went to the first and said, "Son, go and work in the vineyard today." And he answered, "I will not," but afterward he changed his mind and went. And he went to the other son and said the same. And he answered, "I go, sir," but did not go. Which of the two did the will of his father?' They said, 'The first.' "

In this parable Christ does not say that it is improper to make good resolutions, but He warns us against trusting in them. Many begin the new year without God. He says right out: I will not serve God this year! And see, he is soon conquered by God's mercy, returns with tears, seeks grace, and becomes a true Christian. On the other hand, many pass the first hours of the new year in great devotion, but they soon forget the Lord and live on without God. Now which of the two does the Lord's will?

Perhaps many will say: If the good resolutions we make are worth nothing in God's eyes, what should we do? What more can God demand of us? How can we please Him?

How we can not only please God but which is also the only way, God Himself has revealed when He testified about Christ, "This is My beloved Son, with whom I am well pleased" (Matthew 3:17). Here it is: It is only in Christ in whom the Father is well pleased; only through Him does God accept us all the days of our life. We will celebrate not only the Christmas festival but all others, even New Year's Day, properly when we celebrate it in faith in Christ. "Seek ye Jesus and his light, All things else will help you naught," has meaning also today. Therefore, let me urge Christ upon you today. Perhaps there are some among us who on Christmas found no joy in Christ; oh may I therefore still succeed in convincing you today!

The text: *Luke 2:21*

It is a noteworthy coincidence that the civil new year comes just eight days after the celebration of the birth of Jesus Christ. On this day Christ received the sign of circumcision and the sweet name of Jesus. This coincidence certainly reminds us that Christ must also be the center of our new year's meditation. Permit me therefore to show you today that

We begin the new year properly when we begin it in faith in Christ.

1. Because then we do not have to carry the sins of the old year over into the new, and
2. Because then we are also properly prepared to meet the fateful future.

I.

Those who are children of this world, in whom no desire for eternal nor concern for their soul's happiness and salvation has as yet awakened, who are concerned solely about this life, think that they start the new year aright if they expect to get richer in the new year, and experience new pleasures and joys. For the most part these children of the world begin the new year of grace with worldly vanities, with dancing and playing, with laughing and joking.

Those who make this their greatest joy are to be pitied. Alas, they grope in the darkness; the light of divine grace has not risen. They do not know that God has intended an altogether different joy for them. They do not know that their riches are actually nothing but a burdensome care, their joy nothing but an empty shadow, their hope nothing but an idle dream. They do not know how fortunate, how blessed they could be if they only knew what belonged to their peace.

Who will deny that our greatest need for starting a true, happy, and blessed new year is that we do not have to carry the sins of the old year over into the new? Tell me, is not he with all his wealth very poor if he lacks the most necessary wealth of all, God's grace? How can he be truly happy, if he lacks the sweetest of all joy, the forgiveness of his sins? How can he be at peace today, if he has the most disturbing doubts, fearing that God is angry with him, that He is not his reconciled Father?

Certainly, only he can begin the new year joyfully and blessedly if he firmly believes that not only has the sun arisen, but that the sun of divine grace has risen upon him. Only he can begin the new year in a happy frame of mind if he has this comfort: all the sins which you have committed in the past are forgiven; they are buried in the depths of the sea. Today you can cheerfully draw near to God as a child approaches his father, for the guilt of all your sins is eternally erased!

How is it that we can speak that way today? We cannot earn favor with God. If we today wanted to, if we could shed rivers of tears, we could not wash from our souls even one sin that we committed in the old year. If we imposed on ourselves the most difficult work of repentance, we could not satisfy the offended righteousness of God. If we could experience the deepest contrition and repentance, yes, if we could even here experience the pain of hell because of our sins, we could not appease God for one evil thought. What is done is done, and no human work or suffering can undo it.

There is only one—only one who has made that all-propitiating atonement for us all. There is only one whose blood, and be it only a drop, can obliterate the blood-red guilt of all sinners, and this one is Jesus Christ, the most holy God-man. Today's Gospel reading teaches us this.

Our text says that when He was an eight-day-old infant He was circumcised according to the divine Law. Because this holy Child permitted this insulting deed to be done to Him, He was obedient to the divine Law, fulfilling its most humiliating demands as though He were a sinner like we. Jesus Christ did not need this for Himself. He was the most holy Son of the living God, not a servant, a subject; of His own free will He subjected Himself to that which was demanded only of us men. Thus He erased those sins that we committed by the transgression of the divine Law. The drops of blood that Christ shed at His circumcision were the down payment for the infinite guilt of the whole sinful world.

Though the blind world may mock at the circumcision of Christ because in its eyes it is such an offensive deed, it does not know that it mocks the most amazing divine love—their own salvation. Do not allow yourselves to be sidetracked from rejoicing in Christ's circumcision. If the angels in heaven are astonished that God's Son, whom they worship, descends into such depths of shame and contempt in order to redeem men, should we not rejoice that He does that for our sakes? Should we be offended at His deep humility? Far be it! Christ's deep humility is our greatest comfort.

If in the past year you have sinned through pride and this depresses you, and you do not wish to take this sin with you over into the new year, then believe in the Christ Child and rejoice in Him. Through His deep, free-willing self-abasement He has erased your shameful self-exaltation.

If in the past year you have sinned by loving the world; if you have striven only for money and goods; if you have wanted only good days; if you pursued the vain joys of this world and now you regret that you have squandered this time of grace, preferring the world and its goods to heaven and its treasures; if today this lies heavily on your heart and now you wish that you do not have to take your sins along into the new year, then believe on the Christ Child and find joy in Him. By His innocent pains He has atoned for your sinful joys. By His denial of all earthly things He has atoned for your sinful striving for them. Seek in Him forgiveness, in Him grace, in Him rest. You will not seek in vain, for in Him you can have all these things.

Yet who can name all the different sins by which we all in the past year have transgressed God's Holy Law? No matter what name they have, be they few or many, be they only sins of weakness or ever so serious and great and inexcusable, if we do not want to take them along into the new year, if their burden so depresses us that we yearn to be free of them and enter the new year as pardoned, reconciled children of God, then let us in faith and joy embrace the holy Christ Child, who for us submitted to the most humiliating of all divine Laws. No law that we have transgressed can then condemn us. God Himself, whom we have offended, cannot be angry with us. All the sins that we had committed will have disappeared like the old year did.

Oh, how easily the account against every one could be cancelled today! How easily he could find grace for his sins of not only the past year but all the bygone years of his whole life! What a blessed, peaceful, and joyful new year all could celebrate today! Is there still one among us who does not want to turn to Christ? Is there only one who wants to say: Let me enjoy the world first; and after I am tired of this joy, Christ can become my joy!? One can scarcely deem this possible.

Should there be one who thinks like that, I ask him, "Who can guarantee that the new year will not be your last?" When you begin this year, you can never be concerned about the past; you cannot first turn to Christ in faith. If Christ has not by that time been the comfort of your faith, then He remains your avenging Judge. Nothing will erase the sins of your past life; they will follow you to the throne of God and remain with you forever and ever. Therefore, today, today, while the Father draws you to His Son, do not willfully resist Him.

Ah, does perhaps someone else say: I would gladly believe, but I cannot. Instead of confidence, doubt lives in my heart; instead of trust, fear; instead of joy, worry and dread? If you yearn for Christ and His grace, feeling at the same time that you have no power to seize Him in firm faith, this is no sign that you are without faith. It shows merely that your faith is weak and that you do not want to be deceived by a *false* faith.

Is it not true, you do not want a *false* comfort, you want to have Christ Himself? Is that why you complain of your lack of faith? Happy are you! Your yearning for faith is also faith, for God's Word says, "O LORD, You hear the desire of the afflicted" (Psalm 10:17). Continue with this desire; say to Christ with that afflicted father, "I believe; help my unbelief" (Mark 9:24). He will in the new year at His hour give you also a stronger, more happy faith. Finally, you will be able to cry out like Mary, "My soul magnifies the Lord, and my spirit rejoices in God my Savior" (Luke 1:46–47).

II.

However, we continue. Second, we start the new year in the right way when we begin it in faith in Christ, because then we are also completely equipped to meet the future.

Entering a new year is not like entering a house that may be inspected completely as soon as the door is opened. As a year has days and hours, so it has gates that open to us one by one, every day, every hour. This coming year therefore lies dark before us, like the name of a country that we know well, but which is covered by a heavy fog. As mysterious as the future is, just so fateful will it be. We know in advance that the new year will bring new temptations to sin, along with new joys and new suffering.

But whatever we meet while we live in this time of testing, we know that everything that befalls us will be of great importance, of the greatest influence, whether we will be saved or not.

Isn't it therefore of greatest importance that we equip ourselves for what will come? Can a person act more foolishly than to meet his future fate unprepared, blindfolded? Does not a traveler prepare himself for even a short trip? Does he not make arrangements in case rain, storms, or the dark of night should overtake him while still far from his destination? Does not a captain prepare himself when he goes to sea, getting anchor, compass, and lifeboats? Doesn't he make preparation in case a raging storm arises, his ship founders on a reef, yes, is even completely wrecked? Well then, who wants to be so bold as to begin today's new departure on the dangerous ocean of time unprepared?

But you who do not believe in Jesus, with what are you equipped? You will be tempted by sin and will fall; for without faith man has no power to resist sin; without faith, caught in their net, he must obey the wishes of Satan, world, and sin. You will experience new joy, and if you are without faith, you will forget the joys of heaven and salvation. You will experience cross and tribulation; perhaps God will visit you with sickness, perhaps with poverty, perhaps with shame, perhaps with the death of loved ones at home. Without faith in Christ you will have no comfort, you will quarrel with your Creator, murmur against the Lord of lords. If God should take every precious thing away, in despair you will wish that you were never born. But you who do not believe in Christ, how great your misery will become, if God should this year demand your souls of you and summon you before His judgment throne! How terrible your death will be, how terrible your appearance before God, how terrible your eternity! Then you will wish, but alas in vain: Oh, that I also had Jesus!

Happy are you who have begun the new year in faith in Christ! You who take comfort in this, that today on New Year's Day the wonderful Child once born in Bethlehem received by God's own command the name "Jesus," that is, Savior. Happy are you who have chosen this blessed name for your motto for the new year, for in Him God has assured us of our salvation. Though sins may tempt you, though they may lay new snares for you and devise new wiles against you, as long as you believe, you can have the victory over them. True, you have flesh and blood, but you also have the Spirit which wars against the flesh. You can say with St. Paul, "I can do all things through Him who strengthens me" (Philippians 4:13).

Happy are you! Though you may experience many days of joy, though the world may act as a friend, though great honor and riches may await you, yes, and though the whole world would be given you, all this would not tear you from Christ as long as you hold fast in faith to Him. You will confess that despite everything Christ is and remains your highest good, that you would gladly do without everything but Him, that compared with the sweetness of His grace everything in this world tastes bitter.

Oh happy are you! God may in the new year even test you severely. In poverty, you will find enough riches in the grace of your Savior; in shame, the honor of divine adoption remains yours; in sickness, you have the comfort of the Gospel. And should death come and wreck your ship of life, you will be happy even then! The Rock that your hand of faith grasps will not let you fall, for this Rock is Jesus Christ. Your death will then be but the victorious entry into the mansions of eternal rest.

Today, let everyone pray that the Author and Finisher of faith would not only kindle faith but also cause it to burst into a bright flame. Lift up your anchor; your journey will be successful and you will joyfully and triumphantly land on the shore of the home of the saints.

Therefore, if I should today once more summarize my New Year's wish, it is this: God give all of you faith in your heart, faith for your life, faith for your imminent suffering, and finally, faith for a blessed death.

Yes, may God do that for us all and hear my poor supplication for the sake of Jesus Christ, His Son, our only Savior. Amen! Amen!

SUNDAY AFTER NEW YEAR (1)

MATTHEW 2:13–15

Grace and peace be multiplied unto you through the knowledge of God and of Jesus Christ our Lord. Amen.

Dear brethren in Christ Jesus!

Even seemingly small events in the life of Christ are of such great importance that one cannot study His life zealously enough. The life of anyone else attracts our attention and deserves our admiration only if the unusual distinguishes it. This is not true of Christ. Everything that happened to Him from His birth to His last gasp on the cross is of special significance.

Christ did not live on earth for Himself but for men. Through His suffering He bore all their sins. Through His perfectly holy life He fulfilled the Law of God for all men. Now if we believe on Christ, God will look on us as though we had atoned for our sins ourselves, as though we were as righteous, pious, and faultless as Christ Himself.

It is something wonderful when a man really recognizes that Christ through His life and death became his Savior. However, the blessing of Christ's life will become inexpressibly greater if we consider each circumstance in its sublime meaning, ponder upon it in our hearts, and apply it to ourselves.

The life of Christ, like a beautiful garden, delights us if we but give it a glance and feast our eyes on the whole scene. However, our pleasure will be much greater if we examine each flower and taste each fruit. The life of Christ is like a mine in which one sees gold and silver specimens sparkling everywhere. However, we uncover even more glittering loads of that precious metal the more we use the hammer of attentive meditation. How many in the past 1,800 years have dug in this mine for treasures of eternal life! None have ever come out empty-handed. All have found ever new yields in it. And though all men, yes, all angels, would search in the life of Christ for all eternity, they would still find in it ever new riches and ever new material for admiration and adoration.

Have you experienced what a treasure of wisdom, comfort, and power lies in the life of Christ? If anyone has not, he is not a Christian and therefore not on the way to salvation. He is still blind and dead. The sun of grace has not risen upon him. For a Christian as he compares the world with the life of Christ everything becomes insignificant, because Christ becomes his highest wisdom, his only comfort in life and death. Whoever cannot yet say with Paul, "For I decided to know nothing . . . except Jesus Christ and Him crucified" (1 Corinthians 2:2); "It is no longer I who live, but Christ who lives in me" (Galatians 2:20), is not awakened from his natural sleep of sin. He is not on the way to eternal life. And though he may know the facts of the life and doctrine of Christ, he nevertheless is most unhappy, yes, lost and condemned. True saving faith is not a matter of the head but of the heart; note this well—of the heart! Christ so excites the heart that it finds no rest, no peace, and no joy in anything but in Him. On the other hand, everything that he hears about Christ is precious. Oh, that all our hearts might become warm through Christ's love.

To this end let us upon the invitation of today's Gospel consider one of the many important events in the childhood of our Savior.

The text: *Matthew 2:13–15*

In the Gospel just read we today meet our sweet Christ Child as a poor exile. For your devotion I now present:

Christ's flight into Egypt.

Hear:

1. How deeply Christ humiliated Himself;
2. How important this flight was for the salvation of all men;
3. How instructive and comforting this is for the Christian life.

I.

The events of our Gospel reading took place after the Wise Men found the Christ Child, had given Him gifts, and Mary, offering the sacrifice of purification, had presented her child in the Temple. When the Wise Men had first come to Jerusalem with the question, "Where is He who has been born king of the Jews? For we saw His star when it rose and have come to worship Him" (Matthew 2:2), Herod and all the leaders of Jerusalem became greatly troubled. The leaders of the city thought that if the expected King of the Jews had come, war with the Romans would be inevitable. Herod supposed that he was in danger of losing his throne. What happened? Without anyone suspecting it, the king secretly decided to kill all the newborn children of Bethlehem and thus secure his throne. Nobody, least of all Mary and Joseph, knew about the bloody plan. God alone knew it, as it is He alone who is able to read the very plans of men.

Unaware of any danger, Mary and Joseph retired for the night, while the soldiers were getting ready to kill the children of Bethlehem. Oh, what a heartrending scene awaited the inhabitants of Bethlehem! Yet, while God in His unsearchable counsel permitted the murder of the other children, His holy providence watched over the child Jesus. His life just at that moment was more important than His death.

We read in our Gospel, "When [the Wise Men] had departed, behold, an angel of the Lord appeared to Joseph in a dream and said, 'Rise, take the Child and His mother, and flee to Egypt, and remain there until I tell you, for Herod is about to search for the Child, to destroy Him' " (Matthew 2:13).

Here you see the incomprehensibly deep humiliation of the Son of God. Of Him we read in Revelation, "From His presence earth and sky fled away" (20:11). Here we read that this almighty God, before whom the earth and heaven must flee, Himself flees before a mortal man. We know that He is the Light of the world, the Sun of Righteousness, the Image of God; yet now we hear that He seeks the protection of night, in order to be safe from the plots of a miserable sinner. We know that heaven is His throne and the earth His footstool; yet now we hear that He must hurriedly leave Palestine if He does not want to die a miserable death. We know that He came to save all men from sin, death, and hell; yet now we hear that God Himself orders a poor helpless man to save Him from death, to bring Him to safety, to rescue Him, the Deliverer of the whole world.

To our great surprise we heard on Christmas Day that the Son of God was born in a stall and laid in a manger. Today we see the mystery of Christman deepening. We hear that Christ was not tolerated even there—He was dispossessed even of stall and manger. He was obliged to leave His miserable dwelling immediately. Wrapped in wretched swaddling clothes, He permitted Himself to be carried by His frightened mother. He hurried through the desert to Egypt, to another part of the world.

Had not the angel of the Lord preached at His manger that He was the Savior, "who is Christ, the Lord"? Did not the multitude of the heavenly host loudly exult and sing, "Glory to God in the highest, and on earth peace among those with whom He is pleased"? Where is the glory of God now? Is it not an insult to have to flee? Where is the established peace on earth? Does not the first result of the appearance of Christ in this world so far appear to be the opposite? Where is man's joy in Him? Does this not reveal man's great dislike of Christ, yes, a murderous, deathly, bloodthirsty hate?

Who can therefore grasp the deep humility of the Son of the Most High? How dare we? How can we believe that He actually was the great person whom the evangelist proclaimed Him to be? Can He be our helper in all trouble, if He needed human protection and help in His trouble? Can He be the refuge of our souls, if He was a dispossessed refugee? Can He prepare a place for us in heaven, if He could not be king even in the most humble hut, yes, in the caves of animals? Yes, yes, my friends, as contradictory as it may seem to our reason, this holy Christ Child's very humiliating flight is a wonderful pledge of our eternal salvation.

Hear therefore in the second place how important His flight was for the salvation of all men.

II.

Since earliest times, men were offended at the flight of Christ. To exalt the most holy Child, miracles that were supposed to have taken place on the flight from Egypt were invented. The story is told that the holy family was attacked by robbers; one of them was so moved by the heavenly glory surrounding the Child, that he rescued Him from his infamous fellows, returned Him to His mother, and said, "Child, now *I* have delivered you; if you ever can do something for me, think of what I did for you." And this robber was supposed to have been the malefactor, to whom Christ on the cross promised the comfort of paradise. The story is also told that as the Child came into Egypt all the idols in the land immediately fell and broke.

As delightful as all these stories are, these inventions that should take away the offense show that the inventors had not recognized the meaning of

Christ's abject flight. As deeply humiliating as it was for the Savior, just so important was it for the salvation of men.

Christ did not flee because He had been too weak to defend Himself. Not only could God the Father have rescued Him by a miracle, not only were all the holy angels ready to defend Him, but the Child Himself could have protected Himself, had He wanted to use the glory that was imparted to His human nature by its union with the divine. But Christ did not want this. Of his own free will He submitted to the great disgrace of fleeing before a human being in order to become our perfect Savior.

This flight is a part of the whole work of redemption. For that reason it was not only prophesied by Hosea, as we read in our text, that God would call His Son out of Egypt; not only did Abraham, Isaac, and Jacob and his sons have to emigrate to Egypt as the type of Christ, but a divine messenger from heaven must appear to Joseph in a dream and command him to flee into Egypt. If we therefore consider the flight in the proper way, it cannot cause our faith to waver but must rather found, strengthen, and establish it.

Why did Christ flee? First, He thereby won our return to paradise. On account of our sins we fled from God and finally were expelled from paradise. But after the innocent Christ permitted Himself to be driven out of Judea, the Promised Land and His legal kingdom, we no longer have any reason to flee from God, even though we are sinners. Now all, Jews and Gentiles, have access in One Spirit to the Father. Now the door to the heavenly paradise and the promised new earth is opened.

Through His disgraceful insulting flight Christ has atoned for our pride, our impertinence, and our sinful insolence. Because of this flight, in which Christ was constantly driven from place to place, He secured for us sinners security from all the enemies of our soul. On this flight the child Jesus passed by Mount Sinai, where God had given His stern Law that Christ had come to fulfill. He was carried past those places where previously the brazen serpent was set up and the first Passover lamb was slain, both of which prefigured Christ. Yes, in that Christ fled before His persecutors, He earned pardon for all His enemies, even for the most wicked sinners. Though a person may have hated, persecuted, and sought to kill Christ, if that wretched man, confessing his sins, turns to the fleeing Christ in faith, he will find grace and complete forgiveness.

In short, Christ says to us as Joseph who was sold by his own brothers into Egypt said to them in a friendly way, "Do not fear . . . you meant evil against me, but God meant it for good, to bring it about that many people should be kept alive, as they are today" (Genesis 50:19–20). Christ's flight into Egypt also had such a wonderful result that our true heavenly homeland now stands open to all. By Christ's disgrace, honor has been won and given us; by His misery, glory; by His poverty, riches; by His persecution, security; by His wandering about, an abiding home in the mansions of our heavenly Father.

Had this flight not taken place, had not all righteousness been fulfilled by Christ, woe to us! We would have to flee restlessly before God; we would never find peace.

Let us therefore now hear in the third place how instructive and comforting this is for the Christian life.

III.

Christ flees in order to save His life for the salvation of the world. First of all, we see that we dare not unnecessarily venture into danger. We must also seize every opportunity for flight if we can do this without injury to God's honor and the welfare of our neighbor, or if God Himself gives us the opportunity to save our life. In the first centuries there were Christians who (in order to receive the martyr's crown) of their own accord revealed that they were Christians. But this was a false zeal. This suffering was self-imposed. It had no promise of grace. God cannot reward it, but rather must forgive it. We also see that if a person can save his life and does not because he relies on God's protection, his false trust only tempts God. If the very Son of God, who could have very well helped Himself, did not despise the means given men, how much less dare we?

Furthermore, the persecuted Child fled. Those to whom the Child was entrusted must flee with Him. We should learn the lesson that those who accept the little child Jesus in faith dare not expect rest and good days. No, only too soon will he experience great distress as Mary did. Not only will the world soon find out that he is a Christian, but it will also hate, persecute, and attempt everything conceivable to take his faith away. We should take comfort from the example of the persecuted Savior and His mother and gladly go the way of the cross upon which Christ preceded us. Then we should rise and quickly flee with Jesus. We should take care not to enter into an intimate friendship with the unbelieving world and live in its sins and vanities. We should separate ourselves only the more from it by piously walking in Christ and rather lose everything than Christ.

We hear, moreover, that no sooner did the angel and the Wise Men reveal Christ than He also soon again hid Himself. Not only the unbelieving world but even the believing shepherds lost sight of Him. This still happens. Today we feel Christ in our hearts, then the very next day He often hides Himself from us and it seems as though He has left us. What should we do? Our text tells us. It refers us to the prophecy of Hosea. If in those times anyone clung to this prophecy, he was soon delivered from his trial. Hence, we must to this very day seek Christ in the Word if we no longer feel Him in our hearts.

Finally, we also hear that all the plots of Herod, clever as they were, accomplished nothing. This miserable enemy of Christ quickly perished, but Christ remained alive. The enemies of Christ still experience this time and again, and they will continue to experience it until the end of time. Even today they conceive the most cunning plans to wipe Christ and His Word from the earth, but all their wisdom will come to naught. As far as they are concerned, they will reap a frightful reward. Men can drive Christ away; He forces Himself on none. But they will never push Him out of the world. If Christ is not accepted in one place, He enters elsewhere. Yes, as He once returned to hostile Judea who had rejected Him, so He today ever and again seeks those who have sent Him away. With unflagging love and friendliness He offers them anew the treasures of His grace.

Hence, let us take courage during this wretched time of almost universal apostasy. Christ once again fled to Egypt while His enemies no doubt exulted at having rooted Him out. But take comfort! He still lives and His Church remains, even though all the world should conspire against Him. So let us follow Him faithfully and attach ourselves to the Holy Family. Though Christ may always lead us through deserts, we will finally come with Him into our true homeland. Amen.

SUNDAY AFTER NEW YEAR (2)

MATTHEW 2:13–23

Grace and peace be multiplied unto you through the knowledge of God, and of Jesus Christ our Lord. Amen.

Greeting in our Savior, dearly beloved hearers!

If we inquire how it happens that the precious Gospel of Christ is preached to so many who do not wholeheartedly receive it anyhow, do not cling completely to Christ, and would rather remain in their sins, what would we find? A very common reason is the belief that clinging to Christ completely means losing too much.

If a distinguished man were to cling to that despised Christ, he thinks, "Should I give up the respect and great honor that I have generally enjoyed and be despised from now on as a fool, a devotee, an enthusiast? No, I can never do that! I would lose too much."

If he who preciously planned day and night how he could become rich, if he already has seen his earthly wealth increase, if he should now give up all trying to become rich and seek first the kingdom of God and his righteousness, he thinks, "How can I let go of all those wonderful opportunities for becoming a rich man honorably and for Christ's sake be satisfied with no more than food and clothing?! Oh, no! This loss would be too great. There is always time later on to tear myself free from all these earthly cares!"

If someone should be asked to make a complete break with a pet sin, tear even the last strand that still binds him, become free, and surrender himself wholeheartedly to Christ, he thinks, "Alas, that is too difficult. It is impossible for me to make this sacrifice. That is demanding too much of me."

Of a truth, that is the how most people think who do not surrender completely to Christ. This is the main defense that Satan has erected to keep thousands upon thousands of souls imprisoned.

Ah, what an outrageous lie Satan and his heart tell! To think that one believes that he loses anything by associating with Christ! Oh, what a fearful delusion! Nothing is lost, but much is won—not only in heaven but already here on earth. Solomon says and experience confirms it, "The cheerful of heart has a continual feast" (Proverbs 15:15). However, one has a merry heart, a confident spirit, a pure happy conscience only if he turns completely to Christ and makes room for no other love than the love of the grace that Christ brings. Blessed is he who has finally conquered himself! He will then see that his honor was smoke, his wealth a golden chain of slavery, and his joy in sin a pleasant poison for his soul. In Christ he again finds a thousandfold everything which he denied for his sake. Oh that there might be none among us who, if he were previously deluded that it would cost too much to become Christ's possession, would remain in this delusion!

In today's text we find a warning example in Herod. He feared that in accepting Christ he would lose his throne and be robbed of all his glory and joy. And so he persecuted Him and murdered a great number of children just to kill Christ. Alas, he did not kill Christ but only himself, his soul, and his salvation. Let us now consider this horrible deed in greater detail for our warning and admonition.

The text: *Matthew 2:13–23*

My friends, the text just read contains three events worthy of consideration, the flight of Christ into Egypt, the murder of the children of Bethlehem, and finally, the holy Child's return into His homeland. A year ago we directed our attention chiefly to the flight into Egypt. Let us therefore choose as the subject of this year's consideration:

The murder of the children at Bethlehem.

We consider:

1. The unfortunate tool by whom this was done;
2. The good reasons why God permitted it to happen; and finally,
3. The important meaning that it still has for us.

I.

My friends, there have been and still are enemies of the Christian religion who claim that the murder of the children at Bethlehem is only a fable. They say that since Josephus, the Jewish historian who reports much of Herod's deeds and fate, does not mention the fact that this king also ordered the murder of a number of children in and about Bethlehem, it did not happen. It is self-understood that this does not confuse Christians. What they find in God's Word they consider more certain than if they had seen and heard it themselves.

The reason why the enemies deny the truth of the story of the murder of the children at Bethlehem is stated in such a way that it must appear laughable even to an unbeliever. Is it not laughable to argue that because one writer mentions a fact about which another is silent, this fact is not true? We must mention that not only Matthew but also a *heathen* historian, Makrobius by name, reports the story of the murder of these children.

And if one knows but a little of the character and deeds of Herod and takes that into account, it becomes clear why Josephus mentions other facts from Herod's life but remained silent about the murder of the children of Bethlehem. In comparison with the many other atrocities perpetrated by Herod, Josephus considered this shameful deed scarcely worth mentioning.

When Christ was born at Bethlehem, the Jewish nation, as you know, was under Roman rule. The Romans had appointed Herod, surnamed "the Great," as king in Palestine. True, by birth he was not a Jew but an Edomite, that is, a descendant of Edom or Esau, the brother of Jacob. At least outwardly and, it seems, with a certain amount of conviction, Herod embraced the Jewish faith.

This king, who according to our text was the unfortunate tool who caused the murder of the children of Bethlehem, is known in history as Herod the *Great*. However, his greatness consisted in nothing else than in great unheard-of sins—yes, truly devilish outrages. At the time of the birth of Christ Herod had ruled for almost thirty-six years. He enlarged the temple at Jerusalem, making it a most splendid structure. Not only that—in order to please the Romans he also profaned the Holy City by heathenish idols and statues. During his whole reign he was a suspicious, cruel, and bloodthirsty tyrant. If Herod merely suspected that anyone could become dangerous in any way, this person immediately died a violent death. Gradually, by his bloody commands, he put out of the way almost all of his relatives who could ascend the throne after his death. When his wife and sister showed sorrow over these deaths, they also fell victim to his bloodthirsty wrath. Yes, the wicked king even had three of his sons publicly executed when he doubted that they loved him. Even Caesar Augustus remarked that it was safer to be Herod's pig than his son.

Josephus relates all this and adds that in the last years of his reign Herod commanded that besides many other people his oldest son, Antipator, be murdered, after he learned that many expected a miracle-working king of the Jews who had been predicted by the prophets.

Now when we consider how inhuman Herod was, we cannot be surprised to hear what is also related in our today's text. When the Wise Men from the east had revealed to him that a miraculous star had appeared, when by God's arrangement announced the newborn King of the Jews, Herod commanded them to go the Bethlehem, search diligently for the child, and when they found Him to report back so that Herod could come and worship Him also. But with the suspicion of harboring a rival, dark thoughts of murder immediately arose in Herod's wicked heart. But the Wise Men, warned by God, had not returned. Herod called them deceivers with whom perhaps the Bethlehemites had entered into a secret alliance against him. In order to kill that mysterious child whom he feared so greatly, he commanded that all children in and about Bethlehem who were two years old and under be killed immediately. He who with an untroubled mind could order the death of his own sister, his wife, and his sons, in addition to hundreds of others, was certainly even less troubled by the moaning of the poor little children and the heartrending lamentation of their mothers.

The death of this first persecutor was as loathsome as his life. Scarcely had he ordered the murder of the children then God sent him a hideous sickness in which he was to have a warning of his fate in eternity. All the members of his body began to rot and swell. His whole body dripped with matter from which crept great numbers of loathsome worms. Still he lived on, and one could scarcely see the places in his face where his eyes moved. At the same time a putrid stench arose from his body. In this condition the miserable king had himself carried in a sedan chair to Jericho to bathe in the warm water that is found nearby.

Finally, Herod realized that he would not recover. Far be it, however, that his conscience should be awakened at least a little. On the contrary, it became very evident that God had visited him with the terrible fate of a hardened heart. What did he do now that he saw himself before the gates of a fearful eternity? He commanded that his most trusted soldiers be brought to him. Overwhelming them with gifts, he left them in charge of the execution of his last testament. Since he feared none in Judea would mourn his death, he had thought of a plan to cause the land to lament greatly even after his death. Herod's faithful soldiers were immediately to arrest the most distinguished of the kingdom. The moment Herod would die, they were to bury them alive as traitors. Shortly thereafter the wretched king stabbed himself and thus in silent despair he passed from temporal pain into eternal torment.

Thus he departed from this world who in most devilish cruelty had cold-bloodedly murdered a great number of children just to kill Christ.

II.

Permit me to show you now in the second place why God permitted the murder of the children at Bethlehem to take place.

My friends, God's wisdom is so great that no person can guess all of God's reasons in letting evil or good, great or small things to happen. Certainly, it would be highly impertinent to want to name all the purposes for which sake God permitted that most terrible event which is related in our text to happen. In order that we also can wonder at God's wisdom in this case, God Himself has given us clear signs in His Word in which we must seek the mysterious purposes of why He permitted this.

We find the first in Matthew, "Then was fulfilled what was spoken by the prophet Jeremiah: 'A voice was heard in Ramah, weeping and loud lamentation, Rachel weeping for her children; she refused to be comforted, because they are no more'" (2:17–18). We see from this that the martyr's death of the children at Bethlehem was clearly predicted by Jeremiah. It therefore is an unmistakable sign that the Child born in Bethlehem of the Virgin Mary is the promised Messiah, the Savior of the world. When Rachel, i.e., the Jewish mothers living in Bethlehem, loudly lamented the bloody death of her dear children, she was a herald in tears that the awaited king of grace had arrived.

Does someone ask: Why did God predict Christ's coming through such a terrible sign? I answer: God could have chosen another sign and could have also made a different prediction. However, He also knew in advance that the fathers and mothers of Bethlehem would not accept the holy Christ Child but push Him out into a stall. They would not ask about Him and because of His humble appearance would disown and reject Him. God therefore decided to permit the cruel inhuman tyrant to murder their children. God knew in advance that His Son would soon be rejected; He also wanted to reveal quite soon what a great sin this is. If the inhabitants of Bethlehem did not wish to rejoice in the gracious Christ Child, then they should weep and lament over the corpses of their own children at His righteous judgment.

Another wonders: Of what were the poor children guilty that they must be sacrificed because of the malice of their parents? I answer: We cannot by nature reconcile ourselves to the inscrutable ways and incomprehensible judgments of God. To our reason it appears most unjust that God visits the sins of the fathers on the children until the third and fourth generation. But we must remember that such visitations of parental sins on the children is a dreadful punishment for parents but not at all for the children. On the contrary, for the children, especially if they die early because of the sins of their parents, it is nothing but inexpressible gracious kindness. Tell me, what did the children of Bethlehem lose that even in their cradle they died violently? How would they have been helped had they lived as long as their parents? Surely, they would have to die anyhow. And must we then not fear that these poor murdered children would have been seduced to follow the sins of their parents? Must we not fear that if God had not taken these children away early in life, they would have rejected Christ their Savior? Would they not now be lamenting eternally with their parents? What will they do now? Oh, certainly, someday in all eternity we will hear these very children praise God that He killed them to become the first martyrs of Jesus Christ! Someday we will hear them laud God that while there was still time He so graciously took them from the land of seduction into eternal security, from a life of sin into the life of perfection, from this world of misery into perfect glory and salvation.

They lost nothing but gained infinitely more. They were the first sheaves that were brought into the granary of heaven through the grace of the Savior who had now appeared. For Christ's sake they had lost their earthly life; in return they found their eternal heavenly life. Upon their short crying and sobs there followed eternal laughing and rejoicing. After their short struggle, eternal rest and victory. They received an eternally radiant unfading martyr's crown.

There are still more reasons why we believe that God permitted the murder of the children at Bethlehem. God wanted to have men know that the Christ Child is quite different from other children of men. The holy Child may be in great danger with other children, but though hundreds and thousands of other children would not escape, God's watchful Fatherly eye and His wonderful protecting hand over the Christ Child should be most clearly seen. Although the most bloodthirsty tyrant of all should lay traps for Him with such cunning that it appeared impossible for his bloody design to fail, all his cleverness to trap this Child must nevertheless be foiled.

Finally, God wanted to show the world in the sudden death of the innocent children the nature of the kingdom, which the Savior would establish on earth. It would not be a kingdom of visible glory but an invisible kingdom of the cross; its subjects would suffer and struggle but they would find eternal heavenly riches, grace, forgiveness of sins, righteousness, life and salvation.

III.

This leads me in the third place to the important meaning that the murder of the children of Bethlehem has for us even today.

We learn the important doctrine that if we want to remain with Christ, we must expect only the cross, persecution, misery, and death. As soon as we let the world know that our heart and mind lives in and around Bethlehem, we must be ready to find even now a Herod who lays traps for us; we must seal our confession with patient endurance, yes, with our blood.

At the same time we should learn from this story that to reject Christ out of fear of the cross, as the people of Bethlehem did, will not free us from suffering. Or to say it another way, our laughing here will be turned into eternal howling there. We therefore have the choice: either suffer here with Christ like the children of Bethlehem and someday enter with them into glory, or first rejoice here without Christ like the fathers and mothers of Bethlehem, and then weep with them, yes, enter without Christ into the land of eternal tears.

And still more! When Herod prepared the bloodbath in Bethlehem, he did not want to pass as a persecutor of the pious. He called the Wise Men deceivers and the Bethlehemites traitors. Let us learn from this the procedure of Christ's enemies. If you are a Christian, do not hope that the world will admit that it hates and persecutes you for Christ's and the truth's sake. No! With all their unjust persecutions they still pretend that they do you evil with every right, that only because of your sins are you suffering as a scoundrel.

My friends, the murder of the children of Bethlehem not only gives us earnest doctrine but also rich comfort. It comforts us when God even today permits our dear children to suffer. He shows us that God wants to exalt Himself through the suffering of our children; they also should become martyrs for Christ; they also should bear the cross after their Savior; they also should enter into glory through tribulation.

If you stand at the sickbed of one of your little children and your weak heart is at the point of breaking because of their suffering, do not murmur against your God! He, the most tender heavenly Father, loves your children more than you can; just because He loves them He lets them often suffer so severely and bitterly here. Someday they are to reap much with joy; they must therefore sow here with many tears. Someday they should be most glorious; God therefore often submerges them here in great misery. Only wait! What causes your tears now will some day serve as an object of joy for you and them in eternity. Oh, therefore say even at the bed of pain of your beloved children, "My Jesus, as Thou wilt; Oh, may Thy will be mine!" (*TLH* 420:1).

How the suffering of the children of Bethlehem comforts us when we ourselves must suffer much here, when we are often assailed with the thought that God is angry with us! In those little children we can clearly see that God often lays great suffering not only in wrath upon the unbelieving world to punish them for their sins; He also out of love lays suffering upon His own beloved children in order to glorify them. As certainly as the bloody death of those children was not a punishment but a glorious deliverance, the greatest grace that God could show them, so dare also we believers in Christ not go astray concerning God's Father-love when He lays so many and such severe suffering upon us. The very ones whom God loves He scourges and chastens. Those whom He someday wants to glorify He first hurls into the heat of misery; those whom He someday wishes to bring to the feast of victory, He first permits to struggle; those whom He someday wishes to comfort eternally, He first permits to grieve. Amen.

Epiphany Season

The Epiphany of Our Lord (1850)

Matthew 2:1–12

Lord Jesus Christ, we laud, we praise, we worship You that, when our fathers did not know God and were without hope, outside the commonwealth of Israel, strangers concerning the promise, and sitting in darkness and in the shadow of death, You rose upon them as a bright morning star. Today it still shines over us, their children's children. But see! darkness still covers a great share of the earth and gross darkness many people. Break forth also over them as the Sun of grace and truth; may they walk in Your light and their kings in the brightness which has risen upon us. To that end bless the work of Your servants in all lands; awaken ever more people who will say, Lord "here I am, send me!" (Isaiah 6:8). May also many hearts be awakened today to share in the work of the conversion of those who are still far away from the truth. Hear us for the sake of Your glorious name. Amen.

Dear friends in Christ!

If one superficially ponders how God distributes His Means of Grace among the nations, it is easy to think that He has always limited His grace to one particular nation. This, though, still dominates Jewish thinking today. They suppose that they alone are destined to salvation; they think that God has rejected all heathen. But this error is contrary to God's honor.

Divine revelation assures us of the very opposite. It says that God's grace is worldwide, including all men. We are told "there is no injustice with the LORD our God" (2 Chronicles 19:7). Peter and Paul repeat this in the New Testament in the same words. In Ezekiel 33:11 this is stated even more clearly: "As I live, declares the Lord GOD, I have no pleasure in the death of the wicked, but that the wicked turn from his way and live." Paul expresses the same in the words, "[God] desires all people to be saved and to come to the knowledge of the truth" (1 Timothy 2:4); and Peter, "[God is] not wishing that any should perish, but that all should reach repentance" (2 Peter 3:9). From this it is very clear that God does not want the death of a single heathen. He is not willing that even one heathen be lost, but that each of them come to the knowledge of the saving truth.

God, however, was not satisfied with even such proofs of His universal grace. From the beginning of the world He clearly revealed that the Redeemer promised in paradise was for all nations, hence for all the heathen as well. Yes, the Lord said to Abraham, Isaac, and Jacob, that through one of their descendants not only *their* family and nation but *all* nations and families of the earth should be blessed. Jacob on his deathbed called the expected Savior the ruler (Genesis 49:10) to whom the *nations* would cling. All the holy prophets from Moses until Malachi invite all heathen to wait for, to hope for, to take comfort and rejoice in the Messiah as their comfort. As soon as the forerunner of the Savior was born, God opened the mouth of Zechariah to rejoice that the dayspring from on high had visited the Jewish people, "to give light to them that sit in darkness and in the shadow of death" (Luke 1:79).

God did not promise the Redeemer only for the Jewish nation but for the heathen as well. On three different occasions He announced this counsel of grace to all men and called them into His kingdom of grace. The first time the Gospel was proclaimed to all men was in paradise through Adam; the second time through Noah; and the third time through the apostles, who were commissioned to go into all the world to preach the Gospel to every creature. They actually carried out this command so that Paul could assert, "Their voice has gone out to all the earth, and their words to the ends of the world" (Romans 10:18). In another passage he says that the Gospel is "proclaimed in all creation under heaven" (Colossians 1:23). These are the three different eras in which the Gospel was preached to *all* peoples and to *all* nations of the earth.

Of course, God chose the Jews before all other nations as His own, established a covenant of grace with them, and most important, gave them His revealed Word. Paul answers the question, "What advantage has the Jew?" by saying, "Much in every way. To begin with, the Jews were entrusted with the oracles of God" (Romans 3:1–2). Yet God did not wish to give His grace to the Jews alone and deny it to the heathen. The Jews should hold the light of divine revelation not for themselves alone but for all nations. For that reason God had the Jews live in Canaan, the center of the world. For that reason He let them be moved from country to country, from nation to nation, and be scattered throughout the world. For that reason He did such great extraordinary signs and wonders among them, the news of which resounded to the ends of the earth. The Jews were to be like a city on a high mountain, like a beacon built on the highest peak to shine far and wide. Thus the heathen world, sunk in idolatry, should again have the opportunity to come to the knowledge of the true God.

It is, of course, true that despite all of God's arrangements to give the heathen His saving Word, countless millions were deprived of God's Word through the guilt of their ancestors. They sank back into the night of heathen ignorance and superstition. Why did not God see to it that it would be brought again every time to the descendants of those who had suppressed and rejected the Word?

One reason is known from the procedure often observed in not allowing His Word to be preached to those whom He knows in advance would reject it. When, for example, Paul wanted to remain in Jerusalem, the Lord said to him, "Make haste and get out of Jerusalem quickly, because they will not accept your testimony about Me" (Acts 22:18). Had God known that if those living in the darkness of heathenism would accept His Word, He undoubtedly would have let it be preached to them (cf. 10:33–48; 16:9–10).

We cannot blame God that so many millions, who never heard a thing of their Savior, have already died; we must view this as a righteous judgment on these heathen, who as God foresaw would not receive His Word. Yet all these forsaken heathen, languishing in despair and hopelessness without God's Word, loudly accuse those Christians who indifferently and lovelessly are unconcerned about the salvation of the heathen. The conversion of the heathen is and remains a duty to be shared by everyone who calls himself a Christian. Even though the neglected heathen are lost because of their sins, God still demands their blood from the hands of Christians. Mission work is an obligation of Christians.

The text: *Matthew 2:1–12*

The Christmas text related the revelation of the newborn Savior to the people of Israel. Today's text just read related the first revelation of the newborn Savior to the heathen. Hence, in the past twelve days we have, so to speak, celebrated the Christmas of the Jews. Today we celebrate the Christmas of the heathen; this concerns us above all, we who descend from heathen ancestors. Therefore, we are in order to mention today that work by which ever more heathen should be brought to the knowledge of their Savior; I mean mission work. For that reason let my theme today be:

Mission work, a Christian obligation

I will show you

1. Why mission work is an obligation of all Christians, and then,
2. Why this work is especially our obligation.

I.

My friends, the first fruits of the heathen were led to Christ in a wonderful manner. In an eastern country far from Judea, probably Persia, a supernatural star appeared to several Wise Men. God had revealed to them that this star portended the birth of the King of grace, long expected by the Jewish people. Immediately the Wise Men set out for Jerusalem, the capital of the Jews. Upon arrival they asked, "Where is He who has been born king of the Jews? For we saw His star when it rose and have come to worship Him." What happened? King Herod immediately summoned all the chief priests and the scribes, asking them where according to the Scriptures the Messiah would be born. After they showed him from the prophet Micah that He must be born in Bethlehem, the king directed the Wise Men to this little town. They followed his directions and, lo and behold, they found Him whom they sought, fell down before Him, worshiped Him, opened their treasures, and afterward, carrying the eternal treasure of saving knowledge in their hearts, they returned home.

The amazing thing in this story is that the Wise Men were led by a supernatural star to Judea. Yet what is still more amazing is that God did not choose the star to lead the Wise Men directly to Bethlehem but first detoured them. Herod with his chief priests and scribes must first show them from God's Word that Bethlehem was the place where Christ could be found.

The all-wise God had most wise, most important reasons for proceeding thus. Without a doubt one was this: God wished to show for all time to come that it is not by miracles nor by stars nor by angels nor by extraordinary heavenly appearances, but through men, yes, through His established Church, that He wishes to lead the heathen to His dear Son; in short, mission work is the obligation of the Church, of Christians.

Unfortunately, only too many, even good Christians, treat mission work indifferently. They think that they can either do mission work or leave it undone; they can either interest themselves in it or not. And they argue that since today the needs within Christendom are greater than can be met, mission work is really a burden. Therefore, in these distressing times Christians should not be concerned about that. They feel that we should discontinue mission work in order not to hinder progress in other important areas.

But such Christians err. The Christian Church is a debtor to the whole world still living without Christ. She must kindle the heavenly star of the Word and lead the heathen to Bethlehem. This is pictured to us not only in our reading today. All Holy Writ clearly evidences this.

When Christ departed this world, He said to His disciples, "Go therefore and make disciples of all nations, baptizing them in the name of the Father and of the Son and of the Holy Spirit, teaching them to observe all that I have commanded you. And behold, I am with you always, to the end of the age" (Matthew 28:19–20). Of course, Christ with these words made all humanity their field of operation. But they were not the only ones to whom these words applied. They were the root of the tree planted by Christ, which should finally overshadow the whole world. They were the representatives of the whole Church. It was, therefore, really the *Church* of all ages whom Christ commissioned.

It is the Church upon whom He laid this great obligation. It is the Church to whom Christ entrusted His Word. That is why Christ also added the promise, "And behold, I am with you always, to the end of the age." The apostles have long since died, and though they filled the whole world with the sound of the Gospel, millions still sit in darkness and in the shadow of death. The words exhorting loudly, "Go therefore and make disciples of all nations," still resounds in the ears of Christ's Church. It will continue to resound until the fullness of the Gentiles has entered Christ's kingdom, that is, until Judgment Day.

But who is the Church? The Church does not consist only of clericals, the priests and bishops, but of all Christians. Hence the word of the Lord, "Go therefore and make disciples of all nations," applies to you, yes, you who through a living faith have entered the communion of the Church. You have taken over your share in the universal obligation of the Church. You have promised to do mission work to the best of your ability.

This work, however, is not only an obligation of Christians because Christ has expressly said it is. Even if Christ had not spoken a word, Christians would recognize it as their responsibility.

Now tell me: Does not every Christian owe God a debt of love? But can a Christian say he loves God, if he can calmly see Satan, the enemy of God, holding millions of people captive? Can a Christian say he loves God if he can calmly see that the greatest miracle of God's love is still in vain? That in vain He became a man for them, in vain suffered for them, in vain sweat blood for them, in vain died on the cross for them, in vain redeemed, atoned, and won salvation for them? Can a Christian say he loves God if he can calmly see that millions do not know God, serve Satan instead of God, blaspheme instead of praise God? Dishonor His name instead of sanctifying it?

No, as certainly as the love of God remains a Christian's debt even in all eternity, so certainly is a Christian also obliged to share in the work of missions. Satan's kingdom must be destroyed and his booty which he robbed from God taken away. On the other hand, God's kingdom, the kingdom of light, grace, righteousness, and blessedness must be increased and thus the whole world become ever more full of His praise, His honor. You who because of indifference are no friend of missions, you who will not contribute of your possessions toward the advancement of this work, you still do not love God; where there is no love, there is no faith; where no faith, no grace; where no grace, no salvation.

A Christian is obliged to love not only God but also His brethren. Paul writes, "Owe no one anything, except to love each other" (Romans 13:8). Are not all poor wretched heathen also our brothers and sisters? Has not one God created us? Do we not have one father? One mother? Are not all of them flesh of our flesh, blood of our blood, bone of our bone? Can Christians, therefore, say that they love their brethren when then can calmly see that millions of their brothers and sisters die without God, without light, without grace, without comfort in suffering, without hope in death, in sins, in blindness, in God's wrath and displeasure, in inexpressible misery of body and soul, and finally in despair go to hell thus to be eternally lost body and soul?

Never! He who sees his neighbor fall into the water and does not rush to give him a hand does not love his neighbor. And does he show love if he sees millions of his brethren swallowed up in the flood of eternal death and does not hurry even a little bit to help them? He who sees his brother's earthly goods on fire and does not hurry to save what he can does not loves his neighbor. And does he show love if he sees the eternal fire wrap itself around the souls of millions of his brothers but does nothing to quench this fire?

Yet I doubt that in this short time all of you are convinced that mission work is an obligation of the Christian, an obligation that Christ has not only expressly imposed upon His Christians, but which is already contained in the obligation of love to God and one's brother, an obligation that continues into all eternity.

II.

Permit me to continue and show you that mission work is our special obligation, whose repayment God today demands more earnestly than ever.

There were times when Christians wished in vain to contribute something for the conversion of the heathen, when almost all heathen countries were closed to Christians, when Satan had barricaded almost all nations and continents behind seemingly insurmountable walls. Christians could do nothing but pray that God would have mercy on their lost brethren and open the closed doors. These times are passed. Today Christians have access to almost every land and kingdom on earth. Growing world trade has opened the doors of all the nations of the world and all the islands of the sea to Christians. Faster ships have moved continents closer together. The barrier of languages has fallen more and more.

To be sure, the world does not suspect that all these great changes have a greater purpose than the one it pursues. These changes are to make a highway for Christ's kingdom. Since it is now easier to send the heralds of the Gospel to all corners of the world, the obligation of Christians to carry on mission work zealously grows each day. Obviously, God wants the fullness of the Gentiles, that is, the elect of heathenism, to enter into His kingdom of grace, and, as John says, "gather into one the children of God who are scattered abroad" (11:52). Christians should therefore use the more faithfully and carefully this wonderful time of grace to bring into Christ's fold the many sheep who are still wandering in this world.

Of course, not all should and can go out as missionaries to those places where darkness still covers the earth and gross darkness the people. However, if God has led you to that place where opportunities offer themselves, you have to fulfill the duties of your spiritual priesthood over against the heathen. But to leave one's present calling and devote oneself solely to missions, one needs not only special gifts but also special, unmistakable indications that it is the will of the Lord. Therefore, when Martin Bucer wished to make it a conscience matter for Luther to interest himself more in England, he wrote to the prince—it was the year 1538—

"That Dr. Bucer indicates, 'Go ye therefore, and teach,' that we do with *writings*. We have no command to leave our present call any further."

If not all are to be missionaries, we nevertheless are to encourage those in whom we discover the necessary gifts to do this work of love, while we according to our ability provide the necessary means. Even now there are missionaries working in our country who can continue to work only if we open our generous hand. Oh, my friends, what excuse will we offer God if we have given nothing to carry out that holy and blessed work that is entrusted to us as Christians? Oh, how many thousands of Christians three hundred years ago would have thanked God if the wonderful opportunity had been given them which is being given us!

Not only were there times when Christians had no opportunity to share in this work, there are also at present great numbers of bitterly poor Christians who could not give even a small contribution. This is especially true in our old German fatherland. More and more are impoverished by severe visitations. Many fathers and mothers are eating their crusts with tears, not knowing where they should get food and clothing during the severe winter for themselves and their hungry naked children. How gladly perhaps many of these poorest would sacrifice something for their spiritually impoverished brothers and sisters, yet they have nothing but a sympathizing heart.

It is much different with us. We live in a land of great earthly blessings. Most have somewhat more than they need. Many are overwhelmed with temporal blessings. Oh, let us not forget that we did not receive these blessings to let them lie idle in our coffers, or lend them out for profit and draw compound interest, or provide an easy sumptuous life for ourselves, or deck ourselves out in showy clothes and our rooms with splendid furniture, or build palatial homes, or expand our business endlessly, or buy one tract of land upon another. What we have is not our own. It is God's treasury. We are merely the stewards. Above all the Child Jesus still lies in poverty in His manger. He wants us to join the Wise Men in opening our treasures and laying before Him our gold, frankincense, and myrrh as traveling expenses for His journey into distant heathen countries. The Christ Child comes to us in His poor members, in His poor Church, and in His poor lost sheep among the flock of heathenism. Oh let us not wait until the hour of our death to pay our obligation! Then it could easily be too late.

I must mention one more reason why we must recognize mission work as our special obligation. We live on land from which the original inhabitants were driven away. We live among heathen whose forefathers shortly after the discovery of this land suffered the most shocking cruelties at the hands of men who called themselves Christians. In less than ten years about 15 million Native Americans were murdered like wild animals by the Roman Catholic Spaniards. Hence, do not all the Christians of this land owe these miserable people a huge debt? We live on their hills and dales, we split wood from their forests, we ride on their streams, we pasture our herds on their prairies. Woe to all citizens who wish to do nothing to bring the comfort of the Gospel and its eternal wealth to these unfortunate heathen! How terrified they will be when those who were driven away by us from their homeland will accuse them before God and say: "God! Here they are, our enemies; they drove us from our land, but they did not show us the way to Your mansions! Lord, take vengeance for what they did to us!"

Oh my friends, let us then not be even harder than Herod; at least he showed the Wise Men the way to Bethlehem. Let us take care that the bright star of God's Word is kindled for our Native American brothers. Let us bear in mind that one soul is worth more than the whole world; the world will disappear, but one converted soul lives forever and is eternally blessed in God's eyes. Should, therefore, only a few souls be won, oh, how richly would all the offerings that we brought be rewarded!

God does not become tired of doing good to us; we should not become tired of doing good to our brothers. God permits the Gospel to be preached to the poor especially. Let us then, though we for the most part do not belong to the rich but to the poor of this world, give a little bit of our poverty. It is the same to God whether he helps through little or much. Let us therefore add many more ardent prayers to our small earthly gifts, and God will abundantly bless us.

Praise be His glorious name by the tongues of all nations, forever and ever. Amen.

FIRST SUNDAY AFTER THE EPIPHANY (1845)

LUKE 2:41–52

Grace be with you, mercy and peace, from God the Father, and from the Lord Jesus Christ, the Son of the Father, in truth and love.

Dear friends in Christ!

Only a few have immigrated to this country for the proper motive. Most left their homeland to gain material advantages, earthly riches, or a comfortable living. Only a few have come because they could more easily lead a quiet and peaceful life in all godliness and honesty. And even some of those, who have come because of heavenly riches alone, have acted in gross error. Many supposed that they had to do it to maintain the true Church. This, as we said, is a great error.

The nature of the true Church is such that it can exist in any land under any form of government. It is indeed true, that now and then in our fatherland, the temporal and spiritual authorities did not permit the preaching of the pure doctrine. False teachers and books full of falsehood were forced upon our schools and churches, while here the Church has complete freedom of religion. The experience of all ages proves that the Church is always strongest inwardly when she is most severely oppressed. Persecution always nurtures the best Christians, whereas freedom and security engulf the Church little by little in indifference, security, indolence, and spiritual satiety.

It is especially noteworthy and disgraceful that many believe they had to emigrate for the sake of their *children's* salvation; yet it cannot be denied that here our youth is in particularly great spiritual danger.

Here under the guise of freedom of religion and conscience such horrible blasphemies are uttered against God, His Word, and everything holy on all streets, in all public places, and even spread in the eagerly read dailies, as I dare say happens in no other country of the world. Under the cloak of freedom all sins and shame are committed in broad daylight. The government and its laws, all discipline and order is so insolently defied as scarcely happens in other lands. We must also mention that children have so many ways of earning money and becoming independent, that one must almost be amazed to find children obedient and considerate of their parents. The danger of being misled reaches its peak because here as nowhere else an almost countless host of sects fill the land. They often surround themselves with such a deceiving and holy air that even the elect could easily be deceived and misled.

If those of us who are fathers and mothers honestly wish that our children are not merely successful but above all that they be saved; if we consider the conditions of our new fatherland in the light of God's Word, who must not think of the future with fear and trembling? Who must not cry out in worry and solicitude: "Ah, what will become of my poor children after my death? Will they not be drawn into the maelstrom of perdition and lose their souls?"

Such apprehensions are well-grounded; yet we would sin if we would despair completely. We would fall into the same error that prompted many to leave our old fatherland, the error that one cannot be saved everywhere on earth. Such thoughts be far from us! No, since by God's permission we are here, we should for our comfort realize that God, whose grace reaches as far as the heavens extend, is also here; Jesus Christ, to whom the heathen were given for His inheritance and the ends of the world as His possession, has His kingdom of grace also here; God's Spirit, from whom one cannot escape even with the wings of the morning, moves and works here as well. That word applies: "For 'everyone who calls on the name of the Lord will be saved' " (Romans 10:13). Here is the tree of the Church whose branches spread out over all parts of the earth. Here also God extends His hand toward sinners. Here we and our children can be protected from being misled and be saved.

On the basis of today's Gospel permit me to speak more to you on what parents and children must do to bring this about.

The text: Luke 2:41–52

During the past twelve days we have seen Christ as an infant in the arms of His mother. Now in today's Gospel He is presented to us at the side of His parents in His pious youth. Therefore, join me today in considering:

The holy family, an instructive example
for Christian parents and children

We ask:

1. What does it teach the parents?
2. What does it teach the children?

O Jesus, You so want to bless the preaching of Your Word, that it is strongly urged upon parents and children, that henceforth we faithfully direct our children to You, that our children willingly and gladly permit themselves to be led to You, that when we parents sleep in our graves our children may still as a congregation serve You and bless us as their pious fathers and mothers until You at last will have gathered us all together in the triumphant congregation of Your perfected saints. There we will praise You forever and ever. Amen.

I.

Our Gospel reading today relates the only incident preserved from the childhood of our Savior. Yet this one event suffices to give us a picture of what the whole youth of Christ was like until He entered His public ministry.

The first thing that we learn from our Gospel is the way in which Mary and Joseph discharged their duty as the parents of Christ. We learn that after they had circumcised the holy Child according to the Law, they trained Him with the greatest care; even from age 12 He had to go along with them, when according to the Law of the Lord they traveled to Jerusalem to serve the Lord publicly and celebrate the Easter festival with the whole congregation of Israel.

How instructive this is for us parents to whom God has entrusted children! If Mary and Joseph had to rear the holy Child carefully in whom the Lord of glory was disguised; if even they did not dare think that this Child will develop by Himself without their assistance; if they did not suppose that God would watch over and protect Him, how much more should we recognize our calling in being God's tools in the rearing of our helpless children! If the parents of the most holy God-man recognized it as their duty to bring Him into the house of the Lord, how much more should we recognize our obligation to bring our children who are in need of grace early to the Lord.

Of course, it is not within our power to convert our children, cleanse their sinful hearts, change them, and keep them in God's grace. But we can neglect them and be guilty of the loss of their souls. We should, therefore, be God's helpers if they let themselves be saved. They were not given us to play and joke with, still less to be our servants. No, God entrusted them to us, that we direct them even as children to their heavenly Father. Someday God will demand the souls and blood of our children from us and ask, "Where are My children, whom I have given you?"

Our most important and first duty as Christians is to bring our children immediately after birth to Jesus through Baptism. He said, "Let the children come to Me; do not hinder them, for to such belongs the kingdom of God" (Mark 10:14). But we have not paid our debt when we have done that. No, if our children are baptized, Jesus Himself carries them in His heart. Then we like Mary and Joseph also have a child Jesus in our arms in the person of our child. That should redouble our heartfelt concern over them. Then the salvation of this precious child should be the subject of our daily concern, our sighs and prayers. We should daily and hourly lay him in the arms of

Jesus and, as it were, the love of Jesus and the fear of God should flow into him with his mother's milk.

As soon as the child can understand, we should tell him that he was baptized and explain the great mercy that was shown him. We should teach him to say joyfully: "I am baptized! My Jesus is mine! My sins are forgiven!" We should not wait until our children go to school. No, even before we can send our children to school we should be their daily teacher and guide them to God. They are truly unfaithful parents who allow their child to grow up as it is and set their minds at rest with the fact that in his sixth year he will go to school. The frailer the child is the more important becomes what is sown in his delicate heart.

If we neglect the soul of our littlest child, we probably lay the foundation of later ineradicable ruin. If we do not plant God's Word in their hearts, they only too soon even after Baptism become like an untilled field in which the weed of sin, yes, the thorns, thistles, and hedges of vice, impudence, and shamelessness shoot up rampant. Oh, shame on those parents who bring an unruly child to school. As we said, in these very first years faithful parental training does unbelievably much, whilst neglect during this age brings irreparable harm.

And what should one say of those parents who for a small payment have the opportunity to send their children to a Christian school, yes, tuition free if they are very poor, but who do not use even this opportunity to do something for their children's souls, and consider their children their slaves who must earn them money and for that reason even keep them out of school? Oh, how blind such parents are! How is it possible for them not to know why immortal, dearly redeemed souls were entrusted to them by God! What a terrible responsibility they load upon their conscience by such carelessness! How such conscienceless parents will someday wish that they never had children when they must appear before God with them!

Neither does it suffice merely to send our growing children to school just to be rid of them and thus be relieved of all personal worry about their education. That is in no way enough. What can the few hours at school profit, if we do not carefully see to it that the good seed sown in their hearts is not again smothered by bad example, keeping bad company, and all kinds of other corruption? How can that which the teacher plants in their souls thrive and bring forth fruit, if parents at home do not water and cultivate what is planted by questions, admonitions, warnings, and loving remonstrance?

Granted that parents have done everything for their children they were able to during their school age, their parental responsibility in no way ceases even afterward. But what usually happens? Parents almost begrudge their children even the last weeks for that important day in their lives, when they before many witnesses confess their faith, publicly renew their baptismal vow, and swear eternal faithfulness to the triune God. Or, if they allow this to happen, they immediately afterward mercilessly drive their children out into the world; they do not ask whether their children's souls are in danger or not, just so they find a place where their children can earn more money.

Oh cursed greed, if parents for the sake of filthy profit send their children to a place of such great temptation that they can scarcely escape ruin. Oh faithless parents who send their child, still weak and inexperienced in faith and knowledge, among the sects who blind the child by false human piety in order to win him for a false faith. Oh faithless parents who send their child amongst people who consider one religion as good as the next and so think highly of none, calling zeal for the one true pure religion narrow fanaticism. Oh faithless parents who send their child among impious scoffers where they hear nothing from morning until evening but mockery, slander, and filthy jokes! Oh faithless parents who intentionally let their innocent child work where a host of seducers surround him and almost inevitably set a snare for his innocence! Oh faithless parents who unnecessarily send their child amongst murderers of souls and for weeks and months, yes, a year at a time, do not ask whether their child still carries the Lord Jesus in his heart and confesses him before the world! Oh faithless parents who, if they must let their child go into a dangerous place, never in ardent intercession carry his needs to God and never even with tears beg and admonish him to remain true to his Savior! Oh faithless parents who hire out their child in such a way that during his service he can not even once serve the Lord publicly on the Lord's Day, strengthen his faith by the hearing of God's Word, awaken his sluggish heart, confirm his feeble knees, strengthen his already staggering feet, and return to the narrow way that he had already left!

Yes, they say, "We have had enough worries as we brought our children through school. Now they have to get along as best they can. When we were young, we had to go out into the world." Those who are so indifferent show that when they went into the world, they were overcome by its corruption. They have no concern for their own souls; hence, they are little concerned about their children's soul-needs. Instead of lighting the way by their pious example, by their zeal and earnestness in Christianity, they seduce them by their evil example, by their lukewarm sluggish Christianity to be as ungodly as they are. If you would think of what you do, if you should hear the woe that God pronounces upon such unscrupulous parents, you would shudder.

God says, "Seek first the kingdom of God and His righteousness, and all these things will be added to you" (Matthew 6:33). But you do the very opposite and seek first the riches of this world. God says further, "For what will it profit a man if he gains the whole world and forfeits his soul? Or what shall a man give in return for his soul?" (16:26). But you consider the souls of your children worth a thousand times less than the whole world, yes, what should I say? You sell your children, body and soul, to the servants of the devil to earn a couple of rusty dollars. Christ says, "Whoever causes one of these little ones who believe in Me to sin, it would be better for him to have a great millstone fastened around his neck and to be drowned in the depth of the sea" (18:6). But you offend those very children whom God has laid on your heart. Therefore, woe to you forever and ever!

How will you give account for the neglect of your children? Look at Mary and Joseph. Every year, even though extremely poor, they made the long expensive journey to Jerusalem. They took with them their little boy whom no one could seduce or teach. And when out of weakness they had lost Him, how alarmed they were, how they lamented and cried, sighed and sought for Him without rest day and night until they had again found the Child! Believe this, therefore, woe will come upon your heads if because of greed you plunge the dearly redeemed souls of your children into the least danger. Yes, as Christian parents you will have to suffer a more severe punishment than those heathen parents who threw their children into the red-hot arms of the iron god Moloch.

Father, bear in mind, *God* has placed your child in your arms. Mother, bear in mind, *God* has given you your infant into your bosom. God will again demand His child from you. Woe to you, if you must then become silent at the question: "Where are My children?" Think of Eli upon whom God's frightful judgment fell because he had not reared his sons in the nurture and admonition of the Lord. Not once had he turned a stern eye upon their pranks.

Do not say: "My child will no longer obey me!" Perhaps you allowed the child to grow up without the rod of correction. Even now you are reaping the bitter fruits of your blindness. Hurry to retrieve, if possible, what you earlier neglected.

If you have chastised your children in their youth, you should not suppose that your children have now outgrown your discipline. You must continue to use your parental authority that God has given you and even now make your children obedient; do not cloak and excuse their sins but earnestly punish them. Do not slacken with admonition and warning. Let even your tears speak that, if God wills, the hard hearts of your children may still be softened. But above all, you should cry to God day and night, that He would stir the hearts of your lost sons and daughters and convert them. Yes, if they absolutely despise your parental admonition, you should show that you love Christ more than your children, withdraw your parental blessing, and no longer recognize them as your children.

But you, my dear parents, who carry your children day and night upon your hearts, and still see no results, do not despair; God sees your secret tears. God hears your sighs. He notices the inner yearning of your heart. Only wait for His help. Your grief and toil is not lost. God will either draw your godless children to Himself, as once He drew Augustine who had fallen deep into the service of sin. His faithful godly mother, Monica, had prayed and wept for him more than twenty long years. Ambrose said to her, "It is impossible for a child of these tears to be lost." If your children absolutely are not to be saved, your anxiety and prayers for them will still not be lost, but the blessing of your parental faithfulness will return a thousandfold upon your head.

II.

However, let this suffice of what today's Gospel teaches parents. We now consider the boy Jesus as an instructive example for you, my dear children.

The example of Jesus teaches you, my dear children, two important lessons: first, how you even in your youth serve God, and then, how you should be subject to your parents.

The Son of God could have come into the world as a full-grown man. But He did not want to. He wanted to be also a child and a young man. By His holy childhood and youth He wanted to redeem us from the sins of our childhood and youth and set an example of true pious youth. We should follow His footsteps.

Bear in mind, my dear children, the holy Child Jesus was at the same time God's Son. He did not have to obey the Law and appear in the temple at Jerusalem. Yet He accompanied His parents and joyfully undertook the distant, laborious, and difficult trip. No doubt His poor parents often could not give Him even enough food. Bear in mind, in the holy Child Jesus lay hidden all the treasures of wisdom and knowledge—even the teachers were astonished at His great, wonderful understanding when He asked questions as well as when He answered them. And yet this Child went into the temple as soon as He came to Jerusalem and seated Himself amongst the teachers. It was not the beautiful city with its splendid royal palace, or the gleaming mansions of the rich that drew Him. He paid no attention to all these sights, but hurried into the temple; He wanted to hear and talk about God's Word. Are you like the holy Child? Is God's Word the joy of your heart?

Oh yes, perhaps many will say: "Jesus was God's Son; that was the reason why He was so pious even as a child." But can one demand that of us? I answer: "Yes, my dear children." Many other children have followed the Lord and been like Him. The apostle Paul says that from a child Timothy knew the Holy Scriptures. Almost the very same words describe Samuel and the Lord Jesus, "Now the boy Samuel continued to grow both in stature and in favor with the LORD and also with man" (1 Samuel 2:26). Of the eight-year-old Josiah we read, "He did what was right in the eyes of the LORD and walked in all the way of David his father, and he did not turn aside to the right or to the left" (2 Kings 22:2).

So you see, my dear children, it is possible to be pious even in one's youth. Yes, then it is easiest; one does not yet have so many hindrances, no great worries, not such great desires, not so much work; one is also not so easily hated and persecuted on account of his piety, for a pious child enjoys a good reputation not only with God but also with all people. Everyone loves such a child. Pious children are really fortunate children. A godless child, on the other hand, is most unfortunate. He is an abomination to God, the holy angels do not love him, and even people wash their hands of him.

It is, of course, true that of your own power you children can be pious just as little as adults can. Only Jesus was holy, innocent, separate from sinners from birth on; all other people bring a wicked heart into the world. But see, in Holy Baptism God has also given you His Holy Spirit and cleansed your heart through faith. Only believe on your dear Savior. If you believe that He redeemed and washed you from all your sins, He will also give you the power to walk after His holy example. Oh, follow Him! Like the holy Child Jesus, go gladly and diligently into the house of the Lord. Let also the precious Word of God be your dearest occupation, speak of it, ask and be asked questions about it, and let it be your greatest joy. Whenever evil rascals want to entice you not to go where you would be instructed in God's Word, do not follow them; say with the Child Jesus, "Did you not know that I must be in My Father's house?"

Our text tells us that this most holy Child not only loved God's Word greatly; it especially shows that when His parents found Him and returned home He also "went down with them and came to Nazareth and was submissive to them."

Oh that I could write this word, "And [He] was submissive to them," indelibly in your hearts who still have parents! What humility that He to whom all creatures are subject, before whom all angels and men must bow the knee, was subject to His parents! What wonderful, incomprehensible condescension that He who created the firmament let His foster father employ Him when he wanted to build a small hut for a poor human being!

But also recognize from this what godless children they must be who do not imitate this example and do not wish to be subject to their loving parents! What will Christ say to you who have despised your parents, thrown their admonitions to the four winds, grieved them daily, and not even once regarded their tears and sighs that you wrung out of them by your disobedience? The Savior will say to you: "You disgraceful children. I thought that you would be moved to obey your parents, if you would hear that I, your God, Lord, and Savior, was subject to My parents. But see! even My example could not melt your disobedient, obstinate heart and move it to childlike obedience. Woe to you forever and ever! Yes, depart from Me, you cursed, into everlasting fire prepared for the devil and his angels." Alas, how those who were godless and disobedient children will wish that they could once again become young! They will think: "Oh, how gladly we would obey our parents!" But it is too late. Therefore, in heartfelt repentance and firm faith pray God *today* that He would forgive your disobedience for the sake of the holy obedient Child Jesus. God will then be gracious to you and help you to become better while there is time. Do not listen to those who would deceive you by saying that obedience is a heavy yoke. That is Satan's voice. Listen rather to the faithful voice of your father and mother! Their voice is the voice of God; their wrath is God's wrath; their blessing is God's blessing; their curse is God's curse.

Ah yes, bear in mind all you children, what Solomon says, "The eye that mocks a father and scorns to obey a mother will be picked out by the ravens of the valley and eaten by the vultures" (Proverbs 30:17). And finally, bear in mind, what God Himself says in His Holy Law, " 'Honor your father and mother' (this is the first commandment with a promise), 'that it may go well with you and that you may live long in the land' " (Ephesians 6:2–3); cf. Exodus 20:12.

God grant that these precious promises can be fulfilled in us all, here in time and hereafter in eternity. Amen.

———◦◦◦———

SECOND SUNDAY AFTER THE EPIPHANY

JOHN 2:1–11

Grace and peace be multiplied unto you through the knowledge of God, and of Jesus Christ our Lord. Amen.

In our Savior, dear Christian friends!

God instituted marriage for the temporal and eternal well-being of man. While the first man was still in paradise, God wanted to establish the first family bond. God then said, "It is not good that the man should be alone; I will make him a helper fit for him" (Genesis 2:18). And after God had completed this work, He Himself led the first bride to the first bridegroom. He Himself pronounced the benediction on this first pair. David says to every pious married couple, "You shall be blessed, and it shall be well with you" (Psalm 128:2).

If we question those who have married, what would we find? Unfortunately, not a few regretfully think back to that hour when at the altar of the Lord they so joyfully gave the promise of faithfulness until death. At first they hurried to make the vow that like an indissoluble bond of love they thought was so lovely, so blessed. And scarcely was it made when lo! aversion, regret, and despondency filled their hearts. The honeymoon was hardly ended when it seemed as though their sweet dream was shattered by a bitter, painful awakening. They think: "The wonderful dawn of the first days of my marriage I interpreted as the beginning of a beautiful happy life. Alas! it was only the forerunner of gloom and sorrow." If countless married people do not say it, they at least think: "Oh, if I had never taken this step! Oh, if I could only return! Oh, if I could only be free again! Now my life's happiness is sold forever."

Tell me, how come? First, Satan often meddles without a person suspecting it. Many could still be so happy but they consider their marriage an unhappy one. Marriage is God's ordinance; Satan, this enemy of human happiness, hinders the happy progress of this blessed institution. He often attacks Christians, concealing the good things and the blessings of God which they enjoy or could still enjoy. Even a Christian has to arm himself daily with God's Word and prayer, that he does not become unthankful and misunderstand the Fatherly guidance of his God in his marriage.

That so many have not yet found peace of soul in Christ is undoubtedly another cause for so many unhappy marriages. They seek in marriage happiness and rest for their empty hearts. Whoever seeks this in marriage seeks in vain. Even this state can never satisfy the yearning heart of man. A person must be saved in Christ and His grace. If a person has acquired this treasure, then his married life will also become a quiet, peaceful, and happy one. Yes, the less a Christian seeks his happiness in his marriage but in Christ alone, the happier his marriage will be.

Finally, many do not know from God's Word how they should begin, conduct, and view their marriage. Many begin and conduct it without God; hence, they can expect to be unhappy and unblessed. On the other hand, others who do enter this state with God think that a happy marriage has no troubles. They want their spouse to be free from weakness and frailties and their married life without cross and trouble. They do not bear in mind that in this life, nothing—nothing—is perfect except God's Word and grace. They do not bear in mind that no one has ever found a perfect spouse. They do not bear in mind that in every other relation they would have to bear still other, if not the same, frailties of their spouse. They do not bear in mind that as the other partner must bear their frailties, they are obliged to bear his. They really do not bear in mind that here God guides us from imperfection to eternal perfection, from frail union to earth to perfect communion in heaven, from suffering to joy, from trouble to heaven, from tears to eternal laughter.

However, my friends, marriage is far too important to skip studying it in the light of the divine Word. Since today's Gospel on the marriage of Cana invites us to view marriage as God sees it, let us accept this invitation.

The text: *John 2:1–11*

The Gospel reading of the marriage at Cana gives us occasion to direct our attention to the state of matrimony. Marriage appears to be a secular matter and not for the Church to consider, but we must consider that for a Christian all earthly relationships have a higher meaning, that there is a relationship between the kingdom of God and his soul's salvation. The Word of God must shed its light on marriage. A Christian is very much in need of instruction on marriage from God's Word. Of course, Christians should be *in* the world, but not *of* the world; they should do earthly things not with an earthly but a heavenly mind. Perhaps many suppose that instruction in marriage is profitable only for a *part* of the Christian congregation; but he who is not yet married can be kept only through the Word of God to enter it some day in a way pleasing to God, and he who never marries will find that everything in the Word of God benefits all, if only they pay attention to it. Hence, permit me to show you

The dignity of marriage in the light of God's Word.

God's Word makes two things clear to us:

1. How highly God honors marriage, and
2. How men must honor it.

Lord God, heavenly Father, by the institution and preservation of the holy estate of matrimony you seek the well-being of men. You have revealed your gracious will for this relationship in Your Holy Word. Give us grace to ponder and learn to know this important subject in the proper light. Show all unmarried young men and women how this important union may be made in Your name; show all who are fathers and mothers how they may use this state to Your glory and their salvation. Yes, by Your Holy Word grant now that there may be ever more pious families and family altars; that all wounds in our households be healed, all self-made misery end, and all unsuccessful marriage successful. Lord, do this, for You made light out of darkness, good out of evil, blessing out of a curse. May goodness and faithfulness meet each other, and uprightness and peace kiss each other. Hear us for the sake of Jesus Christ our Bridegroom. Amen.

I.

Reason can in some measure recognize the honor of marriage. Even reason tells us that without marriage all mankind would sink to the level of animals; on the other hand, through this indissoluble union the whole human race has received countless blessings. If there were no marriage, the whole fallen human race would be given to the lusts of the flesh in all uncleanness; marriage, however, plants decency, modesty, and chastity as nothing else can. Furthermore, no creature on earth is dependent in so many ways and for so long a time after his birth upon the help of others as is a human being. If there were no marriage, millions of children would roam the world as orphans and most would soon die, but marriage unites father and mother in love, and both hold out their hands to their beloved children.

Marriage is the foundation of all other necessary and beneficial estates. Without marriage there would be no union of men into nations; without it no state would last. Nowhere would there be any permanency. But marriage ties one to families, brings about honest relationships, makes home dear, and holds entire races and families together; finally, they expand into nations. What would the world with its thousandfold miseries, with its selfishness, and with its faithless friendships and associations be like without marriage with its sincere mutual love of spouses, with its faithful loving father and mother, with its tender love of children? Without it the misery of this world would be inexpressibly greater. Marriage brings a very natural ardent love into the bitter world and brings to people, who at first are often strangers to one another, a wonderful inward friendship that shares each other's miseries and joys. It is clear, even reason must recognize and admit that marriage works an inexpressible wholesomeness upon society. Consequently, we also read that even pagan writers praise marriage as the most beneficial of all institutions.

Yet, the real dignity of marriage we see correctly in the light of God's Word. Now let us hear what today's Gospel has to say.

Jesus Christ is the Son of the living God, come to seek and to save that which was lost. His first thirty years He lived in unnoticed quiet. Finally He entered upon His office of Messiah and began to gather about Him a group of disciples. At this time there was a wedding at Cana of Galilee, probably among the relatives of Mary, the mother of the Lord. Since Christ had just appeared in Galilee, He and His disciples were invited. And what did Christ do? One might have thought that He who had come to found the kingdom of God, a kingdom of heaven on earth, would have declined the invitation. No, He accepted it and honored this wedding not only by His gracious presence, but to reveal His glory He also did His first miracle there. And what was the miracle? Did He heal a sick person? Did He awaken someone from the dead? No, since the wedding guests lacked wine He revealed His glory by miraculously turning water into the most delicious wine. My friends, this most wonderfully revealed the dignity of marriage.

We see four points hidden from reason: First, marriage is a holy institution that God Himself instituted. Second, it is a state that God Himself sustains by His omnipotence. Third, it is an institution whose necessities God

EPIPHANY

Himself provides. Fourth, it is one in which God wants to reveal Himself to men.

An unbeliever considers marriage either a burdensome limitation to his roaming unclean lusts, or at best he views it (as do the honorable heathen) as a beneficial human institution. He sees in marriage nothing holy, nothing divine; he considers it a subject for jokes, and it elicits from him at least a smile if one speaks of holy matrimony.

But the Word of God discloses that man did not institute marriage. It is not dependent upon the laws of the different states. It is not a human invention or a mere traditional arbitrary custom. No, from God's Word we see that as soon as the all-wise God had created heaven and earth and the first human beings, He also ordained that the human race is to be propagated by one man and one woman in an indissoluble union until their death.

According to God's clear Word the Lord instituted marriage. The most high Lawgiver says, "You shall not commit adultery" (Exodus 20:14); and, "What therefore God has joined together, let not man separate" (Matthew 19:6). And so it is that before God all fleshly union of the unmarried is adultery. God has threatened to punish this sin as well as the breaking of the marriage bond with nothing less than eternal damnation. We read in the letter to the Hebrews, "God will judge the sexually immoral and adulterous" (13:4); in St. Paul's letter to the Ephesians, "For you may be sure of this, that everyone who is sexually immoral or impure, or who is covetous (that is, an idolater), has no inheritance in the kingdom of Christ and God" (5:5). Oh, what a holy inviolable ordinance marriage is!

That it is a divine institution, God has also revealed by having preserved marriage in the entire world until this hour. How many useful ordinances have been made? However, in time they have fallen and other laws have taken their place. But marriage has lasted until this hour for almost 6,000 years among all the nations of the earth. Many wicked people who have striven to live after their lusts have often used their power, cunning, and art of persuasion to dissolve the laws of marriage; there have even been lawgivers among the heathen who have striven to make a bestial living together lawful. But these states have either soon fallen of themselves, or those who were misled saw such great ruin descending upon them that even the most barbarous heathen have always returned again to marriage. As there has been no nation under the sun in which one cannot find traces of a faith in God, so there is no people so uncivilized amongst whom one does not find

99

traces of the knowledge of the dignity of marriage, despite all the abominations and filth in which they live.

Tell me, my friends, since we see that all men have fallen so deeply; since we see how they have kicked over the traces and have sought the unrestrained freedom of their lusts and desires, what power so manages the world, even darkest heathenism, that the law of marriage could not be completely abolished? Why has no human lawgiver in the long run ever yet succeeded in overriding the marriage law? Why has this law been preserved for all times among all nations, despite all the sound and fury of the unclean spirit and his apostles? Is anyone so blind as to call that blind chance? No, the most high Author of this law must Himself have most ably provided for its preservation. God has with indelible writing deeply engraved in souls and consciences the very law of keeping marriage holy. Yes, marriages are consummated on earth, but they are made in heaven. Even in the marriage of the godless God has His ruling hand; for the one, the spouse chosen without God becomes the scourge of God; for the other, a tool driving him to God. Solomon therefore says, "A prudent wife is from the LORD" (Proverbs 19:14).

God reveals that marriage is His institution, because He in a faithful and fatherly way provides for its needs. What Christ according to our Gospel reading did for the wedding at Cana is an example of what God does for all marriages. When all they lacked was wine—not something necessary, only a means of comfort and cheer—the Lord could not see the bridal pair suffer embarrassment very long but quickly used this opportunity to reveal His glory by miraculously supplying what they lacked.

That is what the Lord always does. Millions of even poorer couples enter marriage with such empty hands that they often do not know where they will find bread and fuel the day after their wedding. But do they not all find what they need? Yes, do not the children of the poorest day-laborers often bloom like roses considering their frugal and coarse food, while the only child of a rich glutton fades away sickly and pale despite nourishing and elegant fare? Must not parents who have reared many children to adulthood confess that according to the proverb the children did not sit with them but they with the children? Must they not with David add, "Like arrows in the hand of a warrior are the children of one's youth. Blessed is the man who fills his quiver with them" (Psalm 127:4–5)? Is not this faithful concern for the needs of the household a way by which God honors marriage as His institution?

But God does still more. As Christ went to the wedding at Cana to reveal His glory through a miracle (John 2:1–12), so He to this very day reveals Himself through marriage to all who do not willfully close their eyes. Without mentioning that God has appointed the parents as the natural teachers and providers for their children and has arranged to erect a family altar in every house; without mentioning that often the husband has led the wife, or the wife the husband or the children the parents to Christ—where would I find the time if I wanted to show you what a wonderful school of manifold experiences marriage is, and thus what a wonderful school of faith, love, humility, patience, gentleness, and all Christian virtues marriage is, with its weal and woe, for all who do not stubbornly resist God? Far be it that marriage, as the anti-Christian papacy teaches, is a hindrance to the service of God and godliness. No, it has with its joys and sorrows become for thousands a way on which they prospered in the knowledge of Christ or were kept and advanced in it, a source of temporal and eternal blessings.

See, this is the fourfold honor with which God has honored and still honors the estate of matrimony: He Himself has instituted it, He has preserved it, He provides for those who enter it, and finally, He makes it a school of faith and love.

II.

The second question arises: How must man honor this estate?

Much could be said on this question. Today I want to call your attention to three important points, which are seldom perceived even by Christians.

The first point to which I direct your attention is this: according to God's Word, parents have a great right over their children. Not only did parents have the right to hire out their children until their marriage to other masters and use their earnings for their own needs, as we read in Exodus 21:7; not only did parents have the right to declare null and void the oath which their daughters made against their will or without their knowledge to God, as we read in Numbers 30:4; not only did parents in the time of the Old Testament have the duty and the power to give husbands and wives to their children as we read in Deuteronomy 7:3 and in the examples of the patriarchs, but also in the New Testament St. Paul writes in 1 Corinthians 7 that the children should not give themselves but the parents should give their children in marriage.

What do those children do who without even asking their parents secretly become engaged, yes even marry? They push their parents from the throne on which God has placed them. They slink away from their parents. They take God-given honor from their parents. They rebel against the home's and the family's God-appointed power. They force strangers upon their parents against their will who are to be their children, heirs, and relatives. And thus they dishonor the holy ordinance of marriage.

Their secret engagements are null and void, even though they sealed them with a thousand oaths! And if they are married even without their parents' consent, such children have entered marriage against God's good pleasure. Their going to the altar, or (as often happens here even among Christians) to the justice of the peace, was a forbidden way, a way of sin, and, if they have done it wantonly and knowingly, a way of ruin, curse, and damnation. If such couples who married against the consent of their parents do not repent, that is reason enough to be damned. Their marriage must be without happiness and blessing.

I remind you of a second way by which man is obliged to honor the institution of marriage. God has revealed in His Holy Word that He considers it an abomination for certain persons to marry. These are all who belong to our closest blood relatives. It would take us too far afield if I were to name all the persons whom God's Word has forbidden to marry. You can find the list in Leviticus 18.

I admit that many suppose that the law of forbidden degrees of relationship belongs to the Old Testament Law, and no longer concerns us Christians. But this is a gross error. These commands and prohibitions do not belong to the ceremonial but the moral law. God says in Leviticus 18 that the heathen have defiled the land by the transgression of these commands, which God calls an abomination—that is why they should be driven out of the land and exterminated. In the New Testament John the Baptist says to King Herod, "It is not lawful for you to have your brother's wife" (Mark 6:18). The apostle Paul declares that marrying one's stepmother is an abomination such as is not known even among the Gentiles.

Therefore, you who want to honor God's holy marriage ordinance, see to it that you do not misuse the freedom of this country and against God's Word marry into your blood relationship. If you are in doubts whether this or that blood relationship is permitted or forbidden, consult Leviticus 18 and talk it over with God-fearing people who are experienced in the Scriptures. Woe to him who through incest knowingly contracts a make-believe marriage, or knowingly remains in it! If such do not repent and tear again the bond that God hates, it would be better if he had never been born.

There is one more point to which I would direct your attention. Many think that marriage is first concluded when they have consented at the altar or before the civil authorities. And so it often happens that those who were betrothed break their engagement by their own choice. They should know that whoever is betrothed to a person with the knowledge and consent of his parents has already concluded the marriage. He is indissolubly bound to his betrothed; the angel calls Mary, the betrothed bride of Joseph, his wife, though he had not yet brought her home, and warns him not to leave her. The marriage ceremony does not first establish the marriage before God, but it only confirms it as a legal marriage before church and state.

Hence of what are they who are properly engaged with the consent of their parents guilty when they faithlessly and thoughtlessly break their engagement? Before God they are adulterers just as well as that couple which after years of married life gets a divorce. Even he who knowingly frees such a rightfully betrothed person breaks the marriage with him. What God has joined together by the holy word of consent no man should separate. As Baptism takes place if it is done according to Christ's institution and no creature in heaven or on earth can annul it, thus marriage is also established if it is concluded according to God's institution by the mutual oath of marital faithfulness until death, and no person or angel can separate what God has thus joined together without great, frightful sin.

Now go home and ponder what you have heard today from God's Word. May God Himself awaken you to receive it in a godly and virtuous heart. Thus you will bring forth fruit in patience, and the holy estate of matrimony will be kept holy also among us; our marriages will be blessed to the glory of God and our own and our children's welfare. We will finally come where the children of God neither marry nor are given in marriage but will be like the angels of God in heaven.

God grant that, for the sake of Jesus Christ our Lord and Savior, praised and blessed in eternity. Amen.

THIRD SUNDAY AFTER THE EPIPHANY (1848)

MATTHEW 8:1–13

Grace, mercy, and peace be with you, from God the Father, and from the Lord Jesus Christ, the Son of the Father, in truth and love. Amen.

Dear friends in Christ Jesus!

Today Lutherans are often harshly reproached as condemning everything that is not Lutheran. However, our Church is unjustly reproached. We cannot deny that there are a few so-called Lutherans who teach that there is no salvation outside the Lutheran Church. All who subscribe to such principles *appear* to be strict Lutherans. Actually, they are not. They have really withdrawn from the Lutheran Church. As far as the heaven is from the earth, so far is our Church from teaching that only those can be saved who have been called Lutherans. The Roman Church teaches that outside of its church no one can be saved. It was against this dangerous error that Luther protested. He declared that the true Church of Jesus Christ is bound neither to Rome nor the Roman Bishop, nor to any place in the world, nor to any person, but alone to God's Word. It is to be found everywhere among all nations and languages.

Our Church teaches that there is only one true saving religion. It is the Christian religion. Therefore, outside the Christian Church you can find neither the true God nor salvation. In Dr. Martin Luther's Large Catechism in the explanation of the Third Article we read, "But outside of this Christian Church, where the Gospel is not found, there is no forgiveness, as also there can be no holiness" (II 56). Furthermore, in the Formula of Concord we read, "In Him we are to seek the eternal election of the Father, who has determined in His eternal divine counsel [Ephesians 1:11–12] that He would save no one except those who know His Son Christ and truly believe in Him" (Epitome of the Formula of Concord 13).

All orthodox Lutherans believe and confess that outside the Christian Church or without faith in Christ there is no salvation, yet nowhere do they maintain that outside the Lutheran Church there is no salvation. No, our Church has never drawn up such sectarian principles. In the preface of our public confessions the Lutheran confessors write the following, "About the condemnations, censures, and rejections of godless doctrines . . . it is not at all our plan and purpose to condemn people who err because of a certain simplicity of mind . . . much less, indeed, do we intend to condemn entire churches. . . . Rather, it has been our intention and desire in this way to openly criticize and condemn only the fanatical opinions and their stubborn and blasphemous teachers. . . . For we have no doubt whatsoever that—even in those churches that have not agreed with us in all things—many godly and by no means wicked people are found. They follow their own simplicity and do not correctly understand the matter itself. But in no way do they approve the blasphemies" (Preface 20).

Thus you see, my friends, that our Lutheran forefathers most decidedly rejected and condemned all false doctrine, falsification of the truth, and deviation from God's Word. Yet they have just as decidedly also confessed that many pious people, many upright children of God and disciples of Christ, are to be found among the heterodox. This important truth is well worth remembering. Now since we are invited to do this by today's Gospel reading, let us direct our attention to this truth.

The text: *Matthew 8:1–13*

In the centurion at Capernaum we find a true believer who has not joined the orthodox. This is most important. Christ Himself directs our attention to it when He says, "Truly, I tell you, with no one in Israel have I found such faith."

The heterodox also have upright disciples of Christ.

We consider:

1. Why we do not have to doubt this, and
2. The purpose this fact is to serve.

Lord Jesus Christ, You have shown us grace by leading us into Your true Church. Let us recognize the greatness of this grace; guard us that in fleshly security we do not rely on this privilege. Let us bear in mind that You have Your righteous disciples also amongst Your enemies; even there You can protect them. Yet You will reject many children of Your kingdom because they were unfaithful. Therefore may we be Your servants not only in appearance but also in truth, remain firm in the true faith until our end, and thus receive the end of faith, our salvation. Amen.

I.

We need not doubt in the least that also among the heterodox are upright disciples of Christ. Scripture has many noteworthy examples. An especially shining example is that of the centurion of Capernaum. He was a heathen. He was awakened to love the Jewish nation, perhaps by the reading of the prophets; according to the report of Luke, the elders of the Jews of Capernaum said of this centurion, "He loves our nation, and he is the one who built us our synagogue" (Luke 7:5). Yet he did not join the Jewish Church.

Capernaum was a very godless city. It was one of those cities, as Matthew writes, in which the greatest number of Christ's miracles had taken place, and yet it did not believe. Christ therefore says it will be more tolerable for the land of Sodom on Judgment Day than for this city. Probably that heathen centurion had been offended at the godlessness and unbelief of the Jews and from weakness of knowledge had not yet joined the visible Church.

Yet what a wonderful faith we see in the centurion! He had a servant sick of the palsy and in great pain. Luke tells us that he thought highly of this servant and therefore, when he heard of Jesus, immediately decided to ask Him to help his servant. But he also recognized his unworthiness most keenly. Not only did he not dare come to Christ but sent the Jewish elders to pray for him, and when Christ immediately promised to come in order to heal his servant, the centurion also had them say, "Lord, I am not worthy to have You come under my roof, but only say the word, and my servant will be healed. For I too am a man under authority, with soldiers under me. And I say to one, 'Go,' and he goes, and to another, 'Come,' and he comes, and to my servant, 'Do this,' and he does it" (Matthew 8:8–9).

What humility, what faith is reflected in these words! Although the centurion most keenly recognized his unworthiness, he does not doubt that Christ's goodness would be greater than his sins. Bear also this in mind: the centurion was certain that Christ could help even from a distance; he would not have to see and speak to his sick servant. Yes, still more: the centurion desired, as we hear, nothing more than a word from Christ's mouth; that was sufficient. He believed with unshakable certainly that, since his own word accomplished so much, *Christ's* word would do much more. Yes, at Christ's word even sickness, death, and hell would have to flee in a moment. In short, nothing was impossible for Him.

Where in all the Gospel stories do we find another faith like that? Nowhere. It was so great that even Christ Himself was amazed and exclaimed, "Truly, I tell you, with no one in Israel have I found such faith" (v. 10). But why does Christ mention Israel? Evidently He wants to say, "Although Israel is God's people, although the Jewish Church is God's true

Church, I have not found there the humble, pure faith which is built upon the Word, which this poor heathen has."

We have in the centurion conclusive proof that Christ has upright disciples among the sects. Yes, often the humblest, purest, and most faithful souls can be found among them, who far excel and shame many members of the true Church.

This centurion is moreover not a unique example in the Holy Writings. We are told that though the Canaanite woman was a heathen, she proved herself such a true heroine of faith that Christ, again amazed, said to her, "O woman, great is your faith!" (Matthew 15:28).

Furthermore, it is noteworthy that the Holy Scriptures repeatedly relate how greatly the Samaritans shamed the Jews. Of those ten miraculously healed lepers the nine unthankful were unconcerned about Christ, and they were Jews. Only one returned to thank Christ, and he was a Samaritan. Whilst a Jewish priest and Levite with loveless, stony hearts passed by that Jew who had fallen among murderers, a merciful and friendly Samaritan helped the wretch. If time would permit, I would add many other examples. I remind you only of the Wise Men from the east, who worshiped the Child Jesus, and of the centurion Cornelius in Caesarea. Why is all this related in the Sacred Scriptures? Certainly (among other reasons) that we should know that there are true children of God, yes upright disciples of Christ, even among the sects.

We can believe that also because of the power which God's Word and the Holy Sacraments have. Let him, whoever he may be, preach the Word of God—be he pious or godless, upright or a hypocrite, the former neither increases its power nor does the latter lessen it. The Word of God is active and powerful and sharper than any two-edged sword. It is always Spirit and life, a power of God to save all who believe it.

To it is always bound the Spirit of God. He enters the hearts and consciences of men through the Word. He causes men to know not only their complete unworthiness but also God's boundless grace in Christ. God's Word kindles in them not only sorrow over their sins but also trust in Christ and the hope of eternal life. Yes, God's Word is so powerful that even a fragment of it, its most necessary fundamental doctrines, can work man's salvation. As the seed grows even if mixed with much chaff, so the Word of God grows, even if many human doctrines and errors are disseminated with it. And as each seed contains in itself the whole tree—its roots, trunk, limbs, branches, leaves, and fruit—so each part of biblical truth contains in itself the whole tree of saving knowledge.

Christ says of the Pharisees who nevertheless taught much error along with the Word of God, "The scribes and the Pharisees sit on Moses' seat, so do and observe whatever they tell you" (Matthew 23:2–3). If therefore also much error is taught among the sects, and the Word of God is preached only in part, nevertheless that which is God's Word retains its divine, enlightening, awakening, converting, comforting power. If only the principal part of the Law is preached along with many errors concerning the Law, it nevertheless remains a thunder that awakens sleeping souls, a hammer that smashes stony hearts. If only the most important part of the sweet Gospel is preached with much false doctrine, it nevertheless remains the heavenly dew that refreshes frightened sinners and instills in them confidence in God's mercy.

And so it also is with the Sacraments. If Holy Baptism is administered according to Christ's institution among those who deem it a powerless ceremony, it remains a Baptism, a washing of regeneration and renewing of the Holy Ghost. If he is baptized, he will be taken up into God's covenant of grace and be reborn a child of God and become an heir of eternal life as long as *he* believes it. And if they administer the Last Supper according to Christ's institution, the guests eat of His body and drink of His blood. He strengthens all believers in their faith, grace, forgiveness of sins, and all the fruits of His suffering and death.

As certainly as among the sects the Word of God, insofar as it is still preached among them, and the Sacraments, insofar as they are administered according to Christ's ordinance, retain their power, so certainly are there also upright disciples of Christ among them. Yes, the greater the temptation of being destroyed by the poison of false doctrine and letting oneself be torn from the rock of salvation, so much the more noble must those souls be who do not surrender the foundation of salvation. For that reason Luther calls those believers languishing under the tyranny of the Roman antichrist "the true patterns of the Christian Church and much more pious than great saints."

Finally, we dare not doubt that Christ has His upright disciples among the sects, because God's Word promises that Christ's kingdom will extend over the whole world. Christ says in our Gospel reading today, "I tell you, many will come from east and west and recline at table with Abraham, Isaac, and Jacob in the kingdom of heaven" (Matthew 8:11). According to this, the saved from all parts of the earth will enter into heaven. Hence Christians must live in all parts of the world. Yes, in the oldest of all prophecies of Abraham and Jacob we read concerning Christ, "[In Him] shall all the nations of the earth be blessed" (Genesis 22:18); and, "To Him shall be the obedience of the peoples" (Genesis 49:10). Moreover, God the Father says to Christ in Psalm 2:8, "Ask of Me, and I will make the nations your heritage, and the ends of the earth your possession." In Zechariah, we read, "Rejoice greatly, O daughter of Zion! Shout aloud, O daughter of Jerusalem! Behold, your king is coming to you; righteous and having salvation is He . . . and He shall speak peace to the nations; His rule shall be from sea to sea, and from the River to the ends of the earth" (9:9–10). Yes, in Psalm 110:2, God the Father says to the exalted Son of man, "Rule in the midst of Your enemies."

How would all these and similar glorious prophecies be fulfilled if Christ did not have His true disciples also among the sects? Has not the true Church always been very small? Have not always great numbers of Christians been enticed to follow false prophets? How small would Christ's kingdom be if He had His true disciples only in the Church of the true believers! Such sectarian thoughts be far from us.

No, wherever the voice of the Gospel has reached, there, according to His promise, the heavenly Word has not returned void. It has won souls for Christ. Wherever Holy Baptism is administered according to the Gospel, the doors of the kingdom of grace have opened and thousands and millions have entered in. Not only in one corner of the earth does Christ have His spiritual temple. The field where He sows the seed of His Word is the whole world. Everywhere He has His true believers. Even in the midst of spiritually proud enthusiasts Christ has His humble pupils. Even in the midst of the self-righteous monks Christ has His souls hungry for grace. Even in the midst of a wicked Sodom Christ has His believing, righteous Lot. Even in the midst of His enemies Christ has His friends. In short, I repeat, even in the midst of the sects Christ has His true disciples.

II.

This is now clear to all. Let us therefore secondly ponder how we should use this fact.

Should we use it to consider truth and error equally good? Shall we consider it a matter of complete indifference to which church or confession one belongs? Should one stay in the religion in which he was born and reared, since one can still be saved as long as he is a Christian? Or does perhaps the fact that even among the sects God has His children mean that one does not have to be zealous for purity of doctrine, that all Christians should call themselves brothers, and that all without further ado unite to form a super-church? Far be it!

Although Christ often extolled the Samaritans, he nevertheless says to them, "You worship what you do not know; . . . salvation is from the Jews" (John 4:22). That many in the midst of the sects come to true faith in Christ and are saved does not happen because they could come to true faith through error but because many err out of simplicity and ignorance. But when they faithfully accept the truth in as far as they know it, their errors will not act to their ruin. They are like those 200 men who joined Absalom and his rebels and yet remained faithful in their hearts to David, their rightful king. God's Word says that "they went in their innocence and knew nothing" (2 Samuel 15:11). Thus they often follow false teachers and their sects and still remain true in firm faith to Christ, their rightful king.

Now whoever for the reason that the simple are saved in the sects, whoever does not seek the truth, yes, wantonly remains in error, yes even leaves the true religion to join the sects, would wantonly abuse God's grace. He would not be guarded by God but be rejected as an unfaithful servant. Error is like sin. One can remain in grace in *sins* of weakness, but grace is taken away in the case of willful and wanton sins. One can also remain in grace despite *errors* of weakness, but deliberate, wanton deviation from God's Word deprives one of God's grace. If we have heard that God has His holy children in all sects, let us praise God's mercy, who sustains so many souls among the sects as He once sustained Daniel in the lions' den; He can render even the poison of false doctrine harmless. But let us not ourselves spring into the lions' den and blasphemously drink the poison of false doctrine; no, let us pray that God may let the pure spring of truth continually flow, sustaining us in the truth until our end.

Christ shows us the *proper* application with the words, "Many will come from east and west and recline at table with Abraham, Isaac, and Jacob in the kingdom of heaven, while the sons of the kingdom will be thrown into the outer darkness. In that place there will be weeping and gnashing of teeth" (Matthew 8:11–12). Why does Christ add this? Beyond a doubt He wishes to warn all who belong to the congregation of the orthodox against the feeling of security.

In carnal security the Jews relied on the fact that they were Abraham's children. They relied on the fact that they were God's chosen people, had the revealed Word of God in its purity, and the temple with the true worship. So when the prophets threatened them with punishment, they cried, "This is the temple of the LORD, the temple of the LORD, the temple of the LORD" (Jeremiah 7:4). And when Christ rebuked the Jews and especially the high priests, scribes, and Pharisees and announced their eternal ruin, their comfort was that they were the true Church; they were in no danger. In our text Christ calls to them, "Many will come from the east and west and recline at table with Abraham, Isaac, and Jacob in the kingdom of heaven, while the sons of the kingdom will be thrown into the outer darkness" (Matthew 8:11–12).

Let that be said also to us, my friends! Let us bear in mind that we who possess the pure evangelical teaching and the unadulterated Sacraments have a great advantage over those who had error preached to and impressed upon them from their youth. Let us not think that it is enough to remain in the true Church only in name and only have the pure doctrine, diligently hear it, approve of it, and praise it. Ah no; let us bear in mind that to whom much is given, much shall be required. The purer our doctrine is, the more highly let us esteem it, the more zealously let us hold fast to it, the more carefully let us guard ourselves against false doctrine. The richer our comfort, which is explained to us from the Gospel, the more faithful let us be in the faith. The greater the spiritual benefits that God gives us, the more ardent let us be in our love, and so much the more let us do good works through which we show God our thankfulness. Yes, if we are children of the kingdom here, happy will we be when we do not walk as children of this world but as children of the kingdom. Someday we will not be cast out but will be received into the kingdom of eternal glory.

That grant us, Jesus Christ, praised to eternity. Amen.

FOURTH SUNDAY AFTER THE EPIPHANY

MATTHEW 8:23–27

Grace be with you, mercy and peace, from God the Father, and from the Lord Jesus Christ, the Son of the Father, in truth and love. Amen.

Dear friends in Christ Jesus!

Reading the history of the Christian Church, we find that men think the Church is always in great danger of being annihilated; yet it has always regained its strength.

How small Christ's Church was when He left the world after His work of redemption! It consisted of no more than a few hundred souls, and most were poor, simple folk. Even the twelve apostles were uneducated, timid men; through the preaching of the Gospel they of all people were to spread the Christian Church throughout the whole world. This appeared to be wholly impossible.

But what happened? Miraculously equipped on the first Pentecost with the gifts of the Holy Spirit, they went out into the world to preach the Gospel to every creature. After no more than about thirty years Paul, who himself became a Christian after being a persecutor, could report to the Colossians that the Gospel was "proclaimed in all creation under heaven" (1:23). A few years later he could write to Timothy, "[God] was manifested in the flesh, . . . proclaimed among the nations, believed on in the world" (1 Timothy 3:16). When all the apostles had died, the Christian Church had already spread over the whole world. There were Christian congregations in all the lands of the world.

If the Christian Church had already been *founded* during the bloody persecutions by the Jews and heathen, then these persecutions really first began after it *had* been founded; the more numerous Christians became, the more the worldly rulers feared that the Christians could become dangerous. Hence, they, and particularly the Roman emperors, decided to wipe out the Christian Church. The Roman emperors and their officials used every imaginable device to torture the Christians in order to cause them to deny Christ and thus exterminate the Christian Church.

They not only beheaded, drowned, strangled, and burned Christians but also dreamed up every possible way to make their death especially frightful and painful. Christians became food for wild animals; they were roasted slowly over a fire, smothered in sewers, crucified head down, and ravening animals were allowed to gnaw at them, killed by thirst. The heathen tore off little by little every piece of flesh from their bones with shells or white-hot tongs. They poured boiling oil and pitch into their mouths. They tied their naked bodies to corpses, threw both into dark and stinking pits, and let them die of hunger and rot with the corpses. In the first three centuries many hundreds of thousands of Christians were killed. When the persecution of Emperor Diocletian and his co-regents ended in the year 310, they issued as a remembrance of their victory over the Christians edicts with the superscription: "After wiping out the name of Christians who wanted to overthrow the kingdom," or, "After the complete extermination of the Christian heresy everywhere."

But was this proud superscription really true? No! Just before a Church Father had written, "The more you cut us down the more we increase. The blood of the Christian is a seed." Yes, the church historian Eusebius wrote, "The very swords at last became dull and broke in pieces as though worn out; the hangmen became tired and had to relieve one another; but the Christians began to sing songs of praise and thanks until their last breath to the honor of almighty God."

All the persecutors died a frightful death. The last such, Emperor Galerius, his body rotting with inexpressible pains, feeling God's wrath, published in the year 311 another edict. He declared that his intention of bringing the Christians back to the religion of their fathers was not attained, and they themselves were only hindered in the worship of their own gods. They should therefore be tolerated and now pray to their God for the welfare of the kingdom and their emperor.

When this fanatic had died and Emperor Constantine became a Christian himself in the year 323, the Christians with but brief interruptions enjoyed complete rest from persecution. But now even more dangerous enemies— false teachers—arose in their own midst. They did not seek the temporal life of the Church but the truth on which it was founded and thus slay it spiritually. But see! no matter how many heretics arose, God always awakened men who exposed the heresy and defended the truth. The Church faced even greater danger through the rise of the papacy. It seemed to have become a worldly kingdom of priests, Christ pushed from His throne, the saving Gospel done away with, and thus the Church surely wrecked. Even the earlier bloody persecutions arose again, and now *in the midst of the Church herself.* But lo! just when all help seemed to be gone, it was at the door. God awakened Dr. Martin Luther, who carried out the work of a complete reformation of the Church.

Alas, today the Christian Church again lies in the dust. It is true that hundreds of millions of men still are Christian in name, but they are either unbelievers who laugh at the mysteries of the Christian religion, or they are the sects who cling to comfortless human doctrines. The true Christians who stand in the true faith are only a very small flock. The enemy of the Church again triumphs and predicts in a thousand writings that the Christian Church will soon be completely wiped out.

What now? Do we have reason to fear that the Church will at last perish? No, no! my friends! According to God's Word, this is absolutely impossible. Our Gospel reading today guarantees that no matter how severely the storms may rage now, Christ's little ship will not be wrecked. Let us now hear and consider this Gospel for the purpose of strengthening us in this belief.

The text: *Matthew 8:23–27*

On the basis of this text, let the subject of today's consideration be

Christ's ship on the Sea of Galilee, a picture of the Church of our times

1. A picture of the dangers in which it hovers,
2. A picture of the members it has,
3. A picture of the protection under which it stands.

I.

The day on which the event related in our text took place was the same day in which Christ had miraculously healed the leper and the servant of the centurion at Capernaum. That we heard in the Gospel reading last Sunday. This had been a day of especially hard work. Matthew tells us Christ that same day healed not only Peter's mother-in-law, but in addition whole crowds of possessed and sick. Evening finally came, and many people still crowded around Him; perhaps they merely wished to see still more miracles. He therefore commanded His disciples to prepare a ship for a trip to the eastern shore of the Sea of Galilee. Whereupon we read in our text: "And when He got into the boat, His disciples followed Him" (v. 23).

In any case the ship was no palatial merchantman, but one of Peter's small simple fishing boats. No vessel had ever carried a more precious cargo than this little boat. It carried something more precious than all the gold, pearls, and precious stones in the world. It bore the Savior of the world and the twelve apostles who were to carry the message of salvation into all the world. It carried the Lord of the Church Himself and its twelve pillars. One can indeed say that had this ship sunk, the Church would have gone down and the whole world would have been lost.

Now one would have supposed that if any ship would have had smooth sailing, then this would have been the one. But what do we hear? We read in our text, "And behold, there arose a great storm on the sea, so that the boat was being swamped by the waves" (v. 24).

"And behold," the evangelist writes. With this little word he shows that something that no one expected suddenly arose. When the ship had thrust from land, the evening sky was clear and bright. Wind and sea were calm, but behold, scarcely had they reached the high seas then suddenly, as we read in our text, "a great storm" arose "on the sea." As we see from the original text, this "storm" was a swell that came from the lake bottom as would arise from an earthquake. The sea suddenly swelled and created waves that, rising and falling rapidly, lifted the ship like a ball, now to giddy heights, now hurling it down into the trough. Mark adds that also a "great windstorm" or a hurricane was added to the storm from the depths of the sea. It seized the little ship and spun it like a top. Sky, wind, and sea seemed to have rebelled.

The result was that the waves not only smote the ship but, as our text says, "the boat was being swamped by the waves." Covered by the sea, it appeared to be destined to sink. All human help, strength, and wisdom were helpless. Even those in the ship, fishermen familiar with the sea, who certainly had passed through many a dangerous storm, feared for their lives.

And what was the most frightening, we read that Christ the Lord, in whose presence the disciples otherwise feared nothing, "was asleep." He seemed neither to know of nor care about the danger in which His disciples were. Yes, Mark informs us that He lay on a pillow near the helmsman. Christ seemed to be the reason why the ship was in this danger. Only one push, and ship and crew would sink into the depths of the sea.

What does our text vividly picture to us? Nothing else than the great danger in which the ship of the Christian Church is at all times, especially in our day. Like a ship, the Church sails from country to country on the sea of time. Christ is the captain. The preachers of the Gospel are the helmsmen. Faith with Baptism is the ship's gangplank, hope its anchor, the cross its mast, and its flag the creed. The Word is the sails. The wind that swells these sails is the Holy Ghost. The Christians compose the crew, and the harbor toward which the ship sails is heaven.

What happened to this ship of the Church? It had no sooner quietly weighed anchor at the time of the apostles and sailed upon the world when, behold, there arose a swell from beneath and a hurricane from above. Hell, world, and heaven itself seemed to have conspired against the ship of the Church and resolved to destroy it. Now the swell of bloody persecution raged; now the hurricane of false doctrine.

If the ship of the Church *always* was in danger of running aground, shattering, and sinking, it is really the case *today*. It is true we today do not groan under the cruel rod of persecution. Yes—God be eternally praised—we here in America enjoy a degree of religious freedom that God has scarcely granted any other land. Nevertheless, here the ship of the Church hovers in greater danger. Our America is not only the land of the sects who preach their false faith everywhere with great show of being the only true saving faith, but also the very enemies of Christ and His Church are here in great power. Unless God prevents it they can, after they are in power, take our freedom from us. In many newspapers and other periodicals they rail at everything holy. They organize secret societies into which they draw the unsuspecting, but from whom they hide their plans. They beguile more and more with their sweet talk of light, enlightenment, progress, and freedom.

Truly, the ship of the Church is again in great trouble. The spirit of the times like a hurricane sometimes lifts it up to giddy heights and sometimes pulls it down into frightful depths. Countless baptized Christians have already fallen away and daily more follow. And what is most frightening, Christ seems again to sleep and watch peacefully how the storm tears the sail of the Word and the flag of the creed into tatters, snaps the mast of the cross, and covers the ship of the Church with the waves of sin and unbelief.

II.

Christ's ship in the storm on the Sea of Galilee pictures not only the dangers in which the Church now hovers but secondly the members it has.

We read in our text, "And they went and woke Him, saying, 'Save us, Lord; we are perishing' " (Matthew 8:25). This tells us two facts about the disciples: first, that they truly believed, but second, that their faith was extremely weak. They had forsaken the whole world and its enticing splendor to follow Christ even into the ship on the sea. And when great trouble and danger befell them and human aid was of no avail, they did not doubt but turned to Christ, awakened Him, and offered this ardent prayer to Him, "Save us, Lord!" Had they not believed that Christ was the almighty Son of God, they would not have turned to Him when only an experienced seaman would know what to do.

Nevertheless, their faith was weak. Had it been a strong faith, they would have thought of Christ's many miracles that they had witnessed. In the middle of the storm they would have, after their prayer for help, certain of an answer, joined in a song of praise and thanksgiving. There would be no room in their hearts for the faintest suggestion of the thought that their ship would sink. With David they would have thought, "Even though I walk through the dark valley of mountain high waves, I will fear no evil, for the Lord is with me."

But what did they do? It is true they pray in faith, "Save us, Lord!" But full of anxiety and fear they immediately add, "We are perishing!" Yes, Mark tells us that several even cried out, "Teacher, do You not care that we are perishing?" (4:38). We see from this that their faith was very weak and no doubt bordered on unbelief. It was no more than a smoking flax and a bruised reed. Hence, Christ did not reject them but rebuked them saying, "Why are you afraid, O you of little faith?" (Matthew 8:26a).

This is the picture of the membership of the Church. There still are (praise God!) people who have left the enticing world, cling to Christ, confess that He is God's Son, and in their troubles in true faith call on Him, "Save us, Lord!" even when man is helpless. Alas, the age of the strong in faith, the heroes of faith, as we repeatedly meet them by name in the first 300 years and in the time of the Reformation, is past. The believers of our times are almost without exception weak and small of faith. Much smaller storms than the storm on the Sea of Galilee, and much weaker attacks and temptations now cause Christians to waver and totter. If a bloody persecution would break out today and Christians were no firmer in their faith than they are now, most would deny the faith and fall away.

Now, my very dear friends, does not this present a sad, hopeless prospect? Must we not fear that the Church will go under after all? Must we not expect that in the last times of the Church increasingly greater troubles, attacks, and temptations are near? Yes, we must expect the latter; but we do not have to fear that for this reason the Church will perish. Christ does not reject even the weak in faith, put out the smoking flax, nor break the bruised reed. For the ship of Christ upon the Sea of Galilee is not only a picture of the dangers in which it hovers and the weakness of its members but also the protection under which it stands. And it is of this that I speak to you now.

III.

It is true that Christ slept while the disciples were in the greatest danger. It seemed as if Christ neither knew of the danger to His disciples nor cared. Yet it only seemed so. Christ did actually sleep but only as a true man. Even then He was and remained the Keeper of Israel who does not slumber and sleep, for according to His divinity He watched; He saw everything that took place, and took care that despite the storm and waves the ship did not become wrecked while He slept. To the disciples He seemed to sleep, only to tempt and test them, to strengthen their faith through temptation, and to make them pray. When Christ was therefore awakened by the disciples' cry for help, He fearlessly let the storm rage on for a while and first stilled the storm in the hearts of the disciples. "Then," we read, "He rose and rebuked the winds and the sea, and there was a great calm" (Matthew 8:26b). This was an incomprehensible miracle. At times it happened in also a natural manner that a hurricane on the sea suddenly stilled. But then the waves would rise for a longer time and only gradually diminish after the wind had been calm for a long time. But Mark tells us, as soon as Christ had said to the wind and sea, "Peace! Be still!" both were immediately and absolutely quiet. The howling winds and the raging sea quieted. It became a glassy surface in which the evening sky quietly reflected the glittering stars; the little ship again sailed peacefully on. All who were in the ship cried out in amazement, "What sort of man is this, that even winds and sea obey Him?" (Matthew 8:27).

Here we have the last picture of the Church of our times. It is an inexpressibly comforting one. We see that though the Church may be like Christ's ship on the Sea of Galilee, though the whole world with all its might may surprise the Church like a sea whipped by the wind, though its sinking may seem to be inevitable, though it may seem as if Christ is asleep again at the helm and His Word the hindrance to the only possible deliverance of the Church, though the very members of the Church seem to be ever so faint-hearted today and in despair cry out, "Save us, Lord; we are perishing!" yes, though many today desperately jump out of the ship into the sea of the world, we nevertheless have no reason to fear and despair. Christ is in our ship, and He does not sleep according to His divine omniscience, omnipotence, and care. When His hour is come, He will arise, chide our faint-heartedness, and say to the world, "Peace! Be still." It will then become absolutely quiet and in triumph the ship of the Church will sail into the harbor of heaven. Christ has promised: "On this rock" (He means Himself) "I will build My church, and the gates of hell shall not prevail against it" (Matthew 16:18). "I am with you always, to the end of the age" (28:20).

Oh, therefore, do not despair, even in these last troublesome times. Do not leave the ship of the Church because you think it will soon go down. Otherwise you will regret it eternally, because outside this ship is no salvation, as once outside Noah's ark there was no deliverance. And as Noah's ark sailed successfully over the waves of the flood and finally, safe and sound landed on the mountains of Ararat, so will also the ship of the Church sail safely over the stormy sea of the world and land on the eternal mountains of divine grace. There, if you have remained in the faith, you will also in amazement cry out, "What sort of man is this, that even winds and sea obey Him?" and will eternally rejoice. For

> *The Word they still shall let remain*
> *Nor any thanks have for it;*
> *He's by our side upon the plain*
> *With His good gifts and Spirit.*
> *And take they our life,*
> *Goods, fame, child, and wife,*
> *Though these all be gone,*
> *Our vict'ry has been won;*
> *The Kingdom ours remaineth. (LSB 656:4) Amen.*

FIFTH SUNDAY AFTER THE EPIPHANY

MATTHEW 13:24–30

Grace be with you, mercy and peace, from God the Father, and from the Lord Jesus Christ, the Son of the Father, in truth and love. Amen.

Dear friends in Christ Jesus!

Here in America everyone has freedom of conscience, religion, and worship. The government never imposes an unwanted preacher upon a congregation. The state favors no denomination; nothing hinders the Church's existence and expansion. Every citizen can live his conviction in complete peace.

Instead of using this freedom to remain with the Holy Scriptures alone, to believe it alone, to teach it and organize divine worship, the wonderful freedom of this country is used mostly to depart boldly from God's Word, to found new sects, thus splitting the Church of Christ more and more. No one wishes to bow humbly to God's Word. Each follows his own idea and seeks a following for his brand of doctrine. Nowadays almost countless factions are fighting one another. When a person immigrates here, he is besieged on all sides with the invitation: Come to us! Here is Christ! Here you find the true way to heaven! Here is the true Church!

If ever there is a country where a Christian must be able to recognize the true Church of Christ, it certainly is our new homeland.

Moreover, it is not enough that here are so many sects—all of whom wish to be the true or the best church. Because there are so many they also try to outdo one another; one through splendor, another through useful institutions as temperance societies and Sunday schools; a third through great and many works for the spreading of God's kingdom, e.g., mission, Bible, and tract societies; a fourth through daily prayer meetings, revivals, and the like.

Woe to him who does not have the true touchstone in this country! Blinded by the glittering pretense of the sects, he will soon become their prey. If he had the true faith before, he will lose his simplicity in Christ and be talked into a false way, into an impure zeal, into enthusiasm and spiritual pride.

Only one thing can keep a Christian from not being drawn into the swift current of sectarianism and be irresistibly swept away. He must find out where God's Word is preached in its purity and the Sacraments administered according to Christ's institution. Whoever does not consider *that* and that alone is lost; he *must* be misled. The Holy Writings themselves tell us that false churches often have a greater air of pious zeal than the true Church. We read that the Israelites were more zealous for the worship of idols than for the true worship. When Aaron made the golden calf, everyone was ready to sacrifice his gold. Afterward they joyfully adored this image. But when Moses urged the worship of the only true God, all were sluggish and listless. And thus it has happened at all times. By nature every person prefers a false devotion. But he is incapable of true worship. Yes, he is so opposed to and loathes it so much that grace alone can take it away and turn it into joy and love.

If a person therefore is seeking the true Church, the only thing he must take into consideration is whether they use only Christ's words. Are they built on the foundation of the apostles and prophets? Is Jesus Christ the Cornerstone? And do they add nothing to and subtract nothing from God's Word? He dare not let himself be blinded by the piety of the sects nor be offended by the failings of the true Church. Our Gospel reading today warns us especially against this last point. Let us therefore apply this warning to ourselves.

The text: *Matthew 13:24–30*

In this important parable Christ presents the kingdom of heaven on earth, His Church. Let us therefore consider today:

How to use the parable of the weeds.

It should serve to

1. Shame those who are offended at the wicked in the Church;
2. Comfort those who are concerned because of the wicked in the Church;
3. Earnestly warn the wicked in the Church.

Lord Jesus Christ, once in gracious humility You taught the people by means of parables; today You still wish to teach us through them. Open the ears of our hearts for Your instruction, that those of us who are dead in sins may be awakened, those awakened be established, and those walking in Your grace be strengthened and comforted. Hear and bless us. Amen.

I.

As long as the Church will exist there will be people who look more to its life than its doctrine. They maintain that if a church wants to be God's Church it must be absolutely pure. There must be no sin, no godlessness, no offense. Every member must be truly devout, born again, pious, and holy. Perfect harmony and peace must rule among them.

In the fourth century a whole sect by the name of Donatists arose in Africa. They left the Church because they believed that the Church must be holy and pure; that the Word and Sacraments have no power if they are administered by an unholy person. A similar group appeared also in Luther's time. They were the Zwickau prophets and Anabaptists. They declared that Luther's reformation was worthless; the matter must be tackled in an entirely different manner—the Church must be thoroughly purged from all sins.

The Donatists came to a sad end. In their false zeal for perfect purity in the Church they committed the greatest sins. Three hundred years ago the Zwickau prophets and Anabaptists came to a terrible end. At first they began their work on a high spiritual plane; many were deceived. In the end they fell into sin, shame, and misfortune.

Even with such warning examples, there are always enough who call that Church the true Church which leads an unspotted life. Not only do many remain in sectarian churches because they see that many sins and offenses appear even in the true Church, but even the *members* of the true Church are often so greatly offended that they reject it, leave it, and would rather stay with the sects who appear to be pious.

Christ told the parable of the weeds among the wheat above all for them. It should shame all those who are offended at the wicked in the Church.

The Church will never be cleansed of all the wicked; Christ compares it with "a man who sowed good seed in his field, but while his men were sleeping, his enemy came and sowed weeds among the wheat and went away. So when the plants came up and bore grain, then the weeds appeared also" (Matthew 13:24–26). Christ Himself has explained what He meant to say. Matthew tells us that when the disciples asked Jesus for the meaning of the parable, He answered, "The one who sows the good seed is the Son of Man. The field is the world, and the good seed is the sons of the kingdom. The weeds are the sons of the evil one, and the enemy who sowed them is the devil" (13:37–39a).

There we hear it from Christ Himself. Yes, He sows only good seed in His true Church. By the doctrine that is preached no one is misled into sin or error, but people come to be true, devout, pious Christians. But what happens? Satan is not idle. He sows tares among the wheat; he does everything possible to bring wicked children into Christ's Church. Some he blinds and hardens that despite the pure doctrine they are not converted. He causes some who were converted to fall away again. He tempts, allures, and entices them not to pay attention to the admonition they receive, to serve the world and sin while members of the true Church, and thus by their unchristian life, bring disgrace on the true Church and her doctrine.

The history of the Church confirms this. Was not the Old Testament Church the true Church of God? But what frightful offenses were common in it. In Adam's Church was there not Cain, the fratricide; in Noah's Ham, the mocker of his father; in Abraham's Ishmael, the scoffer of religion; in Isaac's Esau, the scorner of grace; in Jacob's ten godless sons, who sold their own brother; in Moses' and Aaron's, many thousands who fell into idolatry? Who may enumerate all the offenses by which the Lord's name was slandered by the heathen in the time of the judges, the kings, and the prophets until the coming of Christ? And is it not God's very own people who crucified God's Son? Was not the traitor Judas found among the twelve apostles?

And were there not in the congregations founded even by the apostles people of the same stripe? Were there not among the Corinthians quarrels, an incestuous person, schisms, and factions? Were there not among them as Paul writes, such "who sinned earlier and have not repented of the impurity, sexual immorality, and sensuality that they have practiced" (2 Corinthians 12:21)? Were there not among the Thessalonians those who walked disorderly, did not work but gossiped? Did not the whole congregation at Galatia let herself be led into error? Were not the Laodiceans neither cold nor hot? But did the apostles demand that the pious leave these churches because of the corruption that was found in them? Did they say that the Church was in error, her doctrines false, and the Sacraments weak or worthless? No! After admonishing them to repent they urged them to remain with the Church.

Consequently, if the Church has the pure doctrine, it does not become a false church when sins and offenses are committed. If a church is really Christ's Church, nothing else is possible but that many sins and offenses appear. The purer the teaching is, the more hostile Satan is, and the more effort he puts forth to cover her with shame. Whenever souls are rescued from sin and brought to peace with God through the preaching of Christ, Satan angrily rushes in and tries to makes it appear that sin and misery rule in the Church. Wherever true unity of faith is, there Satan causes such a commotion that it seems as if there were nothing but discord, quarrels, and strife. Wherever the devil is in control, he is quiet; but wherever his authority is taken away by the Word and Sacrament he storms and rages with all the might of a prince of darkness. In short, wherever Christ sows His good seed, Satan will also sow his weeds. Of that we can be certain.

Those who are offended at the Church on account of the wicked, who despise, reject, and leave her, should therefore be ashamed. They are offended at God Himself; they despise and reject Him. He is not ashamed of His spotted Church. He still acknowledges her, if His pure Word and unadulterated Sacraments are found there.

II.

The second question now arises: how should Christ's parable of the weeds among the wheat be used by those who are not offended at the wicked in the Church but are grieved and concerned about them? The parable should comfort them.

The more sincere a Christian is about the salvation of his brother, the more greatly it will depress, grieve, and concern him when he sees that so many offences show up in God's true Church. He will ask: "What is to be done to check these offenses, keep sin down, and adorn the Church with exemplary Christians?"

What instruction does Christ give? He continues in our parable, "And the servants of the master of the house came and said to him, 'Master, did you not sow good seed in your field? How then does it have weeds?' He said to them, 'An enemy has done this.' So the servants said to him, 'Then do you want us to go and gather them?' But he said, 'No, lest in gathering the weeds you root up the wheat along with them. Let both grow together until the harvest' " (Matthew 13:27–30a). What is the lesson that Christ teaches with these words?

Does He mean to say that those to whom the rule of the Church is entrusted should be at ease and do nothing to keep the weeds down? Far be it! For Christ had said, "While his men were sleeping, his enemy came and sowed weeds among the wheat." The upright members of the Church and especially her called and ordained watchmen should not sleep but watch and be concerned that Satan does not sow his weeds of wicked Christians, hypocrites, and false brethren in the Church.

Hence, a congregation should neither receive nor put up with people who want to cling to error or live in sin, people who do not wish to walk as true Christians, submit to God's Word, take leave of sin and the world, and live piously. If a member gives offense by sin, he should be reprimanded. If the offense was secret, the reprimand should be secret. If it was public, the reprimand should be public. If a congregation does not do this, it shares in the sin of its member and cultivates the weeds. Yes, should there be members of a Christian congregation who not only sin publicly but also don't confess their sins and stubbornly persist in them, the congregation must exclude them, cut off these rotten dead members, retain their sins, announce God's wrath and eternal damnation, consider and declare them as heathen and publicans, and avoid their company—in short, excommunicate them.

For it is written in Matthew 18, whoever does not hear the admonition of the congregation, "let him be to you as a Gentile and a tax collector" (v. 17). And it is written in another passage, 1 Corinthians 5:11, "But now I am writing to you not to associate with anyone who bears the name of brother if he is guilty of sexual immorality or greed, or is an idolater, reviler, drunkard, or swindler—not even to eat with such a one." And woe to him, my friends, who lets it go so far that a Christian congregation must retain his sins and excommunicate him. His sins are also retained before God in heaven. He is shut out from the congregation of saints until he repents and is again reconciled with the congregation. We read of every Christian congregation: "If you forgive the sins of any, they are forgiven them; if you withhold forgiveness from any, it is withheld" (John 20:23); and, "Whatever you bind on earth shall be bound in heaven, and whatever you loose on earth shall be loosed in heaven" (Matthew 18:18).

What does Christ mean to say when He said, "Let both grow together until the harvest" (Matthew 13:30)? Christ not only says that until the end of time His Church will never be a glorious kingdom, completely free from sin, defects, and offenses, that Christ will nevertheless sustain His Church until Judgment Day; He also says, first of all, that the Church should not exercise capital punishment on even the most manifest sinner; second, that the Church should not forever deny the sinner her friendship, but if he repents should comfort him with the forgiveness of sins and receive him as a lost child who has been found again. Certainly an excellent direction! Would it not have been frightful if the Church had killed Paul or Augustine while they were still heretics? Both could not have been converted and would not have become such great, wonderful tools, instrumental in delivering so many thousands of souls.

For this reason the true Church has never used the sword against the weeds. Only the anti-Christian, make-believe church of the pope tries that, but under the pretense of rooting out the weeds has rooted out the wheat, and claiming to fight against heretics has fought against the confessors of the truth. Yes, usurping the temporal sword, fulfilling that prophecy of St. John's Revelation, it has finally become "drunk with the blood of the saints, the blood of the martyrs of Jesus" (Revelation 17:6). Its alleged concern for the purity of the Church was nothing else than a zeal to destroy it.

The true Church of Christ acts far differently. By teaching and education she sees to it that the weeds do not take control and choke the wheat. She does not hoe them out with temporal power or premature judgment but lets them grow until the harvest in the certainty that Christ will sustain His Church. In eternity He will present it as the Holy Church, though now it is disfigured and dishonored by sinners.

III.

We hasten to the conclusion and now ask: how shall the parable be used by the wicked in the Church? I answer, as an earnest warning.

How does Christ close His parable? He says, "At harvest time I will tell the reapers, Gather the weeds first and bind them in bundles to be burned, but gather the wheat into my barn" (Matthew 13:30b). According to Matthew's report, Christ has explained it this way: "The Son of Man will send His angels, and they will gather out of His kingdom all causes of sin and all law-breakers, and throw them into the fiery furnace. In that place there will be weeping and gnashing of teeth. Then the righteous will shine like the sun in the kingdom of their Father" (vv. 41–43).

We see that Christ did not give His parable to console those who are the weeds or the wicked. No, Christ consoles only those who mourn over the sins and offenses in the congregation, pray to God because of them, and on their part do what they can that all sins be reprimanded and checked. This parable serves to comfort only pious Christians, for the sins of their false brethren shall not be imputed to them, even if they like Lot lived in Sodom, and like Simeon in Jerusalem. *Here* they have to endure much disgrace because of hypocrites. Even if a false Christian should fall into sin and vice, and he would have to hear from the world, "You, too, are one of them!" they shall someday "shine like the sun in the kingdom of their Father."

But those who by their unchristian life bring disgrace upon Christ and His Word that they confess and upon the Church to which they belong; yes, all who belong to the true Church and act like Christians yet have never turned to God are tolerated by Christians. But on the day of the great harvest they will be separated by the holy angels as weeds from the wheat and thrown into the fires of hell. Then it will be more tolerable for the heathen than for them; they will wish that they had never heard a sermon of repentance and faith; their banishment from God and His triumphant Church, their torment and pain, will be eternal. Christ therefore closes the exposition of His parable with the words, "He who has ears, let him hear" (v. 43b). Christ grant that to us all by His grace. Amen.

THE TIME OF EASTER

Pre-Lent Season

Septuagesima (1852)

Matthew 20:1–16

Grace and peace be multiplied unto you through the knowledge of God, and of Jesus our Lord. Amen.

Dear friends in Christ Jesus!

God's Word reveals everything necessary for our salvation. It opens the very secrets of God's heart. It reveals what God thought and decided upon before the foundation of the world and what He wishes to do for us in eternity.

But what do most do? Not only do countless thousands reject the divine revelation as foolishness, but even many of those who know and accept the Word as God's Word are not satisfied with what is revealed in it. Many want to ponder what God in His great wisdom has permitted to remain hidden from human eyes.

So, for example, many have wanted to fathom how it is possible that against God's will sin, death, and misery have entered the world. Others, how it is possible that God knows in advance all thoughts, ways, and works of man and yet man should not be forced to do them. Others, why God gives one person so many opportunities for conversion and another so few; why He pursues one so long with longsuffering and patience and in the end allows him to find grace in his last hour, while He lets another be snatched away quickly in his sins and be lost. Still others, why God has created also those whom He knows will be eternally lost. And still others, why the merciful God, with whom there is no respect of persons, gives His Word to some nations so richly and so long, while He has let others sit for thousands of years at a time in darkness and in the shadow of death.

Oh folly upon folly! Is it such a wonder that for us weak, shortsighted men there are in God's essence works, ways, and judgments, a thousand things that are inexplicable and unfathomable? We would have to be like God in wisdom and knowledge to understand everything! We must say with St. Paul, "Oh, the depth of the riches and wisdom and knowledge of God! How unsearchable are His judgments and how inscrutable His ways! For who has known the mind of the Lord, or who has been His counselor? Or who has given a gift to Him that He might be repaid? For from Him and through Him and to Him are all things. To Him be glory forever" (Romans 11:33–36).

Miserable is he who does not speak thus with St. Paul but wants to fathom God's mysterious counsel. As he who looks constantly into the sun becomes blind, so must the spiritual eyes of him who wants to look into the depths of God's heart become blind. He must either err completely with respect to God and His Word or fall into all kinds of dangerous error.

In today's Gospel we will be introduced to a teaching that contains impenetrable mysteries. Many to their soul's harm have tried to fathom them, but they have only erred. It is the doctrine of the election of grace, or predestination. Permit me to show you today the correct way in which alone we shall be preserved from every error in considering this comforting doctrine. To accomplish this, we beg the assistance of him in whose light alone we shall see light by silently and piously praying the Lord's Prayer.

The text: *Matthew 20:1–16*

"Many are called, but few are chosen" (Matthew 20:16 [KJV]). With these words the Lord Himself gives us a key to the parable in our reading today. We see from these words that the parable contains information as to what election to salvation really is. Permit me to answer the question:

To what must we hold fast if we do not want to deviate
in any way in the doctrine of election?

I answer, we must hold fast to this, that according to Holy Scripture

1. Whoever is lost is not destined to hell by God, but is lost by his own fault; and,
2. Whoever is saved is not saved by some sort of merit on his part but alone out of pure grace.

I.

My friends, everything that God does in time are realizations of decrees that He has made already in eternity. God does nothing in time that He has not decided to do in eternity. The eternal destiny of man is therefore not decided in time but has already been decided upon before the foundation of the world. God, for example, not only *knows* exactly the number of those who will be saved or lost, but He has also from eternity elected a part of mankind to salvation. In comparison with the lost, the elect are only a few. All these are truths that are so clearly taught in Holy Scripture that no one who believes in the Bible can deny them. The Lord says in our text, "Many are called, but few are chosen." Acts 13:48 says expressly, "And when the Gentiles heard this, they began rejoicing and glorifying the word of the Lord, and *as many as were appointed to eternal life believed*."

All who still consider God's Word the truth are agreed that there is an eternal election, moreover that God did not elect all men; yes, in comparison with the damned He from eternity elected only few to salvation. Yet there are many who, misled by the deductions of their reason, have erred in the article of election.

There is a large denomination that makes the following deductions: Since God has not elected all men to salvation, He must necessarily have destined the rest to damnation. God must not even want to save all men; if God would have wanted to, who could have hindered Him? Who can oppose His will?

Furthermore they say: By nature all men are lost, dead in sin, and opposed to God's Holy Spirit; God must therefore work all good, repentance, faith, and sanctification in them—the beginning and the end, the wanting and completion, the conversion and preservation till the end. If a person is not converted, or if he does not remain in the faith, God must not have wanted to take his opposition away and give him faith or keep him in it; hence God must not have wanted to save him but must have destined him even from eternity to eternal damnation.

Finally, they also conclude: In the Holy Scriptures we read that God hardens whom He wants, that He actually *has* hardened Pharaoh; hence, God must not have wanted the conversion and salvation of such men.

Is this the true doctrine of election? Far be it! We see what fearful, comfortless, and blasphemous conclusions even a Christian can draw, if he is not satisfied with what the Scriptures say, if he begins to draw inferences not based on God's Word, if he wants to build bridges of human reasoning over the bottomless abysses of divine decrees. But, God be praised, God's clear Word shows us that all such reasoning is wrong, false, and empty.

Our human reason can conclude nothing else than this: If God really wanted to save all men, they most certainly *would* be saved. However, since this does not take place, this must be the fault of God's will. Human reason can conclude nothing else, but what does God's Word say? It hurls this reasoning down; it is shown on all pages of the Holy Bible that God has destined no man to damnation but loved all from eternity and wanted to save all.

We read for example in 1 Timothy 2:4–6, "[God] desires *all* people to be saved and to come to the knowledge of the truth. For there is one God, and there is one mediator between God and men, the man Christ Jesus, who gave himself as a ransom *for all*." Moreover, Peter writes, "The Lord is not slow to fulfill His promise as some count slowness, but is patient toward you, not wishing that *any* should perish, but that *all* should reach repentance" (2 Peter 3:9). Furthermore, the Lord Jesus Christ Himself says, "For God so loved the *world*, that He gave His only Son, that whoever believes in Him should not perish but have eternal life" (John 3:16).

Yes, in order that we may not have the least doubt, God even in the Old Testament testified before the world with a precious unbreakable oath with Himself that not one person is shut out from His eternal love. For we read, "And you, son of man, say to the house of Israel, Thus have you said: 'Surely our transgressions and our sins are upon us, and we rot away because of them. How then can we live?' Say to them, As I live, declares the Lord GOD, I have no pleasure in the death of the wicked, but that the wicked turn from his way and live; turn back, turn back from your evil ways, for why will you die, O house of Israel?" (Ezekiel 33:10–11). What can be clearer?

Again our reason could make no other deduction: since all men are by nature lost and God must begin, continue, and complete all good in them, the cause must lie in God if a person is not converted or does not persevere unto the end; God must not have wanted it. But what does God's Word say? The Lord Himself says to the inhabitants of Jerusalem, when they were not converted, "O Jerusalem, Jerusalem, the city that kills the prophets and stones those who are sent to it! How often would I have gathered your children together as a hen gathers her brood under her wings, and you were not willing" (Matthew 23:37). You see, Christ wanted to convert the inhabitants of Jerusalem, but they did not want it.

Although by nature all men are equally sinful and God must first take away their opposition, no one is for that reason lost. When God comes with His Word, He also comes with His Holy Spirit, who wants to remove this natural opposition. Some oppose the working of the Holy Ghost with more than natural opposition; they oppose Him stubbornly and obstinately. Such

God Himself cannot help because God will force no one to be converted. A forced conversion is no conversion.

Hence God says as He does in Isaiah, "Why will you still be struck down? Why will you continue to rebel?" (1:5); or as we read in the Proverbs of Solomon:

> Because I have called and you refused to listen, have stretched out my hand and no one has heeded, because you have ignored all my counsel and would have none of my reproof, I also will laugh at your calamity; I will mock when terror strikes you. . . . Then they will call upon me, but I will not answer; they will seek me diligently but will not find me. Because they hated knowledge and did not choose the fear of the Lord, would have none of my counsel and despised all my reproof, therefore they shall eat the fruit of their way, and have their fill of their own devices. (Proverbs 1:24–26, 28–31)

Stephen did not say that the Sanhedrin would be lost because they were dead in sins and by nature could not have wanted the good by their own power, but he says, "You stiff-necked people, uncircumcised in heart and ears, you always resist the Holy Spirit. As your fathers did, so do you" (Acts 7:51). Already in Hosea the Lord says, "He destroys you, O Israel, for you are against Me, against your helper" (13:9). Or, as the original says, "Israel, that you are corrupt, the fault is yours, that you be helped, that is My pure grace." What can be clearer?

And finally, our reason could make no other deduction: since the Scriptures say that God hardens some, God Himself must be the cause that they are not saved. But what does God's Word say? It shows us that God by a righteous judgment punishes certain men with fearful hardening of heart. He does that only to those to whom He had vainly offered grace, who first hardened themselves against His grace, and who therefore are lost past all hope of saving. That is, for example, expressly said of Pharaoh: "Why should you harden your hearts as the Egyptians and Pharaoh hardened their hearts?" (1 Samuel 6:6). Consequently, we are faithfully warned against self-hardening in God's Word: "Today, if you hear His voice, do not harden your hearts" (Hebrews 4:7). I therefore ask you, what can be clearer?

Hence my friends, whenever the doctrine of election is presented as though God did not want to call all men, bring them to faith, and save them, that Christ did not atone for many men; or whenever such thoughts rise in your own hearts, confidently reject them as deceitful, lying, and blasphemous reasoning. Hold fast to the Word of God, which says that He has elected only a few, but at the same time shows most clearly that God does not want that any should be lost. God has destined no one to damnation; God *could* not elect more because He foresaw that many would stubbornly resist His Holy Spirit, throw aside the Means of Grace, and let it bear no fruit in them. They do not want to believe or remain in the faith but want to harden themselves.

It is true that God had in eternity decided not to save certain men, but not because He hated them or because He did not *want* to save them. God rather dealt as a merchant who because of the danger of shipwreck throws his cargo overboard. He does this neither joyfully nor does he consider his costly goods of no value; he does it reluctantly because the storm has forced him to do that. Thus God had to decide to let many men be lost, not with joy in their death but, if I may say so, with pain and sadness because the obstinate impenitence of these men compelled Him to do so.

My dear fellow Christians, do not be so foolish and inquisitive as to try to discover whether according to the secret counsel of God you are elect or not. But ponder this: God has revealed to you in His Word and in His dear Son who died for you whether you are elect. You should see from this that God loves all men, hence God loves also you; God's Son has redeemed all men, hence He has redeemed also you; the Holy Spirit earnestly calls all men through the Gospel into the kingdom of grace, hence He calls also you. In short, the triune God wants to save all men; He wants to save also you.

You should accept God's Word, which tells you of the counsel of God to your salvation. Believe it, do not wantonly resist it, and pray that God preserves you in the faith. If you do that, you are elect. For Christ is the Book of Life. If one does not wantonly tear himself loose from Christ, nothing, nothing can erase his name from the Book of Life. Christ says, "My sheep hear My voice, and I know them, and they follow Me. I give them eternal life, and they will never perish, and no one will snatch them out of My hand" (John 10:27–28). Whoever is lost has therefore not been destined to hell by God but is lost by his own fault.

II.

My friends, if we do not want to err completely in the doctrine of election, we must in the second place believe that according to the Holy Scriptures, whoever is saved is not saved by any merit but purely by grace. As important as it is to believe that *God* does not have a hand in our damnation, so it is just as important to believe that *we* do not contribute a thing to our salvation. As important as it is that we do not blame God for the damnation of many, so it is just as important that we do not rob God of any honor; He saved us purely by grace without any merit or worthiness on our part.

Unfortunately, there are not a few who admit that all who are lost are lost by their own fault. Yet they suppose that God has elected some to salvation because He foresaw how repentant, how believing, how holy and faithful they would be. Whilst others ascribe evil to the holy God, they ascribe good to unholy men; where others blame God, they ascribe merit to man.

To forestall any misconception is the main purpose of the parable in our Gospel reading today. Peter had put the question to Christ, "See, we have left everything and followed you. What then will we have?" (Matthew 19:27). Thereupon Christ not only assured Peter that they would be repaid, but He also told them in our text the parable of the laborers in the vineyard. When Christ says that they who had come to work in the last hour received the same pay as those who had borne the burden and heat of the whole day, yes that these finally through their murmuring forfeited the goodness of the master; and when He adds, "So the last will be first, and the first last . . . for many are called, but few chosen" (20:16 [KJV]), what warning did Christ wish to convey to Peter? Nothing else than this: from being the first, a person can by his own fault become the last and be lost, but that it is God's goodness, grace, and mercy alone if from the last he is made the first, from a sinner a saint, from a called one elect; that a person can forfeit grace, but that he can never earn it or become worthy of it; that also the *pay* for his work in the vineyard of God is not earned but is a *gift* of the free goodness of God.

You see, my friends, that the differences of error in the doctrine of election are very small. If one has avoided the one extreme, the danger is one can fall into the other. If we recognize that God could not elect many to salvation *because* He foresaw that they would not believe, we dare not say that God has elected the others *because* He foresaw that they are better, that they would believe and be converted. It is of course true that God has elected only those of whom He saw this; but that cannot be the cause of their election. Had God not decided to elect them, they never would have come to faith.

Therefore bear in mind: nothing else moved God to decide to let a great number be lost than His foreseeing their stiff-necked opposition. But on the other hand, nothing else than His love in Christ and the misery of the rest of mankind moved God to save them. God did not choose the elect because He knew that they would remain in the faith, but that they are elect is the reason that they firmly believe. God did not elect them because He *knew* that they would be saved, but that they are elect is the reason why they *will* be saved. In eternity God saw in all men only sin, misery, and death; consequently, God did not choose the elect because He foresaw something good in them, but because He elected them is the reason why they become Christians. The free, gracious election of God therefore not only precedes the salvation of the elect but is also the cause of the salvation of the elect—its eternal, immovable foundation.

The Eleventh Article of the Formula of Concord presents this most clearly:

> God's eternal election does not just foresee and foreknow the salvation of the elect. From God's gracious will and pleasure in Christ Jesus, election is a cause that gains, works, helps, and promotes our salvation and what belongs to it. Our salvation is so founded on it that "the gates of hell shall not prevail against it" (Matthew 16:18). . . . Therefore, it is false and wrong when it is taught that not only God's mercy and Christ's most holy merit, but also something in us is a cause of God's election, on account of which God has chosen us to eternal life. (XI 8, 88)

Now you who want to remain in your sins and do not really want to be converted to Christ, you dare not suppose that you can excuse yourselves by claiming that God has begrudged you the grace of conversion and salvation. No, God gladly wants to save you, if only you permit yourselves to be saved. Christ says, "Whoever comes to Me I will never cast out" (John 6:37). This word applies also to you. Only recognize your misery and go to Christ. He will not reject you. Then you can joyfully and triumphantly confess: "God has from eternity elected also me to salvation." If you do not want this, don't accuse God but proclaim your own woe upon yourselves. Then Christ says also to you, "How often would I have gathered your children together as a hen gathers her brood under her wings, and you were not willing" (Matthew 23:37).

God has chosen the elect not only to salvation but also to repentance and sanctification. St. Paul pictures that golden unbreakable chain of salvation by saying, "For those whom He foreknew He also predestined to be conformed to the image of His Son, in order that He might be the firstborn among many brothers. And those whom He predestined He also called, and those whom He called He also justified, and those whom He justified He also glorified" (Romans 8:29–30). Whoever, therefore, does not let himself be conformed to the image of God's Son, let him not be surprised that also the other links in the chain of salvation and election do not concern him.

But rejoice! you who already stand in the faith, who have power to hate sin, who have fled like chicks under the wings of God, who can say from your heart: "Farewell, false world, with your glory. I cling to Jesus, who is my treasure, my wealth, my hope, and my salvation." Even if you have much trouble in connection with your faith, trouble within and without, even if you still feel yourselves very weak and frail, even if you must wrestle much with the sin of your depraved heart, even if you feel nothing but misery in your heart because you cling to Christ, you thereby have a witness that you belong to the elect. What God carries out in you in time is a mirror of the decree that He made in regard to you in eternity. Be happy and comforted and delight yourselves in the crown of righteousness, which is even now reserved for you in heaven.

But first of all, guard yourself against ascribing your salvation to yourself. Do not think that God has elected you because He saw something good in you. No, you did not elect God but He elected you; you did not seek Him but He sought you. He saw nothing in you but sin, misery, and death, but when He saw you lying in death He was moved to compassion over you and said: "You shall live."

You could not help along in the least with your conversion. It was no work of your free will because you had no free will. You were dead in sins. Your conversion was altogether God's work. You could not prepare yourself to receive grace because before His grace came upon you; you could do nothing but sin. You could not take the offered grace yourself. God first had to give you the hand of faith. God had to create the beginning and the perseverance. He alone can also finish this blessed work. So, where is your glory? There isn't any. All glory and honor belong only to Him who out of unfathomable mercy has received you.

It is that mercy never ending,
Which human wisdom far transcends,
Of Him who, loving arms extending,
To wretched sinners condescends;
Whose heart with pity still doth break
Whether we seek him or forsake. (TLH 385:2)

My friends, ponder also the Lord's warning, "So the last will be first, and the first last" (Matthew 20:16). If you remain in the faith, happy are you!

Today you belong to the first. But do not become proud and secure, lest from a first you become a last. If you have not merited salvation by your good works, you can by your evil works forfeit it. Look into the Gospel. You will find that we are all called into the vineyard to work. If you do not want to lose what is given you as a gift and what you have earned, work most diligently—be diligent in the use of the Means of Grace, diligent in prayer, diligent in the battle against sin and the world, diligent in all good works, diligent in the exercise of faith, diligent in the exercise of love, diligent in the use of hope, diligent in patience under the cross.

If you often find it difficult to bear the burden and heat of the day while others live according to the lusts of their flesh; if it often hurts you to fight while others rest; to bear the cross while others have good days; to be mocked, despised, and abused while others live in glory and honor, oh, do not murmur as those first who became the last, but think of the blessed honor when the Master of the heavenly vineyard will say to His steward, "Call the laborers and pay them their wages" (Matthew 20:8). How you will rejoice over the wonderful gift of the good Householder! Then for each hour of work you will receive an infinite reward; for each work of love done in faith an incalculably wonderful pay; for every battle, no matter how small, an eternal glorious triumph; for each little cross an unspeakably wonderful crown; for each little heat of temptation an unending blessed refreshing; for every small insult immeasurably great honor and glory.

Hence, let all of us write deeply upon our hearts the admonition of the apostle Peter: "Therefore, brothers, be all the more diligent to confirm your calling and election, for if you practice these qualities you will never fall. For in this way there will be richly provided for you an entrance into the eternal kingdom of our Lord and Savior Jesus Christ" (2 Peter 1:10–11). To Him be glory and honor forever and ever. Amen.

SEXAGESIMA (1853)

LUKE 8:4–15

The grace of our Lord Jesus Christ, and the love of God, and the communion of the Holy Spirit be with you all. Amen.

Dear friends in Christ Jesus!

There were times when Christians did not enjoy the benefits of being able to gather publicly and there undisturbed hear God's Word and praise and call upon Him. In the Holy Scriptures we read that the believers of apostolic times could gather *only in private homes*; but even here Christians dared hold their services only behind locked doors. And church history informs us that in the first three centuries the most unbeaten paths, forests, caves, and desolate tombs had to be sought out by Christians whenever they wanted to gather to hear the Word of Life and in their troubles pour out their hearts to God.

It is true that at times the kinder heathen kings permitted them to build beautiful churches. Often, however, the very same king ordered these churches torn down. Yes, it repeatedly happened that their churches were set on fire while the Christians were assembled in them; all who worshiped Jesus Christ were burned to ashes. Thus at the beginning of the fourth century, according to the church historian Necephorus, the entire congregation of Nikomedia in Asia Minor were celebrating the joyful Christmas festival when, under the threat of death by fire, were commanded to sacrifice to the gods. All of the members, however, refused. The church was then quickly surrounded, set on fire, and so more than a thousand Christians were mercilessly burned.

Those certainly were trying times, yet it is even more trying when Christians possess a beautiful church in which they can assemble peaceably but in which God's Word is either slandered or falsified. A church in which human fancy and cleverness is preached instead of God's Word is nothing else than an open door to hell, a shambles of Satan. It would be better for one to go into a den of robbers and murderers than into such a church of unbelievers. Thieves would kill only his body, but in a church of unbelievers his immortal soul would be killed.

However, a church in which God's Word is partly preached, or is still read from the Bible as God's Word, though it is falsely expounded and perverted, is a place where many wells of life and comfort are stopped up and souls led over dangerous detours; here also Satan, with generous hand, sows malignant weeds alongside the good seed of the Word of God in the hearts of the hearers to seduce them. Such churches are so dangerous that even Christ says of them, " 'My house shall be called a house of prayer,' but you make it a den of robbers" (Matthew 21:13). If one can go only to such a church, it were better for him to read the Word of his God at home, even if in tearful solitude.

What a blessing if Christians have both—if they not only can go peacefully to church but also if they have a church where God's Word is preached in its purity and the Sacraments are administered according to Christ's institution! Such a church, be it ever so small and plain, is worth more than all the glittering palaces of the great and rich of this world. Such a church is the place where the poor sinner can not only talk with God but also where God speaks to him through the mouth of a man; where God through His Word not only shows him the way to heaven, but also where the very heaven of grace and salvation opens wide to him. Whoever enters into such a church has reason to say with Jacob, "How awesome is this place! This is none other than the house of God, and this is the gate of heaven" (Genesis 28:17).

However, as great as the advantage is which those enjoy who can gather in such a church, we dare not suppose that such blessed people cannot be lost! Alas, no, they hover in great danger as to their salvation. It is this, which I plan to present today for your awakening and encouragement.

The text: *Luke 8:4–15*

We are told in the Gospel just read that a great crowd gathered around Christ to hear Him. That desire was so great that, as our text says, they hurried to Him out of the cities as men otherwise were accustomed to chase only earthly things. Yes, according to Matthew and Mark, the crowd was so great, that in order to find room Christ had to preach from a ship, while on the shore the people silently listened to His sermon. Would you not think that Christ would have called all these hearers blessed because of their great zeal? Yet, what does Christ do? He shows in a parable that only a small percentage of those who diligently hear God's pure Word will be saved. He, therefore, at the conclusion cries out with a warning voice, "He who has ears to hear, let him hear" (Luke 8:8).

For our warning permit me today to answer the question:

Why are so many who diligently hear God's Word not saved?

On the basis of our Gospel I answer,

1. Because many diligently HEAR God's Word, but do not seek to understand it and therefore do not come to FAITH at ALL;

140

2. Because others COME to faith through God's Word, but do not let it take root in them and therefore do not REMAIN in the faith; and
3. Because still others have God's Word take ROOT in them, but at the same time let worldliness come up and therefore bring forth no FRUIT in PATIENCE.

I.

Our Gospel reading today teaches that all men are like a field. As a field of itself bears only weeds, so nothing but the weed of sin grows from the heart of man if the seed of the divine Word is not sown in it. Most men are lost not because they refuse to read or hear God's Word diligently, but because they despise and reject it as foolishness.

If at least those would be saved who diligently read and hear God's Word! But what happens? When many experience how necessary the hearing of God's Word is for salvation, they hear it diligently and zealously; they even read God's Word in their homes. They suppose that is the only thing necessary for salvation. They look at the hearing of the Word as a good work by which one fulfills his Christian duty, shows that he is a Christian, and is saved.

Yet how sadly they deceive themselves! Far be it that they should receive salvation by diligently hearing God's Word. This very hearing hinders their salvation. What was given them for life and salvation becomes a savor of death unto death. Why? Christ tells us that at the beginning of our text. He says first, "A sower went out to sow his seed. And as he sowed, some fell along the path and was trampled underfoot, and the birds of the air devoured it" (Luke 8:5). Christ Himself explains this parable thus: "The seed is the Word of God. The ones along the path are those who have heard; then the devil comes and takes away the Word from their hearts, so that they may not believe and be saved" (8:11–12). According to Matthew's report, Christ also added the words that these are they who hear the word of the kingdom but do not understand (Matthew 13:13).

We see that the Word of God is like seed. If the seed is to be used, it is not enough that it should be sown. It must fall into the ground, germinate, and grow up. If the seed falls on a hard path so that it cannot mix with the soil, the birds of the air quickly come, eat the seed, and the whole sowing is lost.

So it is also with the Word. It is not enough that a person lets the Word be preached to him, that he hears it with his ears. The important thing is that it falls into his heart, that the hearer learns to understand it, and that it shows its divine power in his heart and works true faith in him. If the Word, so to say, lies on the surface of the heart, if it does not enter into the heart, Satan comes and takes the Word from his heart so that the person does not believe and is lost. As the writer to the Hebrews expressly says, "The message they heard did not benefit them, because they were not united by faith with those who listened" (4:2).

Know from this, you who suppose that because you diligently hear God's Word, you must be true Christians and will be saved: Alas, you are sadly mistaken. The mere hearing does not help you at all. If you absentmindedly hear, do not pay attention, and try to understand, Satan, the hellish bird of prey, comes and takes it from your heart so that you do not believe and are not saved.

God has given us His heavenly Word for the purpose of producing a great divine change in our hearts. By God's Word we should be divinely enlightened that we learn to know ourselves. We should see our great sins and regret them. In the light of the Holy Spirit we must also learn to know Jesus Christ as our Savior and believe in Him. If through the hearing of the Word a new light does not once shine upon a person in respect to himself and Jesus Christ, if the divine fire of the Word does not once pierce the heart, so that his heart glows with a desire for Christ, God's Word has been preached in vain. Instead of saving him, the hearing of God's Word will rather become grounds for the complaint that he let this Means of Grace be without fruit.

He who wishes to be saved must, therefore, hear God's Word with great attention; he must try to understand God's thoughts correctly. These divine thoughts must fill his whole heart, bring forth fruit, and create a living faith and a new life in Christ. If you do not wish that, you must surrender the hope of salvation. Christ says, "Unless one is born again he cannot see the kingdom of God" (John 3:3).

II.

My friends, if all those would be saved who once had taken God's Word into their hearts! Most hearers would still be saved, for God's Word is so powerful that at times it enters the heart so deeply that the first shoots of an active faith and life suddenly show themselves. Yet what does Christ in our parable say of the seed of the Word? He says, "And some fell on the rock, and as it grew up, it withered away, because it had no moisture" (Luke 8:6). And this Christ Himself expounds as follows, "The ones on the rock are those who, when they hear the word, receive it with joy. But these have no root; they believe for a while, and in time of testing fall away" (8:13).

There you have the second reason why even so many of those who diligently hear God's pure Word are not saved. It is this: others *come* to faith through God's Word, but they do not let it take root in them and, therefore, do not *remain* in the faith.

The same thing happens to the Word as to seed. There are rocks upon which lies only a thin layer of soil. If one sows good seed in such land, the seed grows up so quickly that one would suppose that he could hope for a bumper crop. However, what happens? If days come when it rains little and the sun begins to shine, behold! the green plants begin to *dry up* just as fast as they first shot up. Why? The plants were able to send out too few roots on rocky land and, therefore, had too little moisture.

So it is also with many who diligently hear God's Word. Many, it is true, are awakened. Through the working of the Holy Spirit they learn to see that they are poor sinners who must be concerned about their salvation. They bid farewell to the world. Christ and His grace fill them with joy. They begin to believe in Him. They become another person. For a time also they show great zeal for Christianity. They are daily on their knees in prayer. They seek out the zealous Christians and talk with them about salvation. They confess their faith before the world.

And should they be lost? Alas, also ever so many of them are lost! What happens? Sad to say, with many the first zeal lasts for a short time only. Either they are again attacked by their old sins and they let themselves be conquered by them, or through unbelief they have doubts, do not earnestly resist them, and thus they become unbelievers again. Or they are enticed by the children of the world to join in this or that which they know is sinful; they begin to cultivate a taste for the lust of the world. Or the world ridicules their faith and gradually they begin to feel ashamed of their Savior. Or they are tempted to indolence and yielding, they cease praying, cease reading, and cease hearing God's Word diligently, cease watching over themselves, and thus they finally fall into spiritual death and weakness. Or, they see how others who want to be Christians live an unchristian life, take offense, and thus finally become like these pretended Christians. Who can name all the ways in which so many lose their faith?

And what is the cause? When most become Christians they do not let God's Word take deep root in them. They hurry over the consideration of their sinful corruption as quickly as possible. They do not let their rock-hard heart be truly crushed. They never really come to an insight of how corrupt their heart is, how weak they are without Christ, and how easily they can fall away again. They never learn to become really frightened over their sins, God's wrath, and hell. They never learn to see the depths of their poverty as poor sinners.

They wish to start being Christians but they never count the cost. Quickly they promise God that they will be different, but they do not know that they can do nothing if God's grace does not give them the power. They are never really freed from a trust in their own powers and have, therefore, begun their Christianity trusting in themselves. Hence, at the first temptation they fall away, openly desert the Word, and leave the community of Christians; or they remain outwardly with Christians but inwardly leave Christ. Alas, they never repent because they considered their previous repentance a deception, or they comfort themselves with the fact that once they repented—and so they are finally lost.

Ah my dear hearers, let us therefore not forget: We are not saved because we once came to faith but because we remain in the faith. We do not reach our heavenly goal because we once zealously avoided the way of the world and sin and went the way to heaven but because we remained on this way until our end. We are not heirs of eternal life because we once were God's children and were united with Christ but because we remained with Christ until our death.

Many a one formerly came with us into this church and heard God's Word diligently. His heart beat fast when the way to eternal life was explained, and lo! now he comes either not at all or seldom; he has fallen and hurries to meet his ruin! Many a one formerly went the way to heaven with us. He quickly became a zealous Christian. But lo! now he lives and rejoices in the world again, as it is written, "Demas, in love with this present world, has deserted me" (2 Timothy 4:10). He turned his back to his Savior, he has fallen, and his goal is eternal death. But must not many confess that once his heart burned in him whenever the Scriptures were explained but now he is indifferent, cold, and dead?

Ah my friends, consider this: how you began your Christianity will not decide whether you will be saved, but how things stand with you at the end of your life. You who have believed for a time but fell away at the time of temptation, return again! It is worth it to pursue a blessed eternity and escape eternal misery! Just think, God holds it against you that you have left your first love. Repent and do the first works. But this time dig deeper. This time lay a deeper foundation. This time let the Word of God take deep root in you. In brief, become poor sinners who cling only to grace, seek only grace, rejoice only in grace. No wind of temptation, no flood of trial will tear down the house of your salvation.

III.

My friends, one more point! Today's earnest Gospel reading goes still further. It tells us that there are Christians who, though they let God's Word take deep root in them, are not saved. We read, "And some fell among thorns, and the thorns grew up with it and choked it" (Luke 8:7). These according to Christ are they who "hear, but as they go on their way they are choked by the cares and riches and pleasures of life, and their fruit does not mature" (8:14).

What the Lord wishes to say is clear. He wants to say that the seed is lost not only when it falls on the beaten path and does not mix with the soil, and is eaten by the birds of the air; moreover, the seed is lost not only when it grows up quickly but being not deeply rooted, withers on the first hot day. The seed is also lost even when it is deeply rooted but falls amongst the thorns that smother it.

The Lord wants to say that the hearing of the Word is in vain not only by those who do not hear it attentively, never learn to understand it aright, and never come to faith. The hearing of the Word is in vain not only by those who receive it joyfully but do not lay the deep foundation of repentance and at the time of temptation fall away, but it can also happen that even those who have laid a deep foundation for their Christianity and have a deeply rooted faith will lose their crown.

Is this actually possible? Without a doubt, for He who is the Truth has said it is, and he who tills the soil knows this. A farmer knows that even if the seed is deeply rooted and sprouts most wonderfully he cannot hope for a harvest if he does not root out the weeds which grow up *with* it.

This is true also of Christians. Though a Christian by God's grace has a heart which is ever so well cultivated, his heart is not completely new, nor completely spirit; it still has something, yes, much, of the old evil way. This old evil way of the heart is not dead and unfruitful but living and powerful and unceasingly sprouts the weed of sin. If even the best and most experienced Christian is not careful, it does not take long for the weed of sin to overrun the seed of the Word and stifle it. There are two special kinds of weeds that threaten death and hell even to a good Christian: either the weed of the care of this world or the weed of the *riches* and *lust* of this life.

A firmly grounded Christian will not fall easily from fear of the mockery and persecution of the world, because he does not trust the enticements and the flattery of the world, and he is offended at the evil life of many who wish to be Christians. This nearly always causes beginners in Christianity to fall. Yet how many a strong hero of faith who has defied the enticing or threatening world, the unbelievers, and the sects, has nevertheless fallen because of care in continued trouble, need, disgrace, sickness, and other misery, or through wealth, good days, honor, and the like! How easily unbelieving care, discontent with one's lot, worldly grief over earthly loss, and misery sneak in and stifle the Word and faith! How easily the gradual love of the world and trust in temporal things is firmly seated in even the best Christian when he becomes successful, and drives the Holy Spirit away again! How easily a Christian falls into the desire to be rich and thus falls, according to the word of the apostle, "into temptation, into a snare, into many senseless and harmful desires that plunge people into ruin and destruction!" (1 Timothy 6:9). Hence be on guard, examine yourself thoroughly every day, root out the weed of sin with God's Word and prayer, and since one cannot root out everything, hate oneself, be ashamed of oneself, and as a poor miserable sinner, hungry and thirsty, draw daily grace upon grace from the well of grace.

Hence, I now ask all of you, does he, who can go into a church in which God's Word is preached in its truth and purity, feel secure and suppose that he is in no trouble or danger? You will, thinking upon our Gospel reading today, all answer: "Alas, no!" In such churches heaven stands open through the Word, but narrow is the way on which one goes to it and straight is the gate through which one must enter in.

Ah, let us not be secure! Above all, you who have not even once diligently heard God's Word, be afraid! If this happens to a green tree, what shall be done to the dry? If the righteous scarcely be kept, where will the godless and sinners appear? You diligent hearers, however, do not only diligently hear God's Word, but try to understand it and let it go down into your heart. And not only that, but also lay a deep foundation in true, earnest, and daily repentance that your faith neither withers nor dries up in the heat of temptation. And not only that, but also watch and pray that you root out the weeds which shoot up in your hearts and bring forth fruit—fruit in patience. Thus our church will not witness against you, but even in heaven you will cry out with Jacob, "Surely the LORD is in this place, and I did not know it. . . . How awesome is this place! This is none other than the house of God, and this is the gate of heaven" (Genesis 28:16–17). Amen.

QUINQUAGESIMA

LUKE 18:31–43

The grace of our Lord Jesus Christ, the love of God, and the communion of the Holy Spirit be with you all. Amen.

Dear friends in Christ Jesus!

"[God] made from one man every nation of mankind to live on all the face of the earth, having determined allotted periods and the boundaries of their dwelling place, that they should seek God, and perhaps feel their way toward him and find him" (Acts 17:26–27). Thus Paul preached in the public marketplace of the world-renowned city of Athens. They are great important truths that the apostle expressed. We see that after God had created the world He did not leave His work but also preserves and rules it.

If we view the nature of this world with the eyes of our reason alone, it appears as if men decide matters by themselves, as if God were only an idle spectator of what men do. If in the light of God's Word we view the doings of men with the eyes of faith, we see something far different. We see, as the apostle says, that God even from eternity has foreseen everything that occurs in time. He has set His goal for everything and decided for every person how long and in what age he should live. While men seemingly begin, continue, and carry out everything according to their own free will, God has them secretly in His hand and so guides them that they must carry out His eternal decree.

Not only does God control the good but also the evil. Either He hinders it or sets bounds to it, or He lets it happen and thereby carries out His judgments of grace and wrath. We have a wonderful example of this in Joseph's brothers selling him to Egypt. They plotted evil against Joseph, but God meant it for good, and thereby carried out His judgment of peace not only concerning Joseph but also His whole chosen people of Israel.

While the world and hell battle and rage against God to take His honor from Him, hurl Him from His throne, and try to destroy His kingdom, these powers must, without knowing and wishing it, fight only *for* God, promote His honor, strengthen and increase His kingdom. We see this in the bloody persecutions of the first three centuries. The Christian Church was to have been rooted out, and just because of that she sent down her roots only deeper, like a tree shaken by storms. When at the Last Day the earthly life of mankind will have ended, the foes of God with terror, but the elect with rejoicing, will clearly see that nothing happened without God's will, that everything, good and evil, had to serve Him, and that He led everything to a wonderful and blessed goal.

How confident the Christian can therefore be! Though something happens according to or against his will, he knows that it happens according to God's good and gracious will. Though he experiences fortune or misfortune, he knows that what God's counsel has decided in regard to him has come to pass. Though he has many crafty and powerful enemies, he knows that without God's permission they could not harm a hair of his head. Though men have robbed him of everything—goods, honor, and joy—he knows that all this is taken from him only through men by his *God*, who can wish him no evil. Though the future may be dark, gloomy, threatening, and dangerous, he knows nothing will come to pass but what God in grace has destined for him.

For our salvation God has decided our destiny, joys, and sorrows from eternity; this is easily recognized, since we all are sinners and must praise God when He leads us through affliction into His blessed kingdom. Does it not remain an insolvable riddle that even the Guiltless, the Righteous, the Pure among those who are not pure, in whose mouth was found no guile, yes, who was the most Holy Son of God Himself, that even *Jesus Christ* entered into His glory through suffering? Our Gospel reading today gives us an answer to this question. Let us now hear the answer.

The text: Luke 18:31–43

My friends, we see in this text that Christ was busy with two kinds of blind men. In the first class belonged a physically blind person who sat by the roadside and begged. His eyes the Lord miraculously, quickly, and suddenly opened with three words, "Recover your sight" (Luke 18:42).

The disciples belonged to the other class. At that time they were still spiritually blind regarding Christ's suffering and death. What did Christ do in order to open also these blind spiritual eyes? He did two things. First, He spoke also to them, "Recover your sight!" Hereupon He called their attention to the fact that according to the prophets He had to suffer and die.

Of course, the disciples did not immediately receive spiritual sight, as the blind beggar received the physical. It costs God Himself more to enlighten, convert, and sanctify a person than to create and heal him physically. However, we know that Christ's second remedy was not forever in vain. When Christ after His resurrection used this remedy again, when He reminded them of the prophets, this worked so wonderfully that it was as though scales fell from their eyes. Christ's suffering and death no longer seemed dark and foolish but became as clear as day, the most blessed truth that they zealously preached to the whole world.

Permit me today on the threshold of the Lenten season to show you

How important it is that Christ's suffering and death
was foretold by the prophets of the Old Testament.

This is important for three reasons. We see from it that Christ's suffering and death was

1. One appointed beforehand by God Himself,
2. One extremely necessary for our salvation, and
3. One valid for all times.

Lord God, heavenly Father, who let the sufferings and death of Your dear Son be foretold by Your holy prophets, let us also know the great secret lying therein to our salvation. Open the eyes of our souls to see that the suffering of Your Son was one foreseen by You from eternity, extremely necessary for our salvation, valid and saving for all times. May not the word of the cross be for us, as for the blind world, foolishness and an offense but become divine power and wisdom. To that end bless the word now spoken in weakness for the sake of Your truth and grace. Amen.

I.

In our day more and more self-educated men maintain that hitherto the life of Christ has never been presented correctly. In the past it has been thought that one sees nothing but divine mysteries in it. What they claim is absolutely wrong. Since Christ was a true man, the only true presentation of His life would be to believe that it is really human and present it that way. They also look at Christ's suffering and death that way; that Christ had to suffer so many and such frightful things happened quite naturally, an accidental, easily explainable matter. Christ had publicly expounded a doctrine that was most offensive to the vicious rulers of church and state. It evoked the bitterest vindictiveness in them. The natural result was that Christ was sacrificed to the cunning, power, and cruelty of His opponents; when He was nailed to the cross He had to pay for His ideas with His life.

However my friends, all these are the useless fabrications of the most blind and wanton unbelief. What does Christ Himself say in our text of His suffering and death? We read, "See, we are going up to Jerusalem, and everything that is written about the Son of Man by the prophets will be accomplished" (Luke 8:31). There you see that Christ's suffering and death was announced long ago by the prophets of the Old Testament. It was determined long ago by God Himself, yes, from eternity and revealed in time through His servants. Christ expressly says it was predicted not *by* the prophets but *through* the prophets by God, whose tools the prophets had merely been. Christ's suffering did not happen as other human things do, which in a certain sense occur accidentally, that is, in such a way that they under other circumstances could have happened another way or not at all. Christ did not suffer and die because His foes desired it, outwitted, and overpowered Him, but because God wanted it and hence because Christ Himself wanted it.

This fact is shown us at other occasions. When Christ appeared the first time in Nazareth preaching publicly, His hearers became so angry that they violently dragged Him to the steep slope of their city in order to hurl Him into the abyss and kill Him. Since the hour determined by God for His death had not yet come, He "passing through their midst, He went away" (Luke 4:30). When later before a large crowd in the temple Christ confessed, "Before Abraham was, I am" (John 8:58), hence that He is the eternal God, the mob picked up stones to kill Him. But since also the hour decided upon by God for His suffering and death had not yet come, He suddenly made Himself invisible. We read, "But Jesus hid Himself and went out of the temple" (John 8:59). Yes, when they finally came to arrest Christ, with three words, "I am He," He hurled the whole armed mob to the ground. Christ thereby shows how easily He could have fled even then had He wanted to. Yes, had it not been His Father's and therefore also His own will to suffer and die, no chains could have bound Him, no army (no matter how great) could have captured Him, no power on earth could have nailed Him to the cross. With a single word, yes, by His mere will He could have crushed and annihilated His foes.

For this reason Peter says in his Pentecost sermon, "Men of Israel, hear these words: Jesus of Nazareth, a man attested to you by God with mighty works and wonders and signs, . . . this Jesus, delivered up *according to the definite plan and foreknowledge of God*, you crucified and killed by the hands of lawless men" (Acts 2:22–23). And shortly thereafter all the apostles in prayer said that Herod and Pilate had done *what God's hand and counsel had determined before to be done.*

There is no doubt, when in our text Christ says to the disciples, that through His suffering and death everything would be accomplished that was written by the prophets, He wishes to teach us and them that it was not accidental, forced upon Him by human plans, but it was predetermined, decreed, and foreseen by God Himself.

Do not suppose that Christ's tormentors and murderers are exonerated from their horrible deed and that the blame rests upon God. No, God had decreed Christ's death. He, however, did not produce the malice of Christ's enemies. Rather, foreseeing it He used it to carry out His eternal decree through them. Just as he who throws a lamb into the jaws of a ravening animal does not first make it ravening but only lets it mangle the lamb, so also the heavenly Father deliberately surrendered Christ, the Lamb of God, to the scribes and Pharisees, the chief priests and elders of Israel, to Herod and Pilate, as to ravening animals. He did not produce their desire for blood but only allowed them to mangle, lacerate, and kill this Lamb according to their malice.

II.

From the fact that Christ's suffering and death was predicted by the prophets of the Old Testament we see that it was also one absolutely necessary for our salvation. Permit me to speak to you of this.

That Christ had to suffer and die is clear from the mere fact that it was foretold by God through the prophets. What God, who cannot err much less lie, foretells *cannot* be left undone; it *must* take place. Christ also wants us to understand that according to prophecy He must die, because this was absolutely necessary for the redemption of the world. "Everything that is written about the Son of Man by the prophets will be accomplished" (Luke 18:31), Christ says in our text. Why does He not simply say, "of Me," rather than, "about the Son of Man"?

Christ is referring the disciples to that one promised Son of Man, namely, the seed of the woman who was promised to fallen man in paradise. He would crush the head of the serpent and it would kill Him by a poisonous wound in His heels. Moreover, Christ clearly refers His disciples to all the prophecies that that Child should be born, that Son given for fallen men. He, as Isaiah writes, should be wounded for our *transgressions* and be bruised for our *iniquities*, yes, His *life* should be sacrificed for sin. Yet why does Christ refer the disciples to this? There can be no other reason than that they should know that His suffering and death is one absolutely necessary for the salvation of the world. Christ wants to say that as certainly as He is that promised Son of man, that is, the promised Redeemer, so unavoidably, so positively, *necessary* is it that He according to the prophets also suffer and die for the redemption of the world.

That we do not err in this matter we see from the many details of the Passion and resurrection stories of the Lord. When in Gethsemane Christ began His spiritual suffering, He said, "My Father, if it be possible, let this cup pass from Me" (Matthew 26:39). But what happened? The cup of this unspeakable suffering did *not* pass away. Christ must empty it. God's answer to Christ's imploring prayer was, "No, My dear Son in whom I am well pleased, it is *not* possible if the world is to be redeemed."

When shortly thereafter Peter struck blindly with his sword in order to free Christ from bodily suffering, Christ Himself said to Peter, "Do you think that I cannot appeal to My Father, and He will at once send Me more than twelve legions of angels? *But how then should the Scriptures be fulfilled, that it must be so?*" (Matthew 26:53–54). And finally, when He was risen from the dead, He said to the disciples on the way to Emmaus who still could not reconcile themselves to Christ's suffering, "O foolish ones, and slow of heart to believe all that the prophets have spoken! Was it not necessary that the Christ should suffer these things and enter into His glory?" (Luke 24:25–26).

Even Christ's enemies had to confirm that here a *divine* "must" prevailed. As Matthew informs us, at first they absolutely did not want to kill Christ at Easter, when so many people were gathered together. When they took counsel on the matter, they said to one another, "Not during the feast, lest there be an uproar among the people" (26:5). But see! God's hour, the hour of the redemption of the world, had struck. Hell was let loose against Christ. Even against their will, Satan's tools and captives *had* to bring that hellish work to completion.

Oh my friends, what an important truth it is that Christ's suffering and death was one absolutely necessary for our salvation!

First of all, we see that God is not at all as most suppose—a loving, indulgent Father. No, He is truly a holy and upright Being. He really hates sin, and His wrath waxes hot on its account down to the lowest hell. Of a truth, sin is no joke to God, no trifle that He is willing to overlook. Had Christ not been willing to take on Himself the sins of all men, to atone for and let Himself be punished for every sin through unspeakable suffering and the most painful death, God could not have saved a single person nor would He have wanted to. Each sin is so offensive to God's holiness, and He is a Being of such strict holiness that He would and could rather let the whole sinful world be lost than let one sin be unpunished. What the Holy Scriptures say of God's wrath and fury against sin are not merely empty figures of speech but the frightful, terrible truth. Man's sweet dream is that God is a gracious Being whom no one need fear; their god is a phantom, a miserable product of their own mind. For how God really is we see in the bloody tragedy on Golgotha, where the only-begotten Son had to atone for the sins of men if sinners should find grace with God.

Moreover, we also see how foolishly they act who wish to remain in one or the other sin and still rely on God's grace. Such people make a devil out of God. For it is not the holy God, but the devil, who pays no attention to sin. He who knows or to whom it is clearly and convincingly shown that something is sin but does not want to leave his sin and still comforts himself in God's great grace sins against grace, tramples on God's Son who had to bleed for his sins, considers the blood of the testament as unclean, and abuses the Spirit of grace. Nothing else remains for him but a terrible waiting for the judgment and zeal that will consume the offender.

You, therefore, who know that Christ had to suffer and die for sin, do not play with any sin, though it may appear as small indeed, or else you will experience in the hour of death, or surely on the Day of Judgment, that your faith was a fancy, your comfort a delusion, your hope a dream.

III.

It is true that Christ's suffering and death were already foretold by the prophets of the Old Testament. This is, finally, so important because we learn from this that it is also valid and comforting for all time. And permit me to speak to you of this.

Many suppose that if faith in Christ's reconciling suffering and death were actually the only means whereby every person can be saved, Christ would have had to come into the world immediately after the fall. How could faith in something that happened 4,000 years after the fall be the only redemption for all the fallen? This objection, however, would have force only if men had known nothing of Christ's redemptive suffering and death during those 4,000 years. That is not the case. Already in paradise help through a suffering and dying man was promised to the first people. Afterward all the prophets most accurately described His reconciling suffering. He, as Christ says in our text, would be "delivered over to the Gentiles and will be mocked and shamefully treated and spit upon. And after flogging Him, they will kill Him, and on the third day He will rise" (Luke 18:32–33). If we go into the writings of the prophets and the prophetic Psalms, we would find all this and many more details of the suffering and death of Christ so fully depicted that it appears as if the prophets themselves had accompanied Christ from Gethsemane to Golgotha.

Why did God have this foretold by the prophets so exactly? First of all, that those who lived *before* Christ came could have the certain comfort of the forgiveness of their sins, divine grace, and eternal salvation through their faith that hoped in the saving, substitutionary, and reconciling suffering of Him who should come. And by this faith all patriarchs, all prophets, and all saints were saved. On the other hand, all who were lost before Christ's appearance were damned only because they wanted to know nothing of that comforting prediction of the prophets, despising and deeming it a meaningless fable.

And after Christ's appearance the predictions of Christ's suffering and death have lost none of their meaning and power. Rather, they become truly meaningful and effective. After all these prophecies were fulfilled to the last letter, so to say before the eyes of the whole world, after He who was crucified in weakness also actually arose in glory from the dead on the third day, with heightened effect the fulfilled prophecies call to all men, "Christ died for our sins in accordance with the Scriptures" (1 Corinthians 15:3). "In Christ God was reconciling the world to Himself. . . . Be reconciled to God" 2 Corinthians 5:19, 20). The prophets' predictions of Christ's suffering and death have become a well from which even at the time of the Old Testament a wide, full stream of grace and salvation flowed forth; they invited all nations to slake their thirst from it freely and without price.

However, in the time of the New Testament, prophecy and apostolic preaching flow as a double stream wherever there are sinners who need salvation by grace. The Crucified, as it were, stands at the center of world history, as the banner of all nations to which the prophets pointed forward and all apostles point back, as to the Lamb of God who bears the sins of the world, who as John writes in Revelation, was slain from the beginning of the world.

Hence, my dear hearers, let this move us in the coming Lenten season to search the writings of the prophets daily and seek therein the suffering and dying Christ. Let us also first of all, as before a mirror, search for the horror of our sins and God's wrath over them. Then let us behold the complete reconciliation of our sins and the riches of divine love and grace. To do this we are all by nature completely blind, but let us with the blind in our text call upon Christ in faith to open our eyes. We will also finally experience the power of those blessed words, "Recover your sight; your faith has made you well" (Luke 18:42). Amen.

LENTEN SEASON

FIRST SUNDAY IN LENT

MATTHEW 4:1–11

Grace and peace be multiplied unto you through the knowledge of God, and of Jesus our Lord. Amen.

Dear friends in Christ Jesus!

Among the doctrines under vehement attack today is the doctrine of a devil, who with hostile intent ceaselessly tempts man. Yes, many even assert that, though they believe in the whole Bible, they cannot possibly believe in a devil—at least not in a devil who can work among men.

On this point there is little debate with one who rejects God's Word. The doctrine of Satan concerns the invisible spirit world, which cannot be elucidated by our reason but by the Word of divine revelation. If one rejects divine revelation, the doctrine of the mysterious power of darkness must also be foolishness. Why should an atheist, a naturalist, and a moralist believe in an evil spirit, an invisible enemy of souls, a tempter, a seducer of men, when he does not believe in the grace and redemption of his Savior? Luther says in his exposition of Peter's words, "Be ready always to give an answer to every man," (1 Peter 3:15), "If you hear people who are so completely blinded and hardened that they deny that this is God's Word or are in doubt about it, just keep silence, do not say a word to them, and let them go their way. Just say: 'I will give you enough proof from Scripture. If you want to believe it, this is good; if not, I will give you nothing else.' Then you may say, 'Ah, in this way God's Word must needs be brought into disgrace!' Leave this to God" (*Luther's Works*, vol. 30, p. 107 [St. Louis: Concordia, 1967]).

The poison of unbelief and scepticism so controls Christendom and has so infected countless people that even those who do not exactly want to reject the Holy Scriptures doubt Satan's presence, or at least his influence on men. However, as certain as it is that there is a God who revealed Himself in the

Holy Scriptures, so certain is it that there is also a devil. Satan is not only named here and there in Scripture, but the Bible describes in detail his origin, essence, characteristics, how he works power over the human race, his kingdom, abode, and his present and future fate. We find the doctrine of Satan in all the books of the Old and New Testament, in Genesis as well as in the Revelation of St. John. The Sacred Writings do not mention Satan incidentally, but the doctrine of Satan is so interwoven in the whole of Christian doctrine that the entire structure would collapse if one denies the existence of that evil spirit. If one denies the existence of the devil, one must also deny the fall of man, original sin, the redemption, Christ, Baptism, yes, the entire Gospel; yes, then one must make a liar out of the prophets, apostles, and Christ Himself.

Briefly, the Scriptures tell us that God not only created man but also an infinite number of higher spirits, the angels, and gave them great glory. They were to serve Him and carry out His commands. However, one of the foremost of these angels fell from God and with him a great host. That fallen angel was hurled to hell in chains. This wicked enemy, however, decided to found a different kingdom in place of the one he lost, to destroy God's creation.

When God had created the first man in His image, Satan tried to make him also disloyal and mislead him into sin. Moses relates in Genesis 3 how Satan succeeded. Man let himself be misled, renounced obedience to God, fell into sin, and thus became a subject of the kingdom of darkness. Sinful parents now beget sinful children. Every man is now by nature not in God's kingdom but in the kingdom of God's enemy. God's kingdom disappeared from earth when sin entered. Scripture says that the prince of this world is Satan, that he ceaselessly seeks to spread ever more sin, error, blindness, darkness, misery, and misfortune. It says he is "the prince of the power of the air" (Ephesians 2:2), and that he "prowls around like a roaring lion, seeking someone to devour" (2 Peter 5:8). He is "at work in the sons of disobedience" (Ephesians 2:2), and "has blinded the minds of the unbelievers, to keep them from seeing the light of the gospel of the glory of Christ" (2 Corinthians 4:4). "For we do not wrestle against flesh and blood, but against the rulers, against the authorities, against the cosmic powers over this present darkness, against the spiritual forces of evil in the heavenly places" (Ephesians 6:12).

God's Word, however, reveals not only the abyss of Satan, but also the depths of eternal love. It reveals not only the power and cunning of that evil spirit, but also the mighty Lord of heaven and earth. It reveals not only our misery in the kingdom of Satan, but also how Jesus Christ, the Son of God and man, conquered Satan, redeemed us from his kingdom, rescued us from the power of darkness, and instituted a new divine kingdom of grace through His blood in which all who believe in Him find freedom and salvation.

Our text today presents a battle of our Redeemer that He waged for us with the prince of darkness. Let us consider it in the present hour for the strengthening of our faith.

The text: *Matthew 4:1–11*

Under the guidance of this Gospel we today direct our attention to:

Christ's victorious battle with the prince of darkness.

We consider:

1. How Christ battled and conquered for all men, and
2. How also a Christian with the power of Christ may overcome Satan.

O Jesus, faithful Savior, who once struggled for us in a severe battle, we are gathered today to ponder that struggle. Oh, grant that at least for the salvation of our souls Your believers might be mightily strengthened in the faith; let all of us embrace you in faith. Oh dearest Lord Jesus, You alone know how many of us still are in the power of darkness. Arise, arise, struggle today for also these souls. Resurrect the dead, establish the fallen, give joy to the despondent, courage to the faint, and so today again be victorious through Your Word. You alone should have the honor, O Jesus, forever and ever. Amen.

I.

A most amazing battle is related in our Gospel reading today. Christ had just been baptized. Heaven had opened over Him as though it wanted to sink to earth. Now we see hell opened beneath Him and with all its power rush upon Christ. How amazing! Once the Son of God had hurled Satan from heaven; here on earth He allows himself to be attacked, led around, laughed at, and mocked by Satan. He does not conquer him by one almighty word as He well could have but through the written Word of God. He, who is the eternal Light, struggled with the spirit of darkness; the eternal Truth with the father of lies; the Most Holy with the spirit of uncleanness; the King of heaven with the powerless captive of hell. The Son of God let Himself be placed by Satan on the pinnacle of the temple; He allows Satan to demand that He worship him. What an amazing struggle!

When we read at the beginning of the Gospel, "Then Jesus was led up by the Spirit into the wilderness to be tempted by the devil" (Matthew 4:4), we see that Christ's struggle was not something accidental. It was arranged by God Himself. It occurred according to God's eternal, gracious counsel. Christ of His own free will now fulfilled it. Had Christ not wanted it, Satan could not have appeared before Him, let alone dare tempt and assail Him.

Christ did not wage this war for Himself. He battled as the Surety, the Mediator, the Substitute of the whole human race, for all men, for us who are gathered here. Through sin all men sold themselves to Satan; all became his servants and subjects of his kingdom. To redeem and save men Christ came as the real Owner of all the souls of men in order to conquer Satan, destroy his kingdom, take his booty away again, free us from his power, and lead all men through the kingdom of grace into the kingdom of eternal glory.

Thus John says, "The reason the Son of God appeared was to destroy the works of the devil" (1 John 3:8). Yes, the first prophecy of Christ, which the first human pair received from God in paradise, was that the woman's offspring (that is, Christ, the Son of the Virgin), would bruise the serpent's head (that is, the devil's). Cf. Genesis 3:15. Of course, Christ did this chiefly through His bloody death on the cross. There the serpent's head was completely crushed.

However, the battle with Satan, which is related in our Gospel reading today, was the beginning. It was, so to say, the first assault. This battle was the first engagement touched off by the Lord of our salvation, in order to tread down Satan under our feet. It was the first defeat of the infernal host to show them that now a Stronger One had come. Scarcely had Christ begun His ministry when immediately He attacked Satan. He did not leave the field until He had won the last engagement for us on the cross and could cry out, "It is finished!" The resurrection immediately following upon it was the victory shout of the world's Mediator, the great Te Deum Laudamus, "We praise You, O Lord." The descent into hell and ascension into heaven were the victor's glorious triumphant procession. Yet all this could not have followed had not Christ won His first battle in the wilderness. This also was therefore a necessary part of the work of our redemption.

We find a wonderful prototype of Christ's battle in the Old Testament. During the reign of Saul, the army of Israel fought the Philistines. The battle was about to begin when behold, a giant of frightening size and strength stepped forth from the army of the enemy, derided God's people, and proposed that he was now ready to enter into a duel with a soldier of the Israelites. If he should lose, the Philistines should be their servants; if the Israelite should lose, they would be the servants of the Philistines. Frightened by the unusual size of the giant, everyone fled. For forty days the giant repeated his threatening challenge and no one wanted to accept it.

But lo, a shepherd lad from Bethlehem Ephrathah, named David, a son of Jesse, finally stepped up and said, "Who is this uncircumcised Philistine, that he should defy the armies of the living God? . . . Let no man's heart fail because of him. Your servant will go and fight with this Philistine" (1 Samuel 17:26, 32). David stepped forward and said to the Philistine, "You come to me with a sword and with a spear and with a javelin, but I come to you in the name of the LORD of hosts, the God of the armies of Israel, whom you have defied. This day the LORD will deliver you into my hand . . . that all the earth may know that there is a God in Israel" (vv. 45–46). Thereupon the lad slung a stone at the giant's forehead, and bleeding, he fell to the ground. With this one victory all Israel was at once rescued and smote the fleeing foe.

As important as David's battle was for the temporal freedom of all Israel, so important and decisive was Christ's battle with Satan for the eternal salvation of all men. If we wish to understand this battle properly, we must imagine that the whole human race was gathered on one side in the wilderness; on the other, the army of the spirits of hell, with Satan, the giant of hell, at their head. We must imagine how Satan challenged man to a duel. There was no one who dared attempt the frightful struggle. They could expect nothing else but to be and remain the eternal slaves of Satan. But see! God's Son, the real David from Bethlehem, stepped up, of humble appearance it is true, yet full of the invisible power of God, as we read in Luther's beautiful hymn "Dear Christians, One and All, Rejoice":

> *His royal pow'r disguised He bore;*
> *A servant's form, like mine, He wore*
> *To lead the devil captive. (LSB 556:6)*

Nothing less than our eternal freedom was at stake. Whether we should remain Satan's subjects, or again be citizens of the kingdom of heaven, God's children and companions, depended on this battle. Had Christ been *conquered* in the wilderness, woe unto us!

However, happy are we! Christ won, won gloriously, not for Himself, but for us. The bonds are severed, and we are free. Everything that we had lost through the fall in paradise Christ had again regained for us in the wilderness. Man ate of the forbidden tree; Christ hungered forty days and forty nights. Man wanted to be like God; the Son of God suffered for it when Satan skeptically and mockingly said to Him, "Are You the Son of God?" The serpent said to man, "Did God actually say?" and misled man by garbling the divine word. Here Satan tried that on Christ. He remained firm, however, and said without wavering, "It is written." The serpent seduced man to pride and presumption, when he dazzled him by promising, "When you eat of it your eyes will be opened, and you will be like God, knowing good and evil" (Genesis 3:5). Satan also tempted Christ with pride and said, "All these I will give You, if You will fall down and worship me" (Matthew 4:9). Christ, however, triumphed; Satan had to leave, "and behold, angels came and were ministering to Him" (4:11).

Now my friends, if you want to be eternally blessed by the battle of your Savior, your heavenly General, nothing more is demanded of you and all men than that you play the part of a believing spectator. The important thing is not that you learn how to fight against sin and Satan from Christ's example, but the first, the most important, the main thing is that you learn to believe that Christ battled for you, in your place, for your freedom and salvation. Whoever knows and feels his sins, whoever knows that hitherto he has served the devil, that he was full of unbelief, contempt of God's Word, pride, vanity, lust, and love of the world, or that he at least has not really battled against the world, flesh, and Satan, let him merely look to his Savior. This Champion from the stem of David has held the field for us. This Lion from the tribe of Judah has conquered for us. Though you may have fallen ever so deeply, though you may have even begged the devil's pardon, free yourself from this disgraceful tyranny. Side with Christ; then you are victor over sin and hell. Then Christ also divides the spoils of war with you— forgiveness of sins, righteousness, life, and salvation.

Ah, you who still serve sin joyfully, you despise the victory of your heavenly King and wantonly remain with that infamous beaten foe. Leave the army of the Philistines and come over to believing Israel. Under the shepherd's staff of the true David you will find victory, life, and well-being. You who find no delight in sin, but remain timid and irresolute because of the poor fight you put up, do you not see the infernal giant slain by the stone your almighty, eternal General hurled? Of what are you afraid? Join the banner of the cross, and though you may be ever so weak, you will stand on the side of the victor! All believing Christendom, rejoice with St. Paul,

" 'Death is swallowed up in victory.' 'O death, where is your victory? O death, where is your sting?' The sting of death is sin, and the power of sin is the law. But thanks be to God, who gives us the victory through our Lord Jesus Christ" (1 Corinthians 15:54–57).

However, my dear children of God, you who already rejoice in the victory of your Prince of Life, who already exercise yourselves in faith in Him, permit me, your weakest fellow soldier in the Lord, to speak on how a Christian with the power of Christ may overcome Satan.

II.

I repeat, the first use that we should make of Christ's battle with the prince of darkness is that we become believing spectators, not fellow soldiers; that we learn to believe that Christ has battled in our place. Whoever has thoroughly learned this can then confidently and joyfully follow Christ into the battles of the Lord armed with faith and the Word.

But this is also certain: whoever has been victorious with Christ will also fight as He did. If Satan crossed swords with the head, his members dare not feel secure. Christ is the general. All believers in Christ are called to active duty in a spiritual war. The God of spiritual Israel is called the Lord Sabaoth, that is, the Lord of hosts. Every Bible passage is a war trumpet that calls the Christians to battle. In Baptism we all vowed "to renounce the devil and all his works and all his ways," that is, to fight against him. Just as Christ was driven into the wilderness immediately after His Baptism to be tempted, so all who are baptized in Jesus Christ should expect nothing else.

Hence, my dear Christian, if you believe in Christ and His Word, if you find comfort in His victory, happy are you! You have chosen the best part. Bear in mind, you are saved but in hope; you are still in the world; you still have sin in you; you still have flesh and blood; yes, most important, you are still in the land of death, a stranger where Satan dwells. He is around you with his assistants and tools; he is busy trying to ruin you again, trying to make you tired and faint, so that you will leave Christ, yield to him again, and let yourself be brought under his scepter. Do not suppose that Satan is far away; he is in his members, the countless spirits of darkness wherever men are, and most fiercely where Christians are. He is at your side in your room when you pray, when you read God's Word. He is around you when you tend to your work. He is next to you when you go to church, hear the sermon, partake of the Sacrament. Wherever you go he tries to tempt and fell you.

Two things are therefore necessary: first, that you recognize the devil's cunning, and second, that you know how you can overcome him. We learn both from the example of our Lord in the wilderness. Satan sought to overcome Christ by a threefold temptation. First, he held his need before Him, in order to get Him to doubt whether He really was the Son of God. "If You are the Son of God, command these stones to become loaves of bread" (Matthew 4:3). He wants to say: "How can You say that You are God's Son when You are in distress?"

When this temptation would not work, Satan placed Jesus on a pinnacle of the temple and said, "If You are the Son of God, throw Yourself down, for it is written, 'He will command His angels concerning you,' And 'On their hands they will bear you up, lest you strike your foot against a stone' " (v. 6). Satan sought to mislead Christ by twisting God's Word. He quoted a Bible passage, but he left out important words. It says most clearly in Psalm 91, "to guard you in all your ways." Satan wanted that Christ should overlook these words and not remain in His ways, but, tempting God, jump down.

When also this temptation would not succeed, he became still more shameless and took Jesus into a "very high mountain and showed Him all the kingdoms of the world and their glory. And he said to Him, 'All these I will give You, if You will fall down and worship me' " (vv. 8–9). Satan tried to blind and win Christ through riches, honor, and the lust of this world.

There you see, my friends, the three main temptations that meet every Christian. Satan either tries to make the Christian despair through poverty, want, trouble, misery, disgrace, mockery, and all manner of misfortune, or he seeks to move him through the falsification of God's Word to all sorts of dangerous errors, heresies, and doubts about God's Word. Or Satan tries to entangle the Christian's poor heart through the illusion of good days, riches, honor, and the lust of the world. Hence, my dear Christians, learn to recognize the art of the evil foe. Satan is all around you and tries all possible keys to open your heart again. If he cannot open it with the key of shame and misery, he tries the key of false doctrine; if that does not open it, he tries the key of lust and good days. Of course, Satan nowadays very often appears in a visible, assumed image, as old and new examples prove, but Satan appears to Christians most often under the guise of money, false doctrine, honor, and earthly lust.

So, my dear Christian, note carefully: If your earthly trouble tempts you to despair of God's goodness and help, if you begin to burden your heart with worries, you may most certainly believe that the devil stands before you and calls to you, "If you are God's child, command that these stones be made bread. Pray yourself into health. Pray yourself free from your disgrace, yes, just let go of your faith, It is worth nothing." Or if you are tempted to doubt one of the precious teachings of your Christian faith, if God's Word is even held before you, do not doubt in the least that Satan stands before you and says, "It is written: He will command His angels concerning you" (Matthew 4:6).

Note well that Satan through false doctrine quotes God's Word, but he garbles it; he tears it out of its context in order to beguile you. It is Satan's method to give us one truth in order to bring in ten errors. Therefore, be warned! Satan seeks to pervert God's Word so that he gives false comfort for sins against conscience. If the sin is committed, he tries so to pervert God's Word as though there were no grace for this sin; he knows how by lock and key to deprive the poor conscience of all comfort. Or Satan tries to pervert God's Word so that it seems to contradict itself, thereby trying to bring doubt into the heart and cause you to fall completely from the truth.

Finally, note also this: if you are in the faith, you will often be tempted to injure your conscience for the sake of earthly advantage, deny Christ, and leave God's Word. Then think that Satan stands before you and calls to you, "All these I will give You, if You will fall down and worship me" (Matthew 4:9). Yes, consider every proud thought that arises in you as nothing else than a being placed by Satan on the pinnacle of the temple in order to push you off.

My friends, you see that Job is correct in saying, "Has not man a hard service on earth, and are not his days like the days of a hired hand?" (Job 7:1). Of a truth, being a true Christian is not an idle sport, no fun or play; it is a continual struggle with flesh, world, and Satan. Whoever dreams of rest, peace, and good days as a Christian deceives himself. Satan is the enemy of all men, but he is the most bitter enemy of believers; he slinks after them day and night to entice them from their fortress and push them into darkness, blindness, sin, death, and ruin.

Now, how should a Christian defend himself? Christ the General takes the lead; His own follow Him. How does Christ do battle? How is He victorious? Satan tempted Him to unbelief and He answered, "It is written." Satan tempted Him to false doctrine, and He answered, "It is written." Satan tempted Him to pride, and He answered, "It is written."

Oh great, important, golden, heavenly, eternal words of the Son of God. Oh that these words could be written with fiery letters across the heavens, so that all men, all heretics, all doubters, all unbelievers, all despairing, all sinners would have to read them every day! Oh that these words could be engraved in our hearts with an iron point and indelible letters. Ah, listen, you who still doubt whether the Word of God in the Old and New Testament is the eternal Word of the living God, listen as the Son of God is tempted by the power of Satan—He simply says, "It is written." With these few words from the writings of the Old Testament He crushes all the entrenchments and bulwarks of the hellish spirit. How else could Christ have shown the world more clearly that the Bible is the imperishable Word of Him who created heaven and earth, that this Word stands fast when everything, everything else perishes!

So, my dear Christians, make that your weapon in all temptations. Learn from your Savior in all of Satan's attacks to answer, "It is written." The Word of God is the sword of the Spirit; if you seize it in faith, you can do battle, and all the fiery arrows of the devil will be put out on the shield of faith. If trouble tempts you, take the verse, "I will never leave you nor forsake you" (Hebrews 13:5). If false doctrine tempts you, simply cling to the Word; do not depart from a letter, otherwise you are lost. If false teachers also quote God's Word, hold Scripture against Scripture, the clear passages against the dark, and imitate your Savior: "Yes, that is written here, but again and again it is also written." If sins tempt you, if they entice you so sweetly and lovingly, simply say, "It is written, 'Whoever makes a practice of sinning is of the devil, for the devil has been sinning from the beginning' " (1 John 3:8). If you are tempted to leave God, say, "It is written, 'if he shrinks back, My soul has no pleasure in him' " (Hebrews 10:38). If you are tempted in regard to your state of grace, say, "It is written, 'Whoever believes and is baptized will be saved' " (Mark 16:16). "The saying is trustworthy and deserving of full acceptance, that Christ Jesus came into the world to save sinners" (1 Timothy 1:15). "Come to me, all who labor and are heavy laden, and I will give you rest, . . . and you will find rest for your souls" (Matthew 11:28–29).

Learn from this that it was not out of stubbornness that Luther did not unite with those who had departed from God's Word. In the year 1529 a colloquy was arranged in Marburg between the Lutherans and the Reformed. Luther, Melanchthon, and others were on the one side, Zwingli and the rest on the other. They debated whether the true body and blood of Christ were in the Lord's Supper. At first Luther said nothing, but during the conference wrote these words with chalk on the table before him, "This is My body, this is My blood." Whenever he took part in the discussion, Luther pointed to the words, saying, "Here it says, 'It is written, This is My body, this is My blood.' " There was no giving in, no yielding. At the sight of these honest men, Zwingli himself was moved to tears and said, "There are no people on earth with whom I would rather be united than with the Wittenbergers." But despite that he remained in his error, and Luther remained with the truth. May we remember Luther for his faithfulness; he followed his Savior. The greatest principle of the Lutheran Church has since then been, "It is written." This is the foundation upon which Christ builds His Church, so that the gates of hell cannot prevail against it.

Now listen to my last admonition, my dear hearers: If you stay with the Word, you remain with Christ. If you remain with Christ, you remain in grace. Grace will lead you to eternal victory. Amen.

SECOND SUNDAY IN LENT

MATTHEW 15:21–28

Grace and peace be multiplied unto you through the knowledge of God, and of Jesus our Lord. Amen.

Greetings in our Savior, dearly beloved hearers!

Job said, "Has not man a hard service on earth, and are not his days like the days of a hired hand?" (7:1). Christ said to His disciples, "Strive to enter through the narrow door" (Luke 13:24). Paul added, "An athlete is not crowned unless he competes according to the rules" (2 Timothy 2:5). We see that struggling, striving, striving lawfully, that is, striving victoriously, are necessary for true Christianity.

Many suppose that when a person is converted, he can take it easy, like someone who has finally arrived in a safe harbor after a stormy voyage. The danger of being lost has passed. His soul is forever safe and need never fear shipwreck. This, however, is an extremely dangerous deception. When a person *is* finally converted, it is then that the battle really begins. When Christ says, "Strive to enter through the narrow door," He means with not only the first repentance but with the whole Christian life until death. All this taken together is the narrow way that leads to life.

If a person is converted, he is not all spirit but still has a good share of flesh. Of course, he is no longer *of* the world, yet he is *in* the world. He is no longer under the authority of darkness. However, he still lives where Satan, the prince of darkness, rules and goes about like a roaring lion, seeking whom he may devour. A converted person is therefore continually attacked by the flesh, the world, and the devil. If he does not continually fight against them, he will fall under their control before he expects it and his faith and salvation are as good as lost. If one does not struggle for his Christianity, he suffers continual defeat.

After conversion, the germ of sin does not remain only in a few but in all human hearts. He who does not believe this because he has not experienced it proves by his life that he has not yet become spiritually alive, or that he has fallen back into spiritual death. But if one feels how he is daily enticed to all manner of sin in thoughts, desires, words, and deeds, and yet does not struggle against them, considering these enticements as insignificant, he also is without the living, saving faith.

At times even a Christian deals unjustly with his neighbor—injures, vexes, and lovelessly judges him. At times even a Christian permits himself to be misled to speculate, yes, even defraud his neighbor in a business deal and swerve from the strict truth. At times even in a Christian anger, hatred, jealousy, envy, or malicious joy fills his heart, for Scripture says we fail in many ways. However, when a true Christian has failed, it is as if he had a sliver that continually pained him. He cannot rest until he has removed this sliver from his conscience by true repentance. Every false step awakens him to an inner struggle. If his attention is called to his sins by a fellow Christian, he does not show a hardened attitude; he soon breaks down, admits his sins, and becomes only the more humble and watchful.

On the other hand, if one falls into sin and it does not disturb him or awakens an inner battle within him; if he does not let himself be reprimanded, flies into a passion when he is reminded, and wants to have good done to him, he certainly is no Christian. His supposed faith is dead. It is not active through love. His heart is not cleansed from dead works; hence, no faith.

Ah my friends, let us not deceive ourselves with a Christianity without a continual battle.

However, though the struggle with the flesh, the world, and the devil is difficult, there is a struggle that is even more difficult, a battle in which the Christian can never stand, yet into which all Christians are at times more or less led. This is the struggle with God Himself. Our Gospel reading today deals with this amazing struggle. Let us therefore today become acquainted with this struggle.

The text: *Matthew 15:21–28*

A week ago in the Gospel of Invocavit Sunday Christ was presented to us as our example in the battle with Satan. In our Gospel reading today, another struggle, the victorious struggle with Christ, with God Himself, is presented in the Canaanite woman. The subject of our consideration today is

The victorious battle of Christians with God.

We consider:

1. How God battles with them, and
2. How they battle with God and conquer Him.

Lord, how wonderfully You associate with Your own. You struggle with them not to conquer them but to be conquered. You alone are the One who gives them power to conquer. You will crown them. Oh, teach us today from Your Word how to struggle with You and conquer, that You can also someday gloriously crown and lead us into Your eternal kingdom. Hear us for the sake of Jesus Christ, Your dear Son and the Lord of our salvation. Amen.

I.

God had chosen to entrust His saving Word to the Jewish nation. Yet we dare not think that God had done this because He did not want to have mercy on the heathen. Far be it! God chose the Jews for the very purpose of preserving His Word for the whole world. That is why God also had His people live at the crossroads of the world, why He brought them into contact with so many nations. The Jews should be, as it were, the candlesticks for the light of all nations. For that reason there were true believers not only among the Jews but also among the heathen; they were not circumcised and received by the Jews, but they believed the promise of the prophets and were saved by this faith.

The Canaanite woman in our Gospel reading today was such a heathen. She had come to faith in the teachings of the prophets, faith in the promised Savior of the world. And this faith had become so active in her that, when she heard of Jesus Christ's words and deeds in the land of the Jews, she (as Mark informs us) firmly believed that this Jesus must be the promised

Messiah. Although living in the midst of idolatrous, wicked heathen, she guarded the treasure of her faith against all the mockery and derision that she undoubtedly suffered from her heathen fellows.

Now shouldn't one suppose that God would have treated this woman, a pearl in the midst of that heathen filth, quite tenderly? Of course. But what do we hear? Now that she had come to faith, a heavy cross was laid upon her. Her daughter was possessed and grievously tormented by a devil. What sort of trouble that was only those know who have experienced it. In comparison with such a cross, everything else is insignificant. It is a heartrending sight for parents to see their dear child distressed and tormented by Satan day and night. The home is empty of all joy, a house of continual sorrow, fright, tears and sighs. Then add to it that as a rule not only the godless, blind world views such a family with malicious joy, but that even inexperienced Christians often pass evil judgment upon those who are so fearfully afflicted.

We hear still more, however. When her trouble reached its highest point, Christ came into the region. When she heard that, it seemed as if a bright star of hope and deliverance had risen in her hour of trial. In the firm confidence that Jesus, who had hitherto helped all the suffering, would help her also, she sought Him out. And the moment she found Him she cried loudly after Him, even from a distance, "Have mercy on me, O Lord, Son of David; my daughter is severely oppressed by a demon" (Matthew 15:22). But what did Christ do? Without bothering so much as to look around He went on, and, we read, "*did not answer her a word.*"

This was something completely unusual. On other occasions Christ not only stopped immediately when a cry for help reached His ears, but He also had questioned them as to what they wanted Him to do. Now, however, He remained silent as though He did not hear, despite the fact that the woman did not lessen her heartrending cries. This was so odd even to the disciples that they came to Christ and asked Him saying, "Send her away, for she is crying out after us" (15:23). They wanted to say: "Lord, do You not hear how this poor woman beseeches you? Will *our* heart almost break but *Yours* remain cold? Grant her request and permit her to live comforted!"

Yet what does Christ do now? He finally does say something, but only the hard words, "I was sent only to the lost sheep of the house of Israel" (15:24). Thereupon the disciples likewise became silent. When, however, the woman did not depart but rather merely stammered the words, "Lord, help me," Christ finally did turn also to her but with the crushing words, "It is not right to take the children's bread and throw it to the dogs" (15:25–26). Thus

He not only flatly refused the prayer of the woman, but also did it in such words that instead of grace expressed nothing but wrath, instead of esteem the deepest contempt.

Here my friends, you have a good example of how God at times struggles with His dear Christians. And we certainly see that, in general, God's struggles with His beloved Christians consists in His treating them as if they were not His dear children, but people about whom He is not concerned, yes, as if He were their enemy rather than their friend.

The first kind of struggle that God wages against the Christian is, as we see from the Canaanite woman, usually temporal distress. If not always bodily torment by Satan then at least it is other bodily misery, be it one's own sickness, the sickness and death of a loved one, poverty, loss of one's good name, the revelation of the faithlessness and falseness of friends whom one trusted, and all manner of other sorrow and misfortune. Far be it that God should keep those miraculously who are converted. It happens very often that as soon as a person leaves the world and becomes a true Christian, nothing prospers; everything fails. It appears as if God were against him in everything and were his enemy from the time that he became a Christian. God's Word says expressly, "Through many tribulations we *must* enter the kingdom of God" (Acts 14:22). And again, "All who desire to live a godly life in Christ Jesus will be persecuted" (2 Timothy 3:12).

Such bodily afflictions, however, are the easiest struggles that God wages with His Christians. In the Canaanite woman we see there is still another, a more difficult struggle. God often does not answer the prayers of a Christian in trouble. He is silent. The distress not only continues but becomes the greater the more earnestly the Christian prays. The children of the world are often quickly freed from their trouble; they murmur against God, rage, and curse, while the Christians who in their misfortune take refuge in God often sink only deeper and deeper.

And at times God is not satisfied even with this. Christ at first not only said nothing to the woman's cry for help, but when He finally spoke uttered only angry words. He said, when the disciples interceded, that He was not sent to the heathen, yes, compared the woman to a dog to whom the bread of the children did not belong. Christians often experience the same thing. Severe temptations of the soul often accompany the cross. God takes away all feeling of comfort. Their heart condemns them and says that they are sinners of whom God wants to know nothing. They are not elect but rejected.

They do not belong to the children of the kingdom but to dogs of whom it is written that they are outside.

Thus God often battles, as He did, for example, with Job and David. Job complains, "I cry to You for help and You do not answer me; I stand, and You only look at me. You have turned cruel to me; with the might of Your hand You persecute me" (30:20–21). And David complains, "But I, O LORD, cry to You; in the morning my prayer comes before You. O Lord, why do You cast my soul away? Why do You hide Your face from me? Afflicted and close to death from my youth up, I suffer Your terrors; I am helpless. Your wrath has swept over me; Your dreadful assaults destroy me" (Psalm 88:13–16). Whereas the godless suppose that they sit in God's lap, whereas they stand as firmly as a palace and are scarcely frightened of hell, God on the other hand often acts toward one of His real children as if He had rejected them. You see, this is the way in which God struggles with Christians.

II.

Let us in the second place hear how Christians should be the victor when God struggles with them.

A matchless example is the Canaanite woman in our text.

The first thing she did in her difficulty is that, when Christ came into the vicinity, she sought Him out, imploring Him with the words, "Have mercy on me, O Lord, Son of David; my daughter is severely oppressed by a demon" (Matthew 15:22). Since we are not informed that she did something before in order to be freed of her trouble, we can conclude that she bore this in humility and patience as a well deserved, wholesome cross and waited for the help of the Lord without complaint. But when her hope rose when Christ came into her region, she prayed for the removal of her almost unbearable cross. On what did she base her petition? She said, "Have mercy on me." She did not base her prayer to be heard on the claim that she deserved it because of her faithfulness in the midst of heathen but only on Christ's mercy. When she called Christ "Lord," she means to say, "I know that *You can* help me." And when she says to Him, "Son of David," she means to say, "I know that You will help me also, for You are the Savior and Redeemer promised by the prophets."

And what did she do when at first Christ not only remained silent when the disciples interceded, but even with a forbidding attitude stated, "I was sent only to the lost sheep of the house of Israel," and apparently wanted her to understand that she did not belong to the elect? The woman did not admit defeat; she simply fell down before Christ and said, "Lord, help me!" She means to say, "I will not search into or dispute concerning God's secret eternal counsel, whether I am elect or not. It appears as if I do not belong to the elect. But what do I care about appearances? I cling to the Word, which offers grace to all sinners without exception."

What, however, did she finally do when Christ assailed her even more fiercely and angrily said to her, "It is not right to take the children's bread and throw it to the dogs" (15:26)? She did two things: first, she acknowledged the truth of Christ's words; second, she availed herself of Christ's own words. She says, "Yes, Lord." She means to say, "You are right. By nature I am a heathen. I am like a dog that can lay no claim to the right of a child." But at the same time she takes Christ at His own words and adds, "Yet even the dogs eat the crumbs that fall from their masters' table" (15:27). She intends to say, "You have not called me a child of the devil but a dog. So at least You mean to grant what one gives a dog, a little crumb of Your grace which falls from the table of children." And behold! Christ was taken in His own words. He was conquered. Therefore, He cries out, " 'O woman, great is your faith! Be it done for you as you desire.' And her daughter was healed instantly" (15:28).

There, my friends, you see in this example how Christians can be victorious over God Himself. The art of their warfare is very simple: 1. Patience and humility; 2. Ardent and unceasing prayer. 3. And finally (and this is their chief weapon) a faith that holds firm in God's Word despite their experience and the feelings of their heart.

If God wrestles with the Christian through affliction, poverty, sickness, death of a loved one, disgrace, or other misfortune, they do not think as do the children of the world and false Christians: "What have I done to deserve this? Why must I experience evil while others who are more wicked than I are happy?" Much less do Christians try to help themselves in the wrong way. No, first they patiently carry their cross and think that it could be far worse; yes, they deserved hell. After that they pray without ceasing. Above all, they take their refuge in God's Word and rely on what is written, "Those whom I love, I reprove and discipline" (Revelation 3:19). "For those who love God all things work together for good" (Romans 8:28).

Should God assail Christians with severe temptations of the soul, should He not permit them to find comfort, should He permit them to feel nothing but darkness, sin, wrath, death, and hell, if they think that they are pushed away from God's presence and cast away even from eternity, they do not stop praying even then.

And if things seem to become worse instead of better, they do not give up praying. Above all, they seize the sword of the Spirit, which is God's Word, and the shield of faith. They own that God is right and say, "I have deserved that He reject me completely." However, they at the same time cling to God's universal promises: "Whoever comes to Me I will never cast out" (John 6:37). "I have no pleasure in the death of the wicked" (Ezekiel 33:11). "Where sin increased, grace abounded all the more" (Romans 5:20).

And see, the temptation in the one case lasts a much shorter time, in another a longer time, but finally they conquer God. The temptation is taken from them and the light of grace and joy once more shines brightly. God gladly lets Himself be conquered. He does not struggle against Christians in order to conquer but to be conquered by them.

Hence I ask you if you have already experienced something of this struggle with God? Have you at times, like this Canaanite woman imploring, sighing, and crying, wrestled with God in the stillness of your chamber? Whoever experienced nothing of this has a bad sign, for God lets every true Christian taste this. An unmolested faith is certainly a dead, empty faith. If you can tell of some struggle with God, I ask you: have you also passed through this struggle victoriously? Alas, many become Christians, but as soon as temptation comes they fall like wormy fruit. If God sends them poverty, they do not bear it in patience with prayer and faith, but they become only the more zealous to seek ways, so to say, of becoming rich to spite God. And so instead of being exercised in faith by the temptation, they suffer shipwreck of their faith. Others, from whom God takes the sweet feeling of grace, lose their Christian faith instead of learning to cling the more to God's Word. They again surrender to the world.

Oh my friends, do not deceive yourselves in regard to your salvation. Do not think that because Christianity preaches pure grace it is a restful and comfortable life. Learn rather that it is a continual struggle, a struggle not only with the flesh, the world, and the devil but with God Himself. Whoever does not engage in this struggle every day but wishes to make the Gospel of grace a comfortable pillow, his entire Christianity with all his Christian air and talk is nothing but an empty pretense. It is a frightening word that Christ says, "Strive to enter through the narrow door. For many, I tell you, will seek to enter and will not be able" (Luke 13:24). If many of *those* will not enter the kingdom of God who actually seek it, what will happen to those who do not once strive for it?

You, you Israels, who with Jacob daily struggle with God, and on your knees before Him say to Him, "I will not let You go unless You bless me" (Genesis 32:26), oh, do not only remain in your spiritual knighthood. Consider that the times will become ever more evil, the attacks ever more fearful, the temptations ever more deceiving and dangerous; therefore, become ever more brave and daring. Do not let the sweet enticing Delilah of this world rock you to sleep but struggle ever more earnestly. You will not regret it. Many victorious battles mean much blessed peace! When some time you will leave the battlefield of this world as victor, you will hear the blessed voice, "You have striven with God and with men, and have prevailed" (Genesis 32:28). Enter into the joy of thy Lord. Amen.

THIRD SUNDAY IN LENT

LUKE 11:14–28

Grace and peace be multiplied unto you through the knowledge of God, and of our Savior Jesus Christ. Amen.

In the name of our Savior, dear hearers!

Though there are *many* realms in which a person can be according to his *body*, there are only *two* realms in which he can be according to his *soul*: God's or the devil's. Every person is in one of these two, whether he is a heathen or a Christian, old or young, learned or ignorant, rich or poor, of high or low estate, beggar or king.

As according to God's Word there are two ways by which a person can enter eternity—the narrow way which leads to life and the broad way which leads to damnation—so there are only two places where a person will spend eternity: the place of blessedness, heaven, or the place of torment, hell. There are only two kingdoms to which every person belongs: the kingdom of light or darkness, the kingdom of faith or unbelief, the kingdom of sin or righteousness, the kingdom of grace or wrath, the kingdom of life or death, in short, God's or the devil's. There is no third. And as there is no middle kingdom, it is impossible to be in both *at the same time*. A person is completely in the one or the other. The Lord states this quite clearly in the well-known words, "No one can serve two masters, for either he will hate the one and love the other, or he will be devoted to the one and despise the other. You cannot serve God and money" (Matthew 6:24).

There are true Christians who are in God's kingdom but in their great spiritual temptations suppose that they still belong to the devil's. They, however, are only a few. On the other hand, the number of those who are still under the power of darkness cannot be counted. Yet they suppose that they are in God's kingdom. Repentant David, who was rescued from great temptation, says of himself, "I had said in my alarm, 'I am cut off from Your sight.' But You heard the voice of my pleas for mercy when I cried to You for help" (Psalm 31:22). On the other hand, the unrepentant Jews of whom Christ testified, "You are of your father the devil, and your will is to do your father's desires" (John 8:44), notwithstanding said insolently and positively, "We have one Father—even God" (John 8:41).

Though even one glance into the kingdom of darkness is frightening, it is highly important to take a look. And since in our Gospel today Christ reveals that there is not only a Satan, but that he has also an organized kingdom on earth, and since those who belong to this kingdom are at the same time clearly described in our Gospel, permit me to speak to you of this kingdom.

The text: Luke 11:14–28

In our text, Christ Jesus victoriously defends Himself against the slander of the Pharisees. They claimed that Christ's astounding miracles were to be explained by the fact that He was not, as other sorcerers were, in league with lesser evil spirits, but with Beelzebub, the chief of the devils. He could therefore drive out even the mightiest of evil spirits. Since Christ on this occasion also revealed that Satan has a formal kingdom and described in detail its nature, subjects, allies, weapons, and practices, and how one is delivered from it, permit me on the basis of our text to speak to you on

The devil's kingdom.

Let me show you,

1. The nature of this kingdom, and
2. How a person is delivered from it.

Lord Jesus Christ, Son of God, You appeared in the world for the purpose of destroying the works of the devil. You alone really stripped the infernal principalities and powers, made a show of them openly, and held a triumphant procession. Alas, thousands, however, still willfully remain obedient subjects of the enemy of souls, whom you conquered long ago. Oh, have mercy on all these unfortunate souls! Show them what a shameful lord they serve, and what fearful wages await them if they remain with him. Tear in pieces the bands of error and sin with which they are bound. Bring them with the finger of your Holy Spirit out of the annex of hell in which they are held captive and lead them into Your blessed kingdom of grace. Lord Jesus, You who have the keys of death and hell, of heaven and life, hear us for the sake of Your victory. Amen.

I.

In our Gospel reading today Christ defends Himself, saying, "And if Satan also is divided against himself, how will his kingdom stand? For you say that I cast out demons by Beelzebul" (Luke 11:18). Herewith He in a general way reveals that there actually is a kingdom in which the devil is king.

Christ in our Gospel reading gives us no information as to the *origin* of this kingdom. But the Holy Scriptures give us sufficient information in other places. They tell us that Satan did not continue in the truth but left his home with the angels who did not keep their kingdom. Hence, the devil's kingdom, unlike God's, has not existed from the beginning. Satan was also during the great week of creation created good and holy. Later on he fell from God with an innumerable host, who were also created holy angels. With them he founded a great kingdom hostile to God in which he, Satan, is leader, head, prince, and king, and in which originally only the fallen angels were his subjects.

As Satan and his confederates became enemies of *God*, so they became enemies of the *works* and *counsels* of God. As soon as the first people were created in the image of God, Satan planned to cause men also to fall from God and drag them into his kingdom of darkness. How quickly Satan carried out this plan and how successful he was, we know from the story of our first parents' fall into sin. The moment Satan injected into man's heart the poison of sin and hatred of God's holiness, he annexed also the whole human race. Since every man is already born a sinner and a child of wrath, he is as soon as he sees the light of day subject to the authority of darkness. In Holy Writ Satan is therefore called a prince and god not only of a few people but also of the world. He is the Old Serpent who deceives the whole world.

As by nature there is no difference between men but all are *sinners*, so all men are also by nature *subjects* of the prince of darkness; the newborn child of the king just as well as the child of the beggar, that of the Christian as well as the non-Christian. Thus the apostle says to the Christians at Ephesus, "You were dead in the trespasses and sins in which you once walked, following the course of this world, following the prince of the power of the air, the spirit that is now at work in the sons of disobedience—among whom we all once lived in the passions of our flesh, carrying out the desires of the body and the mind, and were by nature children of wrath, like the rest of mankind" (Ephesians 2:1–3).

Satan's kingdom was great even before the kingdom of mankind was annexed. But by that annexation it became immeasurably greater, growing greater with every year, yes, with every passing day.

As soon as Satan had brought mankind into his power, God at once promised a Redeemer who would crush the head of the serpent. God actually sent His only-begotten Son and through Him won freedom from the power of Satan for all men. It is further true that through Christ millions of souls were again torn away from the prince of darkness and led back into God's kingdom of grace and glory. Every day ever more are converted from darkness to light, from the power of Satan to God. Yet the number of men who live under the authority of darkness despite Christ's victory over Satan is immeasurably great. Among them, as Christ in our text states, Satan is "a strong man, fully armed, [who] guards his own palace," and whose "goods are safe" because these heathen have not allowed their only Redeemer to enter (Luke 11:21). But not only this—even the most of those who consider themselves members of God's kingdom belong, it is frightening to say, to Satan's kingdom.

The important question arises: who are they? We find the answer in our text. It relates that Christ drove the devil, who was dumb and blind, from one possessed and in a second had given him sight, hearing, and speech. As the people were filled with amazement at this great miracle, some, probably the Pharisees, uttered the fearful slander, "He casts out demons by Beelzebul, the prince of demons" (Luke 11:15). In vain Christ showed them that this statement was not only malicious but also completely unreasonable; if Satan would thus war against himself, his kingdom would not stand and before long he would himself destroy it. In vain Christ reminded them that even their very own children at times used the name of Jesus to drive out a devil; that with this statement they merely condemned themselves. Convinced in their reason and smitten in their conscience, they still clung to their horrible slander.

The first group is presented to us in these Pharisees. Living among Christians and within call of the Gospel, they still belong to the kingdom of the devil. These are all those who in open unbelief or in manifest sin go against their own conscience. To them belong all those who do not know Christianity yet maliciously and unreasonably slander it; or those, if they know the Bible, reject the arguments that they admit for other matters and even against all reason only mock it to scorn. This is clearly a more than human maliciousness and shows that they must do this because they are subjects and prisoners of the devil, to whose kingdom they belong.

On the other hand, others do not slander the teachings of God's Word by word of mouth, perhaps even confess it, but they live in manifest *sin*; the one in gross idolatry, the other in cursing, swearing, perjury, and sorcery; the third in despising prayer, God's Word, and the ministry; a fourth in despising his parents and revolting against the government; a fifth in hatred of his enemy, cruelty, vindictiveness, irreconcilableness, strife, and envy; a sixth in lust, unchastity, gluttony, drunkenness; a seventh in deceit, defrauding, careless borrowing and not repaying, in usury, yes, in thievery; an eighth in lies and slander; a ninth in all manner of tricks and practices under a show of right. All of them know that these are mortal sins by which a person can neither be in grace nor inherit the kingdom of God. In vain they hear or read God's Word; in vain they are often warned, urgently warned and rebuked. They see that they are on the road straight to hell—but lo! everything is in vain. They remain in their sins and still hope for grace. This reveals most clearly a more than natural corruption. It is satanic blindness and shows that all these servants of sin are under the invisible control of the prince of darkness and are obedient subjects of his kingdom.

Our text also pictures some who were not a party to the slander but who also did not side with Christ. It says they "to test Him, kept seeking from Him a sign from heaven" (11:16). They act as though they were ready to decide for Christ—only one thing is lacking. Christ should do a sign just like Moses, who caused bread to rain from heaven, or like Joshua, who commanded the sun and moon to stand still. But what does Christ say? He says, "Whoever is not with Me is against Me, and whoever does not gather with Me scatters" (11:23). We see that they do not belong in Christ's kingdom but in the devil's. They, so to say, wish to be neutral in the war between Christ and the world. They do not want to spoil it for themselves with Christ or with the world. They do not wish to make a complete break with their old Adam or with God; in short, they straddle the fence.

They also wish to be Christians, but they say that they still have this or that which hinders them from doing their full Christian duty. They want to be considered a Christian brother, but when they see that Christians are busy on behalf of God's kingdom and against Satan's in a completely different way than they are, they say that that is uncalled for, fanaticism, enthusiasm; one must accommodate oneself to the times; one must be wise and prudent; it is often better to be silent and give in a bit than to rage, hastily bring Christ's enemies down on one's neck, and plunge into an impractical battle; one does best if one goes the middle way, now and then going to church and communion, but then as much as possible keeping to oneself.

But what is the true cause of this conduct? It so happens that all such without suspecting it belong in the devil's kingdom; he does not permit them to see that fundamentally they are still enemies of the cross of Christ, enemies of His grace, His Word, His kingdom, His Church, His believers. The devil holds them captive in his net; they do his will. He deceives them most shamefully. God says: "Either completely Mine or not at all; leave the devil completely and join Christ, that is the way to do it." The devil, on the other hand, gladly permits his subjects to be a half-Christian, be somewhat pious, do this or that good work, for then he has them the more securely in his power. Such half-Christians are the most unfortunate of all of the devil's subjects, because they are secure. They suppose that they lack nothing, they are going the correct middle road, and they therefore always live in the delusion that they are members of Christ's kingdom. But they go to hell with their imagined faith, while often even Christians suppose that they died to go to eternal life in yonder world, and faithful pastors have even comforted them on their very deathbed.

How great the devil's kingdom is in the very midst of Christendom. In it belong not only all unbelievers and servants of sin but also all hypocrites, all who are not really serious about their piety, all who still have no new heart born through the Holy Spirit, all who do not wish to be fools for Christ's sake, in short, all who do not want to side with Christ in everything. Christ clearly says, "Whoever is not with Me is against Me, and whoever does not gather with Me scatters" (11:23). Christ's kingdom is only a small, despised, scarcely noticed little flock, but the devil's is the great respected multitude, for everything that is great, high, wise, noble, brave, and upright in the eyes of the world belongs to this hostile kingdom.

Christ calls Satan "a strong man, fully armed, guard[ing] his own palace" (11:21). His kingdom is also a strong, fortified kingdom, well equipped with all manner of weapons and strengthened by powerful allies. Among these powerful allies and their weapons belong, above all, the sinful flesh of all men, even of Christians, man's corrupt, evilly inclined heart with its evil thoughts and desires, all evil examples and offenses of the godless, all errors and prejudices of men, all the delightful conceit and glory of the world, its lust, its amusements, its riches and treasures, its honor and glory, its parades with pomp and splendor, its appearance of wisdom—all this is in the service of this kingdom. All authors and propagators of false religion, all originators and defenders of false churches, all philosophers or worldly wise, all writers and unchristian books and publishers of godless periodicals, and the books and periodicals themselves, countless as the sands of the sea, are faithful apostles of the devil. Yes, all unconverted people as a group are his countless standing army for the spreading and maintenance of his hellish kingdom on earth.

As great and strong as this kingdom is, so united is it also. On the surface no kingdom appears to be more disunited than this one, for in it is nothing else than hatred, wrath, strife, discord, lies, slander, deceit, theft, enticement, persecution of the innocent, war, murder, and bloodshed. But this continual battle on earth amongst itself, this eternal war, is in the devil's kingdom nothing else than golden peace. Since it is a kingdom of darkness, lovelessness, hate, sin, maliciousness, and enmity against God, Satan possesses his kingdom the more in untroubled peace the more his subjects battle and lacerate one another.

II.

Now that I have described this kingdom in some detail, it is time to show you how a person can be delivered from it.

If this is to take place, three things are necessary: First, a person must perceive that he has been under the power of darkness. Second, he must be heartily frightened and filled with an inner longing to be delivered from this fearful and shameful power. And third, Satan must lose his right to accuse him before God and must lose the power to rule him.

As little as a dead person can awaken himself from the dead, so little can a person deliver himself from the kingdom of the devil. The first obstacle is that the person does not by his own reason recognize his true condition. Everyone is by nature completely blind in all spiritual things; he does not know the natural enmity of his heart against God. Yes, Satan even blinds him to such a degree that he either does not believe that there is a kingdom of the devil, or that he supposes that he does not belong to it. The most blind in this matter are not those who sit in gross unbelief and manifest sins but who are neutral, who do not openly reject Christ but also do not give their heart completely to Him.

A second obstacle is that because a person's heart naturally loves sin and the things of this world, he does not wish to be delivered from his shameful slavery; yes, he loves the chains wherewith he is bound.

The third obstacle is that the person cannot forgive his own sins. He cannot protect himself from the accusation of the devil. He cannot tear the ties with which Satan binds him to sin, cannot change his heart himself, cannot himself make it love God, and thus cannot free himself from the authority of Satan.

Now where, my friends, can one find deliverance? Not from any creature; only from Jesus Christ, the Son of God and Redeemer of the world. "If the Son sets you free," He Himself says, "you will be free indeed" (John 8:36). As strongly armed as Satan is who keeps his palace with great power and cunning, Christ, nevertheless, as He Himself says in our text, is the "stronger." When he "attacks him and overcomes him, he takes away his armor in which he trusted and divides his spoil" (Luke 11:22).

Christ, however, compels none by irresistible grace to leave Satan's kingdom. "Blessed rather are those," He says at the close of our Gospel, "who hear the word of God and keep it!" (Luke 11:28). Thus He indicates that the means which He applies for the deliverance of souls from Satan's kingdom is God's Word. The finger of God, that is, the Holy Spirit, is inseparably connected with God's Word alone. Many must therefore hear and keep God's Word. If a person does that, the finger of God or the Holy Spirit frees him from the bonds of the devil with divine power.

First of all, the Holy Spirit convinces him that hitherto he had been under the power of darkness, then he works a wholesome fright in him over this fact, and a deep yearning to be delivered from it. Finally, the Spirit calls him to faith in Jesus Christ, bringing him the forgiveness of his sins, filling him with power to hate all works of the devil, all, even the most subtle sins, completely and eternally renouncing obedience to the devil, victoriously struggling against him, and with a new heart walking in newness of life.

God's Word is preached to many thousands. Yet they remain under the authority of darkness because they willfully resist the Holy Spirit. Others let themselves be rescued for a time but become secure, their heart is then, as the Lord says, "swept and put in order" (Luke 11:25), well prepared to receive the old guest again. The unclean spirit returns from the dry places of heathenism to which he had gone. He yearns to sit where Christ was enthroned shortly before: "it goes and brings seven other spirits more evil than itself, and they enter and dwell there. And the last state of that person is worse than the first" (11:26).

There are always several, as the woman in our Gospel, who let themselves be delivered by the Word. When she had heard Christ speak, moved by the Holy Spirit, full of divine courage amongst that mob of Christ's enraged, blood-thirsty foes, she cried out loudly, "Blessed is the womb that bore you, and the breasts at which you nursed!" (11:27). These words show how weak she still was in knowledge. Christ corrected her with the words, "Blessed rather are those who hear the word of God and keep it!" (11:28). With these words Christ testifies that though she is not His earthly mother, she is nevertheless blessed because she heard and kept God's words.

Go, my friends, and do thou likewise! Now you have also heard God's words. The kingdom of darkness is thereby opened and the means to be delivered from it has been shown. Oh, now receive this Word in a good and honest heart and keep it. God has knocked on your heart to enlighten you, give you a salutary fright, fill you with a desire for freedom, draw you to Christ, and equip you with the power of victory over Satan. Oh, do not resist Him! In Baptism you renounced the devil and all his works and all his ways, and promised yourself to the triune God, Father, Son, and Holy Ghost. Renew your most sacred baptismal oath again today! Renounce not only the gross works of the flesh. What does it profit if you are not tied by the prince of darkness with heavy chains but with silken cords? "Whoever is not with Me is against Me," says Christ; "and whoever does not gather with Me scatters" (Matthew 12:30). Renounce the world and its ungodly ways completely; in each and every thing stick to Christ! Otherwise your half Christianity will be lost anyhow, and Christ will say to you, "I never knew you; depart from Me, you workers of lawlessness" (7:23).

Rejoice, you whom God has already delivered from the power of darkness and translated into the kingdom of His dear Son. You are happy people. He who is in you is greater than he who is in the world. You have a good and strong Lord who will continue the good work that He has begun in you until that day. Remain with him! Some day Satan and his whole kingdom with all his subjects will be hurled into the fiery pit, but you will shine as the sun in your Father's kingdom forever and ever. Amen.

FOURTH SUNDAY IN LENT

JOHN 6:1–15

Grace and peace be multiplied unto you through the knowledge of God, and of Jesus, our Lord. Amen.

In the name of our Savior, dearly beloved hearers!

The Jews were not wrong when they supposed that their Messiah would be a great king and found a glorious kingdom that would spread throughout the whole world, embracing all the nations of the earth. In the prophetic writings of the Old Testament this was predicted so clearly that a believing Israelite could get no other idea of the Messiah and His work.

God said to Abraham, "In your offspring shall *all the nations of the earth* be blessed" (Genesis 22:18). Afterwards God solemnly repeated this same promise to Isaac and Jacob. Dying Jacob comforted himself with the thought that some time Shiloh would come from Judah, "and to him shall be the obedience of the *peoples*" (Genesis 49:10). David received the same promise later. The Lord said to him, "When your days are fulfilled and you lie down with your fathers, I will raise up your offspring after you, who shall come from your body, and I will establish his kingdom. He shall build a house for My name, and I will establish the throne of his kingdom forever" (2 Samuel 7:12–13).

As a result of these prophecies, not only the Psalms but also the writings of all later prophets are full of the plainest predictions that the Messiah would be a king. He would found a kingdom that would reach from one end of the earth to the other, in which the sun would never set. For example, in Psalm 89 we read, "I have granted help to one who is mighty; I have exalted one chosen from the people. . . . I will set his hand on the sea and his right hand on the rivers. . . . And I will make him the firstborn, the highest of the kings of the earth. . . . Once for all I have sworn by my holiness; I will not lie to David. His offspring shall endure forever, his throne as long as the sun before me" (vv. 19, 25, 27, 35–36). Moreover, we read in Jeremiah 33:14–15: "Behold, the days are coming, declares the LORD, when I will fulfill the promise I made to the house of Israel and the house of Judah. In those days and at that time I will cause a righteous Branch to spring up for David"; [Luther: and He shall be a *king* and shall rule righteously] "and he shall execute justice and righteousness in the land."

The prophets worked not only when the Jewish nation was in its prime but also when all its glory and hope in the eyes of men were gone as it languished in the Assyrian and Babylonian captivity; even then the prophets foretold the future of the messianic King and His glorious kingdom that would vanquish all other kingdoms. Daniel, who himself was languishing in captivity, writes after he had described the four world monarchies, "And in the days of those kings the God of heaven will set up a kingdom that shall never be destroyed, nor shall the kingdom be left to another people. It shall break in pieces all these kingdoms and bring them to an end, and it shall stand forever" (Daniel 2:44).

And behold! when Jesus, the promised Messiah, was about to be born, even the heavenly messenger declared, "He will be great and will be called the Son of the Most High. And the Lord God will give to Him the throne of His father David, and He will reign over the house of Jacob forever, and of His kingdom there will be no end" (Luke 1:32–33). Yes, when Christ appeared publicly, the very first thing that He preached was that the great kingdom that had been promised was nearing. "Repent," He cried, "for the kingdom of heaven is at hand" (Matthew 4:17). Christ called His whole teaching "the Gospel of the kingdom" (4:23).

Far be it that Christ should have been silent about the doctrine that He, as the Messiah, was a king and had a kingdom. Rather, when He entered Jerusalem for the last time for His suffering, He publicly received homage as the King of Israel; He defended Himself against the offense that the Pharisees took when, scattering palm branches before Him, the people sang to Him, "Hosanna! Blessed is He who comes in the name of the Lord, even the *King of Israel*!" (John 12:13; cf. Mark 11:9). Yes, when Christ stood before Pilate, and accused of an insurrection, was asked, "So You are a king?" He publicly and solemnly answered, "You say that I am a king" (John 18:37).

Hence, there can be no doubt. The Jews of Christ's time did not err when they believed that their Messiah must be a great king and rule the world. But their ideas of the nature of Christ's kingdom, which most (even the best of them) entertained, were all wrong. If only these ideas had disappeared with those times! Yes, even nowadays most Christians have the same Jewish ideas of Christ's kingdom. Today's Gospel invites us to consider this for our warning and encouragement. Let us now, through God's grace, accept this invitation. Let us first entreat God for His assistance and blessing by saying a believing Lord's Prayer.

The text: John 6:1–15

That Christ fed many thousands with a little bread and a few fish is repeatedly told us in the Scriptures. But the specific thing in the story of our text consists in this, that when the people saw the miracles which Jesus did, they not only said, "This is indeed the Prophet who is to come into the world," that is, the promised Messiah, but they also decided to "take Him by force and make Him king," Although now it seems as though this occurred only then, this just is not true. In a certain sense this not only *can*, but it also actually *does* take place only too often today and by only too many Christians. This is also what I propose to show you today, namely:

Even now many want to seize Jesus and make Him a king.

They are all those who

1. Without change of heart want to become and remain citizens of Christ's kingdom, and
2. Seek ease and good days in Christ's kingdom.

Lord Jesus, You are the exalted God-man, King in the three kingdoms of power, grace, and glory. We are all in Your kingdom of power, in which all heathen, yes all creatures, are subject to You and must serve You. Whether we belong to You in the kingdom of grace, You alone know. Hence, reveal to us by Your Holy Word whether we are or not; awaken those of us who are still far from it, that they hurriedly enter it through true repentance. May those who already serve You in it promise You new, greater, more ardent faithfulness, that we finally enter the inner sanctuary of Your kingdom of glory, and with all the angels and saints praise You forever and ever. Amen.

I.

Before Christ fed the people so miraculously He "began to teach them many things" (Mark 6:34). He dealt, as the evangelist Luke adds, with "the kingdom of God" (9:11). We do not read just exactly *what* Christ said in this sermon on His kingdom. But how Christ was accustomed to describe His kingdom, we know from other passages of the Gospels. He usually presented it as something most glorious—for example, He compared it with a treasure buried in a field, to a costly pearl, to a wedding feast, to a great banquet, and so on. Beyond a doubt He spoke then in a similar way of His messianic kingdom.

Christ's sermon of His wonderful kingdom appears to have made a deep impression on the people and filled them with a great desire to belong to it. For what did they do? At the close of His sermon Christ did not, as they might have expected or wished, solemnly admit them as citizens of His kingdom. They probably thought that Christ did not want to start His kingdom immediately because He feared He would have no subjects; they wanted to use force, seize Christ, declare themselves His subjects, and make Him their king.

That this was foolish needs no proof. Since Christ did not *let* Himself be seized by them, but quickly escaped to a mountain in order to avoid their forwardness, it is clear that this whole project was a plan of the flesh and completely against the mind of Christ.

Today all Christians recognize that. Nevertheless, most are guilty of exactly the same folly that Christ's hearers once were. In what does this foolishness consist? Since they wanted to seize Christ and make Him their king, they thought they could be and remain His subjects just as they were, without repentance and conversion, without a change of heart, merely by an outward confession and clinging to Christ.

In what way do most of the so-called Christians think and act differently today? They are baptized; they perceive that Christ actually must be the Savior of the world; they also confess this publicly in that they go to Church and Holy Communion and are with Christians. They suppose that they have made Christ their king and have become His subjects. But as the hearers of Christ sadly deceived themselves, so do countless Christians today—as once Christ did not let Himself be seized by men and made a King, so He does not today.

The condition for entry into the kingdom of Christ is far different than for entry into a political state. One becomes a citizen of a state by going to the place where the state is. One will become a citizen by taking the oath of citizenship, swearing allegiance, obeying the laws of the land, paying taxes, and, if it becomes necessary, joining the army for the defense of the land. The officials do not ask in what conviction or with what sort of a heart one does this.

It is far different in the kingdom of Christ. This is an invisible, spiritual, heavenly kingdom, a kingdom of hearts and souls. It is everywhere—one can be *in* this kingdom everywhere just as well as *outside* it. Wherever a person is, he can enter into Christ's kingdom. However, wherever he may go, he nowhere comes into the kingdom nor closer to it. One enters it only through receiving a new heart. Everything external either does not *belong* in this kingdom or is only a *means* that works the inward change of heart and through which a person should join this kingdom. One can by no good work enter this kingdom. He may work for it ever so earnestly, give ever so much, fight for it ever so hard, yes, suffer ever so much for it, and even let himself be burned; if he does not have that new, changed heart, he would be a tool, a worker, a mercenary, but not a member, not a subject, not a citizen of this kingdom. Wherever you find hearts in which sin no longer rules but is ruled by them, in which Christ really and truly has set up His throne, and which He moves, controls, and rules, there and only there is Christ's kingdom. Whoever has not yet experienced this change of heart, or has lost this changed heart again is not a citizen of Christ's kingdom. If he still wants to be a citizen, he is one who in a foolish way seizes Christ and wants to make Him king. But love's labor is lost! As Christ did not *then* let Himself be seized, so He does not let it happen today.

All of you who do and suffer much for the kingdom of Christ, who work and sacrifice much, who have earnestly separated yourselves from the world, who have denied yourselves much, but who in so doing have no new heart in which Christ rules, yes, you who have absolutely nothing to show for your attachment to Christ's kingdom except that you are baptized, go to church and Communion, yet live like the children of this world, ah, don't be such big fools as to take it for granted that you have become members of Christ's kingdom. You are still *outside*! Christ does not want to be seized by you. And if you *remain* without a changed heart, you will in eternity see with terror that, as He according to our text once vanished from the Jews, He will vanish from you forever and will leave you alone.

Perhaps at this point a poor sinner to whom his salvation is no joke may say: What should I do in order that I might have such a changed heart and become a citizen of Christ's kingdom? The answer is simple, and Christ has given it long ago. He began all His sermons with the words, "Repent, for the kingdom of heaven is at hand."

The first step in repentance is that one from God's Word learns to know what an evil, corrupt, sinful heart one has by nature and become heartily sorrowful and frightened. If a person wants that, he must not only read God's Word with great attention but he must also fervently and diligently implore

God that His Holy Spirit truly expose his wicked heart. He must be serious about it. His resolution to learn to know himself must not be like the morning frost that melts at the first rays of the sun.

It is not enough, however, for him to know the sinfulness of his heart and be filled with shame, remorse, sadness, and hatred of himself. He must then in faith learn to know the Lord Jesus, who is the only doctor for such sickness, who is the real helper and Savior for such miserable sinners. He must in faith comfort himself with His grace and merit. And this matter is not disposed of with the sigh of cold lips, "God, be merciful to me, a sinner!" One must become quite familiar, yes, intimate, with Jesus. He is the true and only friend of his soul. He does so partly by the continual incitement of the sweet Gospel in his heart, partly through unceasing prayer for grace. As Jacob he wrestles with Jesus and says, "I will not let You go unless You bless me" (Genesis 32:26).

Whoever does that will soon experience that Jesus will not only knock, but will Himself open the door of his heart, enter in, change it from top to bottom, erect His throne in it, rule in it as a king, and so spread His kingdom of grace in it. For we do not come to the kingdom of God, but the kingdom of God comes to us. We do not pray, "Let us come to Thy kingdom," but "Thy kingdom come to us."

II.

However, my friends, we continue. Even today many want to seize Christ and make Him king. As we have heard, they not only want to be citizens of Christ's kingdom without a change of heart, but also seek in it only ease and good days. And it is this that we wish to consider now.

How does it happen that though Christ had done the greatest miracles before—made the blind see, the lame walk, the deaf hear, the dumb speak, the lepers clean, yes, the dead alive—that the people had not wanted to make Christ king but only after He fed thousands for the second time with a little bread and a few fishes? This undoubtedly happened because they concluded from the repetition of the miracle, that in Christ's kingdom one could without work find a well-spread table, freedom from want, war, cross, and trouble, in short, ease and good days. Yes, that was the reason why they hurriedly wanted to proclaim Christ king, crown, anoint, and swear allegiance to Him as once they did to David.

This sketches a true picture of most so-called Christians. This seems to be an extremely severe judgment. But judge for yourself! How many baptized Christians are there who are serious about salvation? God's Word says, "Seek first the kingdom of God and His righteousness, and all these things will be added to you" (Matthew 6:33). "If we have food and clothing, with these we will be content. But those who desire to be rich fall into temptation, into a snare, into many senseless and harmful desires that plunge people into ruin and destruction. For the love of money is a root of all kinds of evils. It is through this craving that some have wandered away from the faith and pierced themselves with many pangs" (1 Timothy 6:8–10). If we compare those who bear the Christian name with this word of God, what do we find? What do most so-called Christians do? Do they really seek first the kingdom of God and His righteousness? Are they satisfied with food and clothing? By no means! They want to be *rich, rich*! And even Christianity must serve that end. What they save by not joining in the costly worldly pleasures because they want to be Christians, that they do not give to God; they do not give or lend to the poor, the needy, nor for the purposes of God's kingdom; they quietly save it that their pile might become bigger and bigger; thus they can look into the future with more tranquility and say "I have made gold my trust or called fine gold my confidence!" (Job 31:24). Yes, they secretly practice the most shameful usury and pretend to their needy brethren that they are poor. They say, "Yes my dear brother, I would gladly help you, but believe me, I have nothing myself." But they do not say that *everything* they have left over, they have quickly loaned out at interest.

Others are satisfied if they always have enough bread and fish, like the Jews in our text. A secure, carefree, comfortable life, that is the heaven they seek. God's Word says, "Let not sin therefore reign in your mortal body, to make you obey its passions" (Romans 6:12). "Those who belong to Christ Jesus have crucified the flesh with its passions and desires" (Galatians 5:24). "An athlete is not crowned unless he competes according to the rules" (2 Timothy 2:5). But what do most so-called Christians do? Are they concerned about their sins? Do they seek to understand them ever more clearly? Do they battle against them? Do they despite their flesh diligently watch and pray, hear and read God's Word, that all sins may be purged from their hearts and life and thus grow in sanctification? Not at all! Most of them think: "To be that worried about sin is enthusiasm. That is pietism and Methodism. That is false legalism."

Many also think that they had once before repented and experienced the pain of contrition. Thank God! They are finished with that. What do they really search for in Christ's kingdom? Nothing else than ease and good days, as the Jews who once wanted to make Christ king after He had miraculously fed them. To them, however, Christ said when they later on hunted Him out, "Truly, truly, I say to you, you are seeking Me, not because you saw signs, but because you ate your fill of the loaves" (John 6:26). Thus Christ must say even today to many thousands of Christians: "You do not want to be Christians. You do not want to hear My Word, use My Sacraments, keep your distance from the world, and cling to My church because you have experienced My grace and power against sin but because you seek ease and good days for this world."

Can we believe that such Christians are citizens of Christ's kingdom? Never! Their whole Christianity is only a pretense whereby they deceive only themselves. To be sure, they suppose that they had *faith*, and therefore must be citizens of Christ's kingdom. But they are mistaken. Their faith is an empty pretense and self-deception. Yes, yes, my friends, it is written, "No one can serve two masters, for either he will hate the one and love the other, or he will be devoted to the one and despise the other. You cannot serve God and money" (Matthew 6:24). "So therefore, any one of you who does not renounce all that he has cannot be My disciple" (Luke 14:33). "If anyone comes to Me and does not hate his own father and mother and wife and children and brothers and sisters, yes, and even his own life, he cannot be My disciple" (14:26).

May God have mercy on us all that no one tries to straddle the fence, clings half to God and half to mammon, and divides his heart between Christ and the world. May we all seek only that one thing needful and in such striving not spare ourselves in our earthly calling, live to ourselves, but only for our King and Lord, Jesus Christ. Thus we will also have joy when He is revealed, and not become an object of shame before Him in His coming. Amen.

Fifth Sunday in Lent (1855)

John 8:46–59

Grace and peace be multiplied unto you through the knowledge of God, and of Jesus our Lord. Amen.

In our Savior, dearly beloved hearers!

Thus says the Lord in Mark 3, "All sins will be forgiven the children of man, and whatever blasphemies they utter, but whoever blasphemes against the Holy Spirit never has forgiveness, but is guilty of an *eternal* sin" (vv. 28–29). According to Matthew, the Lord also added, "The blasphemy against the Spirit will not be forgiven" (12:31). The author of Hebrews speaks of the same sin in the following manner: "For it is impossible, in the case of those who have once been enlightened, who have tasted the heavenly gift, and have shared in the Holy Spirit, and have tasted the goodness of the Word of God and the powers of the age to come, and then have fallen away, to restore them again to repentance" (6:4–6). John also mentions this sin. He writes, "There is sin that leads to death; I do not say that one should pray for that" (1 John 5:16).

We therefore conclude that there is a sin which can be forgiven neither in this world nor in the one to come, neither in time nor in eternity; no creature in heaven and on earth, yes, neither God nor men can forgive it. It is the sin against the Holy Spirit.

If one has committed this sin, repentance and conversion is not only difficult but absolutely impossible. He has taken a one-way road to hell and eternal death. Although he lives on earth, his time of grace has run out—every door of grace is closed. The sin against the Holy Spirit is like an incurable cancer—there is no cure; the heavenly physician Himself cannot heal him. No Christian should intercede with God for one who has committed this sin. The holy angels flee from him. God Himself has given him up. The sentence of damnation that God does not pronounce on other sinners until Judgment Day is pronounced on such a person even here. His heart is like an accursed field on which the sun no longer shines and the dew no longer falls. God no longer does a thing to save him. He no longer calls him, no longer enlightens him, no longer reprimands him, no longer awakens him, no longer comforts him. In short, He pities him no longer. God has surrendered him to his perverted disposition. He is already one who is eternally cursed by God here, one irretrievably lost.

The further God departs from such a person, the closer Satan comes. Amid the scornful laughter of all the infernal spirits, Satan takes him captive at his will. He is the assured booty of hell.

Human language is too poor for completely describing his great misery. This world is a big prison in which he as a criminal, a rebel against the most holy majesty of God, waits for eternal death. What a frightful state!

It seldom happens, however, that those who have committed the sin against the Holy Spirit are frightened. Yet it often does happen that those who are far removed from committing this sin needlessly alarm and torment themselves by thinking that they have committed this sin. It is therefore very important and necessary that every Christian knows exactly what the sin against the Holy Spirit is and why this sin can be forgiven neither in this world nor in the world to come.

Since today's Gospel reading gives us occasion to do this, let us now study the true doctrine of the sin against the Holy Spirit with its heart-shaking but also comforting content. May this take place that we all be instructed, awakened, and preserved in the faith.

The text: *John 8:46–59*

About a year before the event related in our text, the Pharisees stated that Christ had a devil and drove out devils through the chief of devils. Even then Christ showed them that by this slander they were beginning the sin that could never be forgiven, the sin against the Holy Spirit. On the basis of this text, let me present to you:

The unforgivable sin against the Holy Spirit

I will show you:

1. Wherein this sin consists, and
2. Why this sin is unforgivable.

Lord Jesus, You do not reject him who comes to You. You came into the world not to judge but save the lost. You are the *only* door to salvation, the only way, the truth, and the life. No one comes to the Father but by You. Whoever does not come to You to know Your grace but despises it, yes derides and slanders it, sins against the Holy Ghost. He erases himself from the Book of Life and enrolls himself in the book of the lost. Even You cannot save him. He has no forgiveness in this world or the one to come, because he does not have *You*, the only Savior of all sinners. O Lord Jesus, guard us from this most frightful of all sins. Do not let us become hardened by the deceit of sins. Make our hearts soft and obedient, a workshop for your Holy Spirit. Someday bring us to an eternal, blessed communion with You in heaven. Amen! Amen!

I.

Perhaps there are no other sins about which Christians have so many false conceptions as the sin against the Holy Spirit. The results are a double one: First, one often sins against men by falsely charging them with this terrible sin and giving up all effort and hope for their conversion. Second, a person often foolishly worries that he has committed this sin himself. Ah, many a poor fallen Christian has despaired at the thought and without availing himself of grace he (for whom there still was help) died miserably. A dreadful example was the Italian lawyer Francesco Spiera, who twice from fear of death denied the evangelical Lutheran doctrine. Thereupon he thought that he had committed the sin against the Holy Spirit, received no comfort, and thus in the year 1548 died in despair.

What is usually supposed to be the sin against the Holy Spirit? Some think that it is persistent impenitence until death; others, every known denial of, every known fall from, the recognized truth. Still others, that it is every willful sin after conversion. Others say whoever has sworn falsely or has conspired with the devil has committed the sin against the Holy Spirit. It occasionally happens that tempted or fallen Christians feel against their will the most frightful blasphemous thoughts. Despite their sighs, prayers, and struggles they cannot free themselves of these thoughts. They accompany them everywhere, even to the Lord's Altar. Usually they suppose that they have committed the sin against the Holy Spirit. Many Christians experience for a while immediately after their conversion the sweetest incitements of the Holy Spirit. Then they suddenly stop. They suppose when they feel no light, no comfort, no power, no life, that they have fallen into that unforgivable sin.

But my friends, these are all absolutely false notions. Christ and the apostles present this as a sin of only a special class of sinners. Furthermore, many thousands after their conversion have again fallen into willful sins and still have returned to grace. We see this in David. When Paul was still Saul, he was a blasphemer of Christ, a bloody persecutor of Christians, and still he obtained mercy. Peter had been an apostle of the Lord for three years. Although he had sworn falsely that he did not know Christ and cursed himself, he found grace again. During great temptation by the devil Job had against his will thought all manner of blasphemies and even had unwillingly uttered them, yet God did not take him to account for them. Almost all Christians have times when they no longer detect the gracious presence and working of the Holy Spirit. In His place they perceive nothing but darkness, the lust of sin, impotence, spiritual death, condemnation of heart and conscience, and God's wrath; to all of them apply the words of Psalm 97:11, "Light is sown for the righteous," namely, for those righteous in Christ through faith, "and joy for the upright in heart."

You see that the sin against the Holy Spirit must be something completely different from what is commonly supposed. Let us therefore examine our text that pictures people who actually committed this sin. How are they described to us?

The Lord had said to the Pharisees, "Which one of you convicts Me of sin? If I tell the truth, why do you not believe Me? Whoever is of God hears the words of God. The reason why you do not hear them is that you are not of God" (John 8:46–47). And what did they do? Do they actually cite an example where Jesus had sinned against the honor of God or the love of his neighbor?

Not in the least. Not once do they even attempt to furnish the proof, but merely speak with satanic impudence, "Are we not right in saying that you are a Samaritan and have a demon?" (v. 48). The Lord gently contradicts this blasphemy saying that he who keeps His word would not see death; with this He irrefutably shows the divinity of His word. They merely repeated their first blasphemy and said, "Now we know that You have a demon! Abraham died, as did the prophets, yet You say, 'If anyone keeps My word, he will never taste death.' Are You greater than our father Abraham, who died? And the prophets died! Who do You make Yourself out to be?" (vv. 52–53).

In their satanic madness these wicked people forgot themselves and betrayed their hearts' innermost thoughts. Previously they had said that Christ had a devil; when He defends Himself, they cry out, "Now we know that You have a demon!" If they recognize, as they themselves falsely say, this "now" for the first time, how could they have said this before? They show that they knew right well that Christ is from God.

Two years earlier Nicodemus answered Christ not only for himself, but also in the name of his fellow Pharisees, "We," namely we Pharisees, "know that You are a teacher come from God, for no one can do these signs that You do unless God is with him" (John 3:2). Christ's countless, unheard of miracles and His quick, powerful words had done the job of convincing them that Christ was from God. Neither fear of that humble Christ, nor the attractions of great earthly advantage, which they could not have hoped to receive, nor error and ignorance were the causes of their battle and blasphemies against Christ—nothing but the bitter, bloodthirsty, infernal hatred against the recognized divine truth. They may not have known that

Jesus was true God, but at least they knew that He actually was the Messiah who had been promised by the prophets. Yet they resolved among themselves: "Such a Messiah we do not like or want!"

When Christ therefore showed His divinity, saying, "Before Abraham was, I am" (8:58), their hearts and consciences were alarmed at the majesty of His person and His words. The presentiment then secretly rose in the depths of their hearts: this is the truth! But, hardened by Satan, they "picked up stones to throw at Him" (8:59). They wished to close forever the mouth of this preacher of the truth, who brought to light the inmost thoughts of their hearts.

This describes those who commit the fearful sin against the Holy Spirit. Not those who in ignorance and blindness blasphemed the divine teaching as Saul; not those who from fear of death denied the faith as Peter; not those who, conquered by their fleshly lusts, have fallen into sin and shame as David; not those who in the blindness of their heart committed all manner of abomination as Manasseh. All these returned to grace and were forgiven. Much less has it been committed by those people into whose heart the devil has shot his satanic blasphemies, or by those who heartily yearn to be free of their spiritual misery.

But if they are really convinced by the Holy Spirit of the divine truth, if they refuse to accept this truth, if out of hatred of God and the truth, hardened by satanic maliciousness they blaspheme it of their own free will as lies of the devil, if they rave and rage against it in a bloodthirsty manner, they have then committed the sin against the Holy Spirit.

God is tired even here of showing mercy to them. They (as the Letter to the Hebrews says) crucify the Son of God anew, mock Him, trample on Him, deem the blood of the testament through which they are sanctified as unclean, and revile the Spirit of grace. God therefore gives them over to the judgment of stubbornness. There remains no more offering for sins, but a terrible looking for of judgment and fiery indignation, which shall devour the adversaries. Even Christ, the High Priest and intercessor of all sinners, prays no more for them. The Holy Spirit no longer works in them. They are stricken from the list of those who can still find grace. This sin cannot be forgiven them either in this world or in the one to come; they are guilty of the eternal judgment.

II.

The question now arises why this sin is unforgivable. Permit me in the second place to give you the answer.

The reason why this sin cannot be forgiven is not that God from eternity predestined him to this sin and the damnation that follows. Oh no. God from eternity predestined no man to hell and eternal death. Paul writes in Romans, "God has consigned all to disobedience, that He may have mercy on all" (11:32). That is, as God finds all men in the like guilty of unbelief, he also wishes to make no distinction but be gracious to all.

Nor is the reason that these sins are too great and horrible for God's grace. No person can fall so deeply, sin so seriously, be so malicious, that the loving God would not be gracious to him if he really desired grace. Paul writes in Romans 5:20, "where sin increased, grace abounded all the more." Even through Isaiah God declared, "Though your sins are like scarlet, they shall be as white as snow; though they are red like crimson, they shall become like wool" (1:18).

Nor is the reason that it is greater than Christ's merit, that Christ had not taken this sin upon Himself, had not reconciled God for this sin. Oh, no! John writes in 1 John 2:1–2, "If anyone does sin, we have an advocate with the Father, Jesus Christ the righteous. He is the propitiation for our sins, and not for ours only but also for the sins of the whole world." Paul writes in 2 Corinthians 5:14, "We have concluded this: that one has died for all, therefore all have died." Peter writes in 2 Peter 2:1 that those who deny Christ "will secretly bring in destructive heresies, even denying the Master *who bought them*, bringing upon themselves swift destruction."

Nor is the reason that this sin is not directed at the person of the Holy Spirit. The *person* of the Holy Spirit is not holier or higher or more inviolable than the person of the Father and the Son. All Three are One, alike the great, glorious, majestic, the thrice-holy God,

The real reason why this sin cannot be forgiven is clearly revealed in our Gospel reading today. The Lord asks the Pharisees, "If I tell the truth, why do you not believe Me?" (John 8:46). And what do they answer? They give no reason, merely furiously reply, "Are we not right in saying that You are a Samaritan and have a demon?" (v. 48).

The Lord does not cease knocking at the door of their hearts. Holding up all the riches of His grace and as it were pouring it out before them, He says, "Truly, truly, I say to you, if anyone keeps My word, he will never see death" (v. 51). Alas, Christ with these words opens all the doors of grace. This very sermon of grace makes them only the more furious. Their reply is a new snarling blasphemy. They *want* no freedom from death through Christ's word.

The Lord then applies one more means, the last remedy, to shake their hearts. He says that He is the eternal God Himself, saying, "Before Abraham was, I am" (v. 58). Far be it that they should recoil from this great word or the abyss of sin that consists in the conscious struggle against God Himself. This enraged them only the more so that in the madness of their malice they picked up stones to kill Him, the Lord of glory, the prince of salvation.

You see, the reason why the sin against the Holy Spirit cannot be forgiven is that it is not the sin against His *person* but against His *office*, against His enlightenment, against His awakening, against His reprimand, against His comfort, against His conversion, in short, against all the workings of the Holy Spirit. If the Spirit wants to direct such people to Christ, the *foundation* and cornerstone of salvation, they reject it. If the Spirit wants to lead them to the *means* of salvation, the Word of God and the Sacraments, they jeer at it. If the Spirit wants to bring them to the *way* of salvation, repentance and faith, they slander it.

If a person rejects all this because in his natural blindness he does not yet know it or because of the fear of persecution and torture, or the prospect of great fortune misleads him, it is still possible for him to be converted and in true faith find again the grace he slandered. But if a person knows full well the counsel of God for his salvation through the writings of the Holy Spirit, yet out of spiteful hate over against the truth voluntarily, willfully, out of pure malice, obstinately, stubbornly rejects, condemns, slanders, and even cruelly persecutes the confessors of the truth, yes (if he can) even Christ Himself, he is then beyond help and becomes like Satan himself for whom there is no salvation. Because he simply is not to be saved, God out of righteous judgment surrenders him to his hardened mind, reserves him for the days of his frightful judgment, and saves him for the eternal fires.

God would save also him but He *cannot*, because he does not *want* to be saved. Christ therefore says to such, like to hardened Jerusalem, "How often would I have gathered your children together as a hen gathers her brood under her wings, and you were not willing" (Matthew 23:37).

Finally, how should we apply this terrible doctrine?

First, for doctrine and warning: Let us be particular about every revealed doctrine of the divine Word. If we are convinced of its truth, let us then for God's and our salvation's sake not resist it. Even if our flesh and blood finds this teaching ever so bitter and offensive, let us willingly and humbly accept it. Whoever knowingly and willfully rejects *one* truth which was recognized as such through the Holy Spirit can reject *all* divine truth offensive to him. Finally, against better knowledge he will slander it, yes, at last cruelly persecute its confessors and thus fall into the judgment of obduracy from which no one can deliver him.

Let us also apply this doctrine for our comfort. Though this doctrine is frightening, it is rich in comfort. It tells us, though a person may have sinned ever so greatly and slandered God, Christ, and everything holy, even the *person* of the Holy Spirit, there is nevertheless still grace as long as he does not knowingly and willfully slander the *office* and working of the Holy Spirit. In short, whoever still repents, still believes, still wishes to have grace has not committed the sin against the Holy Spirit as certainly as God's Word is clear and true and Jesus is the Savior of all sinners. Let him merely come as miserable and laden with guilt as he is, even though he were a person completely worthy of being cursed. God will make him in Christ an eternally blessed person. Amen.

PALM SUNDAY, CONFIRMATION

JOHN 6:67

"Let the little children come to Me and do not hinder them, for to such belongs the kingdom of heaven" [Matthew 19:14]. Thus, Lord Jesus, You spoke in the days of Your flesh! Upon Your command these children were brought to You through Holy Baptism. At Your command they come to You now by themselves. Will You reject them? No, You will not; You cannot do that. A few years ago You received them when they were brought to You as lost children who were not Yours. How can You reject them today when they come to You as Your precious possession who were entrusted to You, as children of Your covenant, as children of Your Church, as lambs of Your flock? You received them when they were brought to You ruined, blind, sick, and dead, full of sin and uncleanness. How can You reject them today when they come to You cleansed and sprinkled with the blood of Your reconciliation? You received them when they were brought to You as infants who could not beg You for Your grace, and, not feeling their misery, lay before You in mute wretchedness. How can You reject them today when they come feeling their misery, praying and weeping for Your grace? You received them when they were brought to You without knowing You. How can You reject them today? They come to You because they have learned to know and love You from Your Gospel as their Savior and faithful Shepherd. Oh, do not shame our confidence in You. Do exceedingly more than we ask and think. Open Your heavens today over these children. Come down upon them, lay Your hand upon them, press them to Your heart, and bless them. Bless them with the fullness of Your gifts, bless them with Your grace, bless them with the power of faith, with ardent love, with joyous hope, and with peace and joy in the Holy Spirit. Bless them with all the weapons of righteousness for a victorious struggle. Bless them with protection from all evil, with patience and comfort in affliction, with a blessed hour of death, and finally with an inheritance incorruptible and undefiled, that fadeth not away, reserved in heaven for them. Amen! Amen! That is yea! Yea! It shall be so. Amen.

In Christ, my dear congregation! Especially you, dear confirmands!

As a loving mother deals with her child in temporal things, so the heavenly Father deals with us in spiritual matters. A mother carries her child in her arms as long as the child is weak and small. Then she carefully leads the child with her hands so that the child does not fall and hurt himself. Finally, when the child is sufficiently matured in mind and body to be aware of the dangers that threaten, she permits the child to walk about freely and chose his own way.

Thus God deals with men. As soon as we are born, He takes us into His arms of grace and guides us (without us knowing it) with His hand of preserving love. However, when we have finally learned to know the way to heaven God will not forsake us. He then confronts us with the questions: "My child, what do you wish to do? Shall I continue to remain with you? On which way do you wish to go now? The broad way or the narrow, the way of life or the way of death? And with whom are you going to side? With Me or the world? Decide now; choose; choose, My child."

God has done that to you, my dear children! You had scarcely come into the world when God through Holy Baptism took you into His arms of grace, cleansed your souls with the blood of the reconciliation, and clothed your souls with the righteousness of your Savior. He filled you with His Holy Spirit and made you His children. He promised to be your covenant God, your Father, Redeemer, and Comforter; in short, He made you blessed and glorious. All this took place soon after your birth without you knowing it, without you wanting it, without you asking God for it with even so much as a word, without the least bit of help from you—yes, you were carried into the kingdom of heaven as in a sleep.

However, it should not remain that way. Now you are grown up and are capable of understanding God's Word. You were educated in it. You had to learn to know your Savior and the way to heaven, in order that at the right time you might yourself publicly declare what you wish to do. This time has now come. Yes, my dear children, an important hour of decision has struck. You know the way that leads to life and the one that leads to death; you must now decide for yourself which way you want to go. You know the difference between God and the world, between Christ and sin; you must now declare which you wish to choose.

That is why you have appeared here today before this altar. That is why your parents and teachers, your sponsors and relatives, your brothers and sisters, your friends and a great host of other Christians have assembled here in the house of the Lord; that is why God Himself with many of His holy angels is present here. All eyes today are directed toward you. Everyone is listening with intense expectation to hear from your lips how you will decide and what you will choose for your whole future life: life or death, God or the world, Christ or sin.

Oh children, what a gracious hour this is! How fortunate you are! Many thousands who are old would like to stand in your place today. Many thousands who are 30, 40, 50, 60 years old tearfully look back on their past life. They remember with shame the day when they also promised faithfulness to God, for they did it thoughtlessly; they did not keep their promise and went a false way; they chose the world instead of God, sin instead of Christ. Therefore, a whole lost life lies behind them, black as the night. Their conscience is wounded and burdened; their heart without peace and rest; their future lies before them like an open abyss. Sighing, they cry out: "Oh, that I might return again to the beautiful, golden, blessed days of my childhood and youth! Oh, that I might once more as a child throw myself down before the altar of the Lord and crying and praying lay the oath of eternal faithfulness in the hands of my God! Alas, what is done is done; what is lost is lost!"

Once more I repeat how fortunate, how fortunate you children are! A lost life, a long dark way of death does not yet lie behind you; but behind you lies the blessed spring-like days of your childhood, a delightful path on which you joyfully walked by the guiding hands of eternal love. Not until now do the bright way of life and the dark, somber way of death open before you; you should now decide which way you want to go. The world has not yet *won* you, and God has not yet *lost* you. Today, first God and the world ask you whom you want to serve. Sin has not yet been able to make you its slave, and Christ, your Good Shepherd, has not yet set you free. Today, first sin and Christ ask you to whom you want to yield yourself.

However, my dear children, before you make this confession, show by brisk and joyful answers to several questions which I will ask, that you actually know the true from the false way and are truly capable through God's grace to decide and choose for yourself.

EXAMINATION — SERMON

In the name of Jesus. Amen.

"Do you want to go away as well?" Thus with sad countenance Christ in John 6 spoke to the Twelve, when many other disciples had just left Him. This is the same question which I feel I must impress upon you, my dear children!

You have declared that today you are prepared to swear eternal faithfulness to your Savior. Alas, many a child has kneeled at this altar, wet it with his tears, and with trembling voice said: "Yes, I will remain with Jesus, with His Word, with His grace, with His Church; nothing, neither pain nor joy, neither honor nor dishonor, neither poverty nor riches, neither life nor death, shall separate me from Him." But before the next Palm Sunday had rolled around he had already left his Savior. With deep melancholy I today think of so many confirmands on whose head I laid my hand of blessing. They were the joy of my heart; like green trees they had grown up in the garden of the Lord. With joyous hopes I took leave of them. I thought, if no one remains faithful, these anyhow will. I had often seen tears tremble in their eyes and roll over their cheeks! But what has happened? Where are they now? The fire of faith and love that was kindled in them is extinguished. They are now cold and dead. They have left Christ and loved the world as Demas did.

I must confess that the thought of these unfortunate children has so depressed my heart that it wants to turn today's joy into a day of sorrow and grief. However, I find in the Gospel of John that the Savior experienced the same thing. What did He do? Sadly He looked at those who were leaving

Him, but He did not give up the others who were still with Him. Trustingly, He turned to His faithful Twelve with the question, "Do you want to go away as well?" And what did they answer? Peter quickly spoke up. Deeply shaken, zealously he cried, "Lord, to whom shall we go? You have the words of eternal life, and we have believed, and have come to know, that You are the Holy One of God" (John 6:68–69).

Now if Jesus were to step visibly before us, what question do you suppose He would ask you? Certainly, He would also ask you: Children, "do you want to go away as well"? And what would you answer Him? Would you say: "My dear Savior, we can no longer remain with You. The world is too enticing, sin is too sweet, Your yoke is too hard, and Your burden too heavy!"? Oh, never! Never! I do not doubt that with all your heart you would as one voice loudly repeat Peter's word.

So let us pause a few moments while I present to you:

Your Answer to Christ's Question: "Do you want to go away as well?"

It is this:

1. "Lord, to whom shall we go?" and,
2. "You have the words of eternal life, and we have believed, and have come to know, that You are the Holy One of God."

I.

"Lord, to whom shall we go?" With this new question Peter answered Christ's question, "Do you want to go away as well?" Peter wanted to say: "Lord, can You really ask us that? Is it possible that we would be so unthankful as to forget Your love, erase these benefits that we have enjoyed with You from our hearts and minds, and forsake You? Where should we then go? Whither shall we turn? Where would we seek the light of truth that we need?" How shall we appease the hunger and thirst of our souls for God's grace and peace? How shall we gratify our yearning for happiness? Where shall we seek comfort in affliction, solace for the misery of sin, deliverance from death, and eternal life? We would look around in the whole creation in vain. We know of no person in the world, no creature in heaven and on earth, to whom we can go and find what we seek.

Peter and all the apostles did not know where they should go if they should leave Christ. Do *you* perhaps know?

It is true that all those who left Christ thought they could find happiness elsewhere. One left Christ and sought happiness in striving after money and other earthly goods; another left Christ and sought happiness in all manner of lusts and desires; another left Christ and sought happiness in the favor and friendship of the world; another left Christ and sought happiness in honor and respect among men; another left Christ and sought happiness in the search after the wisdom of this world. Did they find what they looked for? Alas, no! Either they returned to Christ as soon as they recognized that they were deceived, or they had to confess in the very hour of their death that their search was in vain, that their heart had deceived them.

Judas left Christ in order to win earthly treasure. Yes, he *betrayed* Christ for thirty pieces of silver. But that money soon became like fire in his hands and heart; he despaired and come to a terrible end. Similarly everyone enjoys his earthly goods that he seeks and for which sake he leaves Christ just as little.

David once left his God and Savior and fell into the sin of lust; alas! as sweet as it once was, just so bitter it soon became. Hear how he complained and lamented in his psalm of penitence. The lust of sin became arrows that pierced his heart and conscience, a heavy load that like a mountain pressed him to the ground! He did not *buy* his happiness with the lust of sin, but he *sold* it. At night he watered his bed with his tears; during the day he went about with fallen countenance, bent and bowed and sad. His previous blessed peace, the sweet rest of his soul, was gone.

Solomon left his God and Savior, loved the world, and enjoyed all his pleasures; but scarcely had he enjoyed them when he cried out, "I said in my heart, 'Come now, I will test you with pleasure; enjoy yourself.' But behold, this also was vanity" (Ecclesiastes 2:1). "Sorrow is better than laughter" (7:3).

Peter himself left his Savior for a short time despite his promise, just to get the favor and friendship of the world and save his life; alas! he soon experienced that he had only made himself inexpressibly unhappy; he quickly left the company of the world and wept bitterly.

A well-known German king at the time of the Reformation left Christ in order to be and remain the mightiest and greatest of men; but after he had enjoyed all the honor and glory of the world, he confessed that his crown with its earthly honor was only a burden. He laid his crown and scepter aside. In repose in Christ he sought that peace and happiness, which he had not been able to find in the whole world.

Paul, while still named Saul, left the Savior, who had been preached by the prophets and rejected the Gospel. He sought rest in the wisdom of this world but did not find it; finally, he turned to Christ and he not only confessed, "In [Christ] are hidden all the treasures of wisdom and knowledge" (Colossians 2:3); but he also added, "To know the love of Christ that surpasses knowledge" (Ephesians 3:19). (German: To love Christ is better than all knowledge).

Oh my dear children, you see that without exception all who had left Christ and had sought happiness elsewhere had to confess that they had deceived themselves. So tell me, what will you do? What will you answer the Savior who so lovingly asks you: Children, "do you want to go away as well?" Is it not true that today all of you will answer, "*Lord* Jesus, how can we leave You who loved us from eternity, redeemed us in time, bought us with Your blood, and baptized us? From the time of our birth You have carried us in Your arms and guided us with Your gracious hands. We cannot even express how much You have done for us! But can we be so unthankful as to forget Your eternal faithfulness and mercy toward us? *Lord Jesus*, if we wanted to leave You, *to whom shall we go*? If You cannot make us happy here and save us hereafter, who can? If we do not find in You that after which our souls thirst, where shall we find it?"

If we wanted to go and grab after gold and treasures, what would we gain? What would it profit us if we would gain the whole world and still lose our souls? We would still be eternally poor. Or, if we wanted to go and plunge into the lusts and sins and pleasures of the world, what would it profit us? Our hearts would here remain without peace and hereafter we would have to languish eternally. Or, if we wanted to go and seek the favor and friendship of the world, what would it profit us, even if the whole world were our friend but the almighty God our enemy? Or, if we wanted to go and seek honor and respect among men, what would it profit us, even if here we could boast of the greatest honor? Hurled from our heights, we would in eternity stand ashamed before God and His angels. Or finally, if we wanted to leave You and seek the wisdom of this world, what would it profit us? What would all light for this life profit us without that Light which shows us the way to heaven? Behold, Lord, where should we go if we wanted to leave You? We do not know.

II.

However, my dear children, Peter answered Christ's question, "Do you want to go away as well?" not only by saying, "Lord to whom shall we go?" but in the second place he also added, "You have the words of eternal life, and we have believed, and have come to know, that You are the Holy One of God" (John 6:68–69).

Peter wishes to say: Lord, we could not leave You because You have the words that have gone right through us as no man's words have. You have breathed new life into our dead hearts. Your words not only stir and shake our hearts, but they also refresh, rejoice, and comfort us. Your words have not only shown us the way to eternal life, but they have also enlightened us with the light of eternal life itself. You have filled our souls with the foretaste of the power of the world to come. Your words have not only directed us from the world to heaven, but they have opened heaven and God's own heart. You have made us certain that we have forgiveness of sins and a gracious God, that we are righteous before God and His children, that we have a share in the glory of heaven and are heirs of eternal life. We have experienced in our hearts that You are truly the Christ, the only Savior of the world, the Son of the living God. Now if we wanted to leave You, we would leave life and choose death, leave salvation and choose damnation, leave heaven and choose hell.

You, see my dear children, thus with shining eyes and passionate heart Peter answered the Savior's question, "Do you want to go away as well?" Tell me, can you give a different answer? Must you not also declare and confess before this congregation that even you have often found that Christ's words are not weak words of men, but the words of eternal life? Did not your souls often stir at the hearing of Christ's words, something you never found in the hearing of men's words? Have you not often experienced how God Himself mightily knocked on your hearts at the hearing of Christ's words? Have you not often experienced how God's Holy Spirit moved the foundation of your souls at the hearing of Christ's words, how you began to pray for grace, how He mightily drew you to God, enlightened you concerning the condition of your souls, reprimanded you on account of your sins? Were you not often overwhelmed with comfort, hope, peace, and joy? Have you not experienced in your hearts that Christ's words are God's words, full of life and power, and that He Himself is the only Savior of sinners, the Son of the living God? Have you not often felt that you could have shouted to the whole world: Oh unbelievers, do not reject Christ and His Word; I can swear that He is truly God's Son and the Savior of the world! I have experienced it!?

If the Savior would ask you today, "Do you want to go away as well?" need you reflect any longer as to what your answer will be? No, no, you will, you must, with shining eyes and passionate hearts, not only say as Peter did, "Lord, to whom shall we go?" you will, you must, also add: Lord, if we leave You, we would be like wanderers, who forsook their guide and went into the dark forest upon unbeaten paths only to perish helplessly. We would be like sheep, who forsook the shepherd and his pasture and went into the barren wilderness only to languish. We would be like sailors who forsook the lifeboat and jumped into the raging sea. No, no, we will remain with You, Lord Jesus. "You have the words of eternal life, and we have believed, and have come to know, that You are the Holy One of God."

Oh my dear children, do not say that only today but whenever your corrupt heart, your flesh and blood, or the world want to entice you away from Christ and His words, whenever you are tempted to forsake Christ and strive after gold and earthly treasures or the friendship of the world, or join in the vain lusts and pleasures of the world, or seek honor and respect among men, or even join the sworn enemies of Christ and his Word. Ah, then recall that Christ stands before you again like He does today and says, "Do you also want to go away?"

> *Although all the world should forsake and forget Thee,*
> *In love I will follow Thee, ne'er will I quit Thee.*
> *Lord Jesus, both spirit and life is Thy Word;*
> *And is there a joy which Thou dost not afford? (TLH 366:4)*

RITE OF CONFIRMATION—CONCLUDING TALK AND PRAYER

Thus my dear children, the great work has taken place. Your heavenly Bridegroom has sued for your souls, and you have given them to Him. You have given your consent; the covenant of faithfulness is forever concluded. He Himself was among us and heard your oath. He is now ready to embrace you. Remain with Him until the last breath of your life.

The hour of parting has now struck. We will never again be gathered together as we were in the past months and as we are today. In conclusion I therefore say to you from the bottom of my heart: Farewell, farewell, dear children! I hope to see most of you again in this house and at this altar of the Lord, if God prolongs our life. However, if all of you remain with Jesus, we will see each other in heaven before the throne of the Lamb; then all of you will be clothed in white, wear crowns on your heads, and carry harps in your hands. Then you will be truly confirmed. Then all temptations, all dangers, all works, all struggles will have ended. Then you will no longer cry, "Lord, have mercy on us!" but will join in the eternal hallelujah of all cherubim and seraphim, all angels and perfected saints. Oh, how you will rejoice that you were preserved until the end, that you remained faithful until death! Then you will bless this day and from eternity to eternity give praise and honor and thanksgiving and glory to the Lamb, who was slain and bought you with His blood and kept you unto salvation. Once more I say to you: Until then, my dear children, farewell, farewell!

Now you, my dear congregation, and especially you fathers, mothers, sponsors, brothers, sisters, friends, and relatives of these children, open your loving arms and receive these children from my hands, from the hands of their teachers. Receive them as your brothers and sisters. However, do not say as did Cain, "Am I my brother's keeper?" (Genesis 4:9). Parents, bear in mind, you remain the parents of these children until your death; God will some day demand them from your hands.

You, however, who are not bound so closely to these children through the bonds of blood, bear in mind the word of Christ, "When you have turned again, strengthen your brothers" (Luke 22:32). If you are converted, strengthen these weak children; watch over them. If they are in danger, warn them. If they go astray, bring them back. If you see them fall, lift them up. If you will faithfully do this, you will also someday stand with these children— oh, may it be all of us—as we stand here with them in hope, before Christ's throne seeing the things for which we hoped.

Now that this may take place, let us kneel and in heartfelt devotion and firm faith carry the needs of these children to the Savior:

Lord Jesus Christ, You have asked these children, "Do you want to go away as well?" and they have answered, "Lord, to whom shall we go? You have the words of eternal life, and we have believed, and have come to know, that You are the Holy One of God." They have confessed that they know no other Savior, that they can find deliverance from sin, trouble, and death only in You, light only from You, grace only from You, righteousness only with You, comfort only with You, power only with You, life and salvation only with You. Therefore they want to remain with You until death.

Oh Jesus, remain also with them and do not reject them. Yes, bind them fast to Your heart; for if You do not hold them, they cannot hold You. Even today their resolution and will is very weak; but You have promised to be their strength. They are unworthy sinners, but just for the sake of sinners You have come into the world as a Savior of sinners and not of the righteous. Their souls are sick and frail; but You are a Physician not of the healthy but of the weak and miserable. We well know that none of these children will be completely faithful to You. Forgetting their vows, they will often stumble and fall, but You have promised that You will remain faithful even if we become unfaithful. Finally, we well know that we are entirely unworthy of Your listening to our poor prayers for these children, but we do not lie here before You in our righteousness but in Your great mercy. We pray to You alone in trust upon Your command and promise. Oh, hear us then. These children are not our children; they are Yours. You have bought them with Your blood; if they should be lost, You will lose them.

Oh, therefore have mercy upon them. Keep them in Your truth and grace. When in temptation, be their protection. When in sin, be their throne of grace. When in trouble and temptation, their comfort. When in death, their life. When in judgment and damnation, their Savior and Intercessor.

Oh Jesus, *we* cannot keep them; we therefore place them in Your lap and in Your arms. They are eternally given into Your charge. Preserve them, help them in life and save them in death.

Oh Thou Lamb of God, that takest away the sin of the world and also their sin, have mercy upon them!

Oh Thou Lamb of God, that takest away the sin of the world and also their sin, have mercy upon them!

Oh Thou Lamb of God, that takest away the sin of the world and also their sin, give them Your peace. Amen! Amen!

HOLY (MAUNDY) THURSDAY (1868)

1 CORINTHIANS 11:23–32

Lord Jesus, true God and man in one person! You have withdrawn Your visible presence from Your congregation because You did not wish to be seen but believed on; yet You are not separated from her. You did not leave us orphans. Although You are invisible, You are even today really and truly with us with all Your grace. And that we may find comfort for ourselves in Your presence, You have instituted a supper on the night that You were betrayed in which You give us to eat of Your body and give us to drink of Your blood. Oh, help us that we do not let ourselves be robbed of this comfort but hold firmly to it until we finally see You with our eyes, hear You with our ears, touch You with our hands, and thus enjoy perfect communion in eternal blessed joy. Amen!

In Christ Jesus, dear Christian friends!

The Holy Supper, whose institution we today celebrate, is according to its origin as well as its purpose a feast of love. First of all, out of inexpressible love to His own Christ Himself instituted it. When John reports the last supper that Christ ate with His disciples, he begins this report with the words, "Having loved His own who were in the world, He loved them to the end" (John 13:1). He wants to say: "Not even the nearness of His painful death had caused Christ to forget His disciples nor did His love for them weaken. Rather He felt this way: At His very departure from the world, He wanted to institute and leave behind for His own the greatest memorial of His love." Christ specifically said this, when for the last time He sat down at the table with His disciples to keep the last meal He said, as Luke reports, "I have earnestly desired to eat this Passover with you before I suffer" (Luke 22:15). Though the Savior had been filled with anxiety before His baptism of blood, yet with such ardent longing He had also awaited His last night of suffering. In this night He would repeal the old covenant meal and would institute a new one.

The Holy Supper is a feast of love not only because Christ Himself instituted it out of burning love for His own but, as was said, because of its purpose—to be the source and bond of the most intimate, brotherly love among Christians. Thus the apostle Paul writes, "The cup of blessing that we bless, is it not a participation in the blood of Christ? The bread that we break, is it not a participation in the body of Christ? Because there is one bread, we who are many are one body, for we all partake of the one bread" (1 Corinthians 10:16–17). He also adds, "We were all made to drink of *one Spirit*" (12:13). He means to say: "Because we Christians partake of the consecrated bread that makes us partakers of Christ's body, and the consecrated cup that makes us partakers of Christ's blood, we all become one body and one spirit, almost one person, one individual." All communicants do not divide Christ's body and blood, not even one part of Christ's body and blood. All partake of the one and the same complete body of Christ and the one and the same complete blood of Christ. They thus become intimately united with one another as their body with their soul.

Is not the Holy Supper, then, really a feast of love? Beyond a doubt. As little as it is possible for a person not to love himself, so little is it possible for a communicant, who heartily believes in the mystery of the Holy Supper, not to love his fellow communicants, for he knows that the same body and blood is in them which is in him. We read that because the first Christians continued "in the breaking of bread" they actually were "of one heart and of one soul."

Yet has not this very Holy Supper since the time of the Reformation been the subject of strife, war, estrangement, separation, and division instead of being a feast of love, which should most intimately of all unite Christians? Has not the Church that left the papacy split over this Holy Supper into two warring parties? And is it not especially our Evangelical Lutheran Church that wants to make no peace?

Is it not also true that our Church would rather remain with her teaching of the Holy Supper and sacrifice the peace of the Church than this doctrine? Should she not surrender this point, so that in brotherly harmony she can celebrate that feast of love with all who call themselves Christians? Would it not be in conformity with Christian love, if we Lutherans would let everyone believe and teach about the Holy Supper what he considered right and appear with him at the Lord's Table in peace? Should we not at least at the altar lay our weapons down? Should not all hostility cease at least at the feast of reconciliation?

Or, is the true doctrine of the Holy Supper actually so important that we cannot yield? That we must hold fast to it in inviolable faithfulness no matter what the results might be? Yes, my friends, we dare not, we cannot, yield as dear as we hold God's Word, Christ's majesty and honor, our salvation, and the salvation of all men.

This is the point that I propose to lay on your heart on the day of the institution of the Lord's Supper.

The text: *1 Corinthians 11:23–32*

"For I received from the Lord what I also delivered to you." With this express assurance the apostle Paul begins his report on the institution of the Holy Supper. This is worthy of note. We see that the apostle viewed the true doctrine of the Lord's Supper as a matter of special importance. He considered it especially necessary to assure the Corinthians that he had the true doctrine not by hearsay, nor through tradition, especially not from man, but by direct revelation from the exalted Lord Himself. How important this historical fact must be! The Son of God, who is sitting at the right hand of majesty on high, revealed all its circumstances directly to his witness on earth in the most exact manner! How important must each word be that concerns that act, each circumstance though apparently insignificant! Therefore, let me present to you today that we should:

Faithfully hold fast to the doctrine of the Holy Supper

This is so important and necessary because it deals with three important things:

1. The reliability of the clear Word of God;
2. The real presence of Christ with His Church; and finally,
3. The pledge of the forgiveness of our sins.

I.

Our Faith and salvation depend on whether the Word of God is reliable. If we cannot rely firmly on God's Word without fearing that we will fall into error, our faith would be vain. Our whole Christianity would be like a house built on sand.

To obscure and raise doubts concerning God's clear Word has always been Satan's trick to deceive men. God had said to Adam, "You may surely eat of every tree of the garden, but of the tree of the knowledge of good and evil you shall not eat" (Genesis 2:16b–17). What did Satan do in order to ruin Adam and Eve? He tried to awaken doubt as to this clear Word of God and said, "Did God actually say, 'You shall not eat of any tree in the garden'?" (3:1). And behold, as soon as man let that clear Word of God be darkened, he had fallen and lost his salvation.

God had said to Christ from heaven, "This is My beloved Son, with whom I am well pleased" (Matthew 3:17). Now what did Satan do after he had ruined man in order to ruin also man's Redeemer? He sought to make that clear word of Christ's heavenly Father unclear. Tempting Christ, he said immediately after hearing that voice from heaven, "If You are the Son of God, command these stones to become loaves of bread" (4:3). But Christ did not let the clear Word of His Father be made unclear. Rather, He repulsed all assaults of the tempter with the Word of God and said at each attack, "It is written!"

Now tell me, can there really be a clearer, a more intelligible Word of God than the words of the Lord's Supper: "Take, eat; this is My body. Take, drink; this is My blood"? Do not these words express so clearly that Christ's body and blood are really present in the Lord's Supper and received in, with, and under the bread and wine? Or tell me, what should Christ have said, in order that He might express this mystery? Suppose a person would hand us a cup and say, "Take and drink, this is wine." Must we not take it to mean that wine is in the cup, that it is given us with and under it, and that we are to drink it? Would not he who hands it to us have mocked us when it is shown that no wine was in the cup? Can we, dare we, believe that the dying Savior wanted to mock His disciples and His whole Church when, giving bread and wine and instituting His Testament, He according to His own explanation said, "Take, eat; this is My body. Take, drink; this is my blood"? Not at all!

Those who don't want to believe this mystery appeal to this, that it is also written that Christ is a rock, a lamb, a door, a vine, and the like. If one dares, yes, if one must take *this* word of God figuratively, why not also the words, "This is My body . . . this is My blood"?

This is a futile subterfuge. That Christ is not an ordinary but a spiritual rock, not an ordinary but a spiritual vine, God's Word itself tells us. But where does Christ say that with the body and blood of which He speaks He means only a spiritual, figurative body and only a spiritual, figurative blood, or only a sign of His body and blood? He says the very opposite by adding to the word *body*, "which is given for you" (Luke 22:19), and to the word *blood*, "that is poured out for you" (22:20). Hence, not Christ's spiritual, figurative body or a sign of it but His real, true body is given for us, and not His spiritual, figurative blood or a sign of it but His real, true blood is shed for us!

There can be no doubt: all who maintain that the bread and wine of the Holy Supper *is* not but only *means* Christ's body and blood or that they are not *truly* present; or that not the *true* but only a figurative body of Christ and not the *true* but only the figurative blood of Christ is present in the Sacrament and received in the Sacrament only spiritually by the believer with the mouth of faith, willfully depart from Christ's clear words.

So I ask you who still consider Christ's word as God's word, dare we, can we, say yea and amen to this? Never! If the Words of Institution were obscure or ambiguous, then without danger the one could explain them this way, another that, as long as their explanation would be according to the analogy of faith. But since the Words of Institution are so intelligible, so clear, so simple that they could not be more intelligible, clear, and simple, so that a child can understand them, no person, no angel, in short, no creature dare explain them otherwise than as they read.

If we would concede this, then the reliability of all of God's Words would be lost. If we could no longer rely on the clear Words of Institution, the testament of the dying Son of God and Savior of the world, we could rely on no Word of God. If the clear Words of Institution no longer stand firm, no Word of God stands firm. If we can swerve from the clear Words of Institution because they do not agree with our reason, we can swerve from all words of God which seem foolish. If we can explain the clear words of Christ, "This is My body," as "This only means My body," then we can also explain the clear words of God: Christ *is* God's Son, Christ *is* the Savior of the world, as Christ *means* God's Son, Christ *means* the Savior of the world.

And this is also what Satan has in mind by overthrowing the clear Words of Institution. He does not want to overthrow only *these* but all of God's words. He wants to make us waver, uncertain, and distrustful. Satan is aiming to make it impossible for any Christian to comfort himself in life and death with the word, "It is written," and thus battle against flesh, world and Satan!

This and nothing else was the real reason why Luther held so firmly to the pure doctrine of the Holy Supper. Already in the year 1524 he said, "If someone should show by firm argument, that plain bread and wine were there, one dare not attack it so furiously. Sad to say, I am much too inclined to accept that as certainly as I detect an Adam. *But I am captured and cannot escape; the text is too powerful and will not let itself be torn from my mind with words.*"

Even Melanchthon writes, "I find no reason why we should depart from the meaning that Christ is present in the Holy Supper with His body and blood. It can be that a meaning which is more agreeable to human reason, especially if it is adorned and embellished with sharply contrived arguments, is more acceptable to an idle mind; but how will that stand in *temptation* when the conscience will dispute as to the reason it has for departing from the usual explanation of the Church? *Then these words, 'This is My body,' will be nothing but thunderbolts.* What will a frightened mind then say against it? With what Scripture and Word of God can it protect and convince itself that Christ's words are to be taken in a figurative way?" So far Melanchthon. He also knew that to give the Words of Institution a new meaning agreeable to reason is simply surrendering all of God's Words and letting no Word of God stand firm.

Therefore, my friends, as especially dear as the comfort of God's Word is, with such inviolable faithfulness hold fast to the pure doctrine of the Holy Supper.

II.

However, it is also so necessary and important to do this because in the second place it *concerns the real presence of Christ with His Church.*

Even during His sojourn on earth Christ had given the promise, "Where two or three are gathered in My name, there am I among them" (Matthew 18:20). When Christ had arisen from the dead and was just on the point of going into heaven, as He parted from His own He comforted them once more with the assurance, "Behold, I am with you always, to the end of the age" (28:20). We see that Christ did not belong to those religious founders who gave a doctrine only to their contemporaries, died, and then left behind nothing more than their teaching and example. Furthermore, Christ does not belong to those friends and benefactors of mankind, whose memory continues to live after their death only in the hearts of a thankful posterity. Finally, Christ was not a mere prophet who like John the Baptist was himself not that Light but only bore witness of that Light, or, who like Elijah at his ascension left only his mantle behind for his disciples.

No, Christ is God and man in one person. He had come into this world not to bring a new teaching but to found a kingdom of grace and glory in which He would be king. The Christian Church differs from all other religious organizations in that she has not only the *teachings of her founder*, but she has the *founder Himself* in her midst. Her Savior, her Redeemer, her helper, her protector is not absent from her but is really and truly present at all times and in all places. This is the highest, sweetest, most blessed, and greatest comfort that the Christian Church has. As long as the Church holds fast to this comfort, she cannot despair.

Satan has always raged and stormed more against this comforting doctrine than against any other. In the fourth century, the arch-heretic Arius appeared who denied Christ's divinity; today all rationalists, who wish to make Christ a mere man, battle against it. All of them wish to take away the comfort that the Church has in a living, ever-present Savior who is always with her and amongst her. They all want to convince the Church that Christ continues to live amongst her only in the spirit, merely in memory.

What else do all those do who do not want to believe that Christ is really and truly present in the Holy Supper with His body and blood? They reject that greatest comfort which the Church has. They often say that they are far from denying this because they also heartily believe that even today Christ is with His Church *according to His divinity*; only they cannot believe that Christ is present also according to His *humanity*. Either they want to deceive others or they are deceiving only themselves. Is there a Christ who is at any place God and not at the same time also man? Are there two Christs, a divine and a human?

No. Therefore, if Christ is with her only half and not entirely, if He is not with His Church according to His human nature, He is not with her at all; for Christ is God and man in one undivided person. Heaven and earth, yes, death and hell cannot separate the two natures. And that is the very comfort which the Church has, not that He is merely the holy Son of God, who is a consuming fire to sinners, but that the God-*man*, Jesus Christ, that the Son of God who became her *brother*, that the friendly, most gracious Savior of sinners is with her; that in her midst she has Him who once lay for her in the manger, who once lived for her, suffered, hung, and died on the cross, who once was awakened from the dead for her justification and finally gloriously ascended into heaven for her eternal glorification.

None other than this God-*man* has also promised her to be in her midst whenever she gathers in His name, none other than this *Savior* has promised to be with her all her days until the end of the world; the holy apostles also bear witness that Christ, as the *Head* of the Church, has not only ascended into heaven but is over all heavens so that He fills all things. She, therefore, believes that also the man Christ is not merely enclosed in heaven like another human saint, but is sitting at the right hand of God (which is everywhere), is everywhere also as a man, and is therefore with her is all the fullness of His power and grace.

However, all this they deny who do not want to take the clear, most sacred Words of Institution, "This is My body . . . this is My blood," as they read. For this very reason they deny the presence of the body and blood of Christ in the Holy Supper. They do not really believe that Christ is also bodily present in His Church. They want to turn the Church into a school, whose teacher is dead and who has nothing more of him than his teachings. They want to give the Church only a dead, absent Christ instead of a living, present Christ, yes, only a memorial and sign of Him.

If our Church does not want to let the pure teaching of the Holy Supper be taken from her, the question is not about a controversy over words waged by theologians, nor merely a false exposition of a text, yes, not even about Christ's presence in the Holy Supper; but it concerns Christ's real presence in His Church generally. Woe to us if we intend to yield! We would surrender the most holy things of the Christian Church, the ark of the covenant and the mercy seat of the New Covenant. Therefore, as we hold

Christ's true presence more dear than His mere memory, as we hold Christ Himself dear rather than His spirit, so we must faithfully hold fast to the pure teaching of the Sacrament of the Altar.

III.

We have yet a third reason. It concerns also the *most precious and incontestable pledge of the forgiveness of our sins.*

It is true that in the Holy Sacrament no other grace is given us than that which is given us already in Baptism, the preaching of the Gospel, and the comforting absolution. If a person is baptized with water in the name of the Father, and of the Son, and of the Holy Ghost into Christ's death, God on the strength of His promise receives him into His covenant of grace, grants him everything that Christ has won with His suffering and death, and washes his soul from all the guilt of his sins; and whoever believes it has it. Moreover, when the Gospel is preached, the general pardon that God the Father solemnly proclaimed through the resurrection of our Redeemer is published to all hearers in the name of the great God, forgiveness of sins is offered and given to all hearers; and whoever believes this has it. Finally, if a servant of Christ or a Christian pronounces absolution in God's name upon another Christian, it is on the strength of Christ's promise nothing else than as if God Himself had pronounced this absolution from heaven and had Himself offered, bestowed, and sealed the forgiveness for all sinners; and whoever believes this has it. It might now appear as if every person were sufficiently provided with the treasure of forgiveness; it would matter little if the Holy Supper with its forgiveness of sins were shortened or even completely taken from him.

But this is not true. Really, the Holy Supper is the very crown of all the Means of Grace, which Christ has conferred upon His Christian Church. In the Lord's Supper Christ gives His Christians the consecrated bread with the words, "Take and eat, this is My body which is given for you," and the consecrated cup with the words, "Take and drink, this is My blood which is shed for the forgiveness of your sins." With these words the Savior clearly wishes to say: "Take My body and eat it, not as food for your body but as that body which was given into death for your sins; take My blood and drink it, but not as drink for your body but as that blood of the reconciliation which was shed on the cross for the forgiveness of your sins." Oh, who may express what a glorious, comforting, heavenly, sweet supper the Lord's Supper is? There not only the forgiveness of sins is preached, announced, imparted in words, certified, and sealed to us as in the other Means of Grace, but at the same time Christ gives His Christians His very body and blood as a *pledge*.

Tell me, is not this assurance of the forgiveness of our sins so great that it cannot be made more certain? Can a debtor still be afraid of his creditor, if his warrantor not only pays his debts but even gives him the very sum into his hands with which he has paid his debt? Certainly not! Can a person still doubt that he will have no more trouble with his guilt of sin, that he has a share in Christ's reconciliation, when the very ransom itself, which God had received as the complete payment of the guilt of all men, is given into his hands, into his mouth, and into his heart? No, there can be a no more precious, a no more incontestable divine pledge.

You see, those who do not want to take Christ's words, "This is My body . . . this is My blood," as they read intend to rob the Christian Church of the greatest pledge of our redemption and make merely an empty memorial feast out of the Holy Supper.

So tell me: Is not the pure doctrine of the Holy Supper worth holding fast to even in the future with inviolable faithfulness? Is it not worth earnestly and zealously battling for? Is it not worth suffering all disgrace and mockery rather than surrendering this? Is it not worth sacrificing temporal peace and unity among men than sacrificing this greatest treasure that the Church has?

Yes indeed, my friends! And since God has blessed our Evangelical Lutheran Church above all other churches with the knowledge of the pure doctrine of the Holy Supper, He has also appointed her the guardian and steward of His heavenly treasure in His Christian Church, and likewise out of His wonderful grace helps us keep this great good of the beloved Christian Church. Though all other Christians fall from this doctrine, though they in great blindness mock and slander it as an old papal superstition, let us hold fast the more faithfully to it in these dreadful times of unbelief and apostasy. Let us not be ashamed of this doctrine but joyfully confess it and publicly praise it as the most precious treasure that was entrusted to us. For—never forget it, I repeat!—this concerns nothing less than these three important things: the reliability of the clear Word of God, the real presence of Christ with His Church, and finally the pledge of the forgiveness of our sins.

But above all let us diligently draw near in faith to this table of grace, pluck the fruit of heaven from this new tree of life that Christ planted outside of paradise in the garden of the Church, and draw water of eternal life from this spring of God; we will also be strengthened and sustained in the true faith to eternal life. There we shall eat the true eternal supper with Christ when we will drink of the fruit of the vine with Him in His Father's kingdom. This grant us, Jesus Christ, true God and true man in one undivided person, blessed in time and in eternity. Amen.

GOOD FRIDAY

MATTHEW 27:31–54

Oh Christ, Thou Lamb of God, that takest away the sin of the world, have mercy upon us and grant us Thy peace. Amen. Amen.

In Christ, dearly redeemed hearers!

We are gathered here today in order to concern ourselves with the most serious and, at the same time, the most mysterious, amazing, and comforting subject for man's spirit. We have gathered here in order to arrange a funeral service. And what sort of a funeral service? It is neither the death of a man nor the death of a famous hero, who fell on the battlefield for his country; nor the death of a dear father, a friend, a benefactor; nor the death of a saint, a martyr who died for the truth—this would be important enough for earnest meditation. It is inexpressibly more. We want to celebrate the death of the only-begotten Son of God for the reconciliation of the world.

Today we shall hear what Peter said to those men of Israel in the temple of Jerusalem: "You killed the Author of life" (Acts 3:15). Today we shall hear what Paul wrote to the Corinthians: "They would not have crucified the Lord of glory" (1 Corinthians 2:8); and what he said to the elders of Ephesus: God has "obtained [His Church] with His own blood" (Acts 20:28). Today we shall hear of the shedding of a blood that was not human blood, but as John expressly writes, the very blood of God's Son.

Yes, this time I must preach to you: On this day many years ago the Most Holy Himself died the death of the sinner in order that the sinner might live. On this day the Almighty Himself was conquered by the power of darkness, that weak men—conquered by the depths of darkness, delivered from His power—might triumph eternally. On this day even He whose goings forth have been from of old, from everlasting, came to the end of His days that salvation might be brought again for fallen mankind. On this day the very inexhaustible fount itself, from which the life of all beings flowed, dried up in order to give life to the dead hearts of all sinners. The sun of eternal love set in order that those who were threatened with eternal darkness could shine in all eternity. The eternal Son of the great God poured out His holy blood in order to extinguish the fire of God's wrath over the sins of men; in short, what Paul said: "In Christ God was reconciling the world to Himself" (2 Corinthians 5:19).

Oh, what a subject! It contains the most glorious, the greatest of all miracles of God's love, the most blessed and deepest of all revealed mysteries of grace.

God died on the cross and reconciled the world unto Himself. It is that which the saints in heaven especially extolled and will extol into all eternity. Yes, John tells us in his Revelation, this is the new song that all the elect sing forever. They cry throughout all the heavens, "Worthy are You to take the scroll and to open its seals, for You were slain, and by Your blood You ransomed people for God from every tribe and language and people and nation" (Revelation 5:9). Not only the saints but also the angels in heaven have no more wonderful subject that they should celebrate in song than the death of God's Son; even the angels, John writes, exult with loud voice, "Worthy is the Lamb who was slain, to receive power and wealth and wisdom and might and honor and glory and blessing" (Revelation 5:12). So you see that the day of Christ's death is celebrated not only in heaven by the hosts of many thousands of angels and all the spirits of perfected saints, but it will be celebrated from eternity to eternity when heaven and earth will have long since disappeared.

So today let us also celebrate this great event to the praise of eternal love, which sacrificed itself for us and for the salvation of our dearly bought souls. That this might be, let us implore God on our knees by singing, "Oh Christ, Thou Lamb of God," etc.

The text: *Matthew 27:31–54*

This is the description of how God did not spare His own Son but delivered Him up for us all. If we take the proper view of the picture of Golgotha, which is drawn before our eyes, what would we read as the title to this picture? The words "Be reconciled to God." Yes, whoever will not willfully close his eyes will see this word, as though written by God's hand with great flaming letters, shining as brightly as the sun over Golgotha. Permit me to show you:

Nothing calls to men so urgently, "Be reconciled to God,"
as the death of His own Son.

In this connection, let us ponder

1. The extent of this call, and
2. How everyone should and can follow this call.

I.

When God created man, he stood in the most blessed relation with God: he was God's child, God's beloved, God's friend. But when man fell into sin, all men became God's enemy and God theirs. God is holy; He therefore cannot be friendly with sin.

Most live in the sweet delusion that they are the favorites of heaven, that they are God's favorites, that they are God's friends. They base these thoughts either on this, that God is good and will not be so strict in regard to sin, or on this, that they have lived honorably and uprightly from their youth on, or they conclude this from God's friendliness toward them because He has let them prosper. But all these are false bases, bases of sand. No, most men are un-reconciled with God. And why? There are two reasons: First, some fear to seek reconciliation with God because they suppose that God will reject them. The second is that others desire no reconciliation.

It is true: had God not offered man reconciliation, how would a man dare to step before the great, most holy God whom he had outraged and propose a reconciliation? But after God's Son died for the reconciliation of all men, this death urgently calls to all men, even the most desperate of sinners, "Be reconciled to God."

If God had only *sent* His only-begotten Son into the world to announce and offer a reconciliation, oh, what an urgent invitation even this would be! Yes, if God had sent an angel with the olive branch of peace, with the message of reconciliation, how joyfully should we not believe that the flood of divine wrath is dried up! Yes, what shall I say? If it had pleased God to permit a man to say to us: "Return to me, I am reconciled," how confidently we could and should return to the fatherly arms of God. But according to His unfathomable love God has done infinitely more in order to win our hearts, convince us of His reconciled heart, and awaken confidence in Him. God did not send His only-begotten Son into the world merely to *announce* the reconciliation but also to offer Him as the *sacrifice* to *establish* that reconciliation. This is infinitely more than if God the Father, Son, and Holy Spirit themselves were to come to us with a reconciled, friendly countenance and enfold us in their arms. This is infinitely more than if God in the presence of all men had opened all doors of His heaven and called to them from the throne of His glory: "Enter into My happiness. I will remember your sins no more; they are carried into the depths of the sea. I will be your Father, and you shall be My sons and daughters."

After God let His own Son bleed and die on the cross, no man can doubt that God will receive him if he but returns. Or what is there that could still fill him with fear? His sins? They are paid for by an infinite price, the blood of God's Son. Or God's wrath? Why, He is reconciled through the death of His own Son. Or God's threats in the Law? Why, they are done away with by the cross, transformed into promises of grace and happiness. As certainly as at Christ's death the sun was darkened, so certainly has the sun of grace and righteousness risen over all men. As certainly as after Christ's death the graves were opened and the dead arose, so certainly was Christ's death the death of our death, and the well of water springing up to eternal life. As certainly as at Christ's death the rocks were rent, so certainly did God's own hand tear away the handwriting of the guilt of all men. As certainly as at Christ's death the veil in the temple was torn and the Most Holy Place with its Mercy Seat was revealed, so certainly was the door of the Mercy Seat of God, yes, the Most Holy Place of heaven, thrown wide open to all men. How all messengers of God can say to all men: "Come, come, be reconciled to God!" You should not first ask: "How will I reconcile the Most Holy, whom I have offended?" That has already taken place! God *is* reconciled, gloriously, completely, eternally reconciled; oh, be ye then reconciled to God!

If one does not wish to come now, when does he want to, when will he, come? If he does not want to be confident now, what should, what can, make him confident? If he is not satisfied with the pledge of the death of God's Son, what should satisfy him? If he does not want to follow this inducement to come to God, what should induce him? If the love that drove God's Son to the cross does not drive him to God, what can drive him?

And yet there are not only those who let fear and their feelings of guilt hinder them from accepting the reconciliation, but there are also those who let love of sin and the world hinder them. But also to these the death of God's Son urgently calls: "Oh, let yourselves be reconciled to God!" He calls to them: "What do you who intend to remain God's enemies want to do? Does not the greatness of the love which God has also toward you and which He showed through the death of His Son move you?" Just think—God does not need you, and still from eternity He longed to draw you to Himself and save you. He foresaw your fall; that is why He decided in advance to redeem and reconcile you with Himself. You offended Him, but He did not wait until you would come to Him. He knew that you would never seek Him if you would have to make the beginning. Although the Most High God was offended, He took the lead and offered you the hand of reconciliation first; He also let His own Son die for you to reconcile and admonish you, yes, through His servant earnestly to beg you with tears of love and pity, "Be reconciled to God!"

"Be reconciled to God!" is written on the cross of the Mediator with legible, blood-red letters for all sinners. "Be reconciled to God!" cries every drop of blood that streams from His wounds. "Be reconciled to God!" the cherubim with angels' voices call from the exposed Mercy Seat. "Be reconciled to God!" call the dead who have risen from their graves. "Be reconciled to God!" thunder the splitting rocks. "Be reconciled to God!" calls the earth, quaking and trembling under the burden of the cross. "Be reconciled to God!" resounds throughout all heaven from the mouth of all spirits who have already been taken into heaven by Christ's death.

Woe to him who remains deaf in the face of these thousandfold voices! Woe to him who despises the love that died for him! Woe to him who will not rid himself of his enmity to God and wants to let even the death of God's Son be in vain for him!

For him there is not only no help, but the very blood that here pleads for him for mercy will in eternity cry against him for vengeance. Heaven, earth, all creatures and even hell will witness against him. Everything, God the Creator and all His creatures, will all someday pronounce the sentence of damnation upon him. There the sweet word "Be reconciled to God!" will no longer sound in his ears but "Depart from me, you cursed, into the eternal fire prepared for the devil and his angels." You *ought* to have been saved, but you did not *want* it. You despised the eternal love that died for you, so now taste My eternal, damning wrath. You desired no reconciliation, so taste now rejection. Now atone for your sins yourself in the flames of hell, for your worm shall not die and your fire shall not be quenched.

II.

My friends, all of you must admit that nothing cries more urgently, "Be reconciled to God!" than does the death of God's own Son; now hear in the second place how we should answer this call.

Really, the call, "Be reconciled to God!" means: believe that you are already reconciled with God through Christ; accept the hand of reconciliation that is extended to you and all men in the Gospel. It appears easy to do this, yet it is impossible for us to do this by our own powers. Only the Spirit of God who must work all good within us can do this.

He must first clarify the word "Be reconciled to God!" or in all eternity they will be and remain misunderstood words. Should the Holy Spirit explain these words, He must first show the person that he is *not* reconciled to God but is still God's enemy because of his sins. Afterward, the Spirit lets his reconciliation with God, which is already accomplished, shine in his heart in the words, "Be reconciled to God!"

But you will say: "What should we do that God's Spirit works this in us?" I answer: Use the means through which God's Spirit alone will work all spiritual good—His Holy Word, His Law and Gospel. Read and hear first of all the Law; you will hear what God demands of you, how you should be not only in your deeds, words, and desires, but also in your thoughts, heart, and disposition. If you hear that, you will soon recognize that you have done nothing that God demands of you. Yes, it will become clear to you that you hate the Law of God with its demands and threats, that you are God's enemies. If God's Spirit has brought you to this knowledge through the Law, do not look away from this frightful picture, but think about how deeply you have fallen, how far you have swerved!

Then God the Holy Spirit will awaken in you divine sorrow. The words "I am God's enemy!" will ring in your conscience like the thunder of God's wrath. "I am an enemy of God"; these words will pierce your heart like a dagger. "I am God's enemy"; these words will come down upon you like a flash of lightning from the judgment throne of the Most Holy and crush you. Then you will wish you could hide from God. But nowhere will your conscience find protection, nowhere a refuge from God's angry countenance. Therefore, you will finally cry out: "I am lost! I am lost! Woe is me!"

However, you will be happy if you come this far! This is not the way to ruin but to salvation! If in such a condition you hear the word, "Be reconciled to God!" then God is reconciled through the death of His Son, reconciled with the whole world, reconciled with all sinners, reconciled with you as well—oh, this word will be like music from heaven; you will be like a child who had a dreadful dream. Though he thought he was about to fall into an abyss, on awakening he sees himself in the lap of his loving mother. You will cry out: "Is it possible? Should *I*, a sinner, be redeemed? Should *I*, God's enemy, be reconciled to God? Should *I* have forgiveness, grace? Should *I* be God's child and God my Father? Should God stretch the hand of love and reconciliation to *me*? Should heaven be opened to *me*?" Through the Gospel, God's Spirit will answer yea and Amen to all these questions of joyful amazement. He will teach you to pray the sweet Abba, dear Father! Abba, dear reconciled Father!

You see that this is the way by which every person becomes capable through the Holy Spirit of following the command, "Be reconciled to God!"

Oh, all of you, go this way; the cross of your Reconciler will become your sanctuary in the agony of sin, your hope's anchor in affliction, your victory banner in the battle with sin, world, and Satan, your heavenly ladder in the hour of your death. The divine certainty of your reconciliation with God will recast your heart. Love to God and your brother will enter in. You will cry out in words and deeds, "I will love Him because He first loved me." You will do to your brethren as God did to you. It is true that here you will not always taste and see the glory of your reconciliation. In affliction and temptation the sun will often not shine over the cross of your Reconciler. Even your eyes of faith will become dark, and under the cross you will often shed bitter tears of misery and anguish because of your sin. Only remain under it until your heart breaks. If you will die beneath the cross, how happy you will be! God will carry your soul away from Golgatha in the vale of tears up to Mount Tabor in the land of promise, where the sun of eternal ecstasy shines, where there are no clouds of doubt and sorrow. There you also will join in the new song, "Worthy are You to take the scroll and to open its seals, for You were slain, and by Your blood You ransomed people for God" (Revelation 5:9). Hallelujah! Amen in eternity. Amen.

EASTER SEASON

EASTER SUNDAY

MARK 16:1–8

Lord Jesus Christ! We have joyfully appeared here today. We no longer see You in disgrace and humility because of our sins but in exaltation and glory for our justification. Your form was more offensive than that of other people. You were the most despised and rejected of all, full of sorrows and grief, but lo! disgrace, pain, and suffering have disappeared. Completely transfigured, You today lift up Your head, clothed in divine glory and viewed by angels and men as the fairest of the children of men. You bore a crown of thorns; You had been surrendered into the hands of sinners and the willfulness of Your enemies. Today we see You in triumph, crowned as victor, Your bands torn, and all Your enemies at Your feet. You had been led like a sheep to the slaughter and like a lamb that is dumb before her shearers, but You opened not Your mouth. Today we see You as the conquering Lion from the tribe of Judah. At your voice death, the devil, and all hell tremble and flee. You died forsaken by God, groaning, and bleeding on the cross; today we see You risen from Your grave, and hear You cry out, "I died, and behold I am alive forevermore, and I have the keys of Death and Hades" (Revelation 1:18).

Today we joyfully celebrate this festival of Your glorification. We cease our lamentations over Your sufferings and death, once more seize the harps that we laid away, and sing to you—the Resurrected—joyful psalms of praise and adoration. We implore You to let us also experience this day that You live as our Lord and God, as our Savior and eternal Mediator. Take us with You from the grave of sin, doubt, sorrow, weakness, temporal and spiritual misery, and let us share in Your victory, life, joy, power, and glory. Oh, bring that about in us all through the Word of Your resurrection wherever it is preached this day. Hear us for Your own sake. Amen.

On this happy Easter Day, dear hearers!

The Easter festival is truly a festival of joy. Everyone knows that. However, few know what the real foundation, object, and content of true Easter joy is. I do not speak of those who even on Easter do not seek their joy in the house of the Lord, where the Resurrected is preached, but in the heathen temples of the world. For what can they who have a taste only for the joys of the flesh know of spiritual joys? No, I speak of those people who gladly wish to be Christians, who are versed in God's Word, and who rejoice in it. They often know wherein the true *Christmas* joy consists, but they are still unclear as to the true *Easter* joy.

It is usually supposed that Christendom rejoiced on Easter (1) that Christ after His disgrace and bitter suffering finally came into His day of honor and joy; (2) that by His resurrection His innocence, divinity, and the truth of His words were incontestably confirmed before the whole world; and (3) that thereby the immortality of the human soul and the future resurrection of human bodies was fixed beyond a doubt. All these things are of course reasons for Easter joy. Even the Holy Scriptures praise these points as fruits of the resurrection of Jesus Christ. It says concerning the first point, "[Christ] humbled Himself by becoming obedient to the point of death, even death on a cross. Therefore God has highly exalted Him" (Philippians 2:8–9). The Scriptures say of the second point, "Great indeed, we confess, is the mystery of godliness: He was manifested in the flesh, vindicated by the Spirit" (1 Timothy 3:16); and in another passage, "[Christ] was declared to be the Son of God in power according to the Spirit of holiness by His resurrection from the dead" (Romans 1:4). Finally, the Holy Scriptures say of the third point, "Now if Christ is proclaimed as raised from the dead, how can some of you say that there is no resurrection of the dead?" (1 Corinthians 15:12).

As important as all this is, it does not contain the real complete comfort of Easter at all. For all these three points—the glorification of Christ, the confirmation of His doctrine, and the confirmation of the immortality of the human soul and the resurrection of the dead—Christ's resurrection was not absolutely necessary.

First of all, God could have glorified Christ in another way. Second, as concerning His doctrine and divinity, both were already sufficiently confirmed by His glorious miracles; the immortality of man and the resurrection of the body was fixed beyond doubt long ago by the resurrection of Lazarus, the young man at Nain, and the daughter of Jairus, yes, even by the resurrection of the dead as related in the Old Testament.

The true object of the Christian's Easter joy is an entirely different one. The points which were named are almost nothing more than the frame of the real picture, nothing more than extras to the real gift.

We can conclude this from the very fact that the Holy Scriptures present Christ's resurrection as absolutely necessary for the work of redemption and the salvation of man. The apostle Paul says in the wonderful fifteenth chapter of First Corinthians: "If Christ has not been raised, then our preaching is in vain and your faith is in vain. . . . you are still in your sins. Then those also who have fallen asleep in Christ have perished" (15:14, 17–18). We must therefore conclude that the resurrection of Christ is not only an added stone in the structure of our salvation, but the cornerstone; the resurrection of Christ is not only a sparkling gem in the crown of our redemption, but the very crown itself; without the resurrection of Christ, the world still would not be redeemed.

And so it is. The resurrection of Christ makes it possible for one to rejoice in His birth, comfort himself in His suffering and death, and boast of His cross. The Christian Church sings not only at Christmas, "Were this Child not for us born, We should all be lost, forlorn" (*TLH* 78:2); and she sings not only during the holy Lenten season, "All sins Thou borest for us, Else had despair reigned o'er us" (*LSB* 434:1); but she also sings at Easter, "Were Christ not arisen, Then death were still our prison. Now, with Him to life restored, We praise the Father of our Lord. Alleluia! Alleluia! Alleluia, alleluia! Now let our joy rise full and free; Christ our comfort true will be. Alleluia" (*LSB* 459:2–3).

The resurrection of our Redeemer is a great, glorious, blessed, inexpressible comfort, yes a comfort that one cannot completely reason out! Let us today satisfy our thirst in this inexhaustible well of comfort so that we will not thirst in eternity. But before we do this, let us appeal to the Resurrected Himself for His assistance.

The text: *Mark 16:1–8*

On the basis of today's story I speak to you on:

The great comfort lying in Jesus Christ's resurrection

1. Which this great comfort is, and,
2. What a person must do to enjoy it.

I.

If we compare the festivals that Christians celebrate to commemorate the great deeds of God, we must say that the most consoling one is the resurrection of Christ. Yes, the comfort that lies in this deed of God is so great that a preacher of the Gospel might fear to reveal it.

And I confess that whenever I should preach on the topic of Easter, a great conflict begins in me. What indifference and slowness in caring for our soul's salvation I see among us! How terribly the Gospel of grace is misunderstood and misused by many for feeling secure! Ah, how many seem to comfort themselves right into hell with it!

This brings me to my first thought: "You will be silent about this great comfort; it will bring only injury." But then I always conclude: "You dare not remain silent; God Himself has revealed the riches of His grace in His Word. He does not let Himself be stopped by the fact that so many would misuse it. He thought of those who need this comfort." This thought always gains the upper hand, and it has again today. Yes, following the example of Paul, I will "not shrink from declaring to you the whole counsel of God" for your salvation (Acts 20:27); that includes all comfort that God pours out freely to the world in His Word. The most anxious sinner will then have peace and the pious will better themselves; on the other hand, the hypocrites never become happy about it because the witness of their conscience, even if it sleeps at times, always awakens again.

At first glance the resurrection of Christ appears to be a very delightful story, but not of such great comfort for us. It is easy to think that it was most important for *Christ* to rise from the dead and after unutterable disgrace be carried into the state of inexpressible glory. But how does that concern us?

One thinks that, however, only because one casts a fleeting glance at the story of Christ's resurrection. If we, on the other hand, hear what the Scriptures say of its meaning, we must decide differently. The most important is what St. Paul writes in (2 Corinthians 5:15). There we read that those who live should live "for Him who for their sake died and was raised." We see that Christ not only *died* but also *rose* again for us. In His resurrection, as in His death on the cross, we must consider Christ as the substitute and surety for all men. And, mark this well, this is the key to the secret of the boundless, great comfort that lies in His resurrection.

Let me try to clear this matter up by a parable. Suppose the citizens of a city rebelled against their king. The king takes the field against them and encircles them with his superior might. The citizens see that they cannot hold out and they fear that the king will soon wreak vengeance upon them. So they decide to appeal to the king's grace. If they were to hear that their deputy was thrown into chains, they would become frightened and conclude that the same fate awaits also them. But if they would hear later that their representative was again freed, yes, if they saw the man himself, laden with gifts from the king, accompanied with royal honor, returning on a royal horse, entering the city with the trumpets' blast and songs of peace, what must the citizens conclude? Beyond a doubt, that the king has pardoned them. He wants to show the citizens through their representative how he is disposed toward all and what a mistake they had made.

So it is in regard to Christ and His resurrection. View the resurrected Savior as man's substitute. Consider His resurrection not so much as glory coming to Christ but to all men. Christ had not suffered and died for Himself but for all men; He did not therefore rise for Himself but for all men. When Christ suffered and died, He, as it were, descended into the depths of the sea to find the costly pearl of our redemption. When He rose from the depths of the sea and, as it were, cried: "I have found it! I have found it!" What had He found? The pearl of our redemption.

When Christ suffered and died, He was the Lamb of God who did not carry His own sins but the sins of the *world*. And when He rose, we see no sins in Him; we see that He no longer bears the form of a servant, the form of sinful flesh. He threw off the burden of sin and left it in His grave. Where are our sins? They are carried out of sight of God; they are forever buried.

When Christ suffered and died, He was punished for the sake of our sins; our sins were imputed to Him. Isaiah says, "He was pierced for our transgressions; He was crushed for our iniquities" (53:5). But when He arose, we see Him freed of all punishment. Whose punishment has come to an end? The punishment of men.

When Christ suffered and died, He wanted to pay the debt that our sins had incurred. He says in Psalm 69, "What I did not steal must I now restore?" (v. 4). When He arose, our surety was freed from the debtor's prison and set free. Where is the account book against us? It is torn up; all our sins are paid. God the Father has Himself declared, by the resurrection of Christ, that He will demand no more payment from us.

When Christ suffered and died, He offered Himself on the altar of the cross for the reconciliation of men with God. When God awakened Him, God Himself publicly showed that He accepted the sacrifice of His Son and found it of full value. This proves that God is reconciled with us.

When Christ suffered and died, He as our General, as the Lord of our salvation, as our David, began the great battle with our enemies: the Law, sin, death, and the devil. When He arose, behold! He had fulfilled the Law, conquered sin, robbed death of its power, crushed the head of the devil, the old serpent, destroyed hell, and triumphed over the prince of darkness and his whole array. As His battle was our battle, so is also His victory our victory, His triumph our triumph, His conquest our conquest. They were *our* enemies who lay at the feet of the resurrected Savior.

When Christ suffered and died, God condemned Him to death in our place. When God the Father again awakened Him, who was acquitted by God in the person of Christ? Christ needed no acquittal for Himself, for no one could accuse Him of a sin. Tell me, who was justified in Him? Who was declared pure and guiltless in Him? We were. The whole world was. God's words to Christ, "You shall live!" applied to us. His life is our life; His acquittal is our acquittal; His justification is our justification.

Now you will understand what St. Paul means when he writes in Romans 4, "[Christ] was delivered up for our trespasses and raised for our justification" (v. 25). Now you will understand what he wants to say, when he writes in the following chapter, "Therefore, as one trespass led to condemnation for all men, so one act of righteousness leads to justification and life for all men" (5:18). Now you will understand what the same apostle wants to say when he writes in 2 Corinthians 5:14b: "That One has died for all, therefore all have died." You will now understand why Christ so often ascribes to us what concerns Him, why He says, "Because I live, you also will live" (John 14:19b). "In the world you will have tribulation. But take heart; I have overcome the world" (16:33b).

So, who can completely express what great comfort lies in the resurrection of Christ? It is the absolution pronounced by God Himself on all men, all sinners, the entire world, and sealed in the most glorious way. The eternal love of God reveals itself in all its wealth, overflowing fullness, and brightest splendor in Christ's resurrection. In the resurrection we hear that God was not satisfied merely to send His Son into the world and let Him become man for us.

Yes, it was not enough to give His own Son into death for us. No, when His Son had finished everything that He had to do and suffer in order to earn grace, life, and blessedness for us, God, humanly speaking, because of burning love to us sinners, could not wait for us to come and beg for His grace in Christ. No, scarcely had His Son finished everything, then He hurried to give to all men the grace merited through the resurrection of His Son, to acquit them all from their sins, and before heaven and earth publicly, really, and solemnly declare them redeemed, reconciled, clean, guiltless, and righteous in Christ.

II.

Oh great comfort! Blessed, yes, eternally blessed, is he who knows, has, and enjoys this comfort! However, let me now in the second place speak to you on what a person must do if he wishes to enjoy this comfort.

That question is very easy to answer. You have heard that the comfort of Christ's resurrection consists in this, that God in Christ has already pardoned, absolved, and justified the whole world; He has in Christ's person already awarded it the forgiveness of sins and declared it righteous. Now tell me, what must a criminal—who had been condemned to death, but later without a plea from him is pardoned by his judge—what must he do in order to enjoy the pardon that had been decided upon? Naturally, he can do nothing more than accept the pardon.

What must a beggar do when an immensely rich man gives a great gift without his having earned it in some way, yes, is brought into the house in order that he may enjoy the gift? Naturally, he also must and can do nothing else than accept the gift. Would it not be the greatest folly if the pardoned criminal and the endowed beggar would not want to accept the kindness until they had earned it? Would not both lose their gift forever?

Now here you have the answer to the question: what must a person do if he wishes to enjoy the great comfort of Christ's resurrection? The answer is: he must *accept* the justification, or the pardon, of God that was awarded to the whole world, hence also to him, in Christ's resurrection; he must *believe* it! He can, he dare, do nothing else. Anything extra that the person still wishes to do in order to enjoy the comfort of Christ's resurrection is not only completely lost, unnecessary, and vain labor but also obstructive, hurtful, and fatal. For whoever wants to contribute merely the least little thing to his justification before God disavows God's grace. He forfeits Christ's complete, only valid merit, the only reconciling power of His bloody death and justifying means of His glorious resurrection.

But do not suppose that on my own responsibility I dare make the way to heaven as simple as that. First, the doctrine itself teaches that—since God has awarded His grace to the world through Christ's resurrection, it can be enjoyed only by accepting it, through faith in it. Second, God's Word also expressly says this. Here belong all the passages of Holy Scripture which demand faith alone and which attribute to faith in Christ's resurrection alone righteousness before God, all redemption, and salvation. St. Paul writes in Romans 10, "(That is, the word of faith that we proclaim); because, if you confess with your mouth that Jesus is Lord and believe in your heart that God raised Him from the dead, you will be saved" (vv. 8–9). Now you have heard it from the apostle's own mouth. And if we went into the story of Christ's resurrection, we would see this in the example of all the apostles. As long as they did not believe in Christ's resurrection they were comfortless. But as soon as they believed this joyful message, comfort, peace, joy, and life entered their troubled hearts.

With Isaiah I today say to you, "Come, everyone who thirsts, come to the waters; and he who has no money, come, buy and eat! Come, buy wine and milk without money and without price" (55:1). Oh, may none of you let this Easter comfort be preached to you in vain. All, all lay hold of it quickly while God has His table of grace still set. The time might come when you need the Easter comfort but you cannot find it.

You who have hitherto clung to the world, to its vanities, goods, joys, and honor, oh, learn to be ashamed of these worldly, fleshly, low desires at the open grave of Christ. He returned to life with that inexpressible glory that is destined for you. Hurl the lust of these worthless things away. Wish for the grace that your Savior brought you from His grave. He gives you true joy; He gives you true wealth; He gives you true honor!

And you who have continued to live in willful manifest sins, oh, repent today! Just think, with your sinful life you have shown that you have despised the grace that God has awarded you. If you have regarded what this means, "Christ has arisen also for me," you will not serve sin any longer. Depart from sin today, rise with Christ from the grave of your sins, and seek your desires now in the boundless grace of your Savior who rose also for you.

But you, who have hitherto stayed away from the well of grace because you felt yourself too unclean, go to it; do not be so foolish any longer! You ask: "Will God be gracious to me if I come to Him?" How dare you ask that, since you have been pardoned long ago as far as God is concerned in the resurrection of Christ. All that is merely lacking is that you have not taken that pardon. How could God in His Word award salvation only to faith if it had not been already won and given to men? One does not believe in something *so that* it happens but because it *has* happened! Open your eyes and see it, open your hearts and believe it. Then you will enjoy this great comfort, which, like a crystal stream, flows from Christ's grave to all sinners.

And you who have already been so wise as to drink from this stream, celebrate a real festival of joy on this day and drink deeply from it! Practice today to imitate the apostle in saying, "Who shall bring any charge against God's elect? It is God who justifies. Who is to condemn? Christ Jesus is the one who died—more than that, who was raised—who is at the right hand of God, who indeed is interceding for us" (Romans 8:33–34). The more confidently we learn to say these words to the world, to the accusations of our heart, and in defiance of the devil, the more able we will be to join in that song of triumph, " 'Death is swallowed up in victory.' 'O death, where is your victory? O death, where is your sting?' The sting of death is sin, and the power of sin is the law. But thanks be to God, who gives us the victory through our Lord Jesus Christ" (1 Corinthians 15:54–57). Whoever practices this in life can in faith also cry out with that old cross-bearer Job even in death, "For I know that my Redeemer lives, and at the last He will stand upon the earth" (Job 19:25). Now Jesus Christ help us all to have such a happy and blessed departure in faith through the power of His glorious resurrection. Amen.

SECOND SUNDAY OF EASTER

JOHN 20:19–31

Grace be with you, mercy and peace, from God the Father, and from the Lord Jesus Christ, the Son of the Father, in truth and love. Amen.

Dear friends in Christ Jesus!

One of the distinctive teachings of our Evangelical Lutheran Church is that the Christian Church and its called servants have the power to forgive sins. Our Church has never, shall we say, timidly and ashamedly, but rather with great earnestness and joyful resolution confessed this to the world. We read in Luther's Small Catechism: "Confession has two parts. First, that we confess our sins, and second, that we receive absolution, that is, forgiveness, from the pastor as from God Himself, not doubting, but firmly believing that by it our sins are forgiven before God in heaven."

The pastor is then commanded to ask each penitent, "Do you also believe that my forgiveness is God's forgiveness?" whereupon the penitent should answer with a confident, "Yes!" In the year 1530, Lutheran princes, lawyers, and theologians were called upon in the name of our Church to present their confession of faith in Augsburg before the emperor and the realm; even there they in no way denied the teaching of the power of the Church to forgive sins but openly confessed it as a precious treasure of the correct, true Evangelical teaching. We read in the 25th Article of the Augsburg Confession, "Our people are taught that they should highly prize the Absolution as being God's voice and pronounced by God's command. The Power of the Keys [Matthew 16:19] is set forth in its beauty. They are reminded what great consolation it brings to anxious consciences and that God requires faith to believe such Absolution as a voice sounding from heaven [e.g., John 12:28–30]. They are taught that such faith in Christ truly obtains and receives the forgiveness of sins" (Augsburg Confession XXVI 2–4).

You see that our Church in her glorious basic confession attaches such great importance to the doctrine of absolution, that he who renounces this doctrine cannot possibly have the same spirit as our fathers who claim the name Lutheran.

As you know, those who deny absolution picture it as something false and dangerous, battling against it every possible way. They explain this doctrine as a relic of the papacy, an invention of tyrannical priests, a pillow for carnal secure people who do not wish to be converted. Perhaps many a weak Christian has had doubts raised by this blasphemous language. What should we do? Should we decide that our Church has been wrong in this point? Should we renounce it and start a new reformation of the nineteenth century? Far be it! If we search God's Word, we would find that in also this teaching our Church stands upon the unchangeable foundation of the divine Word, that all who fight against this teaching fight against Christ, against His Word, against His merit, and against His true Church.

Because our text offers us the opportunity, let us explore this more closely.

The text: *John 20:19–31*

Scripture has three main passages in which the doctrine of absolution has its real foundation: the first is contained in Matthew 16, the second in Matthew 18, and the third in our text today. On the basis of our text, permit me to show you that

They err who deny preachers the power to forgive sins.

By this error

1. The clearest words of Christ are contradicted;
2. The complete atonement of Christ is denied; and finally,
3. Men are robbed of the greatest and most necessary comfort.

Lord Jesus Christ, You have given Your believers the authority to absolve their brothers and sisters from their sins in Your name. You have especially instituted the office that preaches the reconciliation. Graciously protect us that we do not haughtily and self-righteously despise Your comforting institution. Recognizing Your love to us in it, may we use it to the comfort and salvation of our souls. To that end bless the present sermon for the sake of Your death and resurrection. Amen.

I.

The error of denying preachers the power to forgive sins is greater than one might think. It contradicts the clearest words of Christ.

After His resurrection Christ, said to the apostles, "If you forgive the sins of any, they are forgiven them; if you withhold forgiveness from any, it is withheld" (John 20:23). Quite a while before His death Christ had said the very same thing first to Peter and then to all the disciples. To Peter He said, "I will give you the keys of the kingdom of heaven, and whatever you bind on earth shall be bound in heaven, and whatever you loose on earth shall be loosed in heaven" (Matthew 16:19). And a few days later Christ repeated these words to all the disciples when He said, "Truly, I say to you, whatever you bind on earth shall be bound in heaven, and whatever you loose on earth shall be loosed in heaven" (18:18).

In these words the power of forgiving and retaining sins is so clearly conferred upon the Church and her servants that it needs no proof. Those who deny the Church this power commit a great sacrilege. They contradict God's Son to His very face and call His words lies. They commit the very sin by which Satan misled man when he said, "Did God actually say, 'You shall not eat of any tree in the garden'?" (Genesis 3:1).

The words of the Son of God are so clear and powerful that even the enthusiasts often act as if they also believe in the Office of the Keys. But be not deceived by such admission. They say that Christ gave the apostles only the power to reveal the conditions under which a person should receive or be excluded from the forgiveness of sins. But who has ever heard that one

237

forgives sins by stating the conditions under which he could receive forgiveness? That is not explaining Christ's words but refuting it, not expounding but perverting it, not opening its sweet comfort but taking it out and locking it up, in short, treating it as a joke, treading it underfoot.

But, they say, where did the apostles absolve as do the preachers of the Lutheran Church? I answer: it is true that at the time of the apostles there were no chancels from which the formula of absolution was read; true, they had no confessional where the hand was placed on the head of those who wanted to go to communion and the forgiveness of sins pronounced after their confession. Although we do not find this *method of procedure*, this rite, this *ceremony* of the Office of the Keys in the apostolic Church, we find the same facts.

When the apostle Paul writes to the Corinthians, "Do not be deceived: neither the sexually immoral, nor idolaters, nor adulterers, nor men who practice homosexuality, nor thieves, nor the greedy, nor drunkards, nor revilers, nor swindlers will inherit the kingdom of God. And such were some of you. But you were washed, you were sanctified, you were justified in the name of the Lord Jesus Christ and by the Spirit of our God" (1 Corinthians 6:9–11), what else is this but a public absolution that Paul pronounced upon the repentant Corinthians? Yes, whenever the apostles assure the Christians, "For in Christ Jesus you are all sons of God, through faith" (Galatians 3:26), "For by grace you have been saved through faith" (Ephesians 2:8), and so on, what else is this but the Lord saying to the man sick of the palsy, "Take heart, My son; your sins are forgiven" (Matthew 9:2)? Furthermore, when Ananias said to Saul, "Arise and be baptized and wash away thy sins" (cf. Acts 9:10–19), what else is this but as if Ananias had said: "Let me absolve you"?

The apostles gave themselves the power to forgive sins, and they also exercised it. In 2 Corinthians 2 we read that an incestuous person was punished by the whole Corinthian congregation so severely that he stood at the brink of despair. What did the apostle Paul do? He wrote the following to the congregation: "For such a one, this punishment by the majority is enough, so you should rather turn to forgive and comfort him, or he may be overwhelmed by excessive sorrow. So I beg you to reaffirm your love for him. ... Anyone whom you forgive, I also forgive. *Indeed, what I have forgiven, if I have forgiven anything, has been for your sake in the presence of Christ*" (2:6–8, 10). My friends, can it be more clearly stated that the apostles in Christ's stead and in the name of the congregation actually forgave sins?

This evidence is so clear that many foes of absolution dare not deny that at least the apostles had the power to forgive sins and used it. But they question: "How will one prove that today's preachers of the Gospel also have this power?" Does not St. Paul say in another passage, "Are all apostles?" (1 Corinthians 12:29).

I answer: it is true there is a great difference between an apostle and a present-day minister of the Church. The apostles were infallible; present-day ministers are not. The apostles had the power to do miracles and prophesy; present-day ministers do not. The apostles were called directly by Christ; present-day ministers are called mediately through men. The apostles had the call to go into the world; present-day ministers are limited to the field of the congregation which they are assigned. But as far as the office of preaching the Gospel is concerned, there is no difference. Or does the word of the Lord, "preach the Gospel" apply only to the apostles? Does the command, "Baptize them in the name of the Father, and of the Son, and of the Holy Ghost" apply only to the Twelve? Does His command, "This do in remembrance of Me" apply only to the chosen disciples?

No; speaking of those to whom they would preach, Christ especially said, "Teaching *them* to observe *all* that I have commanded *you*" (Matthew 28:20). As certainly as that command to teach, baptize, and celebrate Holy Communion concerns the Church of all ages, as certainly as all that was commanded the disciples should be kept, so certainly is also the command and promise directed to the Church of all times, "If you forgive the sins of any, they are forgiven them; if you withhold forgiveness from any, it is withheld" (John 20:23). And just as certainly do the words of Matthew 18 apply to the Christians and churches of all times: "If your brother sins against you, go and tell him his fault, between you and him alone. If he listens to you, you have gained your brother. But if he does not listen, take one or two others along with you, that every charge may be established by the evidence of two or three witnesses. If he refuses to listen to them, tell it to the church. And if he refuses to listen even to the church, let him be to you as a Gentile and a tax collector" (vv. 15–17). I say, as certainly as these words are directed to the Christians and congregations of all times, just so certainly are also the words that immediately follow: "Truly, I say to you, whatever you bind on earth shall be bound in heaven, and whatever you loose on earth shall be loosed in heaven" (v. 18).

II.

This great error is so ruinous because it also denies the complete redemption of Christ.

It is true, my friends, that the sectarians also express the truth that Christ has completely redeemed all men. One dare not, however, let this blind and persuade him to believe that they actually believe and preach this truth. It is only too clear that if they *express this once* they *deny* this truth a *thousand times* by the way they teach salvation.

For what does this mean: Christ has completely redeemed us? It means that Christ has done and suffered everything for us that we should have had to suffer and do in order to be saved. We do not have to blot out our sins; Christ has already blotted them out. We do not have to reconcile God; Christ has already reconciled Him. We do not have to merit God's grace; Christ has already earned it for us. We do not have to fulfill the Law for our salvation; Christ has already fulfilled it. We do not have to procure a righteousness that is admissible before God; Christ has already procured it. We do not have to conquer death, the devil, and hell; Christ has already conquered them for us. We do not have to earn our own worthiness in order to enter heaven; Christ has already earned it for us. In short, we do not have to complete the work of our salvation; Christ has already completed everything, drained the cup of our deserved suffering to the very last drop, paid our debt to the very last penny, and done the will of God to the very last letter.

Now what can we conclude? This, that this can, yes, must, be preached to all men. Preaching the Gospel is merely saying to all men: Sinners, rejoice! Christ has already blotted out your sins. Christ has already reconciled you with God. Christ has already earned God's grace for you. Christ has already fulfilled the Law. Christ has already procured a righteousness for you which avails before God. Christ has already conquered death, hell, and the devil. Christ has already earned the necessary worthiness for your entrance into heaven. In short, Christ has already completed the work of your salvation!

Do not suppose that you must first reconcile God through any suffering and atone for your sins. Do not suppose that you must do good works, that you must save yourself by your repentance, by your remorse, by your improvement, by your struggles, by your wrestlings. No! This has already taken place. You should merely receive what Christ has already done and suffered for you, appropriate it, comfort yourself with it, believe it, walk and remain in this faith, and finally be saved through this faith.

You see, since Christ has completely redeemed all men, the Gospel is nothing else than the preaching of the forgiveness of sins or announcing it to all people, to which God Himself says His Yea and Amen in heaven. In a word, it is a general absolution that is brought by men to the whole world, sealed with Christ's blood and death, and confirmed by God Himself through His glorious resurrection. Just because the Gospel is an absolution for all men because of the completed redemption of the world, a preacher can and should assure every person who desires forgiveness that in God's name his sins are forgiven.

What do they do, who deny to preachers of the Gospel the power to forgive sins? They deny them the power to preach the Gospel to all men in its true meaning. They deny Christ's complete redemption that is the preaching of the Gospel. Yes, they who deny the power of forgiving sins lack faith *in* and the true knowledge *of* that perfect redemption. If someone believes that Christ has blotted out the sins of all men, how can he take offense when a preacher or a layman says to one who confesses his faith in Christ: "Thy sins are forgiven thee"? If someone believes that Christ won grace for all men, how can he take offense when a preacher of an ordinary Christian assures a person who believes this: "You have also found grace"? If someone believes that all men are already reconciled through Christ's death and justified by God the Father through His resurrection, how can he be surprised that in God's name through absolution this is actually given him by a preacher or a Christian brother, and that nothing is asked of him but to accept it in faith as though he heard the voice of God Himself?

Our Church teaches in all its purity and fullness that Christ has completely redeemed all men, that a person is righteous before God and will be saved alone by grace through faith; for that reason our Church has also held fast to the precious doctrine of absolution. As long as the doctrine of justification alone through faith shines brightly in our Church, so long it will not let the comfort of the absolution be taken away. However, if one does not have the article of justification alone by grace through faith in its purity, infernal darkness must enter, one must deny the power of absolution, and with it the perfection of Christ's redemption.

III.

Finally, this error is so great because it robs men of the greatest and the most needed comfort. Permit me to speak to you of this.

It seems as though there would be sufficient comfort left even if absolution were rejected. Do not also the opponents of the absolution have the Gospel? Do they not also have Baptism? the Holy Supper? It is true they have these if they have not denied and rejected these things according to their essence. However, because they reject the power of absolution, they remove the comfort that they all contain. Is not the comfort that lies in the Gospel this, that the Gospel gives forgiveness of sins to all who believe it? Is not the comfort which lies in Baptism this, that Baptism "works forgiveness of sins, rescues from death and the devil, and gives eternal salvation to all who believe this, as the words words and promises of God declare" (Small Catechism, Baptism)? Is not the comfort of Holy Communion this, that in "these words, 'Given and shed for you for the forgiveness of sins,' ... forgiveness of sins, life, and salvation are given us" (Small Catechism, Sacrament of the Altar)? But the opponents of absolution take this comfort, the very heart, out of all these Means of Grace and leave their hearers nothing but the empty shell.

Do not suppose that I accuse the sectarians of something of which they are not guilty. Sad to say, it is only too true. Do not they themselves publicly say: "Whoever relies on the mere Word has a dead faith. The letter kills, the Spirit, the Spirit who makes alive must do it"? Do they not even blasphemously teach that about Holy Baptism? Do they not say: "How can washing with water help you? That is a powerless ceremony; the Spirit, the Spirit must do it"? And do they not speak just as contemptuously of Holy Communion? Do they not say: "What does the eating and drinking of Christ's body and blood profit you? Must you not partake of His spirit, which is the true nourishment of your souls"?

My friends, do not believe that only the rejection of absolution is involved in the question whether a preacher has the privilege of daring to say the words: "I forgive you your sins in the stead of Christ." No; this denial has a deeper foundation. It deals not only with the question of whether the Word of God is merely a direction to true Christians and whether the Holy Sacraments are merely powerless ceremonies, but whether both Word and Sacraments are actually the means, the tools, the hands through which God offers, gives, and seals to us grace and the forgiveness of sins. The question involved is whether a person can actually rely on the Word of the Gospel and the promises that are united with the Sacraments as on God's voice, even if one's heart and conscience says No to God's promises and condemns us. It therefore confirms the highest, the greatest comfort we sinful human beings most need.

Though the sects may reject this comfort, let us hold the more firmly to it. Though false teachers may despise us for doing so, let us not despise God who has given us this means for imparting and assuring us of His grace. Though enthusiasts may rely on what they do and suffer and experience, on their prayers, on their struggles and wrestling, on their self-denial, on their visions, on their feelings, on their repentance and sanctification, we will rely on what God has done for us and what He gives us in His Word and Holy Sacraments.

Undoubtedly also among the sects there are many true children of God who are in the state of grace and will be saved. But they will not be saved through their great exertions, nor through their many works, nor through their prayers, running, and chasing, but alone through this: that they find no peace in all their efforts and finally come before God naked and destitute, relying alone on the Word of grace.

Let us therefore not wait until we are nearly in our last hour to reject all our doings, works, righteousness, and worthiness before we hold fast alone to the Word and Sacraments. Let us even now begin to throw this ballast overboard, so that our little boat does not sink in the storms of temptation and death. Let us build on that word that announces grace to all in preaching and imparts it to us especially in the absolution. Let us build on our Baptism by which we have been received into God's covenant of grace—for this covenant stands firm forever. Let us build on the comfort of the Holy Supper whenever we partake of it. There Christ gives us His body and blood as pledges that we have a share in His redemption.

That gives us that comfort which will remain even if our heart condemns us; that gives us that very comfort in the hour of death, even if our whole life accuses us and the world and Satan appear against us; that gives us comfort for the Day of Judgment, for God will, He must, keep what He has promised.

THIRD SUNDAY OF EASTER

JOHN 10:12–16

The grace of our Lord and Savior Jesus Christ, the love of God the Father, and the communion of the Holy Spirit be with you all. Amen.

Dear friends in Christ Jesus!

Our Gospel reading closes with the words, "So there will be one flock, one Shepherd" (John 10:16). Today they are almost generally taken in Christian circles as a prophecy that the time will come when all heathen, Jews, and Muslims will be converted. Then all will belong to the Christian Church. Every human being will bow the knee before Christ. The Christian Church will no longer be split by sects, and all denominational names will cease. All strife will end, all swords will be beaten into plowshares, all spears into pruning hooks, peace will rule in all lands, and all sinners will be brothers in the unity of faith and love. Many also suppose that Christ Himself will come again at the beginning of this golden age, take possession of the whole world, found a glorious kingdom, and rule visibly over His believers. This will last for a thousand years at the close of which the end of the world will come. The word of Christ, "So there will be one flock, one Shepherd," is of special comfort to many Christians in these most troublesome times, in these times of asking and seeking, conflict and strife. The hope of such a heaven on earth cheers thousands today. They say to those who do not want to share such a hope: "Do you not see that the promises are being fulfilled, that the darkness which lies over the nations is lifting and the barriers erected between Christian congregations are falling? Do you not see that today the messengers of the Gospel go out into all the world to preach the word of the kingdom? Do you not see how Christians, who formerly did not associate with one another, now desire to live in one church? Do you not therefore see that the prophecy, 'So there will be one flock, one Shepherd,' is being fulfilled?"

If the best explanation were always the one that agreed with the desires and the sweet dreams of our hearts in apparently seeing a startling confirmation in what is occurring today, then they would be expounding that passage correctly. Whether we have found the true meaning of a passage is not decided by whether it agrees with our heart and experiences but with the analogy of the Holy Scriptures. The opinion that Christians and the Christian Church will triumph in the last times, and that the Church, finally free of all strife and oppression, will become glorious and even here enter into her rest disagrees with all of Holy Scripture. It disagrees with those passages dealing with the nature of Christ's kingdom on earth, the hope of Christians in this world, the last times, and Judgment Day. According to Holy Scripture, the kingdom of Christ on earth is a kingdom of the cross, His Church a militant Church; it teaches that *all* who wish to live godly in Christ Jesus *must* suffer persecution and *must* through much tribulation enter into the kingdom of God; it teaches that the flock of Christ is a small flock, that the majority go the broad way, and that few find the narrow way of Christ; it teaches that the life of the Christian here is hidden in God and that it will first be revealed in the glory of heaven.

The hope of the Christian should not be directed to this world but to heaven. Christians should not be comforted by the hope that things will sometime become better on earth but in heaven. They do not have the promised rest on this world but in the world to come. The righteousness for which Christians should wait will not be on the old world and under the old heavens, but on the new earth and under the new heavens. Nor will the last times be a time of glory but of the greatest distress and universal apostasy. If the last days were not shortened, no person would be saved; the last days will be like the days before the flood and Sodom and Gomorrah. Scripture says, "Nevertheless, when the Son of Man comes, will He find faith on earth?" (Luke 18:8). Whenever the Scriptures speak of that which is still to be expected before the end of the world, it does not comfort us by saying that the Church must first appear in her glory, but it points out the opposite. St. Paul does not say the day of Christ shall not come except the thousand year kingdom first come, but, "unless the *rebellion* comes first" (2 Thessalonians 2:3). Nor dare a Christian ever be secure, because Judgment Day could come any second.

You see that all these important articles of the Christian faith would be overthrown; we dare not understand that word of Christ, "So there will be one flock, one Shepherd," in such a way. We cannot hope for a glorious era for the Church of Christ. No! The Church of Christ will be and remain until the end of the world a kingdom of the cross and Christian cross-bearers, who yearn for rest in the heavenly homeland; yes, the nearer the end of all things comes, the more severe will be the battle facing the believers, the more the little flock will be tested in the fire of the last afflictions and temptations. And finally, far be it from us that we should let the hope of a glorious kingdom of Christ on earth reassure us; then in an unexpected hour, the day of Christ will like a snare surprise all who live on earth.

You wonder, then, how that word of Christ is to be understood, "So there will be one flock, one Shepherd"?

The text: John 10:12–16

The Gospel just read says that Christ is the Good Shepherd. Christ Himself mentions three proofs. First, He shows that He gives His life for the sheep. Second, He knows every one of His sheep, that is, He cares for, feeds, guides, and protects each one. And finally, He goes after the lost and wandering sheep and tries to bring them back to His flock, for He says, "And I have other sheep that are not of this fold. I must bring them also, and they will listen to My voice. So there will be one flock, one Shepherd" (John 10:16). Let us today dwell especially on this last point of Christ's pastoral office,

"There shall be one fold and one Shepherd."

We seek

1.   The true meaning, and
2.   The correct application of these words.

I.

Christ says, "So there will be one flock, one Shepherd." In order to understand these words properly, we must go back into the times before Christ; that which Christ prophesied had not yet occurred. In the times before Christ we find mankind divided into two flocks. The one group was the huge number of heathen nations who went to hell without the knowledge of salvation, without the promise, without hope, in short, without God. The other flock was the family of the patriarchs and finally the nation of Israel. God Himself had elected them, revealed Himself to them, instituted a covenant of grace with them, sent prophets to them. To them He had given His Word and especially the promise of a Messiah, a Savior from sin, death, and hell.

The huge number of heathen were like a flock that wandered about and languished in the desert of the world without a shepherd. On the other hand, Israel was a flock that was shepherded on the green pasture of His Word and was given to drink from the fresh waters of His promises. God's flock was also strictly separated from the heathen through a distinct descent, a distinct country, and a distinct Law.

Though before Christ's coming there was a great and high dividing that separated God's flock from the rest, through His prophets God revealed long before Christ's coming that this dividing wall would not last forever. In time it would fall; the heathen would also share in the promised salvation, and thus there should be one flock and one shepherd. God had said to Abraham, "In your offspring shall all the nations of the earth be blessed" (Genesis 22:18). Dying Jacob said, "The scepter shall not depart from Judah, nor the ruler's staff from between his feet, until tribute comes to Him; and to Him shall be the obedience of the peoples" (49:10). David said in Psalm 72, speaking of the Messiah, "May His name endure forever, His fame continue as long as the sun! May people be blessed in Him, all nations call him blessed!" (v. 17). The prophecy in Isaiah 2 agrees with this: "It shall come to pass in the latter days that the mountain of the house of the LORD shall be established as the highest of the mountains, and shall be lifted up above the hills; and all the nations shall flow to it, and many peoples shall come, and say: 'Come, let us go up to the mountain of the LORD, to the house of the God of Jacob' " (vv. 2–3). Finally Zechariah prophesied of Christ, "He shall speak peace to the nations; His rule shall be from sea to sea, and from the River to the ends of the earth" (9:10).

However, the prophets also declared that the Messiah would not turn the heathen into Jews. Rather He will tear down the old dividing wall that existed between Jews and heathen. He will make one fold, the people of the new covenant. The prophet Jeremiah said of the time of the Messiah, "In those days, declares the LORD, they shall no more say, 'The ark of the covenant of the LORD.' It shall not come to mind or be remembered or missed; it shall not be made again. At that time Jerusalem shall be called the throne of the LORD, and all nations shall gather to it, to the presence of the LORD" (3:16–17). The same prophet confirmed this when he wrote, "Behold, the days are coming, declares the LORD, when I will make a new covenant with the house of Israel and the house of Judah" (31:31). In what this new covenant would consist, God stated through the prophet Ezekiel thus, "For thus says the Lord GOD: Behold, I, I myself will search for My sheep and will seek them out. As a shepherd seeks out his flock when he is among his sheep that have been scattered, . . . I will set up over them one shepherd, My servant David, and he shall feed them: he shall feed them and be their shepherd. And I, the LORD, will be their God" (34:11–12, 23–24).

Now if we compare these predictions of the prophets with Christ's word, "And I have other sheep that are not of this fold. I must bring them also, and they will listen to my voice. So there will be one flock, one Shepherd" (John 10:16), the true understanding of Christ's words becomes clear. He really wishes to say: "You see, I am the Good Shepherd whom the prophets have promised; although I am sent only to the lost sheep of the house of Israel, I am not sent *for* them alone. The whole sinful world is the flock which I want to take to myself and whose shepherd I want to be. Therefore, '*I have other sheep that are not of this fold.*' They are not of the people of Israel, not of the Jewish Church. They are the poor lost heathen who hitherto were outside the commonwealth of Israel and strangers to the testament of promise. '*I must bring them also.*' I must open the barriers that have separated them from the people of God that they also may come, '*and they will listen to My voice.*' I will have My Word preached also to them, and they will accept it in faith. Hence there will then be '*one flock, one Shepherd.*' The former difference between Jews and heathen will cease, for I will build one Church, which is no longer tied to one distinct nation, one distinct land, one distinct Law. The whole world will be the ship of My Church, and heaven will be her harbor. In all places she will open her gates wide through Baptism and through her the believers of all nations will enter in as one people."

You see, the promise of one flock and one shepherd will not go into fulfillment in the future. From the moment the Holy Spirit revealed to the disciples that God does not regard the person, but that in all nations whoever fears God and does righteously is accepted; that the heathen must not first become Jews in order to belong to the people of God; that every person becomes a citizen with the saints and belongs to God's household through faith in Christ; when the apostles turned to the heathen and said, "Come, for all things are now ready!"; when this call of God spread from land to land, when everywhere great crowds of heathen believed and were baptized; when in all places and corners of the earth Jews and gentiles gathered in one spirit and faith; when all tongues of the world praised God and the Father of our Lord Jesus Christ, then had happened what the Good Shepherd had announced beforehand as the work that He had come to complete. Then He had attracted the other sheep that were not of the fold of the true Jewish Church. They had heard His voice, and there was "one flock, one Shepherd." No land, no river, no sea, no mountain, no language, no system, and no climate sets limits now to the elect flock of God. Through faith in Christ millions of people from all nations, ages, peoples, and stations were now united into one congregation, which is of one heart and one soul under their invisible Lord and Head, Jesus Christ.

And so we read as the apostle writes to the Ephesians, "Therefore remember that at one time you Gentiles in the flesh, called 'the uncircumcision' by what is called the circumcision, which is made in the flesh by hands—remember that you were at that time separated from Christ, alienated from the commonwealth of Israel and strangers to the covenants of promise, having no hope and without God in the world. But now in Christ Jesus you who once were far off have been brought near by the blood of Christ. For He Himself is our peace, who has made us both one and has broken down in His flesh the dividing wall of hostility. . . . He came and preached peace to you who were far off and peace to those who were near. For through Him we both have access in one Spirit to the Father" (Ephesians 2:11–14, 17–18). He also writes in his letter to the Romans, "For there is no distinction between Jew and Greek; for the same Lord is Lord of all, bestowing His riches on all who call on Him. For 'everyone who calls on the name of the Lord will be saved' " (Romans 10:12–13).

You see, that, that is the fulfillment of the promise, "So there will be one flock, one Shepherd." Therefore, do not indulge in the enthusiastic hope that according to these words, there will still be a mass conversion to Christ before Judgment Day, a final complete union of all Christians, and that Christ will found a glorious kingdom on earth. Such a hope is not only grounded on human thought alone, it is also highly dangerous and harmful. It necessarily so blinds the eyes of the Christian that he does not see the true condition of the Church in these last days of affliction; it makes him uninterested in the difference between truth and error; it diverts the heart from the yearning for heaven and eternal life and draws it down to earth with its yearnings and hopes; and finally, it hinders the daily and hourly preparedness for death and Judgment Day.

II.

Now after we have the true understanding of Christ's word, "So there will be one flock, one Shepherd," the question now arises: what is the true application of these words? Permit me in the second place to answer that question.

If it is Christ's will that all people gather into one flock, there cannot be two or more but only one true Church on earth. We really apply Christ's word correctly when we hold fast to the old apostolic faith: "I believe in the one, holy, Christian Church." We are to seek this one true Church and remain with it. In our times especially some cherish the delusion that there are many true churches; the different sects are only different divisions of the same Church; each has the truth only in a different way. Yes, today many go so far as to maintain that even the Christian religion is not the only saving faith; or that faith is of no value as long as a person acts according to his conscience, loves his fellow man, and is upright and fair to all. He will then be saved no matter what he believes. Many preachers go so far as to misuse Bible passages to extenuate such terrible religious indifference. All these ruinous thoughts that undermine and overthrow religion and piety are judged and rejected through Christ's word, "So there will be one flock, one Shepherd." We see that Christ has only one fold, and He is the only Shepherd of the souls of men. If a person does not belong to the one fold and is not under the one Shepherd, there is no second flock in which his soul can find pasture. His soul is still like a poor lamb that disappeared from the flock, wandered about without the shepherd, without pasture, without water, and finally dies. He who has not entered the Church is still not on the way to heaven, is still without hope, yes, without God in this world.

Moreover, we correctly apply Christ's word, "So there will be one flock, one Shepherd," when we hold fast to the faith that the true Church is united only to Christ and His Holy Word. Since Christ's Word has already sounded to the ends of the earth, His Church is to be found throughout the world. As many in our day falsely expand the Church of Christ, others on the other hand often falsely wish to limit it. The Roman Catholic Church ties the Church and salvation to Rome and the Roman Bishop. She condemns all who do not want to be subject to his supreme power and the authority of his appointed bishops. On the other hand, sectarians bind the Church and salvation to their sects and customs, attitudes, works, and holy practices; they condemn all who do not want to be recast in the form of Christianity that their sect considers the only true one.

Christ's word, "And I have other sheep that are not of this fold. I must bring them also, and they will listen to my voice. So there will be one flock, one Shepherd" (John 10:16), overturns all these barriers through which the Church should be separated anew. Only one thing is necessary in order to belong to the one fold that will be saved, and this one thing is to listen to the voice of Christ, know Him as the only Shepherd of his soul, and remain with Him. Hence, my dear hearers, you see that if you want to be saved, *that* is the only way.

You, whoever you may be, are invited by Christ to go this way. Know that you have erred from God's fold through sin and are lost. Hear Christ, the Good Shepherd, calling to you in His Word, "I am the Good Shepherd," come to Me; and he who comes to Me, I will not cast out. If you know that hitherto you have gone the wrong way; that of yourself you cannot seek and find the way to God and heaven, though you may be old or young, rich or poor, wise or simple, one who has merely made a false step or a deeply fallen sinner, yes, even if you were the greatest of all sinners, listen to the friendly gracious voice of Christ, the Good Shepherd, and in faith come to Him. You will then belong to the one fold under the one Shepherd. Let the others go another way. You remain on the way that your Shepherd leads you. You will be saved. Let the others pin their hopes on other things, on their works, on their sanctification, on their pious practices, struggles, improvements, feelings, experiences, and the like; pin your hope on your Lord Christ. Doing this you will never be ashamed. Whoever is with Christ is in the true flock and the true Church; his salvation is unshakably firm.

Finally, we really apply Christ's words, "So there will be one flock, one Shepherd," when we use our gifts, calling, and circumstances to see to it that this promise is fulfilled in our day. Although Christ has most gloriously fulfilled His word through His apostles, He does not want to stop fulfilling it as long as He prays for grace for the world. It is Christ's gracious will that His Shepherd's voice resounds ever louder where countless hosts of unfortunate heathen still wander about without God and hope. He wants more and more to be led to the green pastures of His Church and added to His blessed flock. It is also Christ's gracious will that the flock which has already answered His call be ever more closely united in Him and every hedge which Satan has built between the sheep of His flock be broken down. And Christ wants to do that through those whose eyes He has opened to see the misery of the heathen.

Oh my dear hearers, recognize your holy calling in doing your part so that ever more you may be called to Christ's flock. Diligently consider the unspeakable misery of the poor heathen in your prayers; do not forget to support the great work through your generous gifts. Let the misery of all Christendom touch your hearts. She should be a flock that rests peacefully about Christ, the Good Shepherd, but look at her fold! Ah, it is a battlefield! What lack of union! What divisions and separations! How the majority of Christ's sheep today groan partly under mercenaries who do not pasture them but only live opulently off them, partly under proud priests who rule harshly and sternly over them! Partly under heretics and false prophets, who have come to them in sheep's clothing but inwardly they are ravening wolves! Do not think that any sacrifice that you must bring is too great. You must contribute something that the light which has been given us be placed on a candlestick to enlighten others; perhaps many of our sincere brothers will then be rescued from the bonds in which they now groan, perhaps unknowingly. We must see to it that ever greater peace be in Christ's Israel, that as it pleases the Lord a friendly evening star will arise in this midnight hour until finally the great Shepherd of the sheep comes and will lead His triumphant flock into the heavenly fold.

To that end may He help us all for the sake of His eternal Shepherd's faithfulness. Amen.

———◦◦◦◦———

FOURTH SUNDAY OF EASTER

JOHN 16:16–23

Grace be with you, and peace from God our Father, and from our Lord Jesus Christ. Amen.

In our Savior, dearly beloved hearers!

There are people who wish to be Christians and yet are almost always sad. Their faces almost never light up in joy. They go about gloomy and cross, a burden to themselves and others.

And what is the reason? One person becomes ill-humored because he sees others get ahead almost without trouble and work, are happy and rich, while he cannot get ahead, yes, is even pursued by all manner of misfortune. Another sees himself misjudged; the honor to which he thinks he is lawfully entitled is denied him. A third because he has powerful enemies for whom everything prospers, while his rights are suppressed. In other words, the reason for their sadness is that their affairs are not as they wish. And if one asks them: "Do you think that you are justly angry?" They answer, if not in words then in their hearts, as did the prophet Jonah when Nineveh did not fall as he wished, "I do well to be angry, angry enough to die" (Jonah 4:9).

Christians may seem to have very good reasons for being dissatisfied with their lot, and be more sorrowful and angry than joyful and calm.

My friends, though the vain *joy* of the world is ungodly, worldly *sorrow* is even more sinful. As pious joy is the image of God, so worldly sorrow is the image of Satan. It is the very opposite of faith. Though it often assumes the appearance of Christian earnestness, it is anything but this. Worldly sorrow is, first of all, really secretly murmuring against God, the Ruler of our life. It is a fruit of pride and self-righteousness. Whoever has really known that he has merited hell because of his sin finds it impossible to be dissatisfied with his lot, no matter how untoward it may be. He recognizes that he has prospered more than he deserved. The word in Jeremiah's Lamentation applies to him: "Why should a living man complain, a man, about the punishment of his sins?" (Lamentations 3:39).

Worldly sorrow is also against the love of one's neighbor. He who is almost always humorless and gloomy becomes a burden to those who are associated with him. Instead of being his brother's comfort and assistant on the trouble-filled road to eternal life, he renders his pilgrimage only the more difficult. But above all, such a person in the final analysis hurts himself. For if worldly sorrow begins to rule his heart, faith and love must depart. The Holy Spirit, who is a Spirit of joy and peace, can no longer live in that heart. It is, to speak quite frankly, the certain way to eternal sorrow in hell. The apostle Paul says that quite clearly in (2 Corinthians 7:10): "Worldly grief produces death."

Christ, therefore, calls His Christians blessed not only when they are persecuted for righteousness' sake, hated, reviled, and rejected for His sake, but He also adds, "*Rejoice* in that day, and leap for joy, for behold, your reward is great in heaven" (Luke 6:23). All the apostles demand the same of Christians. Peter writes, "Rejoice insofar as you share Christ's sufferings" (1 Peter 4:13). James writes, "Count it all joy, my brothers, when you meet trials of various kinds" (James 1:2).

What the apostles asked of Christians, they also practiced themselves. When they had been scourged by the Sanhedrin at Jerusalem because they confessed Christ, we read that "they left the presence of the council, rejoicing that they were counted worthy to suffer dishonor for the name" (Acts 5:41). Yes, Paul confesses, "In all our affliction, I am overflowing with joy" (2 Corinthians 7:4). Not only did the great apostles act that way but even the ordinary Christians. The writer of the letter to the Hebrews gives us this glorious testimony: "You joyfully accepted the plundering of your property, since you knew that you yourselves had a better possession and an abiding one" (Hebrews 10:34).

Now if a Christian should be happy, yes, skip for joy even in the greatest and most severe affliction, is it not disgraceful if a Christian gives way to sorrow and ill-humor when his affairs do not go just as he wishes? He gives poor evidence that he has the faith that conquers the world.

Yet as ungodly and harmful as worldly sorrow is, there is another sorrow that is not harmful but most wholesome—yes, absolutely necessary. That is the godly sorrow over one's self, over one's sins. This sorrow is the way to joy. "For godly grief," writes St. Paul, "produces a repentance that leads to salvation without regret" (2 Corinthians 7:10). And it is this we wish to consider today.

The text: *John 16:16–23*

The words that were just read belong to the last words that Christ spoke to His disciples. The sum of these words is that sorrow awaited them, but that in the end they would have joy in time and in eternity.

Therefore, permit me to show you that

Godly sorrow is the only way to true joy.

1. To the joy of faith in time, and
2. To the joy of sight in eternity.

God, You are a wonderful God. If You want to make us alive, You first let us taste death. If You want to lead us to the light, You first let our darkness become clear to us. If You wish to endow us with power, You first let us experience our weakness. If You want to make us saints, You first make us sinners. If You want to exalt us, You first lead us into the deep valley of humility. Only through the pains of repentance do You lead us to the comfort of faith. Only through hell into heaven, through crying to laughter, through sorrow to joy. Oh, therefore help us to follow You whenever You want to lead us on this amazing way. May we hold still whenever You place Your healing hands on the wounds of our conscience, nor resist Your Spirit of grace whenever He wishes to work on our souls. You always mean well with us. Even Your severe blows are only the blows of love. For by the things that hurt us You seek nothing else but our salvation. If we do *not* let ourselves be led by You, but want to go our own way according to the lusts of our flesh, we are lost. Hence, bless now the preaching of Your Word that it may make us all willing to be led in the wonder of Your grace, and remain under Your discipline until finally we enjoy those pleasures that no one will take from us. Amen.

I.

In our Gospel Christ shows His disciples the way in which their faith will be tested and exercised and strengthened and preserved until their entrance into eternal joy. The way in which this happens is also the same way in which true faith is born in the heart. Which is the way that the Lord prescribes for His disciples? He indicates that with the words, "Truly, truly, I say to you, you will weep and lament, but the world will rejoice. You will be sorrowful, but your sorrow will turn into joy" (John 16:20). Sorrow—not worldly sorrow but godly sorrow—is the way to faith.

There can be no other way. True faith is not only a dead accepting as true of all that which is in the Bible; a person whose heart is still unbroken can have that. True faith is rather a heavenly power worked by the Holy Spirit, by which one comforts himself in firm confidence in Christ, whenever the conscience is disturbed over sin, God's wrath, death, judgment, and hell. It is a power through which a person is born again, the love of sin rooted out, his heart cleansed and renewed, and love to God and one's neighbor poured in.

This miraculous change cannot take place in a person as long as he is unconcerned about his sins. Christ compares the birth of true faith with the temporal birth of a child, saying, "When a woman is giving birth, she has sorrow because her hour has come, but when she has delivered the baby, she no longer remembers the anguish, for joy that a human being has been born into the world" (John 16:21). Christ wishes to say: This is also the case with the joy of faith. Without the labor pains of true repentance, it also does not come into the world. It is impossible for the plant of faith to spring up and thrive in a soul in which the thistles and thorns of indifference toward sin still grow luxuriantly. It is impossible for the oil of divine comfort of faith to enter a heart that is still stony and unbroken. It is impossible for the soothing salve of the Gospel to show its healing power as long as the wounds of sin fester. The Holy Spirit is the doorkeeper of Christ's fold, but this Spirit of Holiness cannot open the door to one who is still a lover of sin. Christ is a physician of sick people. Whoever goes to Him without painfully feeling the sickness of his sins and without seeking a cure for them from Him is only pretending. The Gospel of grace is a meal of grace. Whoever does not hunger and thirst after righteousness merely acts as if he eats this meal. He deceives only himself.

If true faith with its heavenly joy is to enter a heart, the person must, as God says through the prophet Jeremiah, first "Know and see that it is evil and bitter for you to forsake the LORD your God; the fear of Me is not in you," (Jeremiah 2:19). If a person is to learn to exult without hypocrisy with David, "Bless the LORD, O my soul, . . . who forgives all your iniquity, who heals all your diseases" (Psalm 103:1, 3), he must first have been able to say sincerely with him, "For my iniquities have gone over my head; like a heavy burden, they are too heavy for me. . . . I am feeble. . . . I groan because of the tumult of my heart" (Psalm 38:4, 8).

Repentance and sorrow is not necessary because it is so meritorious in God's eyes. It is necessary because no person as he is by nature can truly believe; only one who is really and truly frightened because of his sins seizes Christ in faith, so that he can then truly say: I know that my sins are forgiven, and I know that I hate sin, and, "I walk slowly all my years because of the bitterness of my soul" (Isaiah 38:15), into which my sins have hurled me.

You see that not only those who ignore the Christian faith ignore Christ, ignore God's Word and Church, and hope in vain for salvation. Many so-called Christians have never experienced true sorrow over their sins. If they imagine that they have faith because they not only go diligently to church and the Holy Supper but also conduct their family altar at home, their hope of being saved is also vain.

Sad to say there are only too many who wish to be Christians but do not have an earnest concern and dread of sin. At times in their daily life they are not strictly conscientious, yes, even dishonest. Or they do not always stick strictly to the truth; if they are in a difficulty, they tell a little white lie, as they call it. They are slanderers. Or they gladly speak evil of their neighbor behind his back. Or otherwise they act lovelessly toward him. Or now and then they act like the vain world. Or they secretly cling to the god mammon. Or their greatest aim is their own honor. Or they give way to a certain amount of rage. They cherish certain impure lusts, or envy, or hatred, and irreconcilableness.

Because of all this their conscience is now and then restless. But they always seek to convince themselves that this is only a weakness, a trifle; they are still in God's grace. They therefore suppress their agitated conscience and rid their minds of the matter as quickly as possible. However, if they are reprimanded by their brethren, what do they do? Instead of humbling themselves, they deny or excuse or extenuate their sins; from this time on they (if not openly then secretly) resent him who reprimanded them, while outwardly they remain friendly toward him.

Should such people be Christians? No, of course not! When a true Christian has fallen into sin, he has no rest day or night until he is cleansed through Christ's blood and Spirit. Often the smallest sin makes him so miserable and anxious that he does not know where he stands. Whence does it come, that many suppose that with all this halting between Christ and Belial, they are still in the faith? Their faith was not born by true sorrow over their sins; it is a miserable delusion that cannot stand either in temptation or in death, a delusion more dangerous than open unbelief.

Ah, if only such souls might not be found also amongst us! Perhaps not a one of us belongs to those godless of whom the Scriptures say that they are not frightened of hell for one second. Are there not, however, several among us who, even if they are now and then disturbed, still have never found that true godly sorrow over their sins, which thoroughly converts the heart?

Ah, you unhappy people! Perhaps you have heard and read a thousand times that to obtain grace a person must first repent, then believe, and through faith come to a new life in God. You can perhaps recite this by rote. But you have never experienced it in yourselves! You comfort yourself with a faith without repentance. Ah, are you not afraid that your knowing without doing will bring you a frightful end? Do you not know that in your hour of death your pretended Christianity will collapse like a house of cards? Are you not concerned that the pricks of conscience, which you suppress, could in the face of death become the flames of despair? Do not resist the Spirit of God any longer. Pray God for that true godly sorrow, which alone is the way to the joy of true faith in time.

II.

My friends, a person can have experienced this sorrow and joy and still forfeit eternal joy. Therefore, permit me to show you, in the second place, how continued divine sorrow is also the way to the joy of seeing in eternity.

Undoubtedly the disciples had experienced true godly sorrow over their sins when they came to Christ. Nothing else than the misery of their sins could have driven them to Him. Perhaps only Judas the traitor followed Christ to gain some earthly advantage. Though much weakness still clung to the others, they sought above all their souls' salvation in Christ. Peter in the name of all answered the question, "Do you want to go away as well?" by saying, "Lord, to whom shall we go? You have the words of eternal life"

(John 6:67–68). This answer could come only from the knowledge of the misery of their sins, as we see when Christ had on one occasion miraculously blessed Peter; in the deepest feeling of sinfulness, he cried out, "Depart from me, for I am a sinful man, O Lord" (Luke 5:8).

Now why does Christ predict sorrow for them even in the future? Because nothing else was possible but that they must experience this, because Christ's suffering and death was necessary. God's absolute power and wisdom consists in this, that He does not, because of another matter, have to do something against His will as we men. No, what God lets us experience we experience because it is necessary and wholesome for us in this way and no other.

Thus it was also with the sorrow of the disciples. To be sure, it had its outward cause in Christ's suffering and death, and in the withdrawal of His visible presence, as well as in the enmity and rage of the world. *God's* aim, however, was that the disciples should be led on the way of sorrow to eternal joy. Undoubtedly if God had let them experience only spiritual and temporal joy, they all would have been lost. They could not have borne the great honor of their office and the glory of their gifts, by which they far surpassed all men, even the prophets; they would have become secure and proud. But the sorrow into which they were continually reduced by their faithful God preserved them. When Paul repeatedly begged for deliverance from his severe worries and afflictions, he received this answer from God, "My grace is sufficient for you, for my power is made perfect in weakness" (2 Corinthians 12:9).

God did not lead only the disciples on this way. He goes that way with all His Christians. When at the beginning of our text the Lord says to the disciples, "A little while, and you will see Me no longer" (John 16:16), He gave a short description of the life not only of the apostles but also of all Christians. Of course, their life is not a continual unbroken sorrow, but a continual interchange of joy and sorrow. The basis of their *joy* is that they *see* Christ, that is, that they are *certain* of His gracious presence. The grounds of their sorrow is that at times, yes, that they often do *not* see Christ; they become *uncertain* of His gracious presence.

Christians experience not only the afflictions common to their age, but because they are Christians they go through special trials, such as disgrace, contempt, persecution. But that is not really the subject of the Christian's sorrow. If Christians sorrow over their cross, that is only a weakness of their flesh, yes, more a worldly than a godly sorrow. Their afflictions should really bring joy and not sorrow.

No, the Christian's sorrow consists in something entirely different. True Christians know of no greater treasure in this world than God's grace and living according to God's will. This alone makes life worthwhile, turns a vale of tears into a place of joy. However, as long as they live on earth, they never progress so far that they can either comfort themselves without interruption in God's grace or perfectly fulfill the will of God. They are not yet entirely spirit, but still have much flesh in them. Today they believe with complete confidence, but by the next morning it is as if their faith were extinguished like a light. The old unbelief again forces its way into their heart.

As soon as their *faith* becomes weak they lose their *power* to battle against their sins, love God and their neighbor, serve Him, and even deny themselves. If they do not immediately fall from grace, this always brings on such a severe struggle that they must groan with Paul, "Wretched man that I am! Who will deliver me from this body of death?" (Romans 7:24). And the Christian lives through many such days when he must wage this conflict. Often there are also longer periods of time during his life when he feels, and feels so painfully, well nigh only his unbelief and sinfulness, that his heart is almost always full of groans. The remembrance of his past, a glance into his present life, fills him with sorrow; the thought of the future with sorrow and fear.

Many suppose that when a person becomes a Christian, he must always live in joyful faith and love. That is by no means true. Even the fathers in faith, an Abraham, a David, a Paul, a Luther, have sighed more than they exulted. The true nature of the outer and inner life of a Christian is expressed in the words of Christ, "A little while, and you will see Me no longer; and again a little while, and you will see Me" (John 16:16). Now one experiences certainty, then doubt; now rest, then unrest; now power, then weakness; now joy, then sorrow—in short, a continual conflict. Only false faith is without temptation. True faith is always tempted.

He who experiences nothing of this, yes, does not experience something of this daily, has a sure sign that his faith is only an empty powerless fancy.

How fortunate are they who must confess that they have almost never completely freed themselves of trouble, sorrow, and worry of heart! If they can speak of almost nothing else but their incurable corruption; if they must speak to God with that hymn which concerns the good they did think, speak, and do, "If something good is in my life, Then it is truly thine," happy are they! Without the feeling of the misery of their sins and the sorrow of their heart, they would never remain with Christ but would soon become secure, proud, and self-righteous. The sorrow that ever and again visits them is the means that God uses to keep them with Christ. Oh blessed is he who allows himself to be kept with Christ in this manner. He is on the road to eternal life, as Christ expressly says at the close of our text, "So also you have sorrow now, but I will see you again, and your hearts will rejoice, and no one will take your joy from you. In that day you will ask nothing of Me" (John 16:22–23).

Oh my dear brethren, let us then gladly go the way that the Lord leads, the way of godly sorrow. His aim is joy in time and eternity. Many times in the trouble of your souls the question still escapes our weak heart: Ah, Lord, why? But on that day when we shall see God and reap the joyful harvest from our tears, we will ask God nothing but will laud and praise Him that He has led us through suffering to eternal glory, through trouble to eternal rest, through sorrow to eternal joy. Amen.

FIFTH SUNDAY OF EASTER

JOHN 16:5–15

Grace and peace be multiplied unto you through the knowledge of God, and of Jesus our Lord, Amen.

In our Savior, dearly beloved hearers!

In our days the principle is not seldom expressed that one cannot demand more of a person than he can produce. Whether anyone has done right or wrong, and whether he will some day stand or fall before God depends on whether his actions measure up to his convictions or not. If a person does something because he thinks that it is good, then it is good.

The result of this principle is, first of all, the greatest religious indifference. They suppose that little or nothing depends on one's faith and religion. God is just as pleased when a heathen venerates and worships the sun, moon, stars, human beings, animals, or idols, as when a Christian venerates and worships the true God in the true faith, as long as the heathen believes that these creatures are his gods whom he must serve.

That principle has another result: those who entertain that thought are completely at ease when they have acted according to their conviction and suppose that they are justified before God and man. If God's Word demands that they recognize that they are great sinners, and if they are admonished to repent, very often they say: "What evil have I done? From my youth on I have followed the principle to do right, fear no one! What else, what more would God want from me?"

Nevertheless, my friends, as widespread as the principle is today, so completely false is it.

Yes, if a person does something evil when convinced that it is evil, it is a much greater sin than if he had done the evil falsely believing that it was something good. The apostle Paul, comforting himself somewhat, says, "Though formerly I was a blasphemer, persecutor, and insolent opponent. But I received mercy because I had acted ignorantly in unbelief" (1 Timothy 1:13). After Peter had said to the Jews at Jerusalem, "You killed the Author of life," in order not to hurl them into despair he adds, as it were to excuse them, "Now, brothers, I know that you acted in ignorance, as did also your rulers" (Acts 3:15, 17).

Yet we dare never conclude that because a person considered a matter right, it is right! The Lord says, "That servant who knew his master's will but did not get ready or act according to his will, will receive a severe beating" (Luke 12:47). But He immediately adds, "But the one who did not know, and did what deserved a beating, will receive a light beating" (12:48a); he will nevertheless be punished.

And God's Word goes even further. It shows us that true piety and fear of God consist not in acting according to one's thoughts, nor at one's discretion, nor according to one's intention, nor according to one's conviction; the great ruin of men consists in doing what they do according to the thoughts of their heart and the judgment of their natural reason. Yes, God surrenders those men to a fearful punishment to do what they consider most proper. Thus we read in Isaiah 58:13–14: "Not going your own ways, or seeking your own pleasure, or talking idly; then you shall take delight in the LORD." And St. Paul describes the condition of the unconverted as one in which they fulfill "the desires of the body and the mind" (Ephesians 2:3). Isaiah therefore demands not only, "Let the wicked forsake his way," but also adds, "and the unrighteous man his thoughts" (55:7). Finally, in anger the Lord says in Psalm 81:12 of His people: "So I gave them over to their stubborn hearts, to follow their own counsels."

A person who acts contrary to God's Word is not justified because he has acted according to his conviction. He is condemned. The thoughts, the intentions, the principles that each person has by nature are the very things from which every person must be converted if he wants to be saved. Not the convictions of our natural reason as to what is good and evil, and wherewith one can stand before God, avail before God, but the conviction that God gives through His Holy Spirit.

Our Gospel reading today tells us what this correct conviction is. Let us become better acquainted with it.

The text: *John 16:5–15*

When the Lord had disclosed to His disciples that He would soon leave them, they were so thunderstruck that they became completely silent. Frightened, they thought that, forsaken by the Lord, it would be impossible for them to carry out their commission and convince the world of what they were to preach to it. The Lord therefore says in our text, "But now I am going to Him who sent Me, and none of you asks Me, 'Where are You going?' But because I have said these things to you, sorrow has filled your heart" (John 16:5–6). Hereupon the Lord gives them this comfort: "Nevertheless, I tell you the truth: it is to your advantage that I go away, for if I do not go away, the Helper will not come to you. But if I go, I will send Him to you. And when He comes, He will convict the world concerning sin and righteousness and judgment" (vv. 7–8). The Lord means to say: "Do not suppose that when I go, that is, when I suffer and die and finally ascend into heaven, you cannot fulfill your commission. No, unless I suffer and die you could not do it; the Holy Spirit would not come and reprove the world through the Gospel of My suffering and death, of My resurrection and ascension, that is, He could not convince them of that which you should convince them. But if I suffer and die, the Holy Spirit will come and through the Gospel preached by you give the world the true conviction of sin, of righteousness, and of judgment."

Permit me to stop right here and on the basis of the word of the Lord in our text speak to you of

The conviction that the Holy Spirit alone works.

1. Of sin,
2. Of righteousness, and
3. Of judgment.

I.

My friends, there are above all three things of which every person who should be saved must have the proper conviction: first, which sin really condemns a person; second, which righteousness avails in God's sight; and third, which judgment God will hold.

First of all, which does the world believe is the sin that actually condemns?

There are many different convictions about this. Some suppose sin is only a weakness and sickness of the human nature. As a person could not be reprimanded because his body is sick, a person should not be reprimanded because of the sin-sickness of his soul. They also suppose that many live so wickedly and coarsely because of their lack of education, their poverty, the false principles that were instilled in them, or the prevailing tendency of their temperament that they inherited from their wicked parents. God does not impute all their sins to them, but when they die will make even better people out of them.

Others suppose that it is true that there are sins that damn men in God's sight. These are the gross sins, such as theft, fraud, robbery, cruelty, murder, adultery, fornication, false oath, endless cursing, blasphemy, drunkenness, gluttony, and the like. The others find sins against the second table, and above all those against the first table they suppose God overlooks.

Finally, still others go somewhat deeper. They believe that those hidden sins against the love of God and one's neighbor are damnable sins, but they suppose that if a person regrets them and seeks to better himself, these sins are atoned for.

Now which is the proper conviction of sin, which alone the Holy Ghost gives? The Lord states that in our text when He says, "When He comes, He will convict the world concerning sin and righteousness and judgment: concerning sin, because they do not believe in Me" (John 16:8–9).

A noteworthy statement! Does the Lord mean to say that the Holy Spirit will reprove the world only of unbelief, because nothing else will be reckoned as sin? Far from it! The Lord wishes to say: "When I have gone to the Father, that is, when I will have finished my suffering and death, arisen, and ascended into heaven, the Holy Spirit will preach through you to the world: 'People, there is no difference; you have all sinned and come short of the glory of God. But see! God became a man, took on Himself the sins of all men, bore their punishment, and completely blotted out all sins through His bitter suffering and death. All who believe in Him will not be lost but have eternal life. He who believes and is baptized will be saved. He who does not believe will be damned.' " Through such preaching the Lord means to say the Holy Spirit will first reprove the world "concerning sin, because they do not believe in Me."

What does this mean? This: the Holy Spirit will convince the world through that apostolic preaching that by nature they lay in sin and damnation. That is why the Son of God had to become a man, suffer, and die in order to blot out their sins and damnation. After this had taken place and grace was offered to all men, then came the chief sin, the greatest sin, the sin of all sins that gives its power to condemn to all other sins, the sin which again opens hell and closes heaven, the sin on whose account man really is lost in unbelief which rules in all men by nature. "For," writes St. Paul, "God has consigned all to disobedience, that He may have mercy on all" (Romans 11:32).

There, my friends, is the Holy Spirit's twofold judgment over sin. First, he explains to man that everything he thinks, desires, wishes, speaks, and does is by nature damnable sin but such for which there is still help. One must confess them and believe in Christ who atoned for sin. But, second, if a person does not accept this preaching of grace, if he does not want to throw himself into the dust before God as a lost and condemned sinner and cry for mercy, if he does not believe in him who justifies the ungodly, then the Holy Spirit does not lift His first judgment upon the sins of that person; He declares that that person is not only a condemned sinner but also irretrievably lost.

Oh, my friends, that at least all of us would let ourselves be convinced by the Holy Spirit! It is terrible enough that we all became sinners and through sin enemies of God, burdened with His curse, children of death, condemned to hell and eternal damnation. Woe to us, if we wish to deny this! Woe to us if we do not accept the means, the suffering and death of His Son, which is used by God to deliver us! We then do not struggle only against God's righteousness. We battle against His grace and surrender ourselves to righteousness without grace, which means our inevitable damnation. For whoever does not believe is not first judged but is judged already. God's wrath does not first descend upon him but remains upon him. Nothing, nothing in heaven and on earth can save, deliver, and reconcile him.

II.

We continue, and in the second place direct our attention to the proper conviction that only the Holy Spirit works of righteousness.

As there are many who consider no sin damnable, so there are also many who imagine that they need no righteousness in order to be saved. Most concede, though, that the person who comes to God must also be righteous.

Now what do all men by nature believe is that righteousness which avails before God? A great variety of opinions are to be found. The one supposes he is righteous when he does what one requires of a good citizen. Another, when he outwardly fulfills what his religion prescribes. A third goes deeper and supposes that in addition one must have an upright heart. Yet he also hopes to have such a heart.

What is the correct conviction of that righteousness which avails before God, which the Holy Spirit alone works? The Lord tells us in our text when He continues, "[the Holy Spirit] will convict the world concerning sin and righteousness and judgment, . . . because I go to the Father, and you will see Me no longer" (John 16:8, 10).

What a wonderful statement! Should Christ's going to the Father—His life, suffering, death, resurrection, and ascension—be that righteousness with which we alone can stand before God? Yes, it is this and this alone and nothing else than this. It cannot be our works before our conversion, because they are nothing but sin. It cannot be our faith, for faith is God's work and can never become ours. It cannot be our sanctification after conversion, because that is incomplete and spotted with thousands of sins.

Only one among all men was perfectly righteous before God through His own works—the man Christ Jesus. He was righteous not for Himself, for He is God Himself and does not need His righteousness. He gives it away, presenting it to all who desire it, to all who receive it, to all who believe in Him. In order to convince us of that, the Holy Spirit says to us in the Gospel, "Christ is the end of the law for righteousness to everyone who believes" (Romans 10:4). "He made Him to be sin who knew no sin, so that in Him we might become the righteousness of God" (2 Corinthians 5:21).

Certainly this is a wonderful righteousness indeed. It is not one's own, but the righteousness of another. It is not in man but outside him. He cannot earn or merit it but must let it be given to him by grace. It is not seen on earth but only in heaven. It is a righteousness that no one who wishes to be pious has, but only a poor sinner who considers himself lost and condemned has.

Ah, miserable man, you who do not willfully wish to be lost. Do not laugh at this righteousness. Though you may consider it ever so foolish, it still is and remains the only one in which alone even you, whoever you are, can stand before God. Ah, if only you do not wish to step before the Holy God in your own righteousness! You will not stand before God but will be confounded. Even the heavens are not pure before God and the righteousness of all men is like a filthy rag.

You who already despair of yourself, who already cry out with David, "Enter not into judgment with your servant, for no one living is righteous before You" (Psalm 143:2), seek your righteousness only in *this*, that Christ goes to the Father. Do not say: "How dare I consider myself righteous? I see no righteousness but only sin in me." Just for this reason Christ says, the Holy Spirit would reprove the world of righteousness, because He goes to the Father and we "see Him no longer." It is a righteousness that is not seen but apprehended through faith in the invisible Christ. No matter what your heart may say against it, Christ's suffering, death, and resurrection is your righteousness. That is the conviction that the Holy Spirit Himself holds up before you. As little as you would contradict the Holy Spirit, so little contradict His witness, that Christ is your righteousness. And be convinced even when everything else deceives. He, the Spirit of truth who proceeds from the Father, guides you into all truth and, declares Christ, does not deceive you.

III.

One more point remains about which the Holy Spirit alone gives the true conviction, namely, the judgment. Let us in the third place direct our attention to this point.

Of course, among the unbelievers there are those who are not even afraid of God's judgment; they suppose that no such judgment is to be expected, or that God will not condemn them. They are only a few. Conscience preaches too loudly that a day is coming when God will reveal the hidden counsels of the heart. Most men either don't want to be reminded of the judgment of the Last Day, or they think of it with fear and trembling. No person is able by his natural powers to await that day with joyful anticipation.

In view of this judgment, of what does the Holy Spirit seek to convince the world? The Lord speaks of that: "[The Holy Spirit] will convict the world concerning sin and righteousness and judgment, . . . because the ruler of this world is judged" (John 16:8, 11).

As the preceding were, so are these also wonderful words. They may sound threatening, but they contain unspeakably great comfort surpassing our understanding. The Lord means to say that the Holy Spirit will convince the redeemed of the world through the Gospel that Satan is conquered, their accuser is rejected, and through God's judgment is already hurled into the abyss. If one is freed of his sins through faith and shares in Christ's righteousness, he does not have to fear any judgment, any accusation of the devil, any hell, any damnation. For him Judgment Day is the day of complete redemption, the day of his victory and triumph, the day of the revelation of his freedom and glory in Christ, the conqueror of Satan.

Blessed is he therefore who has let the Holy Spirit bring him to this conviction through the Gospel! He has climbed the highest peak of faith. What the world must fear with trembling, that he hopes for with joy. What embitters temporal life for the world, that makes his sweet. What makes death difficult and frightful, that makes his easy and pleasurable. In the face of death he can exult with Paul, "The time of my departure has come. I have fought the good fight, I have finished the race, I have kept the faith. Henceforth there is laid up for me the crown of righteousness, which the Lord, the righteous judge, will award to me on that Day, and not only to me but also to all who have loved His appearing" (2 Timothy 4:6b–8).

So my friends, free yourselves of the thoughts of your heart in matters of salvation. Let the Holy Spirit give you the proper conviction through the Gospel. Your path will then lead from sin to faith, from faith to righteousness, and from righteousness to glory; you will experience that the golden chain which the apostle Paul weaves in Romans 8 is really unbreakable: "Those whom He predestined He also called, and those whom He called He also justified, and those whom He justified He also glorified" (Romans 8:30).

To Him, the esteemed Holy Spirit, together with the Father and the Son, be praise, honor, and thanks in time and in eternity. Amen!

SIXTH SUNDAY OF EASTER (1845)

JOHN 16:23B–30

The grace of our Lord Jesus Christ, the love of God, and the communion of the Holy Spirit be with you all. Amen.

Dear friends in Christ Jesus!

Prayer is one of the most precious privileges that Christians possess through Christ. Through prayer they are not only in gracious communion with God, but it is also a first-rate weapon in the battle against the flesh, world, and Satan. Prayer is a comforting refuge in anxiety and temptation, a rich storeroom in which they can find everything needed for their spiritual and temporal wants.

In these last Noah-like times there are countless people who reject prayer completely. They consider themselves enlightened, strong spiritually, and say, "God already knows all we need. It is superfluous and absolutely silly to lay this need before the All-knowing in prayer."

Nothing can be more foolish than this objection. We pray not because God must first be told of our needs and wishes but because God commands us to pray. Praying is proof of our submissiveness, a confession of our conviction that everything comes from God, that God owes us nothing, and that we must thankfully receive everything from Him as gifts of His grace and goodness. We read of this in Luther's Small Catechism in the explanation of the Fourth Petition: "God certainly gives daily bread to everyone without our prayers, even to all evil people, but we pray in this petition that God would lead us to realize this and to receive our daily bread with thanksgiving." We find even among blind heathen many who know (by the light of their natural knowledge) that prayer is necessary for divine worship. These heathen will some day arise on Judgment Day against many so-called Christians of our day, accuse them before God, and condemn them through their example. Yes, it often happens that those who despise prayer, who want to be regarded as strong people, involuntarily cry to God in moments of great trouble. How many who when not in danger brag that they believe in and fear no God! How many of such boasters have despaired in the terrors of shipwreck, have terror-stricken thrown themselves on their knees and called on Him whom they perhaps just an hour before had denied and whose Word they had ridiculed!

There are many who do not reject prayer completely, yet they say that the only benefit is that in this way man's heart is filled with thoughts of divine things, diverted from the material, and thus bettered. They deny that by prayer God permits one to obtain something that He would not have received. They say: "Should God let something else happen than what He had decreed from eternity, because such an insignificant creature as man desires it?"

We must answer in this way: It is true that prayer exercises a wonderful, wholesome influence on our heart. This power is by no means the only one which prayer has, however. If it is offered in faith, it is a key to God's Fatherly heart and all the treasures of His grace. And if God hears our prayer, He does not have to change His eternal counsel as we shortsighted men imagine. God has also from eternity foreseen if and what we would ask of Him. He has included even the hearing of our prayer in His eternal counsel; with incomprehensible wisdom He has woven it into the plan of the government of His world and Church.

My friends, do not let yourselves be robbed of the comfort that believing prayer in Jesus' name can conquer heaven itself and get everything that you implore God for. The Gospel for today's Prayer Sunday invites me to speak of this certain hearing of a proper prayer.

The text: *John 16:23b–30*

The first verse of the Gospel just read gives us the subject of our sermon today. The Lord says, "Truly, truly, I say to you, whatever you ask of the Father in My name, He will give it to you" (v. 23b). On the basis of these words I will speak to you of

The hearing of the prayer offered in Jesus' name

1. Upon what it is based, and
2. How it is prayed.

O Lord God, grant that the instruction which will now be given on the gracious way You answer our prayers be richly blessed in all hearers. Awaken especially those who are in all manner of distress and temptation, so that they neither stop praying to You nor cease complaining to You of their trouble; in firm confidence may they wait for Your unfailing help. Move those among us who have never earnestly called upon You through Your Word to confess their inexcusable disdain of Your unending goodness, become believing, diligent, and earnest suppliants, and thus finally join the host of those who laud and praise You unceasingly before Your throne. Hear us for the sake of Jesus Christ. Amen.

I.

Christians have the comforting assurance that their prayer in Jesus' name is always heard. Their faith has irrefutable grounds. It makes them absolutely certain that they do not deceive themselves in this matter.

Christians are always certain that all their prayers will be heard because God commands them to pray. Had God not *commanded* it, it would be unheard of audacity for a man to speak with God—the creature with the Creator, the clay with the potter—to pray to Him and, so to say, prescribe something. As a subject can confidently ask for something from even the sternest king, yes, if he does not want to offend him, *must* ask him when this king has himself invited him to ask for something, so the servants of *God* can and should confidently ask for everything that they need from their heavenly King.

In countless passages of His Word He gives His servants the command to call upon Him. Not only does the Son of God say in our text, "Ask, and you will receive," we read in Psalm 50, "Call upon Me in the day of trouble; I will deliver you, and you shall glorify Me" (v. 15). David knew the unchangeableness of God's command very well; he appeals to God's own command when he prayed and said, "You have said, '*Seek* My face.' My heart says to You, 'Your face, LORD, do I seek' " (Psalm 27:8). Whenever you Christians bow your knees before God you must say in your heart: "If I consider that I am dust and ashes, I certainly would not dare step before You, O great God. Your own command, however, calls me into Your presence. That is why I come in humble obedience in the confidence that You will hear me. It is impossible for You to mock me. It is impossible for You to command me to ask for something that You want to deny me."

A second reason must be added: God has not only commanded us to pray but has also solemnly *promised* to hear us. Christ not only swears in our text with a double oath, "Truly, truly, I say to you, whatever you ask of the Father in My name, He will give it to you" (John 16:23b), but He also says in another place, "*Ask*, and it will be given to you; seek, and you will find; knock, and it will be opened to you. For everyone who asks receives, and the one who seeks finds, and to the one who knocks it will be opened. What father among you, if his son asks for a fish, will instead of a fish give him a serpent; or if he asks for an egg, will give him a scorpion? If you then, who are evil, know how to give good gifts to your children, how much more will the heavenly Father give the Holy Spirit to those who ask him!" (Luke 11:9–13). What God says through the prophet Isaiah is in agreement, "Before they call I will answer; while they are yet speaking I will hear" (65:24). Here belongs what John says: "This is the confidence that we have toward Him, that if we ask anything according to His will He hears us. And if we know that He hears us in whatever we ask, we know that we have the requests that we have asked of Him" (1 John 5:14–15). Yes, David goes even farther and says, "O LORD, You hear the *desire* of the afflicted; You will strengthen their heart; You will incline Your ear" (Psalm 10:17).

If a Christian ponders these and many other promises of God, he cannot doubt that God wants to hear his prayer. Though his heart may always object: "How can you compel God to do what you desire!" he can confidently answer: "I do not have to compel God. Out of unending love, God of His own free will has already bound Himself through His promises. He is faithful and true. What He promises He must keep. The divine honor of His own name demands that. He cannot become a liar. If I wanted to doubt whether He *could* do what He wanted to, I certainly know that God is almighty. He can create what He wishes. Nothing is impossible for Him. He can do more than we can ask or think. He is rich enough to supply all wants, wise enough to find a way out of the most intricate circumstances. He is mighty enough to snatch us from every danger. He has power to turn the very heart. He speaks, and it is done. He commands, and it stands fast. He calls into existence what does not exist. In short, He is a God who helps and a lord's Lord who can deliver even from death, yes, from the abyss of hell."

Though no one can deny that God hears the prayer of all believers, no suppliant could rely firmly on God's command and promise if there were not a third reason: Christ's merit and intercession. If a person wishes to rely on God's command and promise, the knowledge and feeling of his unworthiness and sinfulness would frighten him away. His conscience would say: "It is true that God has commanded us to pray and promised to hear us." God also says that He does not hear the sinner. Are you not a sinner? Are not your hands, which you lift up to God, much too stained? Is not your heart full of ungodly desires? Are you not an enemy of God through your transgressions, unfaithfulness, and impurity? How dare an enemy ask for gifts from his enemy! Yes, saints will be heard, but sinners—never! Oh, how unfortunate would we be if our faith would not have another reason for believing that our prayer will be heard!

But thank God! His Word in no way commands us to look to our feelings and our own righteousness and worthiness in prayer but to rely entirely on Christ's merit and intercession. Christ says in our text, "I do not say to you that I will ask the Father on your behalf; for the Father Himself loves you, because you have loved Me and have believed that I came from God" (John 16:26b–27). With these words Christ does not mean to say that He does not wish to intercede for His apostles. Rather He says that Christians should not suppose that He, Christ, alone can pray and be heard, and that they dare not try to pray. No, just because they believe in Him, their prayer is acceptable for His sake and will certainly be heard in whatever they ask God.

Therefore, my dear Christian, do not be so dejected by the feeling of your vanity, your sinfulness, and your misery, that you doubt your prayers will be heard. Though you may not be worthy of being heard, your Christ who intercedes for you is worthy. Bear in mind that faith in Christ makes even you so dear and precious in God's eyes that He can refuse you nothing. Your Savior is your continual Intercessor with God. He delivers your petitions to the heavenly Father. Is He not able to obtain a gracious answer? As little as the heavenly Father can refuse His dear Son in whom He is well pleased, so little can He refuse your petition, you who sigh and implore your heavenly Father in His Son's name, that is, in trust in His valid merit and intercession.

We must also add that a Christian is driven to pray by the Holy Spirit Himself. For as St. Paul says, He helps our infirmities and intercedes for us in the best way with groanings that cannot be uttered. Now is it possible that God would not hear that prayer, which He Himself awakened in us through His Spirit? Would God not hear Himself? This is impossible. As certainly as it is God Himself who prays in the Christian, so certainly will God give him a gracious answer.

The last reason that every Christian has for praying is that he never steps *alone* before God. All believing Christendom, the entire Holy Christian Church, prays unceasingly for all men and especially for all her true members, as we see from the Lord's Prayer. She stands day and night before God and brings the daily sacrifice of her prayers and thanksgiving into His holy presence. Since Christians are in the most intimate communion with one another and are all members of one body, one prays for all and all for one. Courage may fail a weak Christian when he looks only upon himself. But when he recalls that every day millions include him in their Lord's Prayer, that he is in the rank and file of a great host of countless believing petitioners with whom he appears before God, this must strengthen him.

And so it is that we can be certain that the hearing of the prayer in Jesus' name has an unchangeable basis. It is based on God's command and promise, on Christ's complete perfect merit apprehended in faith, on His continual intercession, on the intercession of the Holy Spirit, and finally on the intimate communion between all believers and saints on earth.

Oh how blessed is a Christian! There is no necessary and wholesome benefit for body or soul that he cannot receive through prayer, and there is no harm, be it ever so great, that he cannot avert through prayer, for his prayer is heard at all times. This, however, takes place in different ways. And this is the second point on which I will now speak.

II.

The first way in which prayer is heard is by God giving the Christian what, how, and when he asks. If according to His eternal wisdom God sees that that for which we ask is beneficial in the manner, and at the time for which we desire it, He does what we wish. In that case He often brings help in a way that no man could have devised or suspected. He often directs things so that even the circumstances and the men who were opposed to our wish must assist Him. Yes, God performs a great miracle, if it is necessary that our hope in Him should not be ashamed.

How many examples of such noteworthy answers to prayer we find in the Holy Scriptures! Through prayer Jacob obtained guardian angels as his traveling companions; through prayer Joshua lengthened the day and Hezekiah, who was deathly sick, his life; through prayer Solomon became the world's wisest man; through prayer Elijah closed and opened the heavens; through prayer Daniel closed the jaws of the lions, and Shadrach, Meshach, and Abednego thwarted the fire's power; through prayer the malefactor on the cross entered paradise immediately, old Simeon received a peaceful journey home, and the crushed publican the assurance of his state of grace. Through prayer the whole city of Nineveh averted the divine judgment that threatened; through prayer the heathen Cornelius had the pure Gospel preached to him; through prayer the congregation at Jerusalem caused Peter to be freed from his imprisonment by an angel.

If we examine the history of the Christian Church, we hear that through prayer pious Monica caused her lost son, Augustine, to be brought around by

God's grace and made a pillar of the Church; through prayer Luther awakened three who were sick unto death: Melanchthon, Myconius, and his wife; yes, as in faith he himself asserted in advance, delayed in his lifetime the religious war which threatened. Yet, who may mention all the wonderful answers to prayer through which God has so decisively revealed His truth to those who pay attention to it!

It certainly is not to be denied that God does not always answer immediately. He often leaves the suppliant to wait. If a Mary says to Jesus, "They have no wine," He answers her, "My hour has not yet come" (John 2:3–4). That is only another way of answering. For the help that God has delayed is not necessarily denied; if He does not help in every fix, He helps when it is necessary. God often wisely delays. He alone knows the hour in which the help or good things for which we prayed are beneficial to us. Through delay He seeks to awaken our earnestness in prayer. Do not be frightened, my dear Christian, if you do not immediately receive that for which you implore God! Think of Jesus: He was heard at all times, yet in Gethsemane He had to wait for His Father's help. He did not let the cup pass by immediately. Jesus had to descend even deeper into the waves of anguish. But what did He do? Did He become impatient? Did He become despondent? No, far from it! He prayed ever more fervently. Follow His example, and finally you will also joyfully see God's help.

Finally, God has another way of hearing prayer, and that is the best: He does not give us what we ask for, but something else, and then always something better. A person often supposes that God does not want to hear him at all. Job sighed, "I cry to You for help and You do not answer me; I stand, and You only look at me. You have turned cruel to me" (Job 30:20–21a). Moreover, Jeremiah prayed, "You have wrapped Yourself with a cloud so that no prayer can pass through" (Lamentations 3:44). Oh, to be sure, my friends, when things do not become better as we pray but apparently only worse, those are times of severe testing. We should then direct our eyes to the hand of God; He is always helping, only not as we think.

Does He not grant our prayer when He gives us something better than what we desire? Was Paul not heard when he begged for deliverance from the buffeting of Satan and received instead the assurance of grace? Was Moses not heard when he begged to be admitted into the earthly Canaan, and instead was taken up into the heavenly Canaan? Was David not heard when he prayed for the life of his little son and he entered into eternal life? Was not the prodigal son heard when he prayed to become a servant in his father's house, but instead was received as the dear son of the family? Or is not our prayer answered when we receive a palace instead of the hut we prayed for, much instead of little, great things instead of insignificant, something eternal instead of something passing?

Many will perhaps say that though this is good, God does not really grant our prayer when we do not receive what we ask for. St. Paul answers, "We do not know what to pray for as we ought, but the Spirit Himself intercedes for us with groanings too deep for words. And he who searches hearts knows what is the mind of the Spirit" (Romans 8:26–27a). We often do not understand our own prayer. With our mouth we pray for a certain gift that would do us harm; the Holy Spirit, however, who lives in us, sighs without our knowing it for something else more beneficial, better, greater, and God who understands the purport of even our hidden petition, gives us the better thing. Does He not therefore truly hear us? We must guard ourselves against praying unconditionally for an earthly gift or trying to force something from God, when we do not know whether it is good for us. Rachel is a warning example. She stormed God's throne in prayer for children, and see, the Lord finally answered her prayer, but the hour of the birth of her child was the hour of her painful death.

Nevertheless, we should pray in firm faith. Our believing prayer is never in vain. Every such prayer is a seed from which here or hereafter precious fruit follows; it is an empty pail that is lowered into the vale of divine goodness and will be drawn up filled to the brim. In all trouble or misery, be it small or great, confidently take your refuge in prayer. It will not be in vain. Never tire in prayer but in all anxiety pray continually. Pray in the church with the congregation, pray in your homes with your families, pray in the quiet, pious solitude of your chamber, whether you walk or stand, eat or drink, work or rest, alone or in company, happy or sad, at least in the hidden chamber of your heart, and God, as the Lord expressly says, will reward you openly.

You, who could not and did not desire to pray to be heard because your conscience is not yet cleansed from your dead works through faith in Jesus Christ; you who still are God's enemies through your love of sin, who never ask for His grace and help; you who at the most babble now and then with your lips, sometimes say many empty words, sometimes put God off with short cold sighs, recognize from your wretched miserable praying that this is not real praying; you do not even desire that for which you pray. Recognize from this that you still are not Christians; for a diligent earnest suppliant and a Christian are one and the same. Repent, therefore; recognize your unconverted, ungodly, fleshly ways and pray God for the spirit of faith. You will then also receive the Spirit of grace and prayer. How gladly God would pour Him over you! Do not, however, grieve Him through new sins, but follow His holy guiding; you will then go through this world praying, daily make new blessed experiences of God's answers. He will finally hear also your last prayer and will lead you through death from danger into security, from this miserable world into the blessed heaven.

May Jesus Christ help us all in that way. Amen.

THE ASCENSION OF OUR LORD

MARK 16:14–20

O Jesus, how glorious is Your name in all the earth! For our redemption You not only descended into the lowest places of the earth but also ascended with divine majesty over the heaven of heavens. As You did not come into this world poor and miserable for Your sake, so You also did not leave it in glory and honor for Your sake; as You did not struggle for Yourself, so You were also not victorious for Yourself but for us whose sins You bore and whose righteousness You became.

That is why You still make known Your great deeds to men; that is why You have again today given us the great grace of being able to gather and hear of Your victory.

Gracious, universal, and glorious Savior, let not today's preaching of Your glory be in vain. Let every person know that he shares in Your being received into heaven and seated at the right hand of the Father.

O Lord Jesus, all of us are already victorious *with* You because You are our Head and the Lord of our salvation. Drive away our unbelief, which supposes that Your ascension does not concern us. Give us that faith, which says not only when You hung on the cross but also now that You sit on Your throne: You are mine! Hear us, King of heaven and King of sinners for Your own sake. Amen.

In the Ascended Christ, dear hearers!

We are gathered here before God to commemorate a great, precious, and glorious fact. Today we celebrate the coronation of our King of grace, Jesus Christ. I mean, the festival of His glorious ascension.

It would be reasonable that today everyone who knows that he is baptized into this great Lord and Savior should joyfully enter and leave the house of the Lord. Yes, it should be reasonable, because we find the believers of the Old Testament happily praising God when they merely foresaw this day in the spirit. David cries out, "Clap your hands, all peoples! Shout to God with loud songs of joy! . . . God has gone up with a shout, the Lord with the sound of a trumpet. Sing praises to God, sing praises! Sing praises to our King, sing praises! For God is the King of all the earth; sing praises with a psalm! God reigns over the nations; God sits on His holy throne" (Psalm 47:1, 5–8). The author of Psalm 68 also rejoices and says, "The chariots of God are twice ten thousand, thousands upon thousands; the Lord is among them; Sinai is now in the sanctuary. You ascended on high, leading a host of captives in your train and receiving gifts among men, even among the rebellious, that the Lord God may dwell there. Blessed be the Lord, who daily bears us up; God is our salvation. Selah. Our God is a God of salvation, and to God, the Lord, belong deliverances from death. . . . O kingdoms of the earth, sing to God; sing praises to the Lord, Selah to him who rides in the heavens, the ancient heavens; . . . Ascribe power to God, whose majesty is over Israel, and whose power is in the skies. Awesome is God" (68:17–20, 32–33a, 34–35c).

You see, thus believing Israel rejoiced when it thought of the future ascension of the Messiah. The Church of the Old Testament really believed that His ascension was something that did not concern only Christ but all redeemed, because it was the keystone, the brilliant crown, of the entire work of redemption.

And so it is. If we consider the ascension of Christ only as the happy conclusion of His being freed from all suffering, all disgrace, all imperfection, all persecution and, as it were, receiving the reward for His faithfulness unto death, we would consider it without its real profit. We must in faith gaze after the Ascended as our Redeemer. We must see ourselves triumphing in Him and make His whole work the foundation of a joyful faith. Then, and only then, do we enjoy the blessed fruit that it should bring us.

The text: *Mark 16:14–20*

The Gospel just read briefly relates the story of Christ from His resurrection until His entrance into glory. As the heart of all commissions that the Lord gave the apostles in this time, Mark mentions this, "Go into all the world and proclaim the gospel to the whole creation. Whoever believes and is baptized will be saved, but whoever does not believe will be condemned" (Mark 16:15–16). "Believe in Me" is the last testament of Christ, which at His departure He left behind for all men; He afterwards immediately confirmed and sealed it with His glorious ascension. Therefore, consider with me today:

The ascension of Christ is a sure foundation of our faith.

1. It bases our faith on the perfect deliverance from all our enemies, and
2. It bases our faith on the continual gracious presence of Christ with His congregation.

I.

Through the fall of our first parents all men have come under the power of three great enemies: sin, the Law, and death. Men became subject to the authority of sin. The Law pronounced the sentence of damnation; death obtained the power to swallow them up. These three enemies are most closely united with one another. They bind men as with *one* chain. The apostle describes this in the words, "The sting of death is sin, and the power of sin is the law" (1 Corinthians 15:56). First sin makes death the king of terrors; the Law then gives sin the power to condemn us.

No human power was able to conquer these foes. Man had become their powerless, defenseless prisoner. If God had not taken pity on men, they would have been lost. However, the Son of God undertook the astonishing task of freeing them from their prison. And what did he do? He was made sin for us, submitted to the Law in our stead, and sprang into the jaws of death for us. He took the sins of the whole world upon Himself. He fulfilled the Law and thereby earned for us a perfect righteousness. He permitted death to swallow Him up and conquer Him through the power of His almighty life.

When Christ rose victoriously from the dead, the entire fallen world triumphed with Him, the sins of all men were erased, eternal righteousness won, hell destroyed, death disarmed, life and immortality brought to light, and deliverance by God the Father Himself sealed to all men in the most wonderful manner. All our enemies lay at the feet of Him who for us had entered the arena against them.

Only one thing remained if Christ should be our perfect Savior. After He had defeated all our enemies, He had to be installed as their absolute Lord. The scepter of omnipotence must be given Him; He must be crowned with heavenly glory; He must ascend the throne of divine majesty. The prophecy of the second psalm must be fulfilled, where the heavenly Father says, "As for Me, I have set My King on Zion, My holy hill. . . . Ask of Me, and I will make the nations your heritage, and the ends of the earth your possession. You shall break them with a rod of iron and dash them in pieces like a potter's vessel" (Psalm 2:6, 8–9).

And this took place through Christ's glorious ascension and His sitting at the right hand of the Father, which followed and was connected with it. Christ as victor then held not only a public triumphal procession through the gates of heaven, but He also became the absolute Lord over sin, the Law, death, the devil, and hell. For that reason He ascended in divine splendor from the very place where in bloody sweat He waged His severest conflict against these enemies, the Mount of Olives.

If we want to consider the ascension of Christ correctly, we must view Christ as the substitute and forerunner of the whole human race. David was a prototype when he killed the giant Goliath. As all Israel was delivered from the Philistines through the victory of David, so all sinners were made lords with Christ over sin, the Law, and death through His triumphant ascension. This is expressed in Psalm 68: "You ascended on high, leading a host of captives in Your train and receiving gifts among men, even among the rebellious" (v. 18). St. Paul states the very same thing in Ephesians 2: "But God, being rich in mercy, because of the great love with which He loved us, even when we were dead in our trespasses, made us alive together with Christ—by grace you have been saved—and raised us up with Him and seated us with Him in the heavenly places in Christ Jesus" (vv. 4–6). As we all are resurrected in Christ and justified by God in Him, so we have also already ascended with Christ into heaven and become lords over all our enemies in Him. And as certainly as sin can no longer harm Christ, no law condemn Him, no death rule over Him, so certainly are we also freed from their prison and translated into a heavenly life with Him, if only we believe it with our whole heart.

This shows us what a secure basis we have for a joyful faith in the ascension of Christ. If we do not want to believe that sin, the Law, and death lie at our feet, we must deny completely the ascension of Christ, deny that He, who ascended into heaven, is our Savior, our Redeemer, our Brother, our Head, our Lord—deny that His labors for us have such a wonderful result.

If our sins wish to worry us, we should not let them cause us to despair, but look in faith to the ascension of Christ and say: "Sin, you are conquered. You will not conquer me anew, but as my captive you should make me cling only the more firmly to my Savior. He is ascended into heaven and I with Him, because I lay hold of Him with the hand of faith and am baptized in His name."

If the Law wants to condemn us, we should ignore its sentence and say: "You are fulfilled; your demands are completely satisfied. God's Son subjected Himself for me; you have lost all your power to subjugate me, for there is nothing with which you can reproach me. Yes, He has ascended to the highest throne and is now your Lord. I do not receive my sentence from you but from Him, and it is grace, mercy, forgiveness!"

If death wants to frighten us, and hell open its jaws for us, we do not have to fear; through Christ's ascension they have now become empty phantoms. Confidently we can and should mock them and say, " 'Death is swallowed up in victory.' 'O death, where is your victory? O death, where is your sting?' . . . But thanks be to God, who gives us the victory through our Lord Jesus Christ" (1 Corinthians 15:54–55, 57).

II.

Furthermore, the ascension of Christ also confirms our faith in the continual gracious presence of Christ with His congregation. And this is the second point that I now wish to present to you.

In our day especially, it is generally believed that after His ascension Christ is no longer on earth with His human nature. Consequently, the doctrine of the ascension is misused to deny that Christ's body and blood are truly present in the Holy Supper.

This error rests upon a completely false conception of the real nature of the ascension of Jesus Christ, Son of God, and Son of man. It is mistakenly supposed that Christ ascended into heaven just as Enoch or Elijah did; He now lives in a certain place in heaven, as is believed of all the other saints.

We must note, first of all, that we are much too weak to grasp and fathom the real nature of Christ's ascension. We do not even have an idea of what the Scriptures call heaven, for it says that heaven has no time or space. Yet our mind has absolutely no conception of something not bounded by time and space. The Holy Scriptures do not once say that Christ only ascended into heaven; it rather speaks this way: "He who descended is the one who also ascended *far above all* the heavens, that He might fill all things" (Ephesians 4:10). Now who can begin to grasp this mystery (to say nothing about describing it)? Bear in mind that the ascension of Christ is like the sun. The more clearly one wishes to look into it, the more it blinds our eyes, so that finally we see nothing. This work belongs to those that we are not to *fathom* but in childlike faith simply to believe what the Scriptures say of it. The more simply we hold to what the Scriptures say of it, the more faith-strengthening this mysterious article becomes.

What do the Scriptures say? They do not tell us that Christ is circumscribed by heaven as other saints are, but that He fills all things; not that He *was* received by heaven, but rather that He *has* received heaven, yes, that He has ascended *up over* all heavens, and, as our text says, "sat down at the right hand of God" (Mark 16:19).

What does this mean? If we do not want to go astray, we must consult the Scriptures. It says that God led Israel out of Egypt with His right hand, and hurled Pharaoh with his army into the sea. It says in Psalm 77:10: "I will appeal to this, to the years of the right hand of the Most High." (German: "The right hand of the most High can change all things.") It says, "If I take the wings of the morning and dwell in the uttermost parts of the sea, even there Your hand shall lead me, and Your right hand shall hold me" (Psalm 139:9–10).

From this it is clear that by God's right hand the Scriptures understand His omnipotence, omnipresence, rule, and eternal divine majesty and glory. That we are not mistaken in this exposition of Christ's sitting on the right hand of God the Scriptures again show us. St. Paul says, "He worked in Christ when He raised Him from the dead and seated Him at His right hand in the heavenly places, far above all rule and authority and power and dominion, and above every name that is named, not only in this age but also in the one to come. And He put all things under His feet and gave Him as head over all things to the church, which is His body, the fullness of Him who fills all in all" (Ephesians 1:20–23). And even in Psalm 110 we read, "The LORD says to my Lord: 'Sit at My right hand, until I make your enemies your footstool.' The LORD sends forth from Zion your mighty scepter. Rule in the midst of your enemies!" (vv. 1–2).

Naturally, all this is not said of Christ's divinity but of that nature in which He went about in the form of a servant, His human nature. His divine nature could be neither humbled nor exalted, experience neither ebb nor increase of its glory, as Psalm 102 expressly says of the divine nature, "You are the same" (v. 27).

Now decide for yourself whether according to Holy Scripture Christ is no longer with us according to His human nature. Far be it! To be sure, He left the world in such a way that He no longer walks among us like a human being, visible, touchable, and occupying space, as once He did with His disciples. Christ could in this sense say, "I came from the Father and have come into the world, and now I am leaving the world and going to the Father" (John 16:28). The angel also could speak in this sense, pointing to Christ's empty grave: "He has risen; He is not here. See the place where they laid Him" (Mark 16:6). We speak in this sense at the close of the Second Article of the Apostles' Creed, "From thence He will come to judge the living and the dead."

But be it far from us to believe that this applies also of Christ, what Abraham said to the rich man in hell: "And besides all this, between us and you a great chasm has been fixed, in order that those who would pass from here to you may not be able, and none may cross from there to us" (Luke 16:26). Be it far from us to believe that Christ is King in a kingdom from which He is separated, and which He can rule only from a distance.

No, Christ has taken a local *departure* from His disciples. With His glorified body He truly lifted Himself ever higher and higher, as far as the eyes of His disciples could reach. But that should only assure them of the truth of the great change which now took place in the state of the man Jesus. We dare not suppose that, when the clouds received Jesus like a triumphal chariot and hid Him from the sight of the disciples, He now continued to rise slowly ever further and further from the earth and raised Himself up above the starry heavens. No, as soon as the clouds closed behind Him, He in that instant also entered into the state of divine majesty, appeared in heaven full of glory before all angels and saints, and also as a man began to share in the omnipotent and omnipresent rule over heaven and earth and all creatures.

If we consider the ascension of Christ in this way, oh, what a firm basis for a joyful faith we then have! Far be it that Christ should have withdrawn Himself from His congregation; He has rather come close to us. We need not first go to Judea to seek Him. No, shortly before His ascension He promised, "Behold, I am with you always, to the end of the age" (Matthew 28:20). Through His visible entrance into His invisible glory He confirmed and brought this about. In all places He as God and man is now near us with His grace, with His help, with His protection. If during His sojourn on earth Christ dealt with His Father chiefly for us, now His own attention is continually directed toward us, His redeemed, to bring us to faith in Him, to preserve us in it, and to carry out the good work in us until that day when we shall see Him as He is. Christ has not ceased completing His work in sinners; He does not rest in the enjoyment of salvation, resting from His labors as those do who fall asleep in Him. But He has appeared for us before God in the Most Holy Place; as Aaron bore the names of the tribes of Israel on His breastplate when He entered into the Most Holy Place, so also Christ carries the names of all believers on his heart when He appears before God as the true High Priest. There He unceasingly intercedes for His own, rules them, provides for them, and protects them, that the gates of hell cannot overpower them.

Oh, then, let everyone today be awakened to faith in Christ and be strengthened in it through His glorious ascension. Let no one say: "How does this concern me?" If you are a prisoner of sin, the Law, and death, as you cannot deny, then Christ's ascension concerns you most intimately; through His ascension Christ has taken your captivity captive. If you at your death do not want to descend into the eternal prison, then in faith cling to the Ascended. You are then free even here, and someday you will follow Him into His glory. He thought of you when before His ascension He gave the command, "Proclaim the Gospel to the whole creation. Whoever believes and is baptized will be saved, but whoever does not believe will be condemned" (Mark 16:15–16).

Now if in the meantime, before your Savior brings you home into his Father's house, you experience misery, many temptations and dangers of soul, do not give up. Cling to Him who today received the kingdom of His Father. For your sake all power in heaven and on earth was given to Him. He will permit nothing to tear you from His hand and will be your shield and protection until He has placed you among those whom He has delivered, who sing an eternal hallelujah to Him in the temple of heaven.

To Him be honor and praise here and hereafter forever and ever. Amen.

SEVENTH SUNDAY OF EASTER

JOHN 15:26–16:4

Grace be with you, mercy and peace, from God the Father, and from the Lord Jesus Christ, the Son of the Father, in truth and love. Amen.

Dear friends in Christ Jesus!

Among the heathen and Christians there were men who have maintained that all sins are the *same*. It is undeniable that *no* sin is a joke. Each is a transgression of the divine Law, an insult to the great majesty of the eternal, holy, and righteous God. Each merits eternal separation from God. Nor can one deny that there are *degrees* of guilt. For certain sins one can have forgiveness and be in God's grace; other sins necessarily exclude one from God's kingdom and His blessed communion. Not only does God's own Word make this distinction clear, but to deny it would destroy all the comfort of the Gospel and lead the sincere to despair. No person is so pure and holy; sin will be found in him as long as he lives.

To be sure there is a great difference among sins. There is the difference between *actual* and *original* sins. All men are born with the latter; it is a sinful *state*, the ruin of the whole human nature, soul and body, intellect, will, and inclinations. Among the *actual* sins there are sins of weakness and sins of malice, sins of willfulness, sins of rashness and dominant sins, willful and unwitting sins, forgivable and unforgivable sins.

Sins of weakness are those one commits only out of the weakness of the human nature. His earnest intention is to serve God without sin; he is sorry over the least mistake, seeks forgiveness for it, and after the misstep becomes ever more wary and watchful. *Sins of malice*, on the other hand, are intentional sins in which the person delights. If the person loves and cherishes them above others, they are called pet sins. If sins are of such a nature that one merits temporal punishment but knows how to escape it, or if one oppresses the poor and forsaken still more, uses their misery and defenselessness, and is still unpunished, these are called *sins which cry to heaven*; finding no judge on earth they cry to the all-knowing and righteous Judge in heaven for vengeance, as the innocent blood of Abel, the sweat of the poor, and the tears of cheated widows wrung from them by usury.

Sins of rashness are those into which a person is hurled either by his temperament or through a sudden, unexpected, severe temptation; so Peter was suddenly hurled into his denial by the temptation of the fear of men and death. On the other hand, ruling sins are those in which the person lives and walks and which he without a strong temptation willingly follows. These are also called *mortal sins*. He who is thus governed by sin can have no faith, no spiritual life, nor stand in God's grace. He is not ruled by God's Spirit, and therefore is spiritually dead.

Forgivable sins are all those in which the person is not yet hardened so that he could not feel remorse over them, repentance, a longing for grace, or faith. On the other hand, the *unforgivable sin* is such a fearful hardening against all the impulses of the Spirit of God that the person despises, mocks, and reviles all grace, comfort, and forgiveness unto his end, and wants to know nothing of Christ, His blood and His reconciliation. In Scripture this sin is also called the sin against the Holy Spirit, or the sin unto death for which one dare not pray.

Finally, *willful sins* are those a person commits against better knowledge despite all the dissuasion and reprimands of his conscience. On the other hand, *unwitting sins* are such that a person commits without meaning to, yes, in which he often supposes that he does something God-pleasing.

You see that there is a great wretched variety of sins of every shade, from the fleeting vain thoughts of our heart to the stiff-necked hardening of a Pharaoh and a Judas. Every sin is and remains a revolt against God, the Father of light; no matter how small they may be, they can be forgiven only for the sake of Christ, the Son of God. Even these sins that we commit unwittingly or even suppose that we are doing something good, yes, are doing God a service, are and remain sins. The Lord declares that in our reading today. This is also the subject of today's consideration.

The text: John 15:26–16:4

My friends, in this text Christ foretells the disciples' fate when they will bear witness of Him before the world. He says, "They will put you out of the synagogues. Indeed, the hour is coming when whoever kills you will think he is offering service to God" (John 16:2). Christ says that they would not only be excluded as heretics by those who would pretend to be the true Church, but would also be cruelly persecuted even to death. Their persecutors would not be ashamed of their deed when they would banish the apostles; they would think that they were doing God a service. Particularly on the basis of this last declaration let us consider:

The sinfulness of relying merely on good intentions.

We will see:

1. That the greatest sins are committed with good intentions, and
2. That one's good intentions do not excuse or justify one.

I.

We can accept the truth that when most commit their sins, they are motivated by good intentions. Good intentions are the fruitful mother of countless sins, the chief comfort with which most set their minds at rest in their sins, the excuse whereby they even refuse to repent. It is also the mightiest snare with which Satan traps souls, keeps them deceived, and draws them ever deeper into sin.

What Christ according to our text predicted, "They will put you out of the synagogues. Indeed, the hour is coming when whoever kills you will think he is offering service to God" (16:2), was literally fulfilled only too soon. The Jews especially who arrested the apostles thought that they were committing no sin at all. They had the good intention of warring against the enemies of God, being zealous for the Father's Law, and battling for the true Church and the only true divine worship. Luke expressly reports that Saul, who later became Paul, approved of Stephen's execution (Acts 8:1). Paul himself declares, "I myself was convinced that I ought to do many things in opposing the name of Jesus of Nazareth" (26:9). He was, as he says elsewhere, a persecutor of the Church of God only because he wanted to be zealous for God and His Law. Speaking of the opposition of the Jews toward the Gospel of grace in Christ, he says, "I bear them witness that they have a zeal for God, but not according to knowledge" (Romans 10:2).

Why did countless Christians become martyrs in those ten great persecutions during the first three centuries of the Christian era? Almost all fell as a sacrifice to the good intentions of the heathen. They thought that the Christians must be blotted out because they were enemies of the state and all humanity, enemies of the gods, yes (since they had neither altar nor sacrifice), atheists. They were supposed to be the cause of all the natural calamities that were inflicted by their gods. Tertullian, the teacher of the Church, writes that whenever devastating floods, continuous drought, earthquakes, famine, pestilence, and the like struck, the heathen with one voice cried, "Throw the Christians to the lions!"

Is not all heathendom with its terrible idolatry and unheard of abominations built on nothing else than good intentions? With the good intention of serving the Most High, the heathen carry on the most frightful idolatry: they pray to the sun, moon, stars; they venerate men, four-footed and creeping animals, birds, idols, and other lifeless objects. With good intentions the heathen sacrifice human beings to their imagined gods, pour out the blood of their enemies on their altars, yes, even the blood of their own children. With good intentions they observe the most disgraceful, unchaste, and heinous festivals, because they think that thus they serve their gods in an acceptable way.

The Muslim cold-bloodedly dips his sword in the blood of Christians without his conscience becoming disturbed; he supposes that the more such "enemies" of God he kills, the higher his place in paradise will be.

And how was it possible that the papacy—with all its anti-Christian superstition, with its hierarchy and tyranny of souls, with its rejection of Christ and His only merit, with its idolatrous veneration of the saints, with its cloisters and pilgrimages, with its forbidding the Bible, with its mutilation of the Lord's Supper, with its abomination of the mass, in short, with all its anti-Christian ingredients—could establish itself in the Christian Church, keep itself alive, and spread? Malice and cunning are not enough to hold so many millions of souls captive and erect a structure that defies all time. The first root and thereafter the mainstay of the papacy were the good intentions with which most introduced the abuses. The opinion that they could make men obedient, pious, and save them only this way suppressed the Gospel of the grace of God in Christ, set in its place the teachings of works righteousness; finally, they even went so far as to silence with fire and sword those who witnessed against the abomination of the papacy. They were branded as heretics of the Church of Jesus Christ. And even now the good intentions that thousands of the better informed in the papacy have are the main bulwark that hinders the final victory of the Reformation over the antichrist. They suppose that if one would abolish this or that which one must reject everything will collapse. They follow the principle that the end justifies the means. They think things must remain as they are and are blind to the fact that great numbers are drawn into eternal ruin.

Moreover, if we look at the Protestant Church, it again is often the good intention that does immense harm. The enthusiastic sects war against trust in the Means of Grace, the Word of God and the Sacraments; they are led by the good intention of thus promoting piety and holiness. With good intentions they make a caricature of the whole Christian Church through their enthusiastic follies. The world shrinks from the Church as from the product of an overheated imagination. With good intentions they battle against the pure doctrine, against the true Church, against the faithful servants of God and sincere members and disciples of Christ; they imagine that they are warring against the enemies of true living piety and promoting the work of God.

Even the universal wish to unite all churches without unity of doctrine, the tendency of paying very little or no attention to differences in doctrine, considering all false doctrine as something harmless as long as it does not appear directly opposed to God's Word—this tendency also has its source chiefly in the good intention of rising with united strength against the known enemies of the Church, making more and more opportunities for the kingdom of God, and removing that which has hindered it from extending the borders of Christ's rule.

And who will deny that many unbelievers, even with their warfare against God's Word, against Christ and His Gospel, even with their mocking and blaspheming of the most holy things, with their persecution of true Christians, also have the good intention of actually fighting for light and enlightenment, for truth and justice, for virtue and morality, in other words, for the well-being of mankind?

Finally, the apostles themselves are good examples of the fact that even Christians are still deceived by their good intentions and often fall into the most dangerous ways. Christ had predicted his reconciling suffering. Peter spoke up with the good intention of talking Christ out of such a gloomy notion: "Far be it from you, Lord! This shall never happen to you." There upon the Lord angrily replied, "Get behind Me, Satan! You are a hindrance to Me. For you are not setting your mind on the things of God, but on the things of man" (Matthew 16:22–23). We find in James and John before the outpouring of the Holy Spirit an example of false religious zeal due to a good intention. When the Samaritans had denied the Lord quarters, they cried, " 'Lord, do you want us to tell fire to come down from heaven and consume them?' But He turned and rebuked them" (Luke 9:54–55).

Unquestionably, no sin is so great and terrible, no error so clear and ruinous, no enthusiasm so absurd and senseless, no worship, no church, no sect, no religion, no principle so false and wrong but that it should not be united with and arise from the best of intentions of serving and pleasing God.

However, do not good intentions excuse the erring and sinning, yes, justify them? Not in the least! Permit me in the second place to add a bit about this.

II.

After Christ in our text predicted that men would excommunicate the disciples and cruelly persecute them, supposing that they were doing God a service, He adds, "And they will do these things because they have not known the Father, nor Me" (John 16:3). Christ says for the comfort of the disciples that their persecutors would not be considered God's friends because of their good intentions; no, their intentions make it clear that they are still in their natural blindness without knowledge of God and their salvation. They are still enemies of God; yes, through their continued opposition to the enlightening power of the Gospel, they have fallen into the judgment of an unconquerable delusion and obduracy. Far be it therefore that Christ should excuse or even justify those sins that were committed with good intentions. He calls it the revelation of a sinful condition, the poisonous discharge of a poisonous well, the fruits of the most fearful servitude of sin.

True, with these words Christ cannot mean to say that there is no difference between a sin committed with conscious malice or with good intentions. Christ, you know, expressly says to Pilate, "Therefore he who delivered Me over to you has the greater sin" (John 19:11). And on the cross Christ in His petition for those who crucified Him mentioned their ignorance to His heavenly Father with the words, "Father, forgive them, for they know not what they do" (Luke 23:34). Christ says of the city of Capernaum, where He had so often preached and done miracles in vain, "But I tell you that it will be more tolerable on the day of judgment for the land of Sodom than for you" (Matthew 11:24). And Paul says of himself, "Formerly I was a blasphemer, persecutor, and insolent opponent. But I received mercy because I had acted ignorantly in unbelief" (1 Timothy 1:13).

Yet with these words neither does Christ want to justify Pilate, His crucifiers, and the people of Sodom, nor does Paul want to justify himself. Christ means to say that those who did not know the Lord's will, will suffer fewer stripes, but stripes nevertheless, and Paul says the ignorant idolatrous heathen who "have sinned without the law will also perish without the law, and all who have sinned under the law will be judged by the law" (Romans 2:12).

Even among those who do evil with good intentions there is nevertheless a great difference.

In the first class belong those who have God's Word but willfully resist the Holy Spirit; they remain in their blindness, yes, finally become so blinded that they deem the greatest crimes a service to God. This was the case with the Jews of whom Christ speaks in our text. Just before Christ had said, "But when the Helper comes, whom I will send to you from the Father, the Spirit of truth, who proceeds from the Father, He will bear witness about Me. And you also will bear witness" (John 15:26–27a). When Christ in the following verses says of the Jewish persecutors of the apostles, "And they will do these things because they have not known the Father, nor Me" (16:3), He declares that their good intentions are the result of willfully resisting the Holy Spirit. The false church of the papacy also belongs to this class. Woe to her! With good intentions she rejects God's Word, substitutes the doctrines of men, persecutes the true Church with excommunication, and, where she can, with fire and sword! Her good intentions will as little excuse her before as it did the Jews who rejected Christ; they will condemn her acts as willful blindness, enmity against God, Christ's Word, and grace.

Those who know nothing of God's Word and consider the most terrible sins as virtues compose a second class. But they also are not excused. We dare not forget that even the most ignorant heathen and all unbelievers carry God's Law in their conscience. "They," writes Paul, "are a law to themselves, even though they do not have the law. They show that the work of the law is written on their hearts, while their conscience also bears witness, and their conflicting thoughts accuse or even excuse them" (Romans 2:14–15).

But what do they do? They "by their unrighteousness suppress the truth" that was still living in them from their birth (Romans 1:18). They go contrary to the voice of their conscience so long until they become so blind and dead that they consider the greatest abomination the most God-pleasing service. Woe, therefore, to all heathen and unbelievers! All their horrible sins, which were committed with good intentions, will damn them. They will have to confess that at first their conscience reprimanded them; only repeated sinning against their conscience hurled them into their dreadful indifference and more than natural blindness.

Finally, Christians who believe God's Word and yet do wrong now and then out of good intentions compose the third class. They also are not excused. For why do they mistakenly do evil, as though it were something good? Because they do not let God's Word guide them in *all* things. God first of all demands that everyone makes only His Word his rule and guide, departing from it neither to the right hand nor to the left.

In the second place, God expressly warns against following one's heart or human commandments and opinions. "The intention of man's heart," writes Moses, "is evil from his youth" (Genesis 8:21). "Whoever trusts in his own mind," Solomon writes, "is a fool" (Proverbs 28:26). God warns through the prophet Malachi, "So guard yourselves in your spirit" (2:15). Christ says, "In vain do they worship Me, teaching as doctrines the commandments of men" (Matthew 15:9). Yes, when Saul had with good intentions offered a sacrifice, God said to him, "To obey is better than sacrifice, . . . Because you have rejected the word of the LORD, He has also rejected you from being king" (1 Samuel 15:22–23).

Not even Christians are excused, if they do not serve God according to His Word but after their good intentions. Though they may show the greatest zeal, the deepest devotion in such self-elected service, and impose the heaviest burden upon themselves, it is all in vain. They follow a seducing leader against whom God has in His Word warned them so often and so earnestly.

My friends, let us not be more merciful than God Himself. Though an unbeliever may suppose that with his sins he is serving God, in His Word God has passed the sentence: "He that believeth not shall be damned." Second, and above all, let us guard ourselves against following our hearts or the laws and opinions of men rather than God's Word. It is God's Word alone according to which we shall be judged. God's Word must therefore be the only rule and guide of our faith and life, the only lamp for our feet and light for our path. Then we will not go astray; or if out of weakness we should err, this light will always lead us back to the true way. May the humble prayer of that faithful lad Samuel be and remain in our hearts: "Speak, LORD, for your servant hears" (1 Samuel 3:9).

May God through Jesus Christ our Lord and Savior help us. Amen.

PENTECOST

JOHN 14:23–31

O God, through Your servants, the holy prophets, You promised, "For I will pour water on the thirsty land, and streams on the dry ground" (Isaiah 44:3). "In the last days it shall be, God declares, that I will pour out My Spirit on all flesh, and your sons and your daughters shall prophesy, and your young men shall see visions, and your old men shall dream dreams" (Acts

2:17). It was long ago today when You fulfilled this precious promise. Today we appear in Your sanctuary to celebrate this deed of Your faithfulness and truth, and as a congregation laud and praise You for it. But, O Lord God, Your promise is yet not completely fulfilled. The dry soil of many millions of hearts still waits for the streams of Your Spirit to flow over them; even our thirsty souls await Your gracious rain that it may enliven, water, and quicken us.

O, therefore, come, come Lord God Holy Spirit, and ever more enlighten the world. It is still sitting in darkness and in the shadow of death. May it know Christ its Savior, accept Him, and remain with Him. On this holy day visit especially Your Church; fill her with Your heavenly comfort, so that she does not despair in these last times but valiantly struggles and holds out until she can triumph in the eternal Sabbath with the angels of heaven. Amen. Amen.

My dear hearers, beloved in Christ, and effectively called through the Holy Spirit!

There is on earth an amazing kingdom that is small indeed but whose jurisdiction covers the world. It has its secret members in all the kingdoms of the world. There is an amazing nation in which all the languages of the earth are spoken. It is gathered from all the nations of the earth, yet it lives under one King by one code in lasting peace enlivened by one Spirit. There is an amazing city among whose citizens are slaves and free, rich and poor, kings and beggars, yet they are equal, equal in wealth, equal in power, and equal in the hope of the glory which they await. There is an amazing temple that all the world knows, into which all the world is invited to enter, yet which no mortal eye has seen. Founded upon an eternal foundation, it is erected of unknown stones and is supported by invisible pillars. There is an amazing general who, weaponless, goes through the world. Although continually warred upon by the whole world, hell, and traitors in His own midst, He is nevertheless unconquered; yes, He is victorious even in defeat, triumphant even in death.

There is an amazing fellowship among men. They are tied together by a mysterious bond; it is the most despised in the eyes of the world but in the eyes of God His most precious treasure. They seem to be forsaken by God, and yet they are the only ones in whom God dwells. They are always anxious about their sins, and they are the only ones who have forgiveness of their sins. They consider themselves the greatest sinners, and yet they are the only ones who are clothed in a righteousness that avails before God. They pass for the greatest fools, and yet, enlightened by the light of truth, they are the only ones who are truly wise. The world considers them the scum of humanity and would gladly be rid of them, and they are the only ones for whose sake the world still stands. They seem to be the poorest, and yet they are the only ones who have all true treasure, who alone can make this poor world rich, who alone possess the true remedy for all the misery of this world and the fear of death, and to whom alone the keys of heaven are entrusted.

Now what is this amazing kingdom and nation, so small and yet so widespread, so diverse in its members, and yet so united? What is that amazing city, whose citizens are so unlike and yet so alike? What is that amazing temple that is so well-known and at the same time invisible and so unknown? Who is that amazing general, who is so defenseless and yet so victorious and unconquerable? What is that amazing mysterious fellowship among men that seems to be so miserable and yet so glorious, that seems to be so poor and yet is so rich, yes, that makes many rich?

It is *the Church*, or God's congregation on earth, whose birthday we celebrate today. We were told at Christmas and Easter what amazing love God first had to show just to be able to gather a church, a congregation of redeemed, justified, and elect from the fallen and lost human race; Pentecost tells us how this Church of grace and salvation for all nations was launched after the Son of God had become the Cornerstone.

Let us therefore today study this divine miraculous edifice somewhat more closely.

The text: John 14:23–31

Christ here speaks of a dwelling of God on earth—of those who are this dwelling of God, of its characteristics, and of its wealth and treasures. This is what other passages of Scripture call the house of God, *the Church*. Undoubtedly this section was chosen as the text for Pentecost because on this day the Christian Church, the Church of the new covenant, was launched through the miraculous outpouring of the Holy Spirit upon the apostles of Jesus Christ. Let us now under the guidance of our text seek to answer the question:

Which Church was launched on Pentecost?

In so doing we ask,

1. Who belongs to this Church?

2. What are the characteristics by which they can be recognized? and finally,

3. What are the treasures the Church has?

I.

The usual answer to the question "Who belongs to the Church?" is "All those who are baptized." Others demand something more and say that one must also publicly *confess* the Christian religion in word and deed; one must recognize and say that the Christian religion is the true one, take part in the gathering of Christians for divine worship, and observe the religious customs of the Church. Finally, others go still further and say that the Christian life is part of this.

I am convinced that even among us not a few would give no other answer. Perhaps they wonder who else can and should be reckoned as members of the Church, than he who is baptized, confesses the Christian religion, and behaves like a Christian?

Yet what does He say, He who alone decides, the Lord of the Church, Jesus Christ? He speaks this way in our text, "If anyone loves Me, he will keep My word, and My Father will love him, and We will come to him and make our home with him" (John 14:23). These are most noteworthy words. While the Lord otherwise ascribes everything to faith, here He does not say: Whoever believes in Me, but, "If anyone LOVES Me." And the Lord does not let even this be enough but adds, "He will KEEP MY WORD." He continues, "And My Father will love him, and We will come to him, and make Our home with him." This means nothing else than: "We will make him a member of the Church."

So according to Christ's own words only they belong to the Church of the new covenant who not only *know* Christ, speak much and often of Him, and believe that He is a Teacher of the truth, but who also *love* Him. Moreover, only those who not only *have* Christ's word, diligently hear it, and seek and search in it, but who also *keep* it.

The Lord does not at all mean to say that true faith is not enough in order to be a member of the Church. In other passages of Scripture, the indwelling of God and membership in the Church, yes, salvation, is expressly ascribed to faith. In our text Christ wishes to impress that only a faith which is not a dead head knowledge makes one a member of His Church. His faith must be a divine power, which changes the heart of man, melts it, and fills it with holy fear of every sin and impurity. And his faith also fills the heart with *love* to Christ, a love consisting not only of words but also an inner living power showing itself in deeds. It is a love that not only makes one willing but also capable of *keeping* Christ's word. The Lord expressly adds in the following verse, "Whoever does not love Me does not keep My words" (v. 24). One who lacks faith cannot become a temple of God, a member of the Church.

Not only do the heathen, the Jews, and the Muslims not belong to the Church of Christ but also all those in the Church who have no love for Christ. For example, there is much in a church *building* that does not *belong* to it. Either it is an embellishment, or furniture, or a defiling stain. If he does not love Christ and really keep His Word, he does not belong to it but is (perhaps because of his gifts and honorable life) a beautiful but dead picture, or, if he lives an unchristian life, only a blemish.

The Christian Church is like a field of wheat. Weeds grow up along with the wheat. They often are more colorful than the wheat itself; they are watered by the dew of heaven just as well as the wheat; the sun shines upon them just as well as on the wheat and ripens for the harvest. In the same way many are like weeds on the wheat field of the Christian Church. They do not belong to it, even though they are watered by the heavenly dew of the Gospel as are the members of the Church; the rays of eternal truth shine upon them as on the true members, ripening for the eternal harvest. The weeds, however, are not stored in the granary at harvest time but are tied in bundles and thrown into the fire.

So all those who here were *in* the Christian Church but did not love Christ and keep His Word, will not be brought into the granary of heaven, even though they were baptized, knew Christ, had sort of a faith in Christ, yes, outwardly led a Christian life. But they will be separated from Christians and cast into the fire. Oh my friends, we will with terror see that very many will be found among such weeds, many whom we considered the best wheat because of their knowledge, usefulness, or honorable life. Ah, when I think back how especially in the last years our congregation has progressed in temporal things but retrogressed in love to Christ and the keeping of His Word, my heart trembles at the thought of the harvest. I feel compelled to say: "My dear brethren, let us not feel secure because we are *in* the Christian Church. Let us rather earnestly examine ourselves in the present festival of the Christian Church to see whether we love Christ and keep His Word." If we have fallen, we can then arise again in true repentance, return to our first love, and at the cry "the Bridegroom comes," arise with rejoicing and follow the Bridegroom into the marriage hall of the Church triumphant.

II.

We have the answer to our first question about the individual *members* of the Church. Let us now answer our second question about the Church as a whole: what are the marks by which she can be known?

Since only those who love Christ and keep His Word belong to the Christian Church, it is composed of a host of people whom only God knows; only the Lord, the searcher of the heart, knows His own. No man can look into the heart of another. No one can see the love of Christ that lives in the soul of another. No person can perceive the motives of another's acts that alone decide whether a person really keeps Christ's Word or only seems to. In other words, though the Church consists of people, it must be a host invisible to us, since no man can tell those who love Christ from those who do not.

And so it seems impossible to know which is the Church of Christ and where it can be found. But it only seems so. For is not God also invisible? But are there not countless signs by which we can recognize His presence everywhere? Do not the heavens declare His glory and the firmament His handiwork? Is not, as the apostle writes, God's invisible essence, that is, His eternal power and Godhead, seen so that one can perceive it in the creation of the world? Yes, we can and should feel after and find Him in His works. The rolling thunder is, as the royal singers say, the rolling of His chariot and the light His garment.

Is not the Holy Spirit invisible? Nevertheless, could one not on the first Pentecost become conscious of His presence and notice that He came upon His disciples? Did one not hear it in the roaring as of a mighty wind that descended from heaven? Did one not see it in the flames that appeared in the form of tongues over the heads of the disciples? Did one not perceive it in the glowing, divine, powerful sermon of the great deeds of God in languages that the disciples had never learned?

The same is true of the Christian Church. She is an invisible kingdom extending over the whole world; she consists only of true disciples of Christ. But there is a sign by which we can most certainly know where she is to be found. The Lord Himself indicates this sign when He continues in our text: "And the word that you hear is not Mine but the Father's who sent Me. These things I have spoken to you while I am still with you. But the Helper, the Holy Spirit, whom the Father will send in My name, He will teach you all things and bring to your remembrance all that I have said to you" (John 14:24b–26). The Lord comforts His own at His imminent return to the

Father, saying that when He will no longer walk and talk with them, the Holy Spirit will teach them everything and remind them of all the words that He said to them. Now what does Christ say will never be taken from His own and will never fail them? What does He say is inseparable from His Church and at the same time a positive sign by which it can be known? His *Word*, His Gospel.

And my friends, it can be nothing else. The Church is the communion of all true believers and lovers of Christ. Nothing else can make a person a true believer and lover of Christ than His Gospel; thus nowhere else than where this Word is can the Church of true believers be found. As you look for wheat only where you have planted the wheat seed, so you also find true Christians, the Church of the new covenant, only where the heavenly seed of the Word is sown.

It is true that the wheat often smothers. One cannot with absolute certainty conclude that where good seed is sown one can also expect a good harvest. Here the spiritual seed of God's Word differs from the wheat seed. We read of the spiritual seed: "So shall My word be that goes out from My mouth; it shall not return to Me empty, but it shall accomplish that which I purpose, and shall succeed in the thing for which I sent it" (Isaiah 55:11).

The Word of God will never be preached in vain. It happens that wherever God permits His Word to be preached, He knows in advance that there are at least a few who will believe it, love Christ, and keep His Word. Wherever God gives His Means of Grace, the pardoned are certainly there also. Wherever there are those who are *called* by God's Word, a number of *elect* to eternal salvation are there also. Once when the newly converted Paul wanted to preach in Jerusalem, the Lord protected Him and said, "Make haste and get out of Jerusalem quickly, because they will not accept your testimony about Me" (Acts 22:18). Wherever the candle of the Gospel burns, the Lord certainly has a number of His own there also. In short, wherever there is a *visible* congregation, in which God's Word is preached in its purity, there certainly is also an *invisible* Church of true believers.

As the column of smoke announces the presence of fire and as the rising sun announces the arrival of the day, so the preaching of God's Word in any place announces the presence of the true Christian Church. Everything else that is extolled as marks of the Church, be it the outward holiness and the great works of its members, the long duration of its existence, the derivation of its beginning in unbroken line from the apostles themselves, or whatever it is—all this can deceive. However, the mark of the preaching of the pure

Word is infallible. Where this is found, there is still today the workshop of the Holy Spirit; there even today we hear that rushing as of a mighty wind in which the Spirit descends from above. He is as powerful through the preaching of the Word as He was long ago on the first Pentecost. By the Word He calls, gathers, enlightens, sanctifies, and keeps the Holy Christian Church with Jesus Christ in the one true faith. Stay where you find the pure Word, for there you find the true Zion of the new covenant, the New Testament Jerusalem, the true temple of God—in other words, the true Church of Jesus Christ.

III.

Does it really pay to seek for the Church of the new covenant, and, having found her, gather around her, risking everything with her? This leads us to the third question that is to be answered: What are the blessings and treasures that she has?

Christ mentions two in our text. He says, "Peace I leave with you; My peace I give to you. Not as the world gives do I give to you. Let not your hearts be troubled, neither let them be afraid" (John 14:27). What is the first blessing that all those have who love Christ and keep His word? It is *peace*.

I admit that Christ here does not mention those blessings that men usually consider great. He says nothing of great honor before men, nothing of earthly riches, nothing of a pleasurable and enjoyable life, yes, even nothing of exemption from suffering, poverty, disgrace, and death. The Lord rather expressly says, "NOT as the world gives do I give to you. Let not your hearts be troubled, neither let them be afraid." Far be it therefore that Christ should promise the glory of the world to those who cling to His Church. On the contrary, He indicates that they would experience very many things that would bring them trouble and fear.

Yet, does not Christ promise something great, something glorious, something enticing to those who love Him and keep His Word? For bear in mind, my friends, when Christ says, "Peace I leave with you; My peace I give to you," He says that God has made peace forever with him who loves Him and keeps His Word. God has forever forgiven him all his sins and become his ally; God now views everything that is inflicted upon such a person, be it good or evil, as though it were done to God Himself. God considers such a person His dear elect child, a subject of His Fatherly love and concern. Having this peace with God we naturally can have only the sweetest inner peace of heart and conscience, that is, the sweet, blessed conviction, that one has nothing to fear but has everything to hope for in time and eternity.

How doesn't it pay to seek the Church of Christ and stay there? Does she not give that peace which all men seek without knowing it? Can this world with all that it offers ever give that peace which soothes the poor restless heart of man? Should we not cast our lot with the Church, since in her one finds that blessing which alone can be called a blessing, the blessing of a heart brought to God's peace?

Oh you poor souls, who must confess that the love of Christ does not yet live in your heart and rule you, that you do not yet keep His Word—must you not also confess that you are still without peace, without rest, without true blessing? Oh, take the big "gamble"! Learn to know Christ, and you will also immediately learn to love Him and keep His Word. Then that peace which Christ has left behind for His Church, which passes all understanding and is better than all the glory of the world, will enter your heart.

But even this peace that contains a whole heaven on earth in itself is not the only treasure the Church has. Christ continues in our text thus: "You heard Me say to you, 'I am going away, and I will come to you.' If you loved Me, you would have rejoiced, because I am going to the Father, for the Father is greater than I" (v. 28). Christ means to say: "Do not be sad, you members of My Church, that I do not remain visibly with you but go to the Father. It is rather the greatest blessing for you, for the Father is greater than I." Christ does not mean to say that the Father is greater in essence than He, for He says in another passage, "I and the Father are one" (John 10:30). "Whoever has seen Me has seen the Father" (14:9). "All may honor the Son, just as they honor the Father" (5:23). No. He means to say that it is more beautiful there with the Father than even here in My kingdom of peace; there with My Father is the kingdom of destination, perfection, glory. Rejoice that I go there, for I am only preceding you to prepare a place for you, and will finally draw all of you to Myself.

That the Church is a *ship* which not only brings peace and security from the storms of the world but which also most certainly enters the harbor of a blessed world; that the Church is a *tree* which grows in this world as though in a nursery, but will some day be transplanted in the soil of heaven; that the Church is like a *vestibule* of the eternal temple, where all the saints gather, see God face-to-face, and live a life in perfect joy without measure and end; in a word, that outside the Church there is no salvation but in her everything is salvation, that, that is the great blessing, the most wonderful treasure which the Church has.

Blessed are all of you who are found in the ship of the Church as those elected out of the old for the true new world. This ship will not be wrecked; despite the gates of hell you will joyfully land on the shores of that land where only the blessed live. Blessed are all of you who are living branches on the tree of the Church; someday you will bloom and become green in the garden of eternal paradise. Blessed are all of you who worship here in the vestibule of the Church of grace; you will also sing an eternal hallelujah in the Most Holy Place in heaven. Amen.

SCRIPTURE INDEX

Concordia
Publishing House
w w w . c p h . o r g

ISBN 10:   0-7586-3889-2
ISBN 13:   987-0-7586-3889-2

9 780758 638892

Church & Ministry/Sermons & Illustrations
53-1196